The Lascelles Family

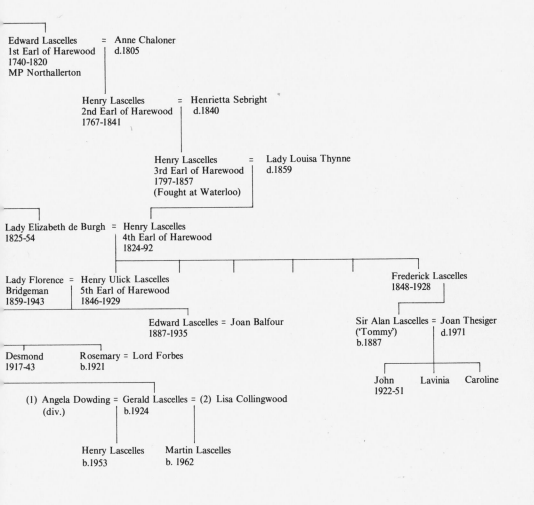

Edward Lascelles = Anne Chaloner
1st Earl of Harewood   d.1805
1740-1820
MP Northallerton

Henry Lascelles = Henrietta Sebright
2nd Earl of Harewood   d.1840
1767-1841

Henry Lascelles = Lady Louisa Thynne
3rd Earl of Harewood   d.1859
1797-1857
(Fought at Waterloo)

Lady Elizabeth de Burgh = Henry Lascelles
1825-54   4th Earl of Harewood
                                       1824-92

Lady Florence = Henry Ulick Lascelles   Frederick Lascelles
Bridgeman   5th Earl of Harewood   1848-1928
1859-1943   1846-1929

Edward Lascelles = Joan Balfour   Sir Alan Lascelles = Joan Thesiger
1887-1935   ('Tommy')   d.1971
                                                         b.1887

Desmond   Rosemary = Lord Forbes   John   Lavinia   Caroline
1917-43   b.1921   1922-51

(1) Angela Dowding = Gerald Lascelles = (2) Lisa Collingwood
    (div.)   b.1924

Henry Lascelles   Martin Lascelles
b.1953   b. 1962

THE TONGS AND
THE BONES

THE TONGS AND THE BONES

The Memoirs of
LORD HAREWOOD

WEIDENFELD AND NICOLSON
LONDON

First published in Great Britain by
George Weidenfeld and Nicolson Ltd
91 Clapham High Street, London SW4 7TA

ISBN 0 297 77960 5
Printed and bound by
Butler & Tanner Ltd, Frome, Somerset

Titania What, wilt thou hear some music,
   my sweet love?

Bottom I have a reasonable good ear in
    music. Let's have the tongs and
    the bones.

A Midsummer Night's Dream, Act IV Scene I

There is no enigma but I feel inclined
to follow Elgar and dedicate this book
'to my friends and relations pictured within'
because it is mainly through them that
I have enjoyed a great deal of my life so
far very much indeed.

Contents

Illustrations

With Marion, my mother and Gerald after Queen Elizabeth's Coronation, June 1953 (*The Times*).

Participating in the blessing the stage ceremony which took place before the appearance of the Azuma Kabuki dancers and musicians, Covent Garden, September 1955 (*Popperfoto*).

Arriving at the *Observer* exhibition of film history with Marion and Dicky Buckle, June 1956 (*BBC Hulton Picture Library*).

In conversation with Maria Callas, June 1958 (*Camera Press*).

Patricia in Italy a few days before I met her (*Lord Harewood*).

Dancing with Patricia in fancy dress at the Opera Ball, February 1959 (*Popperfoto*).

My three elder sons bicycle along the terrace at Harewood, while their cousin looks on, 1963 (*Camera Press*).

Harewood House, north front by T. Malton, *c.* 1788 (© *Earl of Harewood's estate*).

The north front of Harewood House in 1981 (*Lord Harewood*).

Between pages 240 and 241

'Homage to Harewood' – drawing by Coia, Edinburgh Festival, 1962 (*Lord Harewood*).

Talking to Georg Solti and Harold Rosenthal during an interval at the Royal Opera House, Covent Garden, 1964 (*Central Press*).

On holiday in Spain with Patricia just after Mark was born, September 1964 (*Lord Harewood*).

In conversation with conductor Pierre Boulez at the Edinburgh Festival, 1965 (*The Glasgow Herald*).

Neville Ussher with my brother Gerald at Harewood, 1964 (*Lord Harewood*).

My mother pruning roses shortly before her death (*Lord Harewood*).

With Rostropovich and Rozhdestvensky at the Edinburgh Festival, 1965 (© *Paul Shillabeer*).

Escorting the Queen during a visit to York University, October 1965 (*Syndication International*).

Entertaining Dr Klemperer and Barry Tuckwell at my home, 1966 (*Lord Harewood*).

Mark meets his brothers for the first time (*Lord Harewood*).

Posing with the Judge who married us after our wedding in Connecticut, 31 July 1967 (*Popperfoto*).

Our first appearance after our wedding with three-year-old Mark at the Harewood Show, 9 August 1967 (*Syndication International*).

The Bird Garden at Harewood. Patricia and Mark with a macaw (*Lord Harewood*).

Garlanding at Kalki, Madras, 1970 (*Lord Harewood*).

Patricia and some Nepalese children pose for the camera with the Himalayas in the background, 1970 (*Lord Harewood*).

The Queen and Patricia before a dinner in Leeds, Silver Jubilee, 13 July 1977 (*Syndication International*).

At a Leeds United match at Elland Road (*Lord Harewood*).

Partridge shooting with Neville Ussher and Jack Charlton (*Lord Harewood*).

Walking with Patricia in the grounds of Harewood, May 1981 (*Photo: Terry Smith, Colorofic Photo Library*).

Foreword

I HAD ALWAYS thought there was something rather final about writing about one's own life, as if there was nothing left to do except conceivably embark on a second volume. I don't feel that way yet about my own. Nevertheless, when Ronald Duncan, on holiday in 1979 with Patricia and me in Barbados, insisted he and I talk together with a dictaphone between us it seemed churlish to refuse; after all, something might come of it. Some weeks later, I read the inevitably disjointed results with mounting horror; did I *really* talk so ungrammatically – and with such relish for the barely relevant parenthesis? To correct and improve what we had started to do seemed something of a Herculean endeavour and in the end, nettled by the inadequacy of what I read, I started again.

When, two holidays, several weekends and many train journeys later, I had contrived to write quite a lot, someone asked me whether I was recalling the impressions of the time or writing from a 1980–1 point of view, and I replied that I was, necessarily, looking at it all from my present vantage point, and interpreting what I now remember I felt then in the light of what I have experienced or learnt since. I don't really believe that 'total recall' can ever be other than factual – such and such happened at a particular moment – and I think that explanation (as opposed to factual record) must be coloured by subsequent events, changes in one's own point of view, advances in understanding.

I have never kept a diary, except on two visits to India, but the pocket engagement book I have for more than thirty years carried with me records most appointments and has prompted a multitude of memories. Of course, I have been selective and have concluded that quite a lot of what very much interested me at the time need not interest a reader. I have tried, probably unsuccessfully, to avoid the trap of feeling obliged to refer to all the friends and colleagues whom I would not like to offend; in the end, lots remain unmentioned and I must face the consequences.

The story, admittedly in rather general terms, is carried up to the present day as far as Harewood and, oddly enough, my Indian experiences are concerned, but I decided at the outset that my job as Managing Director of English National Opera at the Coliseum counts as 'work in progress' and that to do more than touch on it would be a mistake, on the grounds that it is neither easy nor wise to stand back and publicly take stock of what you are currently trying to do.

Since it has played a large part in my life, there are constant references to music, musicians and musical performance, but I cannot see how that could have been otherwise unless I had set out to falsify my own experience. Like Bottom, whose words I have borrowed for my title, I am no professional musician, more's the pity, but I am a very good listener, and from that position have derived so much pleasure as sometimes to make me feel I should be daily on my knees giving thanks for what in nearly sixty years has come my way.

Acknowledgments

RONNIE DUNCAN STARTED me off and my wife has been indefatigable in deciphering over-corrected typescripts and commenting constructively on them. To them I am particularly grateful, as also to Victoria Glendinning for detailed and invaluable advice, almost all of which I have taken, to Edmund Tracey, Dicky Buckle and Neville Ussher for help over individual sections, and to Anne Wilson, who typed almost all of it with hardly an error and no complaint at all.

Brief biographical notes of many of the major names mentioned in this book will be found from page 307 onwards.

CHAPTER ONE

Growing Up
1923-42

'IF YOU RUN away to leg again, I'll throw the ball at you!' The scene was cricket nets at Harewood; I was the bowler, fancying myself as a speed-merchant too, my brother was the batsman with a safety-first complex, Herbert Sutcliffe was coaching us.

Gerald *did* retreat with the next ball, Herbert *did* throw the ball at him – and it accidentally hit him, as Herbert reminded me years later at a Scarborough Festival match. We were lucky as schoolboys to have the privilege of a coach like Herbert – Wilfred Rhodes had coached us the year before – and lucky too that our parents treated it both as something natural, so that we were not tempted to brag about it, and also as something not available to all, so that we must make the most of it.

Cricket in those pre-war days was a passion with my brother and me, and we practised in the Easter holidays, played at school and whenever possible in the summer holidays, watched Yorkshire's games (and very occasionally a Test match) when we could manage it, which was often, and even pored in the winter over Wisden and the county yearbooks, as well as getting up at unearthly hours to listen to the radio commentaries on Test matches in Australia. Gerald's keenness was a little less intense than mine and neither of us was specially good, though neither by any means a rabbit. We made our runs and took our wickets; we thought about tactics and tried to emulate the great men whom we watched and occasionally met during those summer expeditions.

The Scarborough Cricket Festival in late August and early September was a particular magnet. Herbert Sutcliffe, Maurice Leyland and Hedley Verity, Brian Sellers, Bill Bowes, Arthur Wood and our other Yorkshire heroes were reinforced by leading players from all over – by classical batsmen like Hammond and Woolley and Hendren, by big hitters like Wellard and Jim

Smith, by fast bowlers like Farnes and Voce, and always by the touring teams, Australians, South Africans, Indians – but not that I remember in those days by West Indians. We used to leave Harewood soon after breakfast and motor past York Minster and through Malton to get there by eleven or eleven-thirty. We refused to miss a ball bowled, were often invited to lunch in the President's tent where we met the players, and were usually dragged away by six so as not to be late home for dinner, assuaging schoolboy appetites on the way back by purchase of a choc ice at the stop-me-and-buy-one bicycle-barrows which in those days trundled through any small town and still sold ices made from cream and tasting of what the label described.

I was born in 1923 in London, at Chesterfield House, where South Audley Street runs into Curzon Street. It was once Lord Chesterfield's house and Dr Johnson used to go there; it's sad that it has now disappeared, as photographs testify that it was a beautiful house and would have made a splendid embassy. By the 1930s it had become too big for a private house, and we left in 1931 for a more modest house in Green Street, just north of Grosvenor Square. That was I believe what is called a 'grace and favour' house, in that it belonged to the Crown and was allocated to appropriate persons. My parents were 'appropriate' because my father had as Viscount Lascelles in 1922 married the daughter of King George V and Queen Mary – he told me once that the King had wanted to follow precedent over the husband of a monarch's daughter and make him a Marquess, but he refused on the grounds that Marquisates died out quicker than any other title and he was keen to provide himself and his ancestors with heirs! My father's parents, Lord and Lady Harewood, were still alive and will figure in this book, as will my father's sister, Lady Boyne.

My maternal grandparents came to Chesterfield House while I was being born, and my father, deciding he could not face entertaining them at such a moment of stress, left my aunt (so she told me) to look after them. The King apparently paced up and down regaling them with tales of the wives of his friends who had died in childbirth, a lugubrious performance which would certainly have driven my father away had he risked staying.

In the 1920s, Goldsborough in Yorkshire was our home and we spent most of our time there. We went to London each summer for the season, and, when my brother and I were still young, we spent about a month of the summer at Newmarket, covering a couple of race meetings. I remember it vividly because it was at Newmarket that after much fumbling I learnt how to catch a tennis ball, there that I first had hay fever, which became the scourge of childhood, adolescence and early manhood.

When I was seven or eight I was taken to a hay fever specialist, who nicked my arm in a couple of dozen places and covered it in pollen solutions to discover what I was allergic to. The answer seemed to be everything except cats and dogs and horses, and I returned, first to have the inside of my nostrils cauterized – more frightening in prospect than in reality, though it was surprising to smell one's own burning flesh and not feel it – and then regularly to have the inoculations which were supposed to subdue the dreaded disease and its symptoms of red eyes, sore nose, and constant, unstoppable sneezing. I don't know if the inoculations did any good, but, apart from the army years, I continued with them until I was fifty, attempting to learn after the war to give them to myself, a skill I never properly acquired, so that my second wife Patricia, seeing me once wince with pain and withdraw the needle before remembering to inject the fluid, gave me a simple pistol-like affair designed for diabetics.

Goldsborough is a Jacobean house, near Knaresborough, and still at that time on the edge of the Harewood estate. For generations, the eldest Lascelles son had lived there during his father's lifetime, and it is a sizeable though not grand country house in its own park and in the midst of agreeable countryside, twelve miles from Harewood. It seemed huge to children and, leaving there at the age of seven and not returning until I was over twenty, I was surprised to find everything on a much smaller scale than I had remembered.

My earliest childhood memories are bound up with Goldsborough: smells, which I have since realized are the most evocative of all associations; the melancholy of looking out of a spare bedroom, which became my earliest schoolroom, on to yew trees; the boggy rides in the wood which were once dug up and the cakes of mud roasted, so that the following winter there was a simple brick foundation; the peacocks which roamed the gardens until my father connected a barren year's racing with them and superstitiously decided on their removal; the Guernsey cows from which came our too-rich milk and which roamed the park and terrorized our nanny; the elegant but slightly ludicrous Irish wolfhounds which my mother had been given and which once succeeded to my father's indignation in catching the goat which kept the horses company; the wolfhound puppies which knocked me down when I was six and threatened to lick me to death; the smell of verbena at the most sheltered point of the garden; going to church regularly and learning the collect for the day before setting out.

To Goldsborough belong other equally specific and perhaps more significant memories. Alfred Munnings came to stay to discuss painting my parents, which he later did with fair success, and he visited me in the nursery, offering to draw an animal for me. Some thick paper was produced and I demanded a bull. He started with the ring on its nose and continued tantalizingly, but for a child fascinatingly, with disconnected details – its horns, tail, hooves, back, four legs, the farmer's bowler hat – until the whole had been assembled to my infinite delight. Then, on the back of this paper, because I complained it looked docile, he drew one which had got away and was tossing the farmer in the air. My joy was complete, and my mother had it framed with glass on both sides. I still have it, as well as a sense of gratitude that a celebrity should have given the time to please a small child.

My earliest musical memories are from Goldsborough too. We had a wind-up gramophone in the nursery and used to listen to Chaliapin's record of the 'Song of the Flea' – the acoustic, pre-1925 recording I think, because I remember it as single-sided. My aural image of that famous chuckle of his growing to a guffaw dates from then and owes little to subsequent hearings, frequent though they must have been. I insisted it was played again and again, a tendency I observed years later in my own children when something caught their fancy – maddening for others but I suspect as natural to a child whose imagination has been captured as to demand another strawberry.

More traumatic was to find when I was six my parents playing a record – it must have been Albert Coates's – of the prelude to Wagner's *Die Walküre*. The music seemed to me then and indeed now the epitome of urgency, and when the plight of the fleeing Siegmund was explained to me, I demanded repetition and built up a picture of the fugitive, sometimes running through dark, hostile woods, sometimes through a tunnel of flaming trees. Gerald, to my scorn, ran upstairs in tears, but I insisted on one hearing after another, and the music's threat has lost little for me over the years.

The prelude to *Die Walküre* produced a fear that was mainly pleasurable. Less enjoyable was to go up to bed at Goldsborough past a huge picture by Frans Snyders accurately called 'A horse attacked by wolves and lynxes'. By day, terror was muted, but the horse was rolling on its back and the attack was graphic enough to make running past it in the evening up the half-lit stairs a daunting experience.

Summer meant we were in the south, based in London, which as a child I did not much like, because it was hot and dusty and we were always put to bed too early so that we listened to cars rattling round the streets at the back and couldn't get to sleep. The sound of a taxi in an empty street in the summer still has for me a melancholy clatter which I associate with those

4

days, and one of the luxuries of growing up was to put the light out at one's own chosen time.

Like most small children in those days, I had my tonsils out, curiously enough at home. I must have been four, and I was told without any melodrama to lie on the table where the operation was to take place. The doctor said I was to blow up a football, and the chloroform mask was put over my face to produce a very sharp feeling of choking and claustrophobia. I came out of the anaesthetic to find two nurses I had never seen before whispering together at the bottom of my bed, and my throat was indescribably sore. I don't think I was fed on ice cream; it was not until much later that I heard from a schoolboy contemporary that this had made the operation for him almost worthwhile.

I don't know how that early operation could have been made less scaring, but the knack had been found by the time I had another one, much less routine, about six years later. I had contracted a violent streptococcal infection at school and, since my parents were abroad, stayed with my paternal grandmother before being taken into hospital. I was not feeling at all well so that it may have been easy for the doctor who was in charge and the surgeon who was going to operate to induce a feeling of confidence, but I remember approaching the whole thing with anything but a feeling of dread. New techniques of anaesthesia probably helped too, but I can't believe the ploy about blowing up a football was a good one, not least because at four footballs didn't mean much to me anyway.

I wish I had sharper and more accurate memories of Chesterfield House, which we left when I was eight. It had a spacious marble staircase leading from a marble hall, big enough for a military band to play in when my mother had receptions. There were ices, which we were allowed to sample, made of cream and fresh fruit, and the band played Albert Ketelbey's 'In a Monastery Garden', with which I fell in love and demanded again and again – one of the few childish whims I remember being gratified without demur or admonishment.

We played nearby in Hamilton Gardens, now absorbed into the Park Lane traffic scheme and then only available to a few key-holders but an admirable place for children. From there we watched the rather frequent military parades, which seemed either to go towards Buckingham Palace or else to march past the Cavalry Memorial at the end of Stanhope Gate which made an appropriate saluting base. I once stood there in my grey flannel summer suit and grey flannel floppy hat next to my grandmother Queen Mary, suffering agonies of indecision as to whether to take my hat off when soldiers

5

saluted her or leave it on; after all, it wasn't me they were saluting, and I knew it.

We were annually taken to watch the Trooping the Colour in honour of the King's birthday on Horse Guards Parade, a seemingly endless ceremony associated for me with flowing dresses and big hats and considerable fuss on my mother's part about getting into them in time for it all. We greatly admired my father, riding with my mother's brothers just behind the King and taller and more striking than they were in his red Grenadier tunic and great bearskin cap (our nanny wrongly called it a busby and we were very quickly put straight about that). We went to parties and Miss Vacani's dancing classes, which we intensely disliked, were taken out to tea with friends of our own age, which we enjoyed apart from the dressing up which preceded it, and went annually to the Royal Tournament at Olympia. This was a splendid entertainment for, as they now say but would rather have died than say then, children of all ages. We loved the horses and the musical rides with gun carriages, the occasional spill, the races between naval gun crews, the bangs and the smell of gun powder (or cordite?) which hung about the arena.

We sat in the Royal Box, and here was a snag: shyness forbade that we should ask to go to the lavatory, and no one had the imagination to ask us. I remember peeing in my pants there, which was uncomfortable and shaming, and the bliss of sitting next to my father a year later and his asking the right question at the right time so that the second half of the afternoon was not spent squirming in misery. Perhaps it was a sign of the times that a child could be brought up with so strong and yet so uncertain a sense of decorum that he feared to ask to go to the lavatory.

Chesterfield House is associated too with French and piano lessons in one of the rooms off the drawing room – the French lessons more successful apparently than the piano lessons, since I don't remember the time when French was not somehow familiar and I have never been able to play the piano worth a damn.

My childhood was happy and I tended to enjoy all the things we regularly did. We moved to Harewood from Goldsborough when I was seven, in 1930, some months after my grandfather died, and I enjoyed the life we led there in the country. I had been to stay at Harewood before, and remember well the hip baths in front of the fire, the relative softness of my aged grandfather's beard (he was seventy-seven when I was born, eighty-three when he died), and the gentleness and persistence with which he taught me, when I stayed there in autumn without my parents only weeks before he died, how to eat the delicious pears grown at Harewood – cutting them in half round the middle, removing the core from the centre and then scooping them out with a spoon.

This gentleness seems to have been uncharacteristic, as I learnt later from my aunt that he was by no means easy with any of his children. Perhaps he had mellowed, and anyhow to be allowed at six to eat without nursery supervision with grown-ups who were not my parents was in itself a novel and exhilarating experience. I must have avoided spilling anything or making a fool of myself as these memories are entirely good; not so the first time I ever ate lunch in the dining room at Chesterfield House, when I choked on the skin of the chicken breast I was eating and wished the floor would open and swallow me and my shame.

But my parents can't have been discouraging or discouraged, as a few days later I was there when the young and beautiful Princess Ingrid of Sweden, later Queen of Denmark, came to lunch, and later still when the to my eyes exotic-looking King Alfonso of Spain was our guest, and I rehearsed my bow, which was hardly necessary since we bowed constantly to our grand relations.

My paternal grandfather, the fifth Lord Harewood, seems to have been self-centred and to have brooked little opposition. He refused even after my father had come of age to let him keep his hunters in the stables at Harewood; and after he had once had to help with my father's racing debts, he got his lawyer to draw up a punitive document by which my father acknowledged or paid the debt back as humiliatingly as possible. My father, whom I never knew or heard of nursing a grudge apart from this one, transferred the estate from that lawyer the moment my grandfather died. From the fuss my grandfather made packing away the admittedly splendid and valuable Sèvres and Celadon china at Harewood in 1914, my father said you would have supposed the Germans' main objective was precisely to capture it!

Years later, my father showed me my grandfather's diaries, which were in effect engagement books with entries to do with dining out, travel, trout-fishing, hunting, shooting and his visits to the opera – that, and the invariable Saturday night entry 'Took a pill'. I glanced at the operatic entries, which was why my father showed them to me before throwing them away, and could see from their regularity that he was a genuine addict – but, to judge from such entries as 'Ballo in Maschera. Singing poor apart from Selma Kurz', mainly a canary-fancier.

7

My paternal grandmother, whom we called Dar, was a major feature of our existence until she died just before I went abroad in the war. She was gentle and took pains with children, and I remember walks at Harewood to her Rose Garden, where she laboriously taught me the name of a rose she said she could never remember but which has remained with me to this day: 'Souvenir d'Aimée Terelle des Chaînes'. She told us stories and read to us when she came to say goodnight before she went to dinner. She listened to our nonsense without ever making us feel ridiculous, she respected our confidences and gently interceded with our parents, but never took sides against them; indeed by example she showed us a pattern of behaviour and an unruffled outlook on life and on people which has, I hope, remained an influence. She belonged very much to her generation, wore clothes of a certain style, almost always and whatever the weather with a choker round her neck, and we loved and played endlessly with her jewellery (the family jewellery, which she had retained as my mother didn't need it).

Dar married my grandfather when she was very young and was so astonished to find that at Harewood, unlike Weston in Shropshire where she was brought up, there was no flock of black sheep, that some had to be imported to make her feel at home. We have this St Kilda flock, or rather its descendants, at Harewood to this day. She had the foibles as well as the dress sense of her generation; she dismissed what she thought not quite apt behaviour or the right sort of person with 'Rather troisième, my dear', and had dotty but somehow not inappropriate nicknames for people whose names she could not remember – like 'the little married man' for the china expert Willy King, small and pernickety of manner, who came from the V & A to catalogue what was at Harewood and whose marital status never ceased to astonish her. After the war I got to know slightly his wife, Viva King, but never told her about my grandmother's status-questioning estimate of her husband.

While still at Goldsborough, I had acquired a governess, Miss Vigers, a little round body of whom both Gerald and I became very fond. I suspect she was a good teacher – she certainly took great pride in the good places her pupils took at school – and she made learning interesting, so that I fell in love with the history book and took without too much remonstrance to French and Latin grammar and even that bugbear of my own sons, arithmetic. She hadn't the physique for games but not much fazed her, not even when my father said I should learn to milk a cow, which would be much more useful if I were stranded in the country than my thirteen-times table. So off to the farm I was taken and there buried my head, cap in place, in the cow's side and pulled at its udder until the milk came. It all seemed to me rather scaring and certainly very smelly, but I was proud of the little accomplishment and of being able to tell my father about it.

With Miss Vigers I used to go to the joiners' shop in the Estate Yard at Harewood. This was a hive of activity presided over by Fred Wood, the House Carpenter, who never seemed to tire of showing us round and whose work was constantly interrupted while he made little things for our diversion, though this was not always popular with our parents as he was an expert cabinet maker and his job was no sinecure. The smell of wood shavings was much more attractive than that of the cowshed, but we thoroughly enjoyed at the farm looking at pigs, kept in individual stone sties, not, as now, in great impersonal sheds, and we scratched their backs with the sticks we carried in emulation of the grown-ups. It was about Miss Vigers that Gerald and I used in later days to tell a true story to the effect that we had once seen her just after breakfast answer the house telephone and, finding my mother on the other end, bob reverentially as she said, 'Good morning, ma'am'!

At Harewood we rode our ponies constantly. I had started to ride at six at Goldsborough, taught by my father's Stud Groom, whose name was Griffiths and who once astonished me when, kicked smartly on the shin by my independent-minded pony (whom I already loved and would have taken sides with against anyone), he called her rather strangely but with a wealth of feeling, 'You little vixen!' We rode virtually every morning except Sundays, rain of shine, from the time we went to live at Harewood until the outbreak of war.

Our best friend was the groom, Dick Froude, a retired huntsman who had come to us while we were still at Goldsborough and was a constant companion and confidant until he died just after the war. He had a disposition of rare sweetness, put up with our fads and had a repertory of fascinating anecdotes about hunting and racing. In addition he was persuasive enough to get us to ride tolerably well, to practise jumping now and then, and to get back in time for lunch.

Much store was set on punctuality before the war, for meals, walks, and for the start of our rides, and the threat of being left behind if we were late may have been an empty one but was effective enough to make us keep to time. Another rule was to walk our ponies the last half-mile home so that they arrived at the stables cooler than if galloped. We once found a sheep inextricably fouled in some brambles, and spent twenty minutes getting her out, with the result that we should either be late or have to gallop the last half-mile. We chose to be late, since somehow we did not like to make the sheep an excuse, and were duly berated for our sin against the rule of punctuality.

Out riding, bowler hats were worn with a cord attaching them to our coat collars in case they were dislodged by wind or a bucking pony – a proper sight we looked too, the hats jammed down over our ears and slightly tilted back. On one occasion, stung as we later discovered by wasps, my pony took off out of control at the entrance to Wheatcroft, a great forty-acre field by the River Wharfe and the perfect arena, one might have thought, within which to allow a maddened pony to gallop itself to a standstill. The river was to the north and the field went into a kind of bottleneck at its eastern end. I allowed the pony to gallop the full length towards the bottleneck, believing it would stop at the six-barred gate at the end. In this I was mistaken, and to my astonishment we took off, struck the top bar firmly and landed hard on the other side, separately, the pony on its knees and me on my by now exposed head, the bowler having blown off a couple of hundred yards before. Dick Froude and Gerald arrived unstung a minute or two later, to find me on the ground very bedraggled and rubbing a sore head. The pony was eventually caught and we jogged home, agreeing to say nothing about the episode in case it counted in some way against us.

For days I had a headache which I did not admit to, and must have had slight concussion, but not a word was said to anyone – why, I simply cannot imagine, as we never got more than a scolding and I have no recollections which support the notion that our parents ruled us with a rod of iron. I think more than anything it was a grown-up insistence on undisturbed routine which made us perform actions which seem in retrospect stoical.

Riding was considered so natural a part of life that we even took our ponies with us when we went to stay each autumn with my uncle and aunt, Lord and Lady Boyne, at Burwarton in Shropshire. Burwarton was the only place I ever thought of as a second home, and Rosemary Hamilton-Russell, my cousin and eighteen months older than me, I loved with unquestioning devotion throughout boyhood. We each had a governess in those days, so it was lessons for both of us for two and a half hours after breakfast, riding on the Burwarton Hill for an hour and a half before lunch, lessons and a walk in the afternoon. We invented games of every kind, mostly involving running; the inventing, naturally, usually occupied the period while we were walking uphill, and the running mostly occurred on our way home downhill.

My uncle, who was then in his seventies, seemed a rather nebulous, distant though invariably kind figure, but Aunt Madge was one of the most remarkable people I ever met. She and my father were born eleven months apart and were emotionally very close, and they told me that for the month of the year that their ages were the same they pretended to be twins. Aunt Madge was the longest and in certain ways one of the strongest influences on my life. We adored her as children, wondered at her energy and forthrightness, loved the kindness and ability to turn little things that went wrong into laughter, hated to incur her disapproval and basked in its opposite. I think she guided our childhood fairly firmly, but I almost never remember a cross word from her; she had an easy ability to sway us away from what might be destructive or disruptive towards what seemed to us nothing less than an ecstasy of pleasure. She was more fun to be with than almost anyone I ever knew, and that qualification extends from the time I was six, through half-term parties in London and staying with her early in the war (during which she lost in succession her husband, her mother and three sons) to her many later visits to Harewood.

She was the greatest support to me after my mother died and my divorce became imminent, and then Patricia's and my best friend after I remarried. I think she may have been a dominating, even domineering parent, but younger people continued to adore her, and my own sons, including Mark who was born when she was already eighty, looked forward to her visits to Harewood more than to those of almost anyone else.

She was always close to us, and deeply minded the approach of my divorce. I remember asking her to lunch one day to meet Patricia, before we were married; I picked her up in the car and surprised her by aiming towards where we lived rather than to a restaurant (she confessed afterwards that this made her very nervous). When we arrived she went straight in, embraced Patricia and said, 'My dear, before we go any further, I want to say that I interfered in your lives and I was quite wrong and I hope you can forgive me.'

When her eldest son, my cousin Tavie, was married in 1932, I was a page, dressed in a child's version of the uniform of a Grenadier of 1815. The uniform was preserved, and – part of an uncanny tie between my family and the Battle of Waterloo – my eldest son David later wore it when he was a page at Tavie's son Michael's wedding around thirty years later. The nature of the tie will, I hope, emerge later.

At Harewood life was to some degree predictable – but, provided that predictability included some highlights, what child ever minded that? – and we used to watch football matches in the winter just as we played or watched cricket in the summer. Football for us meant Leeds United, and those were the days of Willis Edwards and Wilf Copping. Edwards had captained

11

England a few years before, and we used to say that he never broke out of a walk, or at most into a trot, but was always *there*. His elegance and timing is a happy memory of my boyhood.

Expeditions away from home in those days were comparative rarities. I have sometimes wondered whether my parents still instinctively thought of taking the car out as if it involved grooming and harnessing and then risked tiring a pair of carriage horses – not because they were hopelessly old-fashioned, but because that was one of the measures of their own childhoods. We went to football matches if there was no threat of fog or snow and, very occasionally, to the cinema, or, before Christmas, out shopping.

Shopping in childhood took us on a very limited round, mostly looking for presents, but it almost invariably included the replenishing of our stock of 'caps' for toy pistols, a major source of pleasure then. Films were a bigger treat altogether, not encouraged if the weather were fine, as my father in particular, though not I think a puritan, believed in the virtues of doing rather than watching and was basically no fan of spectator sports. I quickly came to love the cinema, and in 1937, staying at Sandringham where films were shown in the evenings after dinner, regretted that our visit coincided with the first anniversary of my grandfather's death, which meant there would be no film that night. (On another visit, *Carnet de Bal* was thought to be too sophisticated for Gerald and me, who were thirteen and fifteen at the time.) *The Informer* made a great impression, with Victor McLaglen in a virtuoso performance and the whistling of 'The Rose of Tralee' as one of the motifs of the film, a tune which stuck in my mind until partially exorcized by repeated playing of the records John McCormack and Richard Tauber made of it. I still think it's a haunting tune, and a good film too, for that matter.

Some of these 'expeditions' were made with my father's Scottish secretary, Constance Bliss, of whom we were very fond and who spent time and trouble on us. She had been secretary to Lord Balfour and did not always hide that she thought us rather small beer – English, too – compared to the dazzling conversationalists and great names she met with him. I imagine he paid her more attention too than did my father.

We bicycled locally with her, and we would go by car on summer expeditions up Wharfedale, thus starting a kind of love affair with the incomparable beauty of the Yorkshire dales which is still very much with me. We would leave after breakfast with a huge picnic basket, take off through Otley and Ilkley, past Bolton Abbey and Appletreewick, and often stop at Kettlewell to walk up one of the paths leading to Great Whernside. Sometimes we came back through Grassington and Pateley Bridge,

Nidderdale and Ripon, or we took off through Settle and Aysgarth on a more extended round. Once I had a driving licence, we occasionally made the same expeditions with my mother, and I remember just after the war building an elaborate fantasy with her which involved reconditioning a farm cottage we saw in a particularly favourable spot and making walking expeditions from it at weekends. I don't remember who was to cook; certainly not me, and I do not think it was one of my mother's major accomplishments either.

People came to stay with my parents, and though I was intensely shy, I was paradoxically by no means averse to new company. In our holidays from school, the great party times were York Races in the summer, and then Christmas. Christmas meant a full house of relations, walks with different people to talk to, elaborate games, special food and staying up late – and of course when we were very young it also meant Father Christmas. I never rumbled until long after the event the particular cousin who was dressed up as Father Christmas, though the charade was carried on for Gerald and younger cousins long after I knew it was a grown-up in disguise. But, which grown-up? We played billiard fives in early days and then proper billiards or snooker; there were tremendous snow battles, and presents and church on Christmas Day, sometimes without the necessity of wearing a stiff collar.

Stiff collars fill me still with almost as much horror as they did then. They were seldom comfortable, and always caused a struggle with one's tie. I did not mind tying a black tie round a stick-up collar in the evening, but on one unforgettable occasion, when Gerald and I had announced that we had grown out of our seldom-worn daytime ones, we were made to our infinite chagrin and mortification to put on the evening, stand-up collars to go to some church service in York Minster.

Stiff collars featured too when my grandmother, Queen Mary, came to Harewood for her annual visit in early September. She used to arrive for some reason at Harrogate Station rather than Leeds (perhaps she came from Scotland) and my father used to go to meet her. My dread of formal occasions was brought to a head one year when neither of my parents could go to the station, and I at the age of ten or eleven had to go in their stead. I trembled with fear at the prospect of doing something wrong, such as tripping on the red carpet at the station, or forgetting to take my hat off at the right moment, or put it on, or not knowing where to walk or how to get into the car without causing a commotion. To this day, I am never confident of getting this kind of thing right, and a long walk in public or a solo entrance in prospect fills me with horror. No amount of rationalization on the lines of 'it doesn't really matter' defeats the subconscious suspicion that it does.

King George v, my grandfather, stayed at Harewood and opened the Civic Hall in Leeds in 1933 with great pomp and ceremony, horses and carriage and out-riders and all. My mother was ill – this lasted in all perhaps a couple of years, becoming known in the family as her 'infirm state' – but Gerald and I watched from the side and were later taken to see my grandmother when she got a piece of grit in her eye and the doctor had to roll the eye-lid back to get it out; more dramatic to watch, I suspect, than painful to the victim. Much later I heard that the day's most dramatic event occurred when my grandmother went to the lavatory in the Lady Mayoress's parlour and, because it was badly designed and there was no room for her voluminous skirts with an inward-opening door, had to climb on the seat before getting out.

We saw our royal relations comparatively often and regarded them therefore with awe rather than dread, though my grandfather the King found it so easy to find fault with anyone that what was probably a basic kindness was quite lost in his gruff exterior, added to which the ritual good morning and goodnight peck had to be offered to a beard of astonishing abrasiveness. I don't think he really cared much for children and he had a positive mania for punctuality.

The only person who was allowed to be late for anything, even breakfast, was apparently my mother, who was of course his only daughter, and whose instincts must have been similar to those of her two grandmothers, Queen Alexandra and the Duchess of Teck, each of whom was capable of being up to a couple of hours late for meals, which must have been astonishing even in Victorian times.

We used at Windsor to come down at nine o'clock to breakfast, not to eat – we'd done that – but to play, visibly of course but if possible inaudibly. The King had an African Grey parrot called Charlotte of which he was very fond; it sat at a table by his side eating seeds or the apple core he gave it, sometimes perching on people's hands, including my mother's. Like all parrots, it clung on hard and we were scared of those pinching claws and that awesome beak, so that my grandfather shouted: 'The parrot will see that child's nervous – make him keep still.'

Gerald and I were staying once at Windsor in spacious nursery rooms and contrived to spill a pot of ink on to the writing-table top. I had a brainwave and mopped it up with the little dry sponge which sat in a glass dish on each writing table in case anyone wanted to wipe a nib. Where to put the ink-soaked sponge? Not back in the dish, we thought, so I threw it out of the window, not realizing it would land two floors below on my grandfather's balcony. We were not popular.

The possibility of getting something wrong was, where my grandfather was concerned, raised to heights of extreme probability, and our visits to Windsor for Easter usually provided their quota of uneasy moments. In 1931 he had been dangerously ill and was terrified of getting a cold. I had started to get hay fever and at the end of April, as we went to say goodbye to him in his sitting room after breakfast, I started to sneeze, either from the pollinating grass or sheer nerves, and no amount of assurance that I had hay fever could stop the shouts of 'Get that damn child away from me', which made a rather strong impression on an awakening imagination.

Gerald and I were involved in many celebrations, big and small, at either Buckingham Palace or Windsor. At Windsor one Easter, when I was six or seven, I stood holding my grandmother's hand in awe at my first sight of black people, when King Amanullah of Afghanistan came with his entourage and paid his respects to the King. For years we had a massive gramophone in a mahogany case with his crest on it which he had given to my mother. I believe this visit proved his undoing and he was deposed before he could return to Kabul. But my wonder at all those black people dressed like Westerners and behaving like them and not as I naively expected like cannibals or little black Sambo lasted quite a while.

We went regularly before the war to parties at Buckingham Palace. There were Levées, celebrating my grandmother's birthday, at which a Guards Band played; I was regularly given 'In a Monastery Garden', joined now in my affections by the Londonderry Air. Years later, my friend Morris Smith, orchestral manager at Covent Garden, told me he had played at Buckingham Palace in the late twenties when he was nineteen and newly joined. He played the trombone, as he thought quietly, and his chagrin was intense when an equerry was sent to the Bandmaster to ask him to quieten the trombonist whose stentorian tones were disturbing Her Majesty! He also remembered 'In a Monastery Garden', but did not know it was my fault that it got an encore.

Visits to Windsor at Easter, to Sandringham at the end of our Christmas holidays, and for high days and holidays to Buckingham Palace were rather formal, but we were encouraged to treat them as less than abnormal. This was not completely successful, but it was something of an achievement on my parents' part that it was only after the war that I realized I was Queen Mary's eldest grandchild and that this in itself appeared to have meant more to other people than it ever did to me.

A celebration I remember more vividly than others is that of the Silver Jubilee in 1935. It dominated that summer and some of my memories of it are very positive indeed, like the sound of the bells crashing in together as we neared St Paul's where the service was to take place. I found this thrilling, and was delighted when Benjamin Britten used the bells at the start of the second act of his Coronation opera *Gloriana* nearly twenty years later. Another musical memory of the Silver Jubilee is of the bands along the route stationed a few hundred yards apart, constantly playing 'God Save the King' as different elements of the procession appeared. What was exciting was that as we drove along with my mother in an open carriage we could hear one band merging into another in a brutal kind of counterpoint, which I found much later was done symphonic justice to (with admittedly different tunes) by Charles Ives, the American composer. At the service itself, I was overwhelmed by the anthem 'I vow to thee my country', the tune to Cecil Spring-Rice's words taken from Holst's *Planets*. The melody haunted me for days and, when the record of the service was issued, this part of it was a source of great joy.

Less joyful to both Gerald and myself was the wearing of the kilt, which was the garb my grandfather had decreed we should appear in for his Silver Jubilee. We did not think of ourselves as Scots; we hated trying on the things and resented our not very successful attempts to get them to hang and swing properly. In fact the only thing which relieved our conviction that we had been made complete guys of was the *Sgiandubh* which we each wore in our stocking – a naked, sheathless dagger which had to be put in quite carefully if it were not to slice either flesh or hose. They were very satisfactory to fling into the wooden heads of our beds too, but that was quickly discouraged.

When my grandfather died in January 1936, we were duly overcome by the solemnity of the occasion, by the fact that anything like the cinema or football was banned for us, and then by the cold and majesty of his funeral procession, in which we took part only in carriages, being too young to march with the men. At Paddington we stood waiting to get into the train with my father, who was in uniform. We were to travel to Windsor with him and, noticing a rather bent figure in obviously German uniform with what looked to me like a storm-trooper's helmet, I asked who that old man was. 'Old man!' snorted my father. 'We were at school together and he is four years younger than me!' It was the Duke of Coburg, who sat with us in the train and turned out to be delightful company, which is not surprising since his sister, Princess Alice, was the easiest and most charming of all my mother's older relations.

The procession through the streets of London, with its constantly repeated Dead March from *Saul* and Chopin's Funeral March, each of which I took to my heart, was the most impressive part of the funeral, and the service in St George's Chapel relatively private. I remember the family, led by the new King, filing out singly and bowing to the coffin, which was by then lowered into the grave. Here was a new dilemma. How long to leave before following my father, how long to pause before bowing? Might one even fall in?

The Abdication came during my second half (as we idiosyncratically called the term) at Eton, and I remember in late 1936 seeing a newspaper placard with the words 'The King and Mrs Simpson' and imagining that it was probably someone appealing for clemency for a condemned son. King Edward VIII, who was Gerald's godfather, had even for us as children what we now call charisma, and it was a great shock when at the beginning of December I was summoned to my housemaster's room and shown a letter from my mother which said that he had told his family he had decided to abdicate, that his decision was irrevocable, and that this letter and its contents were to be wholly private between the master and me until the public announcement was made. He said, 'This is very distressing news', and I know I found it as shattering as everyone else. Before the Christmas holidays began, I remember a very hang-dog expedition to London to watch the proclamation of King George VI – hang-dog because of the sadness attending the departure of his brother, not lack of enthusiasm for the new King.

My parents were I think the first of his family to go to see the new Duke of Windsor in exile, in Vienna in February 1937. But the Abdication, its inevitability, the country's reaction, the possibilities still before the ex-King – these things were discussed *ad nauseam* until well after the war. My parents never talked about it when I was present, although I had heard that my uncle, while he was King, had written a stinging rebuke to my father when in March 1936 he delivered a British Legion speech protesting the occupation by Hitler of the Rhineland – how could the King contribute to foreign policy if his own relations made irresponsible statements? I knew that as Duke of Windsor he came every so often to London, when my mother usually saw him with my grandmother at Marlborough House, and all of us knew that he was condemned for putting private life above duty. But it was hard for the younger amongst us not to stand in amazement at the moral contradiction between the elevation of a code of duty on the one hand, and on the other the denial of central Christian virtues – forgiveness, understanding, family tenderness.

I have never ceased to wonder that it was only in 1953, pausing in New

York for a night between aeroplanes (she had been in the Caribbean), that my mother met her sister-in-law for the first time, when she went to pick up her brother so that they might go together to London where Queen Mary was dying. She told me afterwards that she had found her charming, and that was how I found the Duke and Duchess of Windsor when they invited their by now grown-up nephew to lunch at their house near Paris a few years later. It was quite a large party but thoroughly enjoyable, and my uncle and aunt made everyone feel important while going through the motions of giving them a drink and showing them round the garden, of which he was justifiably proud.

Topazia Markevich, wife of the conductor Igor, told me that, staying once in Venice, she was invited to a party at which the Duke and Duchess of Windsor were the guests of honour. Topazia mentioned to the Duke that she knew me, and he asked if I was competent at my Covent Garden job; then could not resist saying: 'It's very odd about George and music. You know, his parents were quite normal – liked horses and dogs and the country!'

Patricia and I saw him once in front of the Ritz Hotel in Madrid, when we were staying there before we were married and he was waiting to be picked up to play golf. By then he looked tiny and I loomed over him, half uncertain as to whether to make a move, but deciding in the end to do so. Perhaps for me the saddest public result of my divorce was that I was not asked to go to his funeral at St George's, Windsor, where nearly forty years before I had watched him bow at his own father's funeral.

I was already at Eton by the time of the Coronation in 1937. To my gratification I was bidden to be a page to King George VI. This was not arduous but involved a number of rehearsals at Westminster Abbey, as much could go wrong; timing and placing had to be of military precision, and nobody was going to let us spoil it. We pages ranged in age from grown-ups, like the descendants of Haig and Jellicoe, to at least two younger than me.

The uniform was less ridiculous than the kilt we had worn a couple of years before, and the rehearsals meant we had to come up specially from school and spend the day in London which was enjoyable (Gerald was a page to Queen Mary). We wore knee breeches and a kind of scarlet tunic which reached to the knees and was bordered with gold braid, but at least it had the merit that several of us were kitted out in it, not just Gerald and me. My cousin Sandy Ramsay, son of my godmother Lady Patricia Ramsay, and I were shortly afterwards pages to Queen Mary at the annual Garter Service at Windsor in the same uniform. Both Gerald and I had Silver Jubilee and Coronation medals as a result of our connections and wore them on our

Corps uniforms at school, to our slight embarrassment and the equally slight mockery of our contemporaries.

Gerald and I are eighteen months apart. I was taken to see him soon after he was born and, word has it, resented him very much. I suppose I felt threatened by the new baby; and later, he was always the favourite of our nannies – perhaps rightly; but I could not be expected to care for that. Certainly it was a mistake on their part to show it, and I remember a moment of triumph when I was punished for something that was wrong – but Gerald had done it, not me.

In later life, we have been relatively close, particularly against the rest of the world. As children, we sometimes quarrelled as brothers can, but the riding, the cricket and the football matches we shared happily, as also the walks and the fishing in the lake for pike, which in the winter we vastly enjoyed.

Gerald was a better fisherman than me and unlike me graduated to fly-fishing for trout. The lake was important to us during our holidays; we rowed on it in summer and for several years in anything like decent weather we bicycled lustily round it before breakfast, returning to the five-course feasts at nine-fifteen which were offered in those days in country houses. In winter, skating was a quite regular feature of Christmas holidays forty years ago, and with luck this included some not very serious ice hockey.

On the lake were regularly to be seen Canada geese, which after the war increased to become a pest but whose hound-noise calls we then (as now) enjoyed; and Whooper swans, a smaller and obviously more vocal bird than the commoner Mute and in our view much more handsome. We took pride in the fact that at that time Harewood was the place furthest south where Whoopers bred, and was on that account mentioned in bird books; in winter the keepers wired them in against the foxes, and we pointed them out for admiration to our visitors. When they nested, Gerald and I noted the sites they had chosen and took care to avoid that part of the lake. Such immunity did not apply to the water-hens which nested all over the lake and whose eggs we used to take and cook for tea.

Our childhood holidays were dominated by the fantasies we invented for ourselves, along more or less James Bond lines but years before that worthy became a folk hero; we postulated an existence of such luxury as to be almost unparalleled in real life but which sustained us through many an otherwise humdrum walk round the woods. My father's brother, Eddy Lascelles, lived nearby, and we found him then sufficiently entertaining to understand when our parents later told us what a tragedy it was his wife refused to have children. When we went with them for walks, I loved listening to the gossip, sometimes political, sometimes about people we knew, and have unhappy memories of the news coming through as we arrived by car at Newmarket one spring that he was critically ill and not likely to last the night. My father set out immediately for Yorkshire, but Uncle Eddy rallied for a few months, to die later that summer of 1936.

Food at Harewood was delicious and we were greedy, and the contrast between the rich fare at home and the plain stuff at school tried our digestions to the utmost. In fact, we had perpetual wind problems. My mother used to have a room in which she undid parcels, kept presents, put away things she did not want to use at the moment and which was a general glory hole; she called it the Little Library and we (including my father) called it the Piggery. Once, we were waiting there to go to bed while my parents looked for a present for someone, when a particularly noisome smell spread through the room. 'I think it must be a dead rat under the floorboards,' said my father. 'There was once one when I was a child and it took them several days to find it – and it smelt just like that.' It died down and could have been forgotten had it not recrudesced. This time my father decided that something must be done, and vast investigations took place until a rat's skeleton was duly found, although everyone was amazed that the part of it which had caused the smell could have disappeared so quickly. Only years later did I discover that Gerald was the cause of it all – the farter with a poker face would go far.

Although I was a hopeless pianist, music already had started to make an impression. King Amanullah's gramophone stood in the Music Room at Harewood and I was allowed under supervision to play records occasionally in the evening. As well as 'The Song of the Flea', there was a duet called 'The Keys of Heaven' sung by Clara Butt and her husband Kennerley Rumford, and its Victorian melody and impeccable sentiments (she capitulates only when he offers 'the keys of my heart') appealed to me strongly, as did the well-worn melody of 'Clementine'. We were taken to a film with Richard Tauber in it, *Blossom Time*, which started where *Lilac Time* left off and included a fair number of Schubert songs sung by one I later came to recognize as a master of *Lieder*. I was convinced Tauber was the greatest tenor who had ever lived, but my grandmother assured me Caruso was much greater and gave me his recording of 'Santa Lucia' to prove it, which it did, establishing a new favourite tune at the same time.

20

We owned a pianola in good working order, and I used to fix the rolls and listen with awe as Paderewski's or Josef Lhevine's fingers worked their magic through the medium of the fretted paper. You could control dynamics and some degree make the rolls go faster or slower, and my enthusiasm often provoked remonstration from my mother as she did her knitting or needlework to the accompaniment of Chopin or the Moonlight Sonata with *my* dynamics and *rubato*. There was a pianola roll of an arrangement of the 'Prize Song' from *Mastersingers* which I discovered had a particular significance in my parents' courtship – precisely what I never knew – and I demanded a record of the real version. I got the money to buy it in Harrogate; the shop produced Piccaver's Decca recording, and that joined my list of early favourites.

I went away when I was nine to a preparatory school called Ludgrove, long before the period when you could admit that you didn't in every respect enjoy school, so the stiff upper lip and the bitten lower lip were the order of the day before going back each term. On the whole, I think I rather enjoyed it all, apart from sometimes being cold, sometimes uncomfortable, and occasionally being punished for not working hard enough. There were certain agreeable unwritten rules: boys were not allowed to mock other boys because of the foibles or the clothes of their parents – if a mother came down in a ridiculous hat, it wasn't done to say so. And if somebody was born foreign, it was not done to point it out.

Ludgrove had other attributes which I liked. It was very much a cricketing school run by people who had played for university, and I was influenced particularly by Alan Barber, a master who had captained Yorkshire a couple of years before I arrived. Games I always enjoyed, and as a bonus – surprising to many I have said this to – I never remember being bullied there. All the same I don't forget the horror of going away to school at the age of nine – a lot of children go earlier than that now – and I think that the notion of boarding school is, on the whole, barbarous. I understand why it grew up in England; I accept that imperial expatriates wanted to send their children home and country people in the past often wanted better than local schooling for theirs, and I know that it works quite well. But the depths of loneliness one could occasionally plumb trying to get to sleep at night are unrivalled in my experience, even during the war. Still, on the whole I enjoyed it, and it was at that soccer stronghold which was Ludgrove – founded by G. O. Smith, the Corinthian centre forward, and Arthur Dunn – that I learned to play and to love football.

My footballing career reached no heights of glory, and perhaps its pinnacle was to captain the Second XI at Ludgrove and at outside right somehow to outrun a left back who was even slower, and score the winning goal. The glory of that moment did something to compensate for the horror of having as captain to call for three cheers for the opposing side at the end of the match, perhaps the first time I had ever raised my voice in public without having been asked a question first. History was my strong point, and before I left I was awarded the school history prize, the master to my infinite pleasure in his speech saying that I knew my history book as well as I knew my Wisden. Schoolboys in my day were not only subject to 'crazes' – yo-yos were 'in' when I went to Ludgrove – but were also collectors of one thing or another. We collected cigarette cards, and somewhere I still have album after album which I acquired while I was there. Perhaps this was the start of a character trait which within five years had me collecting gramophone records.

I had no difficulty with Common Entrance Examination, and I went to Eton when I was thirteen. I was in the house of Charles Rowlatt, an interesting man badly wounded in the First World War; we used to say that he had a tin tummy and a tin plate in his head and that they hurt in bad weather. He was an old-fashioned kind of schoolmaster, a disciplinarian, good at not interfering but also skilful at knowing what was going on. He was on that account a good housemaster, but an odd, remote, rather uncultivated kind of person, very much a bachelor and, my mother used to think, thoroughly scared of women. He thought of the arts as peripheral, and he wouldn't let anyone in the house act in school plays.

It was perhaps to the credit of both Charles Rowlatt and my father that it was not until I was looking through letters I had inherited that I found my housemaster had suspected me (or had written to say he did) of being a fire-raiser. It is quite clear from the tenor of his letters – 'Dear Lord Harewood, I am afraid I cannot take so light a view as you of George's misdemeanour' – that my father refused to take seriously what was no more than an accident. I had been drawing my fire with a newspaper, turned away and found it had fallen and was in the process of setting fire to my waste-paper basket. With some aplomb, as I thought, I extinguished the conflagration with a little water from my water-jug (you can't beat out a smouldering wicker basket), but the water trickled down the oil-cloth passage, was reported, and duly blown up in this manner to my father. Neither parent nor master ever let on to me that I was suspected (quite wrongly) of these tendencies.

Although I didn't in the end want to send any of my children to Eton, this is not to say that I did not appreciate much about it. I started there on the wrong foot, catching measles at the very beginning of April 1936 so that I went up in May a few days late. Those first days were meant for new boys to find their way about, and it must have taken me a year in which to recover from that lost initiation period. I could never, as it were, quite find the place. I was the only new boy in the form I was put into and I was always bottom of it, to my intense irritation, because I had always been near the top at Ludgrove.

What I think we did get at Eton was an education – in the sense that we learnt how to learn, acquired a certain discipline of mind, accepted that not everything had to have an immediate pay-off. We certainly worked quite hard, with early school at seven-thirty both summer and winter, three further periods of schoolwork in the morning, another of preparation before lunch, and on alternate days two more in the afternoon. Supplement this with a fair amount of out-of-school preparation, and it adds up in its own way to a fairly full curriculum. Life was of course much less comfortable than at home, and we have all joked since that the conditions in which we existed at Eton would be condemned in any publicly-owned establishment.

At Eton I quickly gave up trying to learn the piano, to my subsequent regret. Dr Henry Ley was head of music at Eton, and I returned to music study after School Certificate, when we were allowed to discuss and learn about music in something rather quaintly called Extra Studies, which occupied two or three periods of school hours every week. Expert at it even then, I used to work the gramophone for the good doctor, endeavouring beforehand with only partial success to make sure that the two turntables were revolving at the same speed so as to minimize changes of pitch as we switched from side to side for the eight or ten sides of a symphony (78 rpm recordings lasted no more than four minutes per side). Daddy Ley was a kind old man, a splendid organist who had been a fellow student of Stokowski's – and he was the first man to assure me that this and not Stokes (as was popularly rumoured) was his true name. He found it hard to cope with our group, which included tearaways like Humphrey Lyttelton, and he dealt with us by ignoring discipline and pretending we were grown-ups. It didn't work too badly.

One very odd aspect of life at Eton was the Officers' Training Corps. About half the school assembled after lunch on Mondays. We drilled a bit and we used spasmodically to go out for field days, which were the most attractive aspect of the Corps. None of us took it seriously, to the misery of the First World War officer who ran it. We wore a uniform of quite unparalleled hideousness, a sort of crushed mulberry colour said to have originated when a master bought up a huge quantity of left-over cloth somewhere about the time of the South African War, and the colour was retained apparently in perpetuity. An attempt to wind puttees round one's legs so that they stayed up was one of the small problems of weekly life, and the whole exercise seems in retrospect one of almost complete futility.

Every now and then we were inspected, either by a general or some other grandee, and on one unforgettable occasion the Queen (now the Queen Mother) came down to perform this function. I remember my sensation of frozen horror as she got nearer and I was terrified she would recognize me and even speak to me, and the smile I got (and of course did not dare return) hardly put an end to my ill-concealed misery, which she apparently noticed and commented on.

I always had hay fever in the summer, and that didn't help the cricket; I never got into the Eton XI. I can measure my own keenness by a comparison with my eldest son, David, who was a better cricketer than I, and was in the First XI at Westminster as an all-rounder when he was sixteen. At the time of his 'A' levels, we discussed whether he should stay up the following year, and I said, 'Well, you will probably be captain of cricket,' which seemed to me an inducement. But he said, 'That's not a good enough reason to stay here.' He may have got his priorities right, but in the end he needed more 'A' levels for university, stayed on, and captained the XI.

I always longed to be strong and muscular, to be an athlete and more than just a moderately skilful games-player. Football at Eton in those days meant the Field Game, much loved by my contemporaries but to me a primitive, unevolved form of football in which such skills as passing were against the rules. I played it when I had to, which seemed excessively often, but far preferred another Eton game, Fives, played in a court modelled on the space between two buttresses of the Chapel. It is fast and energetic, demands considerable skill, some of which I managed to acquire, and I derived great pleasure from it.

I was very fond of my father, though as a boy I was slightly in awe of him. I admired him as an upright and fair person; as, I thought, a good judge of people, and somebody who was amusing and who took pains at the same time to make serious things palatable, and to teach us not to treat life with the solemnity schoolmasters seemed to encourage. I have always told my own sons that they must remember that everything matters, but also that they must not forget that nothing matters so much as to amount to tragedy, and I learnt it from my own father.

He was a man with a wide range of interests, very much a countryman, who rode and shot well and loved all aspects of country life, which he observed and explained to us as children. He could be very good company and, although he wasn't really wrapped up in children, made life interesting precisely because he did not talk to one as a child. Every evening after tea when we were young he used to read to us from Kipling's *Jungle Book*, dramatically and resonantly, and these readings were much looked forward to.

When we went hunting, our old groom, Dick Froude, came with us and we tended to enjoy ourselves in a middling kind of way. One red letter day, when Dick was ill, my father was going out and said that he would look after us, which simply entailed our keeping up with him. He rode well and without fear, which was more than could be said for us boys. But I think we each separately decided that to show our fear was more frightening than the prospect of jumping without palaver the fences my father jumped. As a result we rode boldly at everything a few yards behind him, and had easily the best day's hunting of our young lives.

At race meetings we were encouraged to look and judge for ourselves, to see why a race had turned out the way it did and how that result had fitted our and our parents' prognostications. We went out shooting too, mostly at Harewood, and I remember my father taking me to alternate with him grouse shooting on the famous Blubberhouses Moor in Yorkshire. He shot twenty grouse at the first drive and, from just as many 'possibles', I got only two at the second; 'You got ten times as many as I did,' I said accusingly. 'Perhaps I've shot ten times as often as you have,' was his rather consoling answer.

When I was very young, my father did embroidery and *petit-point* (he was a Freemason and learnt and repeated his Masonic ritual while sewing). There are several chairs at Harewood covered by him with needlework copies of Gould birds. His passion in the arts was painting, and as soon as he could afford it, he collected pictures. Virtually all the Italian pictures at Harewood were bought by him, and I loved tagging on behind when my parents showed visitors round the house. Occasionally we used to go together to exhibitions, and increasingly as I grew older I found I enjoyed looking at pictures. What he saw there seemed to be immediately worthwhile, well observed, suggestive. Music had always been part of his background. As a young man, he heard Jean de Reszke, later Caruso, Melba and Scotti, and he went frequently to the opera. Paintings and drawings, though, were his major interest.

My father inherited a fortune from an eccentric great-uncle, Lord Clanricarde, whose sister married my great-grandfather, and whose mother was the daughter of George Canning the Prime Minister. My father was wounded several times in the 1914–18 war, and once on leave he was going to lunch at the St James's Club when he recognized his great-uncle sitting in a corner. Lord Clanricarde was not at all popular in London, any more than in Ireland, where he had property; in fact he seems to have been a very disagreeable old man. In any case, my father, out of manners, went to sit with his great-uncle for half an hour before lunch. In 1916 Lord Clanricarde died, leaving all his money to my father, to the great fury of my grandfather.

It was then that my father started to buy pictures and drawings, using as his agent Tancred Borenius, a Finn by birth but by adoption very much a Londoner, who worked at Sotheby's. I remember Tancred Borenius very well from when I was a child and became very fond of him. In fact I took him to the first performance of *Peter Grimes* in 1945, and got to know him well over the years. He was an old-fashioned *savant*, who seemed informed and informative about everything, a cultivated man and excellent company, the first intellectual I got to know.

Old Lord Clanricarde had an apartment in Albany, and was so mean that rumour had it he used to search the dustbins of Piccadilly to see if they contained a decent bit of bread for his lunch. After my father died, my mother showed me odd bits of Lord Clanricarde's mother's jewellery from which Uncle Hubert had broken off a piece to stick on a safety-pin as a tie-pin, sometimes dyeing a diamond with blue ink because he wanted it to look like a sapphire or with red ink to make it look like a ruby. A very odd man.

I went in the fifties to a performance of *Don Giovanni* in Dublin in which singers from Covent Garden were appearing – Joan Sutherland was Donna Anna, Geraint Evans made his only appearance in the title role, famous as he was as Leporello – and I sat in a box with the President of Ireland. He told me he was happy to have me as his guest so long as I didn't tell anyone I was related to Lord Clanricarde, because that was bad news in Ireland.

Neither of my parents showed emotion easily and, though I clung to my mother as a little boy and haunted her sitting room and bedroom at Goldsborough, my declarations of affection were regarded I think as slightly embarrassing and something I would grow out of. I therefore to some degree did so. We did not talk of love and affection and what we meant to each other, but rather – and even about that not easily – of duty and behaviour and what we ought to do, which did not at all encourage spontaneity or a confident, out-going point of view. I was naturally shy, but the behavioural pitfalls with which the great world seemed to be bedevilled undoubtedly contributed to such an attitude. I never felt entirely confident with my parents until I was grown up and had been through the war, and I think they found it as hard to talk in a serious and yet personal vein to us as we did to them.

As an illustration of the degree to which we subordinated our emotions, I remember my amazement when I was told by one of his contemporaries, on my return from prison at the end of the war, that my father had had a row in his club with Sir Robert Vansittart, who was thought to be the architect of Churchill's policy of German unconditional surrender, which my father found not only obnoxious but certain to endanger the lives of prisoners, of whom I was one. My father had let his emotions run away with him on my account and in public! I could hardly believe it.

My parents got on well together and had a lot of friends and interests in common. Someone years later told my first wife Marion that she had always felt sorry for my mother 'married to that cold, hard man', but, though she was doubtless primarily out to make mischief, she had it all wrong. My mother was never so happy to our eyes as children as when she and my father were embarked on some scheme together, as they often were, and my father's advice was sought on every conceivable subject including those on which he could not possibly have been expected to have a view. After he died, we could see with maturer eyes that, without my father at her side, she often found it hard to cope. Until her death she travelled with photographs of him to put out wherever she stayed, and when in later years we would rearrange furniture or a whole room at Harewood, she often snorted to others (but tactfully never to me): 'Well, it was good enough as it was for Harry and me.'

Shyness, I should imagine, was one of the first things people noticed about my mother; gentleness and kindness as well, with in later life a little Hanoverian spleen underneath it all. She was conditioned to communicate only on as uncontroversial a level as possible; I have always believed that this was the result of an upbringing which discouraged direct discussion or any display of emotion. Instead, it encouraged a form of family feeling which was strong, even loving, though it still to my mind substituted superficial regular contact for something closer. That my mother's interest in Family was inculcated early on I have no doubt, as with Queen Mary it was very strong indeed.

My mother responded throughout her life to her upbringing, and maintained family contact by becoming an inveterate letter-writer. She wrote up to a minute before post-time, and we blessed the day when during the war the afternoon post from Harewood was altered to leave at four-thirty in the afternoon rather than the five-thirty my mother had discovered it to be – for my father had declared collection at the house was at five o'clock so that there would be some hope of our getting tea at the proper time.

Most mornings from the time I was twelve until after the beginning of the war my mother used to come riding with us. She rode with skill, and we had a certain sense of pride when we were considered old and responsible enough to go out with her alone and without a groom – an odd source of satisfaction that sounds now!

Gardening was one of the things my parents liked to do together, and when Gerald and I were children we used to go out with them in the afternoon and help reduce unruly thickets of rhododendrons to manageable proportions. To this end all sorts of implements were kept in the basement at Harewood and sedulously cleaned and oiled after use. We pulled up ragwort when we found it on our walks, and in the autumn gathered great bags of Spanish chestnuts which, if there had been a warm summer, made a delicious addition to vegetables at lunch – we always had them as a purée and they gave my mother as much satisfaction as if she had cooked them herself.

When she grew older, it was the pruning of roses my mother preferred to the removal of over-exuberant rhododendrons, and she would go off pruning on a summer evening with a lady-in-waiting while we played tennis.

My father bred most of the racehorses he had in training and we used to go regularly to see the foals when they were born in the months between Christmas and Easter, and then in the summer to watch the mares and foals in one lot of paddocks, and the yearlings segregated by sex in the others. Practice made us reasonably discriminating about those likely to look well and, even more important, move well when grown up, and we became amateur connoisseurs of the pedigrees of the animals we observed year after year from birth through a racing career until they reached the status of brood mares at stud.

As we got older, the demands Gerald and I made in holiday time naturally became greater. Gerald used to play the piano, at first hymn tunes, later jazz, but we still had a lot of spare time at Harewood and used to look for ways of filling it constructively. When I was ill in 1934, my grandmother lent me her portable typewriter and I taught myself to type, not stylishly but fast and relatively accurately. I soon acquired my own, and we started a spasmodic holiday magazine, which we called the *Harewood News* and wrote, typed, duplicated and delivered for something like three years before the war. We indulged every kind of literary conceit from cricket and football notes, through gardening articles, short stories, motoring and railway notes, historical reflections on aspects of Harewood, mostly written by us, occasionally by others. I was an avid follower of racing form, and used to listen to what my father and his friends said. My racing notes therefore occasionally contained a tip, which unfortunately some gossip columnist in a newspaper once wrote up as if my father had written the column. He did not conceal his embarrassment from us.

Worse though was to come in the weeks before the war, when our last edition of the *Harewood News* carried a description of an anti-aircraft gun site near Leeds, which we had been taken round by an acquaintance who belonged to the Territorials. We checked with him and wrote it all up – as was perfectly legitimate, since it had been described in the local newspapers – but unfortunately we specified the number of the sites round Leeds, and that was a piece of classified information. The papers duly noticed our error and proceeded to feature it, speculating as to whether the War Office would find themselves obliged to censure us. As we drove off to watch cricket at Scarborough, in half the towns or villages we went through there were newspaper posters announcing 'Royal Boys in War Office Crisis' and 'Harewood Boys Face Censure', which scared and irritated us in about equal measure. 'Harewood boys' indeed! We were '*Lascelles* boys'! In the end, we got a good-natured letter from somebody at the War Office which described the whole thing as a storm in a teacup and told us of our technical infringement of the rules – but it was not the kind of thing our parents relished.

A major excitement for me early in the summer of 1939 was to go with my mother and grandmother to the opening night of the Covent Garden International season a couple of days before going back to Eton. Beecham conducted *The Bartered Bride*, and Tauber and Hilde Konetzni played the leads, singing wonderfully but even to my unsophisticated eye looking the parts less than convincingly. The glamour of the occasion impressed me greatly – I was probably the only person in the boxes not in a white tie – and I enjoyed the opera as well, although knowing none of it beforehand. Quite a different impression came from *The Magic Flute* in English at Sadler's Wells a year later, when I heard Joan Cross and David Lloyd in a performance of an opera I knew well from records, and remained in a state of pure delight at the grandeur of the performance and the glory of the work.

The war started when I was sixteen and a half and still had a couple of years to go at Eton. The black-out became a feature of our lives, which otherwise went on much as usual, except that the older members of the school dug trenches, filled sandbags and joined the Home Guard, returning from holiday in August 1940 to guard a power station or reservoir during the Battle of Britain, which we could occasionally see going on over our heads. At one point of the war, our parents were staying at Windsor and on Sunday we were invited there to lunch, the invitation going direct to our house-master. He said he could not possibly give permission – it is true that it was unusual, but so perhaps were the circumstances – and I had to get it from the Headmaster myself.

When I was eighteen, before joining the army, I left school and went to work as driver, taker-of-notes and general factotum for the Head of the War Agricultural Committee in the West Riding of Yorkshire, by name W.P. Richardson. I got great pleasure and profit from this job, and W.P. was a man of extraordinary capacity whose kindness to a callow youth will never be forgotten. When I started, he was off with toothache and I was, on his instructions, put to help sort the mail at eight-thirty every morning. I am not sure my driving made a very positive impression on all my passengers, though I remember as if it were yesterday my boss stopping as we passed his house outside Harrogate the first time I drove him and offering me a glass of sherry, all of which I contrived to swallow the wrong way. Five minutes of empurpled coughing was the sort of social gaffe I dreaded. I met a lot of War Agricultural people, farmworkers, Irish ditch-diggers, warp farmers near Goole, Dale farmers north of Skipton, and what little farming lore I have acquired (and mostly forgotten) has been as a result of that apprenticeship. During those six months, I lived at Harewood and learnt to find my way round the West Riding – all signposts had been removed against parachute attack. The first time I was sent from our HQ in Harrogate to Wakefield, I went through Leeds leaving the Queens Hotel on my right and on towards Wakefield, asking six miles down the road for County Hall, only to learn that I had arrived in Castleford.

It was early in the war, and I learnt to drink. It was early in my life, and I fell in love for the first time, but trembled to declare it.

W.P. loved the people who worked for him and one of them was a ditch-digger of dubious sobriety but impeccable skill. He was a true Yorkshireman and did not believe in disguising his opinions. I was primed about this before we went one day ostensibly to check up on what he was doing, really to make him feel wanted. W.P. greeted him and said, 'This is Lord Lascelles', whereupon our friend looked me up and down and asked: 'What? Them from Harewood? Aye, he's got look on 'em', which put me in my place.

To live in the country in the war was to have better rations than in town. We observed the rules rather strictly but took advantage of the pig allowed per household, which provided bacon, an occasional ham, and some pork to supplement the rations. There were pheasants, and we kept edible rabbits – Belgian Hares – in the stables. People came to stay, on their way to visit troops or in connection with their war-time jobs, but I remember virtually no leave home to Harewood from the time I joined the army in 1942 to the end of the war. The King and Crown Prince of Norway – Uncle Charles and Cousin Olaf – came to stay visiting Free Norwegian troops, and, to our great excitement, the formidable General de Gaulle. To him and his ADC we gave *escalope de veau* (in reality Belgian Hare beaten out flat and bread-crumbed; delicious nonetheless) and the best the cellar could provide, and after dinner took him to a film in the hospital, which from mid-1940 occupied most of the house.

Years later, in 1965, at the Buckingham Palace reception after Winston Churchill's funeral, the French Ambassador took me up to the General, now President of France. He remembered in exact detail the events of that single evening twenty-three years earlier, an almost impossible feat considering that the reception was attended by crowned heads and big-wigs from all over the world; I was hundreds down the pecking order, and the Ambassador had had no time in which to prime his chief. But he rolled it all out as if he had memorized it. Perhaps he never forgot anything!

Those six months at Harewood are full of jumbled memories, of Sadler's Wells Opera on tour in war-time conditions, of concerts in Leeds, of Saturday visits to the moors after the grouse. With Sadler's Wells I heard Walter Widdop, the great Yorkshire Wagnerian tenor, in of all operas *Butterfly*; I got to know popular operas, and above all I got to know Joan Cross, who was to become a lifelong friend. She brought a reduced version of their touring *Marriage of Figaro* on a Sunday to the hospital at Harewood; this was a red letter day in my life and a major experience, marred only because my father, a keen Mozartian, was ill in bed and could not hear it. I think the performances were good and I know that Joan herself was a supremely musical and exciting operatic artist. With Lawrance Collingwood she ran the company, and one of the might-have-beens of operatic life in our time is the fact that she spent the best years of her career touring and administering in wartime, not spreading her talents through the world in peace.

I was completely stage-struck in those days, and soon after I left school went with my mother to a Charity Gala at the Royal Hall in Harrogate, which featured many famous people including John Gielgud and Joan Cross.

My mother was the Gala's Patron and asked to see these two, and I actually trembled with excitement at the prospect of meeting them and shaking hands. I don't look back on this with shame as I have never lost that feeling for the magic of the theatre and still tremble with excitement and fear before a first night with which I am concerned.

Sadler's Wells provided most of the opera during that period, but variety of a rather special nature came with a visit to Leeds of a talented touring group with Moussorgsky's opera *Sorotchintsi Fair*. It was sung in Russian with the great Oda Slobodskaya as Khivria, Darya Bayan and Ermo Simberg as the young lovers, Arsene Kiriloff as a splendidly ripe Tcherevik, and with Parry Jones, Otakar Kraus and Marian Nowakowski in lesser roles. I have never seen it since, but caught it twice then in Leeds and again at the Savoy Theatre in London.

The opera habit was fixed by then and my diary entries for 1941–2, apart from engagements, consist almost entirely of broadcasts from Italy, Germany and oddly enough Hungary, and the casts I heard, or half-heard, on radio. My parents must indeed have been forbearing, to have tolerated night after night those stifled groans and static-ridden howls while we dined.

CHAPTER TWO

Guardsman Lascelles
1942-4

A MONTH AFTER my nineteenth birthday I joined my father's old regiment, the Grenadiers. Enthusiasm was perhaps not uppermost in my mind, and my diary rather too plaintively marks the day with the entry 'End of Civilization'.

I went to the Guards' Depot at Caterham, where I was Guardsman (R) Lascelles, 2622986 – I remember the number as if it were still in daily use! Once a week at Caterham you stood to attention by your bed, having laid out all your kit in an exact geometrical pattern for kit inspection. You yelled out your name and number to the inspecting officer and it was a matter of life or death if your socks weren't neatly folded or your mess tin wasn't in the right place. This was a period of intense physical activity, much square drill, some rifle and other military training, and quantities of good plain food. Apart from rather frequent bamboozlement as to the relevance of it all and where we were all going, and indeed sometimes where we actually were, it was not disagreeable.

In fact, the principle of military discipline, based on physical fitness and instant obedience, was something I have never quite forgotten (though not always practised), and it was well, humanely and quickly taught. There was a war on and everyone was in a hurry. Our eight weeks' basic training passed fast, but we were treated by pre-war soldiers to much reminiscence of the trials and tribulations of only a few years back, when the uniform webbing belts, carefully whited over the past three hours, were inspected and then thrown in the coal bucket; when tough men fainted on parade; when the man who went 'over the wall' was held to have admitted failure and not pursued. Such horrors were quite absent from our training, and the life if Spartan was not unenjoyable.

I remember we were allowed a weekend pass in the middle of the training; my mother went to stay at Windsor Castle and I was fetched by car at noon on Saturday for my leave. The bliss of sophisticated food and being allowed to wear civilian clothes for a few hours was slightly spoilt by my total inability to sleep on a soft bed, and by the Windsor driver, who brought me back to Caterham after dinner on Sunday, missing his way in the blackout so that we arrived ten minutes late. I was reported for being late back off leave, and had up to the Orderly Room next day before my Company Commander, who was a First World War officer come out of retirement. When he asked if I had anything to say I said, 'Nothing, sir', which seemed to me the truth, and I got some mild punishment. He stopped me later that morning and asked where I had been and what had happened. He seemed satisfied with the explanation, but at least I had not had to go through the rigmarole about Windsor and the car in the blackout in public.

From Caterham, with the status of a recruit – albeit a Guardsman (R) – I went to Sandhurst, one of the largest officer training establishments in the country. A small bedroom to oneself was a definite boon, and I made one or two friends there, including Derek du Pré, to whose daughter Jacqueline I after the war became godfather. The lectures were boring, the training arduous, and my own comprehension of what was expected militarily less than complete.

Military skills I found did not come easily, and some of the things we were asked to do we tackled with more desperation than conviction. We learnt to ride motor-cycles, which was intriguing for those of us who had not attempted it before. It's not hard to acquire the knack, but rather daunting to be required to ride up a vertical bank after only a few days' practice. Believing that death this way would be no messier than any other, I pointed my machine at the bank, opened the throttle as instructed but without much conviction that it would avert disaster, and found I could charge to the top without real difficulty. This was the only piece of military expertise I ever found I was better at than the next man. But I found starting the bike after it had stalled inordinately hard, and after a few days the calf of my right leg, from the number of times the starting pedal had rebounded on to it, was like beaten steak and I was forbidden to ride for a week.

Nonetheless, I completed the course, was passed fit to be commissioned, and, after a week's leave, went off to Windsor to join the Training Battalion of the Grenadiers, one of half a dozen newcomers categorized as 'young officers', chased round the square and over the training ground by knowledgeable and on the whole benevolent sergeants and by benevolent and on the whole knowledgeable officers.

Not always so benelovent though was the commanding officer of this training battalion. He took a dislike to me, which was of course his prerogative, and showed it when we were on a peculiarly nasty battle course. This involved amongst much else crawling some distance under live fire, and climbing a tree and getting across a rope to another tree – something which I found inordinately difficult, having powerful legs, which enabled me to march forever, but weak arms, which would not raise my own weight more than once or twice. In a state of some exhaustion, I hauled myself up the tree to near the top, where a sergeant was waiting to give a helping hand in case the last yard or two proved difficult. This was all too obviously so in my case, and he leant down only to hear stentorian bellows from the commanding officer: 'Let him fall! Don't give him a hand!' The sergeant reacted with, 'Don't take any notice of the old bugger, sir. Give me your hand and I'll haul', which he proceeded to do, thus saving me from certain injury and earning my commanding officer my intense dislike as opposed to my lasting hatred.

One of my Windsor memories is of my astonishment and delight on finding that a group of senior officers led by the adjutant Dick Briscoe wanted, like me, to hear the BBC's broadcast of *Turandot*, with Eva Turner and Frank Titterton. Another is of a parade in wintry weather when we were drilling on the square and I made the mistake of turning left with both feet in the air. The crash hurt at the time, but by mid-afternoon had resulted in a stiffness that made walking almost impossible. The doctor took a typically military view: send him and his haematoma on leave and let someone else patch him up!

I went up to Harewood with my massively bruised behind, and for days sat on a rubber ring and moved about as little as possible, time agreeably spent going through old copies of *Musical America* which a friend had sent me, at the end of which I knew a great deal more than I ever expected about music in America in the 1930s and indeed about European operatic premières as well. After a few days I began to feel ill, and it was not hard to diagnose jaundice, of which I had only a mild dose, but which the doctor back at Windsor thought had come from rats peeing on our vegetable supplies at the barracks; at any rate, several of us went down with it.

I was at Windsor from October 1942, and then in London for a few months at Wellington Barracks – from the point of view of housing, a slum for all ranks, but close to the theatres of the West End and to Sadler's Wells's London home at the New Theatre, St Martin's Lane, almost opposite the building it subsequently occupied when I became its managing director thirty years later. Sadler's Wells were often in London at this period, and I went whenever I was free. In addition, memory recalls John Gielgud and Gwen Ffrangçon-Davies in *Macbeth*, Constance Cummings and Owen Nares in *The Petrified Forest* (the latter quite changing my view of what to expect from a so-called 'matinée idol'), and, best of all perhaps, Frederick Valk and Bernard Miles in *Othello*, the former mighty of voice in a way I have never since met outside opera in this mightiest of Shakespearean roles. Or was *A Month in the Country* with Valerie Taylor the most enjoyable as it was the subtlest of all the plays I saw at that time?

Otherwise, I remember a period of almost complete loneliness socially – I knew nobody in the battalion at all well – and, from the military point of view, a fog of incomprehension. But that was not quite all. I was due to go on leave, because an injection I had had in the back of my leg for varicose veins had gone badly wrong. The site of the injection had become infected and so painful that, as with my Windsor fall, I could hardly walk. I already had a ticket for an afternoon concert taking place at Wimbledon at which the famous Anglo-Viennese tenor Alfred Piccaver was to sing, and nothing short of a renewal of the Blitz would have kept me from it. I made my way there by underground, my limping (which was entirely genuine) exciting sympathetic comment from fellow-travellers about war-wounded (which I was not), but the opulent sound of Piccaver's voice would have made any discomfort worthwhile. Lotte Lehmann has written about 'his velvety voice which was and still is my great love amongst tenors', and the velvet and the long, sensuous phrasing were still there, even though he was in his late fifties. I could hardly contain my enthusiasm, and the Viennese-born lady next to me let hers rip, so that we compared notes of my recordings and her Viennese memories to mutual satisfaction.

Even complete rest did my 'wound' little good, and the military doctor who inspected the hospital at Harewood once a week felt that surgery could be the answer. This put our admirable local doctor very much on his mettle, and within ten days he had everything healed up and all threat of the surgeon's knife well behind us.

My military exploits on formal occasions were never notable for their *savoir faire*. Returned to Wellington Barracks, I found myself the junior officer, the subaltern, on King's Guard. This effectively meant I was for a day in charge of the detachment posted at Buckingham Palace. There was to be a great parade of one of the women's services in front of Buckingham Palace and the Queen was to take the salute. My job was to turn out the Guard, present arms as she went past, and keep the Guard in the forecourt of the Palace until she came came back through the gates, when we were again to present arms until she had disappeared into the Palace. All went well until the hour-long ceremony was over. I called my little body of troops to attention as the Queen came back through the gates, and then called for them to present arms. Unfortunately she stopped to talk to some people inside the Palace gates and, for what seemed like eternity, my little detachment held the 'Present', not a position you want to maintain indefinitely. How that episode ended I can't remember, but the uncertainty of it and the fear of making a mistake leaves a chill memory.

The Grenadiers had two battalions fighting in Africa, and we were waiting to go out to them as reinforcements. In May 1943, when I had been commissioned eight months and in the army about sixteen, a warning order came through for me and with it another week's leave. At its end, we were put on forty-eight hours' notice to leave but told to take each day as it came. My mother stayed in London, and we sampled every restaurant and went to every concert available – could it have been then that Benno Moiseiwitsch began his piano recital (as was then customary) with the national anthem and then left the stage for twenty minutes while the piano-tuner gave first aid to a note which had irretrievably stuck? – but eventually, with our packs on our backs and bands playing, we marched off to the station and thence by train to Liverpool for embarkation.

I had never been to sea before and I think the overcrowded squalor and stink of that troop-ship produced a dislike for sea travel which I shall never quite overcome. We docked at Philippeville in Algeria without incident, which I suppose is shorthand for saying we were not attacked (though we expected to be) and that somehow, though we got on each other's nerves, we contrived not to quarrel too seriously.

Philippeville gave most of us a quick taste of Middle Eastern tummy, and also introduced us to multi-seater lavatories. We bathed, and those of us susceptible to it came close to collapse with sunburn; we trained a little, and we went incessantly to those over-public latrines. A scirocco blew up at one point and, even though old hands of the Middle East had warned us of the disagreeableness in store, the reality surpassed any expectation, with searing heat as if you were in an engine room and too near hot metal, and a kind of claustrophobia accompanying it which reduced the spirits to zero level. My squitters were at their worst at this point and I was rushing two or three times an hour. It was a curious introduction to the world of abroad, and I could then have little idea of the pleasure new countries would eventually give me.

Within a few weeks I joined the third battalion of the Grenadiers at

Sousse, in Tunisia. They were resting after the campaign, and we worked only from about seven until half past nine or ten in the morning. Our only real function was to provide night guard over a POW camp which was fully set up with an inner and an outer ring of barbed wire, twenty yards apart. To show the inmates we were around and meant business, our instruction was to fire several bursts of machine-gun fire down fixed lines between the rows of barbed wire. The guns were pegged down and the drill was done every night, the bullets winging their way apparently harmlessly into the desert.

It seemed to me an odd and rather pointless custom, several weeks old by the time I superintended it, but mine was an unlucky night; half an hour after our fire-off came the message that a stray ricochet bullet had killed a soldier sleeping in his tent miles away, and that an inspecting party was on its way to see if anything had been different from other nights. Some weeks and a court martial later – I was only a witness, I think – it was decided that nothing had been done amiss, but the experience was rather daunting – and tragic for the victim.

From Sousse in August I was put in charge of a horde of prisoners recently captured in Sicily and on islands such as Panteleria. They were now on their way to Algiers, where I was to hand them over to Americans. There were about 1,500 of them, a hundred or so Germans, the rest Italians, and I had a dozen Guardsmen and a sergeant with me – not so inadequate a number as it might seem as the journey was through open and rather hostile country and escape would have had little point.

The job took us about a week, and I was in charge of the train and its French drivers and stoker. I felt very sorry for the prisoners, herded into cattle trucks with little more than the clothes they wore, and we used to stop every hour or so for a few minutes in the interests of sanitation, signalling our departure with blasts on the whistle and watching as dozens of unguarded enemy soldiers rushed back to the train, pulling their shorts and trousers up as they ran. Food was issued regularly and was no problem, but water was, and I insisted that we got water for them at every station. The French who controlled the stations and manned the train were none too keen about that, but until they produced the water my guard detail and I could stop the train moving, which we did, and with it, since it was a single track line, all the traffic in that part of the world too.

When we got to Algiers, I had to hand over to an American officer. He went down the train counting the prisoners and said: 'You are short on the count.' I said, 'OK, count again.' It takes quite a long while to count 1,500 people, and when he had been conscientiously down again he came up with quite a different figure, still short. The army likes figures, and is particularly keen on making someone take the blame if they don't tally. I doubted if this American was going to be the last to sign for our batch of prisoners and I was quite determined not to be lumbered with losing any, so, with the prospect of another recount and time not on his side, he signed. This journey, with our little attempts at mild humanitarianism, had its ironic overtones, as I spent the last ten months of the war as a prisoner myself.

I was given some leave in Algiers but immediately went down with pleurisy – not something to have in August in Africa, as it is painful in itself, like an acute appendicitis (which I haven't yet had), and liable to be accompanied in that climate by prickly heat. After a day and a half of abject misery, I was given morphia, and the relief and euphoria which followed is something I remember to this day. Thirty-five years later, I went to give a mid-day lecture in Manchester, and before it started an agreeable woman with grey hair came up to me and said, 'You don't remember me. I nursed you in hospital in Algiers.'

In London, I had made friends with an American officer, Jonathan Schiller, who was a musical lecturer with a passion for opera. I saw him again in Algiers, and we went together to a performance of *Werther* in the Opera House, not badly sung even though the small pouter-pigeon of a tenor tripped over the rangy Charlotte's feet after *Pourquoi me réveiller* and so inadvertently turned his declaration of love into something a little more precipitate. The young baritone, René Bianco, went after the war straight to the Paris Opéra, but his singing there never quite fulfilled what my opera-starved ears heard in 1943 as great promise.

This was my only North African operatic adventure, apart from an expedition from Sousse with a friend for a few days' leave in Tunis, memorable for a drive to the ruins of Carthage and a gramophone record shop which yielded a mass of French vocal recordings not available in England – *Voix de Son Maître* of Marjorie Lawrence, Singher, Pernet, Bernac; Polydors of Germaine Martinelli and Tirard; Odéons of Micheletti, Luart, Bourdin and Cesbron-Viseur; and above all the complete *Pelléas*, recorded in wartime under Désormière, with Joachim and Jansen in the title roles. I picked up a wind-up portable gramophone too, and somehow until I was taken prisoner hung on to my primitive gramophone equipment.

For Christmas 1943 we were at Constantine. The third battalion of the Grenadiers was commanded by Algie Heber-Percy, a very curious man, something of a military genius, loved by the battalion, whom he knew to a man, though not by his young officers, whose names and identities he mostly forgot. I think his priorities were not wrong and I admired him as a commander but disliked him for his unpredictable ways with his juniors. There was an element of the pirate in him, as perhaps there is in most good military commanders, and when the battalion captured a German bank during the North African campaign, he kept part of the money – with the knowledge or at least the connivance of his superiors – and sent a truck down to Cairo to buy Christmas luxuries for the battalion. This was typical of his paternalist view of his duties, and it was typical too that he decreed a battalion run on Boxing Day, some four or five miles across country, and equally typical that he waited at the finishing line to ensure that all the officers came in more than halfway up the list, as he had stipulated. It can't have been good for us to over-eat and drink one day and then run it off, but somehow it worked. Most things did with Colonel Algie.

In January 1944, my company went off on a training scheme, arriving after a day of travelling near Philippeville. Next morning, we were planning a programme when the telephone rang and we were told to return to Constantine ready to embark next day for Italy. I was the only officer in my company who hadn't seen action in Africa, and was told that any campaign in Italy would be infinitely less disagreeable than the training for it, if for no other reason than that everyone you were in contact with would be helpful and on your side instead of critical and trying to catch you out.

The Italian campaign had started in the autumn and we were involved only in its second phase, prevented from taking part in the Salerno landing, I understood, by shortage of transport. When we reached Naples early in February, the advance had been held up along a line which included the River Garigliano and was based on the reputedly impregnable Monte Cassino, a mountain topped by a monastery and so strategically placed that it was a regular feature of pre-war Italian military manoeuvres.

The routine was for an Allied battalion or brigade to be based on a particular village, to train from it and maintain it as a headquarters when it was the unit's turn to go up into the line. It was mid-winter, and 'go up' was no figure of speech, since the line seemed to be on the tops of a series of high mountains, and we occupied the near slopes, just above the snow-line and looking across at Monte Cassino some twenty or thirty miles away. By coincidence, I was first shot at (or rather shelled) on my twenty-first birthday, 7 February 1944, and three days later we toiled for most of the daylight hours up the mountain, taking over from a tired battalion in a rainstorm which turned to snow during the night. German patrols were said by our predecessors to be very active, and we tried to be more interested in them than the weather, which was ferociously horrible.

On that trip into the line the weather provided tougher opposition than the enemy, and we returned without casualties. Before our next tramp up the Cerasola mountain I could already feel a fever coming on, but trusted to providence that it would disappear. The climb was fierce and several men of the battalion did not make the top, where snow and (for me) mounting fever made the future seem a little bleak. I could eat nothing, but rumour had it that the weather had deteriorated and that the journey down the snowbound hill was now for a wounded man a twelve-hour carry with the Indian stretcher-bearers; reinforcements were hard to get up, and somehow to report sick after a single day in what was said to be a dangerous position seemed, and indeed was, unthinkable. For three days I was an even more useless fighting soldier than nature and training had intended, but youth and luck kept pneumonia at bay and it was not long before I was perfectly fit again and thanking my stars that inhibitions had triumphed over common sense and kept me there.

Army gossip was blaming the hold-up on what was thought to be an aesthetic reluctance to bomb the monastery at Cassino, which the same rumour insisted was a German observation post. (Do you remember this situation satirized when Allied officers talked languidly of Giotto's towers in Rossellini's film *Roma, Città aperta*, made just after the war?) The army was having casualties, dissatisfaction was growing and taking on class overtones. In due course we watched from our mountain the bombers go in for hour after hour and turn the monastery, which I have often since then been assured (including by the Germans) was not at that time used by the enemy, into a solid mound of rubble from which observation henceforth became not only easy but safe.

The weather was against the sporadic fighting which accompanied the regular use of patrols, and we tended to stay in the line between a week and a fortnight, depending on the deployment possibilities and the undeniable fact that fresh troops are better than troops tired from exposure. Not long after the bombing of Cassino, we were relieved, guided off the hill by night, reaching our new billets at a place called Petrullo at six-thirty in the morning. The march took place on a night dark with rain, down uneven, rocky paths which produced constant falls, and we arrived more exhausted than ever before. I had never had much liking for tea, but the mugfuls of strong, hot, sweet, military liquid ladled out to us at the end of that murderous march were the nearest thing to nectar I have ever encountered.

It was March, and weather in Italy was, to put it mildly, variable. The winter of 1943–4 was said to have been one of the worst winters in memory. Throughout the campaign, right up to midsummer when my participation came to an abrupt end, however hot the days, we always if sleeping out had problems with the cold. The blanket wrapped round one's pack and carried complainingly by day was crucial by night, when we all evolved, with the blanket and the light but air-tight gas cape we carried, some form of more or less cold-proof, private igloo.

I was in Italy for five months before being wounded. I was never abroad before the war, and Naples was therefore the first place on the Continent I ever saw. I had four or five leaves there, and I loved the place then and love it still, even though the drains stink, the food is the worst in Italy and the foreigner then as now was looked upon as fair game. There I first heard Italian opera sung by Italians, there occurred much of value in early manhood, and my debt to Naples is one I would not gladly discard.

The San Carlo Opera House is a truly splendid baroque legacy of the nineteenth-century ascendancy of the Italian opera. Performances at that time were preceded by the national anthems of all the Allies whose base Naples was. There must have been more than half a dozen played, and I once heard Stravinsky's arrangement of the 'Star Spangled Banner', which was found to infringe the American Constitution and forthwith proscribed.

Pina Esca, a strapping young soprano, was our resident prima donna, and very fine she was in *Forza del Destino* and *Andrea Chénier* and as an improbably healthy-looking Mimi, and Augusto Ferrauto was her tenor opposite number, a fine *spinto* tenor who sang everything, sometimes twice a day. I think each paid the penalty of too hard and varied a schedule and their careers failed to outlast the war, but there must be thousands of wartime operatic converts who will bless their names if they can still remember them.

Performances were far from sophisticated, and the chorus stood in an unvarying semi-circle so that you could pick them out individually performance by performance, noticing an absentee by the small gap between neighbours. I remember Ferrauto decorating his intense and exciting Don José with an unwritten 'Ohimé!' on the final cadence of *Carmen*; and I remember sitting one afternoon in a box with the baritone Ugo Savarese, who was scheduled to sing but who was at that period one of the most uncertain starters around, his place often taken by a fine character baritone, by name Ettore Marulli, whose beautiful voice used in a big role to start to get hoarse in the first aria and deteriorate from then onwards.

Food was not plentiful in Naples, and restaurants were therefore disinclined to serve much to occupying forces; but we found one called Ursini, next to the Albergo Patria, a transit hotel, which was kind to us. We ate mostly at military clubs. To one of these, the Giardino degli Aranci, Marlene Dietrich once brought more than a whiff of glamour simply by coming to dine there. From the Giardino degli Aranci we watched Vesuvius erupt, a magnificent sight at night as the lava poured glowing down the mountain's side, with occasional spouts from the summit as more explosions celebrated the most massive eruption for years.

The battalion had a flat off the Via Roma, and there I spent several periods of leave, comfortably and economically, with other officers from the battalion, notably my friend Harcourt Farebrother. He had arrived at Caterham with me, shared in the trials of the troop-ship to North Africa, joined the third battalion with me, shared a billet in Constantine, and was to be fatally wounded the same day as I narrowly avoided that destiny. He was a serious soldier and a good one, but we had otherwise much in common, including a love of music and a sense of the ridiculous. (He told me his housemaster at Winchester had put the boys on to rationing a week earlier than the rest of England *so that they would be prepared for it when it came in!*)

Naples was the provider of bright lights for us, and for me that meant predominantly the San Carlo and its opera, apart from one short period when it housed Irving Berlin's *This is the Army, Mr Jones*, which to my surprise I enjoyed – I was in those days a determined anti-lowbrow (with my ignorance I could not call myself a highbrow). One day I had arranged to call on the great soprano of Verdi's late years, Gemma Bellincioni, the original Santuzza too, who had retired to Naples. To my great chagrin, on this day she was unwell and could not see me; instead, I wandered up the Via Roma, determined to comb every second-hand shop in sight for gramophone records. That meant looking in every drawer of every piece of furniture, examining every pile of discs or books, and for once in my life I was lucky and for a few bob bought a pile of Battistini Warsaws, a de Lucia and a Boronat – treasure trove at any time, and some consolation for the disappointment over Bellincioni.

The mortality rate, or at least the risk of getting wounded, was then very high for officers, so a system grew up whereby the platoon commander alternated in battle with the platoon sergeant, his second-in-command. My platoon was I think eight times in action during the period February to June 1944, not counting abortive actions when nothing happened. Of the eight, I went five times and was wounded the fifth; my original platoon sergeant, Sergeant Treeby, was in battle in Italy twice, winning the DCM for great bravery the first time and getting killed the second. So statistically the risk was rather high.

At the end of March our base was moved to a village called Calvisi, and from there in early April we were sent into Cassino, to occupy ruined houses two hundred yards from the German front line, which involved a silent, nerve-racking entry by night, wondering all the time if a flare would reveal us to the enemy. I tried one morning to bring artillery fire on to a tank which appeared near the Continental Hotel opposite, but we did no better than a near miss; and early another morning I listened on the field telephone to the English side of a scare when a German patrol fetched up at first light on the upper floor of a bombed house of which the British were occupying the cellar. The agitated, sometimes angry efforts by the company commander a hundred yards further back to encourage his platoon commander, who spoke in hushed whispers and expected a hand grenade down the stairs at any moment, made superb broadcasting; but I believe the capture of the German patrol cost three or four English killed. I was only five days in this exposed position, with its forward listening post and its constant artillery or mortar 'stonks', before going back to Calvisi and on leave to Naples.

We were back in Cassino in early May for the last chapter of that long-running serial, though in a less forward area than before, again in the cellar of a bombed house. For twelve nights we mounted standing patrols in front of our position but had no casualties, though we could follow, either by report or occasionally by direct observation, the series of attacks mounted in the final assault on Cassino, which involved not only sweeps from right and from left, but a tank battle to the south (including my cousin Dick Hamilton-Russell's 17/21st) and a daring mountainous attack from behind the Germans' position by the Poles. There were reports on 16 May that the Germans were pulling out and, on the evening of the seventeenth, Allied loudspeaker demands for surrender – too late in the day to be effective, I noted critically in my diary. By ten-fifteen on the eighteenth the town was clear, an operation for which we stood by in order to provide if necessary covering fire.

By five that afternoon we were back in a rear rest camp. I took off my boots by my camp bed and by sheer luck shook a scorpion out of a slipper before putting it on, but whether it was that shock, reaction to the previous twelve days or simply Italian weather which brought on a severe bout of hay fever I shall never know.

Our HQ moved to a place called Potito, and from there, left out of battle, I made more expeditions to Naples to the opera (to see my first *Ballo* and *Aida*), but returned to hear reports that in our absence the battalion had done badly in action and retreated from its position. The new commanding officer had dined with his HQ before the action began, but had hardly anticipated that the first message to go out from Battalion HQ over the field wireless (so I was assured) would be 'The commanding officer's pissed'! Those of us in reserve went up next day to hear that the legendary John Nelson, whom I did not know but who had been with us in Africa, had taken over command – his predecessor had had bad luck, but the army held bad luck a crime.

Morale did not take long to rebuild and we were in reserve as we by-passed Rome, which had, we heard, been captured. We spent 10 and 11 June in a two-battalion attack on a bridge over the River Galantino. Casualties began not far off as we crossed the start line, but I was heartened a little later to meet my old friend the Catholic padre, George Forbes, coming back and assuring us it was pleasanter where he had been than where we were. By midnight we had reached our objective and started to dig in on the near side of a hill, under which at first light we discovered a tunnel, three kilometres long and filled with 1,000 civilians. My platoon sergeant and I got an ovation from them when we went to investigate, but the rain dampened our enthusiasm, though not my hay fever which now turned to asthma as well.

We spent a couple of days resting and visiting the attractive town of Narni before getting the news that an early night was desirable, as on 18 June reveille would be at 0130, an early start to a prospectively active day. We eventually left after breakfast at 0600 and got to within six miles of Perugia, when the leading armour reported anti-tank mines and we were sent to attack Monte Corneo. It had been a day of attacking and capturing minor German positions, most of them abandoned just before we arrived – more nerve-racking perhaps than dangerous but, with the enemy retreating, there was the constant risk of somebody staying behind and catching you from the rear. You could never tell when you arrived at a place, usually in total silence, whether it would be defended or not, whether it had been mined to blow you up after consolidation, or even if your arrival would bring down an artillery 'stonk' on your head.

Although I didn't know until I had a letter in prison, my friend Harcourt Farebrother was killed that day, shot from behind during the advance.

It was a curious day, exhilarating in the speed with which we advanced. The tanks moved through us until held up, when we would abandon our trucks to leap-frog them and try on foot to winkle out what was blocking the way.

Just before nightfall, a fresh battalion took over to consolidate, and we stopped, pretty tired, having walked, run, or been on the move the entire day with little food since breakfast, just frequent gulps from a water bottle. We had fetched up at a manor house, with gardens and a shrubbery. The owners and the other inhabitants of the village emerged from the cellar as we arrived, full of welcome and of course, poor things, very nervous. In an unoccupied country like England (or America) one can have no conception of the fear a group of civilians must have of oncoming troops. If the soldiers have had bad casualties, their morale may be low and their tempers high, and they may be blaming some of the casualties on civilian collaboration with the retreating enemy. If the troops are to be left there for a bit, there is a whole nightmare of possibilities of humiliation, rape, murder, from a group of young men who are surely sex-starved and may be ill-led and out of control.

We dug in round the house, then bedded down, as we thought, for the night (I was inside the house), but around midnight I was sent out on patrol. My commanding officer was John Nelson, who was just as good with those he commanded as Algie Heber-Percy (and better with the officers), and, judging by his subsequent record, a finer senior soldier. After that night, I next saw him in Berlin in 1967, when he was commanding the British troops and on the point of retirement, as sympathetic and dynamic a personality as he had been in those weeks, when his word was life and death to us in the third battalion of the Grenadiers in Italy.

The village was on a main road, and next day the tanks would advance down the road through our front line and on towards Perugia. I was to go with a small patrol of six Guardsmen to protect an engineer officer whose job it was, with me, to walk up the middle of the road and see if anti-tank mines had been planted. The essence of an anti-tank mine was that it didn't go off if you walked on it, only if a tank went over it. But there was a snag: there might be anti-personnel bombs round the tank mines and those would go off at a touch. Our job was to investigate the presence of mines which would be invisible from the battened-down tanks coming in next morning; we were told we should be stopped when we got to the point of furthest advance.

The trouble was nobody stopped us. I thought our own shells were whistling rather close overhead and dropping rather short as we went up the road; and then, instead of an outpost saying 'Halt! Who goes there?', somebody yelled 'Halt! Wer da?', and we realized we had bumped the German line.

We felt rather exposed on the top of the road and needed a diversion to get us across to the other side. I thought to put my rather rudimentary knowledge of the use of the hand grenade into practice, so I pulled one out of my pocket and extracted the pin, which serves to keep a metal band in place. You could hold the metal band indefinitely and even put the pin back again to make it safe, but once you let go of the band, the grenade was primed to go off in five seconds. I pulled the pin out and promptly dropped it into the large pool of water I was inadvertently lying in, so there was no question of replacing it. I lobbed the grenade overhand as far as I could, to be rewarded with the appropriate explosion and a rather noisy aftermath, as it seemed to have landed in a rubbish dump full of tins, which showered the neighbourhood and struck me at the time as irresistibly comic.

Less funny was the reception the sapper and I got when we ran across the road, in my case (but not his) to be riddled with bullets on the other side. I have never quite known whether the gun was fired by a trigger-happy member of our party or by a German in the course of his duty.

I could feel I was hit in several places, high on the inside of one thigh, lower on the other leg, and in my stomach. The main sensation was not of great pain but of a tremendous and disconcerting blow. I was convinced a bullet had gone straight through my stomach, and foresaw with horror rice pudding for the rest of my life. I didn't pass out but felt rather light-headed, and after a bit the sapper, who held me up, helped me get out a first field dressing and hold it to my stomach, in an effort to staunch the flow of blood. He insisted on staying there with me, which seemed wasteful as he was sure to be taken prisoner in the morning, needlessly I thought; but by then I was too tired to argue. I don't to this day know his name and would not recognize him, as our acquaintance was entirely at night, but he was undoubtedly a kind and brave man; the risk to him was great if he stayed, very slight if he went back.

At first light, Germans started to appear and ordered us to move. This I found distinctly painful, but we somehow got up the bank on to the road, at which juncture a barrage of artillery fire started from our side, aimed at the German lines but falling only a couple of hundred yards beyond us. Our captors of five minutes disappeared very fast, taking the sapper with them. I couldn't get far myself and sat down on a tree plainly felled there to impede the tanks in their advance, and hoped the shells wouldn't hit me. The artillery barrage was a cover, and shortly an armoured carrier came up from our side, the Germans having by then disappeared to safety and my sapper friend having dodged them and reappeared; men from my battalion carried me into a nearby farmhouse.

By one of those pieces of ill luck, the corporal stretcher-bearer who was in charge of the party decided I was too badly wounded to move, which turned out to be untrue but was a quick diagnosis on the evidence of the hole apparently just over my heart. In point of fact a bullet had hit me half an inch from my heart, and because I was crouching – 'presenting the smallest possible target to the enemy,' I afterwards said – had gone just under my ribs to emerge through my left hip, hitting nothing vital on the way out. But after six or eight hours of bleeding, saturating my bandage, it gave the impression of a severe body wound. I learnt afterwards that apart from this bullet near my heart, I had another about an inch from my balls, and a third half an inch from my shin, so I escaped rather lightly in the circumstances.

The corporal insisted we stay under cover in the farmhouse until a better means of transport could be brought up. Had they loaded me on to the carrier and taken me back, I could have been in hospital in an hour, patched up and perfectly well by autumn, which indeed I was, but by then the wrong side of the lines.

Quite soon Italian partisans appeared and offered help, but we stayed there too long; the Germans started to return because, with the carrier still in sight, they realized something was up. By that time most of my blood-soaked battledress had been cut away and my various holes bandaged up, and I was sitting rather groggily on a stretcher in the middle of the farmhouse, round which in early afternoon some skirmishing took place. In the end it was captured, together with the corporal and the three Guardsmen whom he had brought with him, but not the sapper officer, who had started back hours before, as soon as the carrier appeared.

When captured, I was stark naked except for my boots, beret, watch and bandages, feeling much the worse for wear and distinctly resentful of any disturbance of the status quo, which in that midsummer heat had begun to seem almost benevolent. It hurt very much by now to lie flat, so four Germans heaved my stretcher up on to their shoulders and carried me away sitting bolt upright and complaining at every jolt – I learnt quickly the platitude about the prisoner of war's potential nuisance value to his captors – like Radames in a provincial and under-costumed production of Aida.

The old adage, that if you strip a dressing off fast, it hurts less, apparently appealed to German front-line doctors. The man examined before me on my arrival at the first aid post was a German who had lost an arm, and they whipped the dressing off the stump very fast – not very reassuring for me because, though I imagine he was quite brave, it is disconcerting to hear a fellow human being howl. They took mine off like that too and I bit into the pillow and managed somehow to preserve, if not dignity, at least silence of a kind, but it wasn't any fun even though I was fairly sure by then that my injuries were superficial.

That first night was spent in pain and with little sleep, but next day, after a painful, undrugged ambulance ride I found myself in a big, modern front-line hospital, at a place called Forlì. I was the only Englishman in it, and at least two Germans in my ward died while I was there. The practice was to rip the dressings off each morning to see how the wounds were progressing, which produced sufficient audible distress to cause a young doctor, who apparently, like the patients, found this treatment unnecessary, to come round and soak the bandages off a quarter of an hour before the older man in charge made his rounds. They say that it hurts just as much, but, believe me, that's untrue.

My wound was a long one, from my heart down under my ribs and out through my hip, which must be about eighteen inches – you could hardly have a longer body wound without doing some serious damage – and the bleeding from it was considerable. Within two or three days, my stomach muscles were turning blue and, as the blood drained downwards, my balls black, and this made movement painful. I could not even drag myself up in bed and felt as though I had been kicked in the stomach by a horse and developed mumps next morning. Still, it all healed up quite fast.

The second day at Forlì, a German officer came to interrogate me in immaculate English, the product it emerged of a boyhood spent at English schools in Tanganyika. He was the Intelligence Officer of the division which had captured me, and he asked various questions, most of which, by no means to his surprise, I refused to answer. He was considerate and obviously inclined to help and was instrumental in getting me a toothbrush, a luxury I had so far lacked. I saw him again to my amazement in 1955, at the opening of the new Hamburg Opera House, when I was there as an official guest representing Covent Garden. He was by then the state premier of Schleswig-Holstein: Kai-Uwe von Hassel, a member of a well-known German diplomatic family. He became before he retired the *Bundestagspräsident* (more or less the equivalent of the Speaker of the House of Commons).

It was certainly not this sophisticated gentleman who first said to me as I lay in a hospital bed of captivity, 'For you, ze var is over!', but whoever was the first was certainly not the last. It seemed to have been learnt as a useful catchphrase and was repeated to us again and again. Nor do I remember which German I first heard say *'Dienst ist Dienst, und Pflicht ist Pflicht'*;* doubtless the context was one of some unpleasant duty unflinchingly carried

*Literally: 'Service is Service, and Duty is Duty.'

out, but I must say that it remains one of the most unwittingly unattractive of all catchphrases.

That June and July, I was in various hospitals in Italy, in Mantua, Bologna and Verona. It was hot and I was recovering. I was alone in a two-bedded room when a comatose body was brought to the other bed and I was told it was a wounded Englishman. He had had an operation and his foot had been amputated. To my amazement, it turned out to be a man I had at one stage sat next to at Eton, by name Ivor Coats. It was my not very agreeable duty to tell him when he came round what had happened, as he had at that time no idea of the nature of the operation.

To look after me, I was allotted a *Sonder-Führer*, who told me that his name was Schmidtmann, which meant, he said – rather fatuously, I thought – 'Smithman', and that he was a clock-maker from Stuttgart. He was tall and slightly lugubrious; he got me to play draughts (at which I thought he cheated) and rather half-heartedly attempted to justify Hitler and his ways, with references to the aftermath of the First World War and his own attempts at getting to university being thwarted because of the number of Jews who succeeded in getting in. He admitted that cruelty was never justified, but was nevertheless convinced it was all the fault of the Jews.

In the Bologna hospital, the Centro Putti, I came near to disaster when a young Italian orderly, with whom I had verbally sparred about Fascism, came in wearing a funny hat with a feather in it and boasting of his connection with a Fascist youth organization. I mocked sufficiently savagely for him to draw a knife and rush towards me, so that only my roars for help apparently prevented a youthful Fascist from carving me to bits. Somehow, I even got an apology from the hospital authorities, but I must admit the breach of manners was mine even if the over-reaction was his. It came I suppose from a conviction that one had somehow to help the war effort even when confined to bed, and to rile the enemy seemed the only means to hand. An older orderly suggested I get away and in touch with partisans in the hills, an intriguing but slightly ludicrous idea since I couldn't even get up on my own to go to the lavatory.

I was taken prisoner on the anniversary of the Battle of Waterloo, in which an ancestor of mine was wounded; my father was wounded on 18 June 1915, precisely a hundred years after Waterloo; and I was wounded on 18 June 1944. We were the three Earls of Harewood who saw active service in the nineteenth and twentieth centuries and the coincidence is at least odd.

The Bologna hospital was run by a gentle Italian surgeon, who performed a dozen operations a day as well as looking after administration, and the work was done partly by orderlies and partly by nuns. The nuns mooned around like heifers, always as far as I could tell in couples, mooing *'Buon giorno'* as they looked vacantly round the door, so it was a surprise to find at Mantua, in what was basically a hospital for English POWs, that the middle-aged nun in charge of the food was competent, prepared to be on her own and looked like someone painted by Ribera. She was cheerful, responsible and ubiquitous, and when a group of TB-ridden Italian soldiers moved in to die (from Polish salt mines, we were told), she used to read prayers for them before breakfast, a noisy procedure which woke me up and raised a longing to get across the corridor, in which the prayers were being said, to the lavatory beyond – I was by now, if limping, slightly mobile. Holding down my embarrassingly short night shirt, I would edge behind her chair and the sister would break off her murmuring long enough to bid me *'Buon giorno'* before returning to the dispensing of spiritual comfort.

Mantua was regularly bombed, and few days went by without an alarm. An American airman lay in a nearby bed, very ill (he died while I was there), but inclined, like Shishkov in Janáček's *House of the Dead*, at all costs to tell his story. He had been shot down and was in an Italian POW camp when the Badoglio armistice was concluded and an announcement made that Allied prisoners were now free. He had taken to the hills and was half-way down Italy when he was challenged by a young man in uniform. He put his hands up in surrender only to find himself shot twice through the middle. Recovering in hospital, he was in a ward on the top floor when it was bombed, ironically by Americans, and he fell through to the bottom.

As a result, he was in a poor way. He spent the time in between narrations assuring us that the Americans did the day-bombing from about 40,000 feet up, which made precision bombing, let alone reading a red cross painted on a hospital roof, rather hard. He knew; he'd done it. As our hospital had a red cross on the roof (we were told) but was within a quarter of a mile of the bridge the bombers were trying to hit, we felt more than a little vulnerable each noon as the place shook and trembled with the impact of that day's near-misses.

CHAPTER THREE

Prisoner of War
1944-5

I was taken to Germany on 17 July 1944, to a camp called Moosburg, outside Munich. I travelled with a couple of Germans, one a sergeant who had been well treated as a prisoner of war of the English in the First World War, and the other a private. Each had had a telegram giving the category of his leave. The worst category signified all your relations had been killed and you had lost your house; the lowest leave entitlement was for a bombed house with no loss of life involved. They were in that category and overjoyed at the prospect of going home to Hamburg, and it struck me as a small price to pay. All this came out as they shared their rations with me, including some delicious parmesan cheese, which was unpopular enough with the Germans to be known as 'partisan' cheese.

We went from Verona through the Brenner Pass to Munich, which had been burnt out by Allied bombs a few days before, so that it looked like a ghost town. The centre was destroyed completely, railway lines and all, and we went by tram from one end of town to the other. I suppose I was obviously English, although (because of my lack of apparel at capture) I was wearing a pair of German shorts and a shirt, and the other occupants of the tram started to spit at me, to the vast indignation of my escorting sergeant who said nothing like that had happened to him in England in the last war and it wasn't going to happen while I was in his charge in this war. I was still on sticks and, only half-truthfully, claimed that I couldn't carry anything – and didn't.

Moosburg was a camp of three or four thousand people, and we lived in the equivalent of Nissen huts, rather chilly at night even in late July. We woke up one morning to be told by the sentry that Hitler had been killed and that the war would shortly end. The guards seemed delighted, but the rumour only lasted about an hour and a half; it transpired that Hitler had survived.

I was moved in the last days of July to Spangenberg, not far from Cassel, and spent a night *en route* in the station jail. The camp was full of colonels taken prisoner in Normandy in 1940, who not unnaturally felt bypassed in their professional careers and were for the most part rather melancholy. I was put with a group of half a dozen commandos from Saint Nazaire, with their commanding officer, Colonel Charles Newman VC, a most remarkable man, still at their head. They were a wartime élite, and I was lucky to make friends with them. One, Ronnie Swayne, was a musician, a flautist, and he and I discussed music in the intervals between reading in the library or walking in the castle moat. He later became an active member of the Liverpool Philharmonic's Committee and after that of the Philharmonia's in London. He brought me up sharp when we were deep in discussion one day by saying that we all generalized about music on the flimsiest evidence, knowing few of Haydn's or Beethoven's quartets, at most one of Myaskovsky's twenty-seven symphonies, and yet were prepared to give an opinion on their output. If we were discussing a writer, we would have read a higher proportion of his work before saying whether we liked or disliked it!

Spangenberg is a superficially attractive castle in a pleasant setting, near a village through which ran a main-line railway. Prisoners with time on their hands were fanatical gleaners and sifters of information, and from Spangenberg were able to transmit it back to England. They told me that two years earlier they had observed, night after night, peculiarly-shaped, tarpaulin-covered objects in transit; and their exactly-observed measurements and timings contributed, London assured them, to location of the launching sites of the v-1 and v-2 bombs directed against England. Nothing like that took place while I was there, but I went once to the town to the dentist. Officers could not by the Geneva Convention be made to work – though we were assured it would be different once the Germans won the war – and we normally had to give parole not to escape whenever we went outside the castle walls. Going to the dentist did not count, and so I had a man with a rifle to guard me. At Spangenberg on 15 September arrived my first letter from home, after a three-month gap without first-hand news, inadequately filled by occasional cables from Switzerland assuring me that my letters were being received.

In that camp, we all read. I had got through Galsworthy's Forsyte novels, which I dare say I wouldn't otherwise have touched, and also most of Grove's *Dictionary of Music and Musicians*, up to S, when I was moved. After the Hitler plot in July 1944, the *Wehrmacht* salute was abolished in Germany and everyone had to give the Nazi salute instead, an occasion of great loss of face for career officers. We heard about this in advance, and when the wretched officer came in one morning and did the 'Heil Hitler' thing, he was greeted with booing and general mockery.

We made friends with the camp interpreter, Dr Bohrer, a civilized person who had been a friend of the composer Hindemith's at Frankfurt, where he lectured in philosophy at the university. He was anti-Nazi – the only German I heard say so in front of other Germans; many claimed it in safe privacy – and so his rank was that of a corporal. He was a loyal German but hated Hitler, and we talked together about music. I saw him years after the war at Harewood, by which time he was a personnel officer for Dunlop in Germany, and seemed just as urbane and kindly as he had in 1944. There was also a solicitous padre at one of these camps and, goaded by his clumsy kindnesses and questioning, in a mistaken moment I claimed to have a 'relative living near Victoria Station', which got around and caused some jocularity.

I was moved from Spangenberg on 11 November, and thirty-six hours later reached Colditz. Prisoners used to refer to Colditz as a *Straflager*, a punishment camp, which irritated the Germans very much, but the fact is that we were counted twice a day at Spangenberg (at nine o'clock and five o'clock), but four times, at unspecified hours, at Colditz. Everyone there either had a 'record' of escape or some other punishable offence. Mine was to have prominent relations.

Before I left Spangenberg, I went to talk to the Senior British Officer, who was a colonel of great seniority and indeed wisdom – one of the few who could still function as if he had not spent the five best years of his career in prison – partly to say goodbye and partly to see if he had any message for his opposite number in Colditz. It turned out that he had. The camp radio, built up over months and functioning now for several years, was the life-line to the outside world – something we all knew – and there was virtually certain to be one in Colditz. What was not quite so certain was whether they knew the changed frequency on which the news was beamed from England towards Germany. They told me the number, and I pulled out something on which to write it down. This caused a *frisson* of horror and I was told I had to memorize it. I did so successfully (rather to my surprise) and went on my way.

The journey by train was uncomfortable and I arrived at Colditz in the evening, to be shoved into a cell with a double bunk, the bottom one of which was already occupied. A cavalry-moustached head poked out which turned out to belong to Dawyck Haig, the Field-Marshal's son. We introduced ourselves – I had last seen him as a fellow-page at the Coronation in 1937 –

and contrived to sleep through the night before being taken off for a shower, a welcome prospect in spite of inevitable overtones of concentration camps. We were then separated and I was put into a large and very cold barrack room.

After about half an hour, the commandant, preceded by NCOs shouting *'Achtung!'* at the tops of their voices, made his entrance. I shambled to my feet but was not wholly prepared for a furious cry from the commandant of *'Warum grüssen sie nicht?'* ('Why do you not salute?'). I suppose I should have grabbed my military hat and saluted him – he was after all a colonel – but the best I could do was an attempt at the vernacular, which came out rather lamely as *'Ach!'* It does after all mean 'Oh', which was all I meant to say, but it evoked less than total enthusiasm. My diary, having no engagements to record, has: 'Am shouted at for some minutes before I have even attempted to open my mouth! Am beginning to suspect the American film Nazis are rather truer to life than I previously thought.'

It was not long before I felt it time to go and report to the Senior British Officer. I was instructed to go to a particular building and up the stairs where I should find his room. I arrived at the bottom of the stairs to meet tumbling down them a figure in air force uniform which I duly caught, to be met with a volley of oaths from the tumbler who was evidently less than steady on his pins. It was the famous Douglas Bader, with two false legs and a propensity not only to fall downstairs but to berate whoever caught him, insisting that he had to make his own way.

Slightly daunted, I went to see the SBO, only to realize that my carefully memorized figures had evaporated. We went through the formalities of a greeting, enquiries about my journey and the last camp, and it seemed I was not going to be asked the dreaded question about the radio frequency. I plucked up courage to ask him whether they regularly had the news and then, getting an answer in the affirmative, to discover when they first learnt the new frequency. Within a week of its change, I was told, to my infinite relief.

The practice of totalitarian regimes has always been to attempt to get at people through their relatives, and this gathering together at Colditz of a little group of prisoners with illustrious connections was an example of that line of thinking. We were known as *Prominente* – our jailers threw up their hands in horror at the suggestion we were hostages – and, apart from Dawyck Haig and myself, there were five other special prisoners: John Elphinstone, a nephew of the Queen's; Giles Romilly, a nephew of Mrs Churchill's; Charlie Hopetoun, the son of the Viceroy, Lord Linlithgow; Max de Hamel, a distant relation of Churchill's, whom he had never met; Michael

Alexander, a splendid character, who had had to claim relationship with the Field-Marshal when he was captured in the African desert behind the German lines and dressed in German uniform. Only his name saved him from a firing squad. Michael was a constant source of ideas, and prison would have been duller without him.

Ours was a tight little group, kept at night in one room and constantly under surveillance. It was all rather pointless and foolish, but they thought we could be useful as hostages, and we had to take this at its face value. We had even worked out what would happen if luck worked against us and the camp were not overrun as the war drove on. We should, we believed, be moved, at first from camp to camp, and eventually to the Final Redoubt. There was some doubt then as to whether the Redoubt existed; it turned out to be no myth, but a rather tangible fortress in Austria. There, we felt, anything might happen. Our prognostications were not inaccurate; we reached the penultimate step.

It was bizarre and rather irritating to read recently a bowdlerized and sensational account of our *Prominente* adventure in *The Valhalla Exchange* (by Harry Patterson, alias Jack Higgins). His *Prominenten* were far more glamorous than us – a French aristocrat who was a commando and a great lover, an English ditto who was no straighter than he should have been (me?), a beautiful French woman of forgivably dubious loyalty, and so on (if my memory plays me false, it is no falser than he played the facts, *our* facts) – and his conclusion is more like the end of *Götterdämmerung* on skis (literally) than our blissfully anti-climactic finish.

Winter in Colditz was disagreeable, because it was a very cold place, now virtually unheated, and because we had exiguous rations. The Germans gave us a bowl of soup with some bread every day and we had, in addition, Red Cross parcels. These, however, by winter 1944 we had decided to ration, having worked out that no more parcels would reach Germany through Switzerland, and that even if they did, the over-stretched German transport was unlikely to carry them to us. A large number were in store, but we thought it prudent to reduce the allowance for December and January to one parcel a week for every six persons (half a parcel a week per person was the ideal). The doctor told us that, with rations and food parcels together, we were on about 1,100 or 1,150 calories a day, just below the minimum diet for a bed-ridden patient. We weren't bed-ridden, and the result was that we were constantly cold, and to go upstairs meant either a pause every dozen steps or a temporary black-out. My diary records that I weighed 83kgs on 9 October at Spangenberg, and 73kgs at Colditz on 20 December, a loss of about twenty pounds in ten weeks.

Small wonder that throughout the winter Colditz's inmates used to group round the camp kitchen door and remove the peelings of the kohlrabi – a coarse vegetable I have hated ever since – in order to re-peel the peel and make the residue into additional soup. Small wonder too that the division of our rations, once we had re-cooked them with whatever there was from Red Cross parcels, was effected by one man, whose accuracy was tested by the simple process of giving him last choice of each slice or plateful. Patricia says that if ever she wants a cake divided into nine or a melon into five, she can always count on my past experience and prison-honed accuracy.

Prominentes lived on the bottom floor of the castle, and the 'mess' I belonged to was up some four flights of twisting turret staircase. In a room at its top were concealed the radio and anything else we did not want the Germans to see, and look-outs were posted whenever the radio was in action to give the alarm the moment a German came into the courtyard; if ever one attempted to come upstairs, a horde of people poured down and by sheer weight of numbers made his ascent a very slow business. We spent a lot of each day in bed, fully dressed, in order to warm the bed and keep the damp out of the sheets, which we sewed into sleeping bags. Reading in winter by day was also in bed, because it was too cold outside and the little fuel we had was kept for the evening.

We weren't allowed to collect wood. In fact the only times I left that camp were on the organized *Prominente* walks, for which we were allowed by the Senior British Officer to give parole. These were uninspiring affairs, partly because the countryside seemed dreary in winter, partly because we were weak and the walks tiring. We jawed away as usual, perhaps a little more fractiously, but we brought back little from the side of the road, because there was little to glean. The walks were infinitely less agreeable than the occasional expeditions we had made in summer from Spangenberg, when we would give parole to go out into the woods to plant trees – the only activity ever suggested for prisoners which we felt was quite certain not to benefit the Nazis! We were given a spade and shown the trees and then left to get on with the digging. One could either work away, or simply lie out in the sun.

Our room, with its seven beds with their straw mattresses, had a stove in the middle, but there was little to burn in it, and that little we kept usually till evening. At a certain time – nine or ten – we were shut in and only allowed out to the lavatory if we attracted the attention of the guard who was posted outside our room and at frequent intervals looked through the spy-hole in the door. We read and we talked, endlessly discussing whatever interested us, in my case often music, in that of the others, literature, philosophy, religion. We were far from a flippant lot, and it was relatively rare that our Scottish lairds, John Elphinstone and Charlie Hopetoun, re-lived pre-war jaunts on grouse-moor or race-course, although John was a dab hand at bird drawings and Charlie's racing reminiscences, when they came, were very much to my taste.

Not least, we discussed our own predicament. As John Elphinstone used to say, we were all right so long as we were in the hands of the *Wehrmacht* and not of the Gestapo, but even the *Wehrmacht* would inevitably discover that to the Allies we were just half a dozen unimportant officers and a journalist (Giles Romilly was not in the army), and their patience might wear thin. And then, there was the bogey of the Final Redoubt.

We talked too about what would happen to us and to the world after the war. The younger ones amongst us were full of optimism and aspirations, sometimes seriously expressed – there was a professional soldier a bit older than me who meant to go far and was reading his Clausewitz – sometimes disguised in flippancy, sometimes too nebulous, as in my case, to be formulated with any substance. It amazes me in retrospect how little we quarrelled, as the claustrophobic atmosphere must have been highly conducive to bickering and over-reaction to often-expressed, sometimes contentious points of view.

Michael Alexander and I used to speculate about our companions. Would X achieve the place in politics he longed for? Was Y's much rewritten novel the masterpiece he had begun to believe? Could Z's theories change current thinking as he was convinced? I was more naive than Michael, who nicely combined idealism and scepticism, but we agreed that some of our fellow Kriegies (from *Kriegsgefangenen* = POW) had in their five years of incarceration lost all aspiration and courage and would settle the moment they got out for a quiet life, the more insulated against the buffets of the world the better.

Colditz was famous as an escaping camp, and prisoners were sent there who had escaped from other camps, as well as the few they hoped to use as hostages. There existed some feeling of shared achievement, at least in terms of having a proven nuisance value, and the camp had far more vitality than Spangenberg, insofar as very hungry people have vitality. No one who was there will forget it, and I often wonder if some of the others, like me, watched with fascination the TV series *Colditz*, which reflected none of the disagreeable side of the castle but quite a lot of its camaraderie, caught some of the physical attributes of the place and dealt with many of the legends in a perfectly plausible if fictionalized manner.

Those of us there simply because of our connections were kept apart at night but had unrestricted contact with the other prisoners during the day. At *Appel* time, we paraded with the others and were counted. It takes some time to count 180 people, and it was all done by one supervising officer with a sergeant and half a dozen soldiers to keep order. In case of an escape (there were none during my time as it was forbidden from England), or if anyone was working on an escape route even as a blind (and we kept this going), the thing was to bamboozle the counting officer into counting someone twice. This was done by doubling round behind the ranks after being counted and getting to the end to be counted again. It was astonishingly often achieved, sometimes as an exercise to prove it could still be done, and sometimes just to irritate the guards.

At Colditz, we had made a number of rules of our own; one of them was that nobody was allowed to gossip with the guards simply to exercise his German. The guards were often disgruntled, always bored, and easy sources of small bits of information which, put together, gave us a better idea of what was going on outside – the state of German food supplies, of civil and military morale, of troop movements, of mounting pressures on manpower. This information could only be evaluated with accuracy by a fluent linguist, of whom there were several in the camp, including the ex-son-in-law of Schacht, the Economics Minister. So it is not surprising that few of us could answer in the affirmative that regular post-war question: 'Did you come out speaking fluent German?'

On our camp radio we received instructions forbidding escape as a result of an atrocity in the summer of 1944. After the plot to kill Hitler, about forty RAF prisoners escaped and the Germans, when they caught them, shot a number out of hand, giving out that there were certain areas of Germany, well-defined but for security reasons unspecified, which ranked as no-go areas; anyone found in them would in future be executed without question. I have always imagined it was meant to save them the bother of rounding up escaped prisoners. But we worked out that 180 of us in Colditz kept busy far more soldiers (around 200) than we could ever, considering Allied numerical superiority, have pinned down at the front. In Colditz, there were more of them than of us; we took some pride in that, and so dummy escape schemes continued to be organized.

Punishment consisted of a specified number of days in the isolation cells, and while I was at Colditz an American colonel, senior officer in an American camp elsewhere, was moved in because he had torn down the German notice announcing – as he said, illegally and against the Geneva Convention – the newly designated security areas. He had been condemned to death for his action and was put in our isolation cells 'to await carrying out of sentence', an idle threat as he (and we) supposed at first, and unlikely to be carried out before we were overrun by the Allies.

Much work had been done at Colditz in maintaining possible escape routes in case of need. At the top of the castle there was a large, bleak dormitory, from the end of which some six or eight feet had been sequestered, the boarding imitated exactly and bunks placed up against the false boarding. Behind was a glider, whose components had been painstakingly manufactured and were waiting to be assembled in order to be taken to the ramparts, launched, and so float over the moat and the outside wall, over the town maybe and out to freedom. I was told that when the Americans arrived some three days after our party left, the freed prisoners assembled and launched the glider with complete success – but I have never met an eye witness to the event.

I spent a lot of time at Colditz reading about music, and even attempting to make it. A senior Swiss Red Cross representative came to see me while I was still in hospital at Moosburg and asked if I needed anything. When I told him I wanted to learn the clarinet, he said his son was a clarinettist (a very distinguished player, I discovered afterwards, by name Anton de Bavier), and within a month a beautiful Boehm arrived together with an English 'tutor'. I started to learn it, but I had got only about half way, so to speak, when we had an influx of French prisoners from further east and possibilities for practice were drastically reduced. But throughout my ten and a half months incarceration, I thought and read about music – we had a good Red Cross library – and by May 1945 I was less ignorant than a year before.

We had too a wind-up gramophone and quite a lot of records, mostly sent through the Red Cross and including all the late Beethoven Quartets played by the Busch and Lener Quartets – I played them again and again, and have since realized that my rather primitive tastes might not in other circumstances have caught up with these masterpieces for another twenty-five years.

I think that by the time I was fourteen or fifteen I had decided that my life must somehow be concerned with music. I became more and more involved, tried to hear it at all times and in all forms and learn more about it, though I have never been a practising musician of any merit whatsoever. From about 1938, music gave me more excitement and pleasure than anything else and, though I didn't say this to everyone because I didn't think they would have approved, I was convinced it would somehow dominate my life. I really wanted more than anything else to work in an opera house – in *any* capacity; I didn't care. That was where I felt my contribution in life would be.

It was easy to make acquaintances, hard to make friends, in the confined atmosphere of a camp. Easy to make enemies too, at least temporarily, but we managed somehow to keep some element of cool, whatever the flare-ups, partly by exercising a certain vigilance over our neighbours, partly I suspect because the low diet kept us short of energy. This too may have been why, in my time in prison, there was little sign of homosexuality, though admittedly I was not looking for it. It must have been in evidence earlier when there was no prospect of a quick end to the war.

By the time I was at Colditz in November 1944, it was obvious the war could not end before spring, but highly unlikely it could last much longer; and such near certainties make a vast difference to one's thinking – even perhaps to one's instincts. Earlier, it had been a question of sticking it out through the pessimism until one could afford optimism as a viable alternative. More than one of us, particularly amongst those who had been in since 1940, succumbed to some kind of nervous breakdown at this last stage of the war; others immersed themselves in writing – novels, theses, solutions to the problems of the world or, in my case, just notes on what I had read.

We had of course nothing alcoholic to drink – beer was issued at Christmas, I seem to remember – but earlier on they had brewed some kind of poteen from potato peelings and drunk it with relish until over-indulgence sent one of the topers blind (only for a few weeks, I was assured). Some had been kept and was doled out at Christmas. Most of this we made into brandy butter for the Christmas pudding; the rest was quite drinkable, certainly potent, and one man – a pre-war *Times* foreign correspondent and, in prison at least, a communist – decided to have all his at one meal, with the result that after dinner his tongue was loosened and with deadly precision he demolished the pretentions of everyone in his mess – the grandest in the camp; the 'Bullingdon', we called them – and revealed what he thought, usually correctly, lay behind each individual façade. There were some bruised egos for quite a time after that episode.

Poker schools, music appreciation groups, philosophy classes, history lectures – we tried every kind of activity, intellectual or otherwise, until in the end the cold beat us. Colditz, I subsequently realized, played Redbrick to Spangenberg's Oxbridge – rougher perhaps, more energetic certainly, and the atmosphere far less rarified.

Half way through the winter there arrived a little party of a dozen Poles, the six senior generals of the Warsaw Rebellion and their accompanying staff. The seniors were old-school soldiers, three of whom had in 1914–18 been in the Austrian army, the others in the Russian, and their manners were impeccable except (we were told by the juniors) when they argued amongst themselves about post-war Poland. They were agreed about the incredible duplicity of the Russians, who had acquiesced in the timing of their revolt and then delayed their entry into Warsaw until the Germans had put it down. But old allegiance and new semi-political convictions went deep, and it was clear that some would welcome Russian hegemony, which seemed inevitable, just as much as others would prefer exile and refuse ever to accept it.

General Bor, who commanded in Warsaw and was the senior, became a friend, and we had long talks in French, which continued after the war when I saw him in London and even occasonally at Harewood, until the dissolution of the Free Poles put an end to his official activities and he drifted off into retirement. His ADC was a bright charmer called Stas Jankowski, and I also struck up a friendship with him. In Poland, he had been very active in the resistance. One of our number, who was at school with me in the early 1930s, had been in a POW camp in Poland, escaped, contacted the resistance and been hidden in Stas's family's house until found there by the Germans and hurried off again to prison. They put him into a Polish concentration camp to await transport to a POW camp, and he later made the tactical mistake of complaining to the Red Cross that he had witnessed, indeed been a victim, of the weekly beating-up which had become part of routine at that camp – of course, against the Geneva Convention, which he was invoking to the Red Cross. Equally illegal was the setting of Alsatians on prisoners under interrogation, which he had also witnessed.

As a result of this testimony to the Swiss, he was for the Germans a marked man and constantly under suspicion. He cared about that very little, but minded very much that, when he was reunited with his old comrade Stas, he heard that Stas's entire family, mother, sister and all, had been murdered because they had been sheltering him. In our camp, the guards' behaviour was correct, but perhaps you needed reminding that the veneer was not very thick.

By early April 1945, the Allies – Russians to the north, Americans under Patton to the south – were no more than five or six days away, and our hope was that we would be left in Colditz until they arrived. But the feeling was that we would be moved, and on Friday 13 April 1945 we deduced that the move was likely to be before nightfall. By then, there must have been a dozen

Americans in Colditz. One of them, John Winant, son of the American ambassador in London, was, the other Americans decided, to take advantage of a prepared hiding place inside the camp and, so to speak, be removed from circulation.

At roll call that night he was missing, and the camp commandant, who had by then received his orders about us, announced that he had no alternative but to take the castle to bits until he found him. Eventually the search was called off when the Americans produced John, who was added to our little group of *Prominentes*, plus the half-dozen Polish generals from Warsaw and their staff; and the whole lot of us were moved out rather melodramatically around midnight, with the courtyard brightly illuminated and the other inhabitants kicking up a remarkable farewell shindig from the windows as we left.

With our few possessions, and two Maori orderlies who had volunteered to go with us, we were put into a bus as if going on an overnight trip from Leeds to London; and in the early hours of the morning we were off, in theory only to another camp, in practice on that journey towards the Final Redoubt that we had all along predicted could have been planned for us. We went through the blackened ruins of Dresden at first light and arrived at Königstein. From here, three or four years before, General Giraud, the rival of de Gaulle, at a cost of something like a million cigarettes, had escaped, lowered down the side of a sheer cliff by means of a knotted rope of sheets – or so we were told.

Our arrival was dramatic, just after dawn. The bus in which we were travelling could go no further and we had to get out and carry our things into the castle. Charlie Hopetoun, removed in spite of remonstrance from hospital to complete the party, was by now too exhausted to carry anything and could hardly get up the rough path. Inside the castle, we were received by a correct-seeming Oberst Hesselmann and offered breakfast. No sooner had we started to eat than another German officer came in to announce formally and with apparent regret that President Roosevelt had died.

It was obvious we should not stay at Königstein, and Oberst Hesselmann agreed that, when the move came, Charlie should be left behind in hospital care. We insisted someone stay with him, but the decision about who it should be was eventually taken out of our hands when Dawyck Haig was laid low with violent diarrhoea, the result I always thought of a prune pudding we had cooked from our Red Cross parcels.

My acquaintance with town jails controlled by the Germans was increased during our journey by the addition of Pilsen to the list, and eventually we reached a place in Bavaria by the name of Laufen. It was demonstrably now a civilian internment camp, and we wanted at all costs to maintain our proper POW status in a recognized military camp. John Elphinstone, who was senior among us, argued until with some show of reluctance we were taken off to a place by the name of Tittmonning.

This camp, an old castle, contained the entire Dutch officer cadre, among whom we found an old friend of two members of our group who had been for a time in the British army. We explained to him our predicament as we saw it: we were a group of hostages being moved slowly but apparently inevitably nearer the Final Redoubt, and we longed to find a delaying factor to prevent them moving us out of the line of the Allied advance. He told us that, as at Colditz, several escape plans had been evolved, one of which we could use. But there was a snag: the only plan which could be put into operation without rehearsal would accommodate only two people – and one of them would necessarily be himself, since guidance was essential if it was to be made to work. As at Colditz, they had tunnelled into the wall, and the rest of us could hole up there and hope the Germans would not deduce that the whole lot of us could never have made it through the wire.

We said, 'OK. We'll draw lots as to who goes.' But here came a second snag. Giles Romilly said he had claustrophobia and could not contemplate a sojourn in the wall, so it had to be he who went with our Dutch friend on the escape, and we who occupied the hide. The Poles, who were of course offered a place, said they felt better off following the working-out of the inevitable without doing anything about it.

The escape was a simple one, a matter of accurate timing of the sentries' routine, of cutting a section of the wire which surrounded the camp, and of keeping nerves under control. With rehearsal, there would have been no problems, but of course Giles hadn't rehearsed it. Nevertheless it worked, and we were all safely holed up in the wall on 20 April when the Germans counted the dummies in our beds. Next morning, they presumed that all six of us had escaped and we were left to sit it out in hiding.

The castle was old, and it had not been hard months before to remove the wooden panelling in our dormitory, burrow into the six-foot wide, rubble-filled castle wall behind it, equip the hide with lavatory bucket, blankets and food for just such an emergency, and then replace the panelling and the bunks in front of it. It had even been possible to attach a wire to the electricity supply so that during the day we could read in the hideout – not of course during the night in case there was a crack that would have given things away. At nightfall, or when Germans were in the building, the Dutch banged on the wall and we turned the light out and kept quiet.

It was cold and uncomfortable, but in its way not without luxury. There was a great tin bucket near the entrance which served as a lavatory, and one person sat upright on its seat. Then there was a three-foot high passage, just wide enough for two to lie in, provided that one lay on his side. Someone else sat at the end on a box, and the fifth was up near the air hole, agreeable by day, distinctly chilly at night. Every two hours we rotated, but because there was no room to pass in the tunnel, if either of the men beyond it needed to reach the lavatory drum it was a question of 'all change'. There were several such changes during the four days and nights we were there, each one something of a test of character.

We passed the time reading – gossip was obviously risky as we could not be certain nothing would be heard by a passing guard down below – and I suppose I showed rather too strong a sense of the melodramatic by taking in the Atlantic Edition of Oscar Wilde's *De Profundis*, which I had been storing up to read. We munched our rations and we attempted to sleep. John Winant lost a little popularity when he pulled out a whole clove of garlic and bit into it, assuring us that it was not only good but kept germs at bay.

After about three nights, we were, we later heard, given away. We could hear rain outside, and the Dutch were taken into the courtyard late in the evening for an unscheduled roll call. One or two of them were about seventy, and to spend the night standing in the rain could hardly have been agreeable. We realized something was up when we heard great blows as of a sledgehammer as the guards went along the walls testing to see what was solid and what false. There was what sounded like an explosion on our part of the wall, and guards with guns and snarling Alsatians peered in at us.

Out we crawled, to be marched through the rain, singly, two guards and a dog to each man and with our hands above our heads through the ranks of the assembled Dutch. We were conducted across the courtyard as if no security could be too tight; but once in the commandant's office, the tension could not be sustained and our reception was curiously low-key. Breakfast was even mentioned, I remember – by the commandant, I suspect, rather than by the security officer, the latter an unattractive individual who had been an employee of Cook's before the war and who spoke quite good English. Fury and relief competed for expression when we came in; he told us that both he and the commandant had been condemned to death immediately our escape was discovered. The commandant added that he himself didn't greatly care, partly because he realized that it was our duty as officers to try to escape, partly because his wife had been killed in a recent air raid and he had no one now left to live for.

We were straight away moved from Tittmonning back to Laufen, on what had been the Austrian border, and there we had guards night and day. We were there seven or eight days, during which time I acquired a pipe, I can't think how, and tried to smoke it, but so unrelentingly that it burnt the inside of my mouth and the enthusiasm was short-lived. Our guard was commanded by a one-armed air force general, a decent enough man, and we naturally asked him where we were going to next. He said, 'This is where you are going to stop.' We had had this kind of assurance before, and one or two of us who were lying on our bunks got up and said, 'Oh well, we had better get packed then, hadn't we?' It was disconcerting two or three hours later to be told by our general, 'I am sorry, the order has come through that you are to be moved.' We didn't see why he should get away with this and said: 'You knew when we asked you earlier, didn't you?' But he said, 'I give you my word of honour as an officer that I did not know.' We said, '*We* knew, and you guessed that we knew, didn't you?' But it was from instinct, not information, that we knew.

Our worry was that the Swiss diplomat who supervised the welfare of prisoners in this camp would lose us; he was our only link with the outside world, the only non-German who knew where we were. He was a funny, tall, untidy sort of fellow, with his tie badly tied, and spots of blood on his collar where he'd cut himself shaving. He had been to see us, full of optimism, at about six in the evening, but if we were to be moved at first light, as seemed likely, he would lose track of us. So we asked that he be informed, and did not believe the reassurance we were given.

It was in a mood of something like despair that we went out into the courtyard on 1 May and there, as if in the last reel of a film, saw an ss officer, such as never entered a pow camp, a fat little fellow with a small car and a peroxide girlfriend. Our bus crept through the gates, and spirits shot up when we made out our Swiss friend, trying to get his umbrella into a tiny car – it was of course raining – struggling with his tie, and waving at us at the same time. The lifeline wasn't yet cut.

We crossed what was once the Austrian border, nosed through a ghostly Salzburg – I looked in vain for the Opera House – and then took an inappropriate road joining Salzburg and Innsbruck: inappropriate because, if the Allies were close to Salzburg, they were nearer Innsbruck. We stopped at a place which Hitler called Markt Pongau but whose real name was St Johann-in-Pongau – he approved of saints' names no more than he approved of German royalty. The weather turned fine and the road led down into a beautiful pine-forested valley. We could see in the valley below a vast camp, well laid out and, from our almost aerial vantage point, judging by the different uniforms we could see, multi-national. As we got nearer, we could see Russians, what we decided were Kurds, and all sorts of Eastern Europeans.

We were put into a hut, a guard was posted, and we got some food – better than usual, presumably because by then we had become, although we didn't realize it, counters in a game being played for high stakes. That afternoon, we were taken for a rather nervous walk in the woods, and we noticed on our return that the guards had turned their guns outwards, instead of pointing them inwards at us. They were no longer stopping us getting out, but trying, as they admitted, to prevent the Gestapo getting in. All the top Nazis were in Berlin, except Kaltenbrunner, the head of the Gestapo. The *Wehrmacht*, which held us and loathed the Gestapo, knew he was after us in his own bid for survival. I suspect the only reason he never caught up with us was the sheer weight of traffic on the road – military traffic retreating from Salzburg towards Innsbruck with good discipline, and a line going the other way from Innsbruck to Salzburg in just as orderly a manner. No one, not even a leading German, could have got through, and helicopters barely existed in those days.

Markt Pongau housed us for the night and next morning we were offered a bath. Then took place an extraordinary episode. Normally, if a German officer came into our room, he was preceded by a tremendous stamping and shouting of *'Achtung!'* and so on, to warn us we should stand up and, if he had a senior rank, salute him. On this occasion, the door opened with no shouting and in came a very large man, tall and built like Goering, and like him covered with medals. He said in German: 'Good morning, gentlemen. My name is Obergruppenführer Gottlob Berger' (*Obergruppenführer* was equivalent to Lieutenant General). 'I am a soldier, but now for the past few months head of the ss.' (This was because Himmler, when fighting started on German soil, was transferred from head of the ss to Minister of the Interior.) General Berger told us that he thought the war was within a day or two of coming to its end; he disbelieved in keeping prisoners pointlessly, although it was his duty to tell us that he had received orders to shoot us. He was going to disobey those orders because he thought them futile and indeed criminal, and had made arrangements to hand us over to the Swiss protecting power, who were coming immediately to take us through the German lines and deliver us into Allied hands. We thanked him for this and he assured us everything would be arranged.

After lunch there appeared a very suave Swiss of perhaps twenty-five, smartly dressed, with a rather la-di-da English accent, by name Werner Buchmüller. He told us he was very glad to be able to be of help; we would leave as soon as possible in his car and the two trucks the Germans had lent him. I remember I sat in his Buick next to him, because his sense of protocol was strictly non-military and my protests that there were generals in the truck behind went unheeded.

Leaving in the mid-afternoon of 4 May with a feeling of total exhilaration – like a child going to its first party – we somehow assumed we should go fast and be in Allied hands in a couple of hours. But it was not like that. We crawled along in a solid queue of military vehicles, with on the other side of the road just as solid military traffic going the other way. We were probably the only non-military vehicle in this cavalcade, and I remember a feeling of awe coming over me at the thought that we were watching the death march of a section of German military might, one half retreating in good order from Salzburg to Innsbruck, the other half just as painstakingly from Innsbruck to Salzburg, each half bound, not for the safety or at least stability it sought, but for prison, rehabilitation and a lifetime in which no German uniform would ever be worn again. So at least I thought. Our fear of course was of being attacked from the air, which seemed all too likely, but we weren't. I suppose we went no more than twenty-five miles in four or five hours before leaving the road for what looked in the gloom like an inn.

By this time our nerves were worn through, and to be met by an ADC and conducted into the inn as though we were a party of visitors, and then invited to have some food and a drink before going on with our journey, was very weird indeed. The whole atmosphere had changed; we seemed to be treated as honoured guests. It was General Berger's HQ, and upstairs we found a pleasant cold meal – ham and salami and beer – laid out for us. Half way through, the general himself appeared and made a speech, and we came close to drinking toasts (but stopped short of that). He presented John Elphinstone with a pearl-handled revolver, and made only one condition for our release. As our guide through the German line he was sending an SS doctor. 'I know that the Allies have threatened to shoot all SS prisoners. This man has been with the SS only a week. He is a doctor and a soldier like me, and I must have your solemn word that he will be looked after and treated properly.' We agreed, and the doctor sat in the front of the car as we motored slowly on through the night until at first light the German troops by the side of the road told him they thought there were no more Germans in front. We put a Swiss flag (a white cross on a red ground) on the front of the car which led our convoy and drove very slowly into no-man's land, an eerie sensation as all we needed was a trigger-happy outpost to think, 'Christ! There's a bloody great Buick coming up the road', and an anti-tank missile would have smashed into us.

For perhaps a mile we saw absolutely nothing. We were going very slowly and eventually we arrived at the American front line, with no fuss, and that was that. Our ss doctor went off to be a prisoner, and we went off to breakfast in the hotel. The Allies had only been in Innsbruck a day, but freed prisoners were already being processed. An hotel room, a bath, breakfast seemed the summit of luxury, and afterwards we were photographed. Rather pleasant we look, untidy but pleasant, with long hair, and uniforms that were less bedraggled than they might have been – battledress is never smart but seldom scruffy.

Released at the same time was another little group, mostly French: Jean Borotra, Vichy Minister of Sport; Colonel de la Roche, who had been head of the French Fascists before the war; the ex-Premier Daladier, looking very down-at-heel and ill, and his wife; Paul Reynaud, also a wartime Prime Minister; and General Gamelin, Commander-in-Chief before the fall of France. I got it into my head that the Poles were in for a tricky time and that they must at all costs not be photographed with any of these people, particularly Borotra, whom we suspected, quite unjustly, of being a collaborator. Speaking of collaborators – later in the morning we walked a bit in the town, and a man rushed up to us with much wringing of hands and said in halting German that he was a Russian opera singer who had been taken as labour by the Germans and he was afraid he would be returned to the Russians and shot. We felt there was nothing we could do, but the episode left an unpleasant taste.

By lunchtime, reaction started to set in and most of us felt pretty shaky. My voice had dried up to a husky whisper. We were able to telephone to England and were told we should fly home within two days, which we did, from Augsburg.

I remember few details of my return to England. My mother was in London, but my father was ill at Harewood and I talked to him on the telephone. I have a feeling I slept the night at Buckingham Palace, I am fairly sure my mother and I dined there, and I do remember smoking a cigar and being undemonstratively sick (in a lavatory) afterwards – I have never really liked cigars since though I had before. I was in London for VE day and on 8 May went home to Harewood and spent the rest of the summer there, sleeping (with some difficulty), putting back a little weight, and recuperating.

CHAPTER FOUR

A New World
1945-6

LOOKING BACK ON the war, I realize my memories of the army are far less unfriendly than I would have expected. In retrospect I can admire such things as its ability to get, by less than ruthless means, more out of people than they set out willingly to give.

The inculcation and use of discipline is interesting, considering that it is mostly taught either on the parade ground or through military trivialities. We used to say in the Brigade of Guards that true discipline, which we believed we had, was valuable, and we followed this statement with a vast claim. Any trained unit, we said, should succeed with a properly mounted attack against equal forces because the odds are on the attacking group in the short term winning; our discipline would sustain us through the *counter-attack*, in which the odds would of course have shifted, and enable us to remain on the ground we had won. It was a large boast, and I must admit that in any action with which I was concerned we were never counter-attacked, so I never saw it proven. But I am convinced that any form of discipline that gets more out of people than they knew they had got is a very positive thing, and therefore, unless it is imposed in some inhumane way (and ours wasn't), worthwhile.

I suppose that is the most valuable lesson I learnt from the war, together with the prison experience of living, for however short a time and even sustained by hope of its short duration, in circumstances of discomfort and malnutrition, the condition even in time of peace of a high proportion of the world's inhabitants.

I stayed at Harewood through the summer of 1945, passing the time in resumptions of friendships, visits to relations, expeditions to see plays in London such as *The Duchess of Malfi* and *Hamlet* (with Peggy Ashcroft,

John Gielgud, Leslie Banks and a host of celebrities), operas such as a moderately-sung *Fledermaus* conducted by Tauber and a fine *Così fan tutte* at Sadler's Wells.

The great musical event was undoubtedly the première of *Peter Grimes* at the reopening of Sadler's Wells, when the company and Benjamin Britten seemed triumphantly to reveal the possibility of something new for opera and even for England. It was nothing less than a new confidence which returned at a blow; audiences (though not all critics) sensed this and were bowled over, and I sided firmly with the audience. I took my family's friend Tancred Borenius to the first night, and on the way in met Edward Dent and William Walton, the former as cynically optimistic as usual, the latter dourly warning of the difficulties surrounding a first opera (virtually none of us knew it was actually Ben's second).

We left in a whirlwind of impressions – of singing lines that spoke newly but were singable and unfragmented; of an orchestra which commented as seemingly none before (I had not yet heard *Wozzeck*); of the use of a traditional framework which allowed the new to hit its target square; of an odd subject which put for the first time on the operatic stage an anti-hero (we did not yet know the term).

The gramophone was of course a factor in the attempt to recapture sanity, as in the past it had always been to retain it, and an immediate pleasure was to find that my admirable batman, whose name was Harry Honeybun, had somehow contrived to get back to me the record collection I had accumulated in North Africa and Italy, still in the mortar box in which we carefully carried them from one base to the next. In August, I shot grouse at Bolton Abbey; and at Oxford on 7 October carried Jacqueline du Pré to the font as her godfather. Before that, my father had asked, gently but insistently, when I thought I should be well enough to rejoin my regiment. I hadn't given it a moment's thought, but wrote off immediately, manoeuvred my return date to take in Doncaster Races, and at the end of the summer was posted to Windsor.

Windsor then housed a de-mob battalion, and on my second morning there I found I was the only officer present at nine o'clock. When I asked the pleasant-seeming Company Sergeant Major, 'Anybody for company orders?' he replied: 'Yes, sir, a lot of people, probably twenty.' Asked what for, he said that they were all late for breakfast parade: 'They all have sleeping-out passes and they were late into barracks.' I asked why, and was told that the train had broken down. 'Oh well, that explains it!', to which came the correct military reply, 'Sir! A sleeping-out pass is a privilege and you will have to stop their passes for a week. They mustn't be allowed to get away with it.' I said, 'They won't be getting away with anything. It wasn't their fault,' and let them all off.

But I wasn't to get away with it either, and two days later I was transferred, this time to Chelsea Barracks in London, which suited me very well; when I wasn't on duty I was able to live in the spare bedroom of my father's apartment at St James's Palace. I was again with a unit full of men waiting to be de-mobbed; and the company officers consisted of an old friend of mine from the time I first joined up, Anthony Gishford, who was about to become a music publisher, Humphrey Lyttelton, the trumpeter, whom I had known at school, and myself. As virtually always in my short military career I was the junior officer, something which neither age nor circumstance ever seemed to alter. One got de-mobbed on a system of points, with age and service abroad totting up the highest score. I was twenty-two and joined in 1942, so was in a relatively low category, unlikely to get out until late 1946.

At this juncture, I was asked to go to Canada as ADC to the Governor General, who was my great-uncle, my grandmother's brother, Lord Athlone. It was the kind of invitation one dreamed of in prison days, though hardly what one would have wanted in wartime. So it was with many a glance over our shoulders – my fellow officers because they would get out soon, I because I was going to a land of milk and honey – that we ran this company.

It wasn't very exacting and we weren't, I am afraid, very exact. A tendency developed for Humphrey and I both to turn up for seven-thirty breakfast parade, which was unnecessary, or for neither of us to, which was unmilitary. Nobody said much about it until a semi-retired colonel, whom we had observed in the mess, looked out of his bedroom window one morning and noticed our absence. He turned out to be the Lieutenant Colonel (the senior-serving Grenadier), whom we had not recognized since none of us knew him, and he did his best from then on to make life uncomfortable, to no great effect admittedly, but just enough to remind us of the schoolboy standards we were trying to put behind us. We used to finish every day at about five o'clock, and Humphrey spent the evenings playing in a dance band, while I tended to go off to the opera, to a play or a film.

One or two odd things happened to me that autumn. The first was that a director of the Bank of England with a German name wrote to ask if I would be prepared to support the application for a review of his case by the General of the German division which had captured me in Italy. The General was apparently a blameless Austrian career soldier, a pre-war family friend of my correspondent, and he was languishing ill in prison under American jurisdiction. I asked advice of my parents and then checked with Buckingham Palace (where my cousin, Tommy Lascelles, was the King's Private Secretary), and wrote to J.J.McCloy, the American High Commissioner in Germany, simply stating that I had through the intervention of the General in question been treated with consideration and decency. To my astonishment I had a reply within a month saying that the General's case had been looked into and he had been sent home. It seemed to me then and still does that these decisions must have been startlingly haphazard, if a letter of such banality from someone as junior as myself could have made the difference between freedom and captivity for an old man accused of no crime.

The other occurrence had more melodramatic overtones. One day in the post there arrived from Germany a packet containing photostat copies of documents and a letter from a German lawyer asking me to testify that Obergruppenführer Berger, the German General who had liberated us, had indeed done what he claimed. He too was now ill and in prison, and I was asked to pass on the evidence and get support from my fellow *Prominenten*, Dawyck Haig, John Elphinstone, Charlie Hopetoun and the rest. It was easy (and truthful) to write what we were asked to write, and my only regret is that I did not have one of the supporting documents photographed before passing it on. It contained all our names, under the German instruction: 'The following Allied POWs are not to be allowed to fall into enemy hands.' What amounted to our death warrant was dated March 1945 and was signed by Hitler.

There is a somewhat deflating postscript to that agreeable no-man's-land of getting back to peacetime – or discovering peacetime for the first time as a grown-up. I was travelling down from the north to London on one of those meandering, post-war trains which took five or six hours for the two-hundred-mile journey, and got into conversation with a pleasant enough man, older than me, who was sitting opposite. We talked about the war and I said I had been a prisoner at the end of it. He knew several people in the same position including some, he said, at the notorious Colditz. I started to describe life there, and mentioned the poker schools in which we played regularly. Some schools allowed high stakes (not the one I belonged to), and the man opposite said: 'I believe there were people who left prison with quite high debts and never paid them. I was told old George Lascelles was one of them, but of course he was moved at the end of the war so perhaps it wasn't his fault.' I was so taken aback at the magnification of my £4 debt that I never revealed my identity to him, and a little later slunk off the train.

I crossed to Canada in winter 1945 in the *Queen Elizabeth* which was still, our few cabins apart, a troop-ship. We had an enjoyable, if sometimes rather comic journey, a suitable prelude perhaps to a period which seems to have been full of 'episodes'. All in all, my five months as an ADC were wonderfully rewarding, not least because they gave me my first taste of adult life untrammelled by rationing or blackouts or restrictions of any kind. Canada had never had those things, and life at Government House was as comfortable as you could imagine – sheltered and over-privileged as well, no doubt.

My only previous experience of the sea had been in troop-ships on the way to North Africa and Italy, and the one thing I knew for certain, in spite of my father's conviction that it was all in the mind, was that as soon as a ship started to roll I felt sick. This was easily cured by lying down, which evoked less opposition on the *Queen Elizabeth* than on troop-ships. I can't say I contributed very much to that journey, but I did meet a fellow ADC, Neville Ussher, who had come back from Canada with the Athlones and who quickly became a close friend and has remained so ever since. He had been so badly wounded at Calais that he was one of some three hundred POWs repatriated during the war, and had been with the Athlones since 1943. He returned with them for their first leave, while in Europe married a French girl he had got to know in Canada, and was coming back to Canada to help see the Athlones to the end of their tour of duty.

Neville and I shared a cabin, and I told him before we left Southampton that before long, if I knew my family, the Athlones would want to be taken down to inspect the engines, and that if I went too the heat and the smells there would undoubtedly bring on sea-sickness. So Neville took HE and HRH down, and later confirmed both temperature and odours. Later still, I astonished him by eating quite a healthy meal in bed, including oysters, while still unable to face the rolling ship. I don't think he quite believed my explanation – that all was well as long as I could remain horizontal – but it was perfectly true, and to this day I can stand any amount of rough air travel provided the seat will tilt back.

By the time we landed in Canada on 20 November the country was snowbound, and it was the start of a winter of unrelieved frost and sun. Our work at Government House was not at all arduous: three ADCs shared the routine (apart from Neville and me, there was a Canadian called John McClure), and only on big occasions were all three on duty. Otherwise we rotated, with one of us in any given week described as 'in waiting', which meant he was on duty at all times; another 'next-in-waiting', which meant

74

that if Princess Alice wanted to go out on her own, he went with her; and the third ADC still in residence but off duty, unless a special occasion demanded a full turnout.

We lived as part of the family and were all welcome at meals, like cousins in a great house, unless there was an official lunch or dinner, in which case, if off duty, we had to go out. The food was excellent, the company very congenial, and the work unexacting, as my aunt and uncle had done their tours and, in the aftermath of war, did not embark on extensive farewell trips. We used to go off and watch ice hockey games every Thursday evening if there wasn't another job.

There were still a fair number of smaller official functions, and people constantly came to see the Governor General. He had a marvellous memory but hardly ever attached a name to the person or place he had in mind. Most people were referred to as 'he' or 'she'; 'there' was the place they came from, and all the time one had to remember that 'she' could be either his sister, Queen Mary, or else Princess Alice. Ministers who knew him well referred to the visits as 'playing Dumb Crambo', because, unless they by luck caught on immediately to what was being referred to, they could skate dangerously and anonymously from one confidence to another, agreeing with the Governor General at every turn only to be asked a penetrating question which brooked no evasion.

There was a story of the lady on HE's left at a luncheon party who came from the provinces of Canada, and, not having been to Government House for two or three years, was understandably nervous. He didn't speak to her for half an hour, which helped her nerves not at all, and then suddenly turned and asked, 'How are they?' She searched for the right kind of answer and produced, 'Oh, very well, Your Excellency,' and he said, 'Yes, yes, no trouble with them at all?', which she took to be a reference to her family, who were grown up and in the services. 'Never, sir.' But when he followed up with, 'I had some difficulties at first', she knew she was out of her depth. Finally he asked, 'Do you never have any trouble keeping them in in the morning?', and she realized that on the only other occasion they had met they had each got a new set of false teeth, and were going through what you could only in the circumstances call teething troubles. But it would have taken a Sherlock Holmes to have deduced at the start of the conversation that 'they' were teeth.

Once, while I was there, he sent for Neville Ussher who was ADC in waiting. 'This fellow Edwards, I think we should ask him to lunch.' 'When, sir?' HE said: 'Tomorrow, there's nobody coming, I see.' So Neville asked, 'Will I be able to get hold of him easily?' and got the reply, 'Oh yes, just ask Edson' (the Canadian Naval Commander who was in charge of the ADCs). Sure enough, a Major Edwards, known to be a friend of HE's, was located and invited to lunch. Neville told the Governor General who smiled and shook his head. 'No, no, no, not that Edwards at all. The other one . . .' So, rather nervous by now, Neville went off, consulted Edson, and together they deduced it must be Colonel Edwards, one of the honorary ADCs, who lived with his wife in Ottawa. That turned out to be wrong too. The right Edwards was actually the Adjutant General, just returned from Europe. We got him, and next day at lunch the three pairs of Edwardses were all lined up, wives next to husbands in order of seniority, and presented. We never made out if they thought it a quirk or a practical joke, but none of them could have known it was a variant of Government House Dumb Crambo.

One had as an ADC to announce the names of visitors clearly and audibly, and on big occasions this was important. Neville knew far more of the visitors than I did, and the great thing was to make quite sure that you teamed up husbands and wives, who were liable to stray even while waiting in a presentation line. On one occasion I distinguished myself by insisting on announcing, 'The Archbishop of Quebec and Mrs . . .', not realizing that he was the Catholic archbishop.

The Governor General and his entourage travelled Canada by train, very comfortably indeed. I remember going to Quebec and sampling in a sizeable dining room on the train the admirable food cooked on board, and sitting in a fair-sized drawing room. The Viceregal party was going once by train across the prairies, sitting in absolute silence before lunch and sipping pink gins. The Governor General was looking out of the window as the train crossed miles of nothing until a solitary house came in sight, and he asked: 'Who lives there?' The Comptroller looked up and rang the bell. A black attendant came in and the question was put to him by the Comptroller. 'I don't know, Your Excellency. Some son of a gun!' The Governor General was perfectly satisfied with the answer, and the story goes that when about six months later he met a man called Gunn who came from that part of the world, he said, 'I know where you live.'

Life at Government House in Ottawa was fun because nobody tried to catch anyone else out; it was a normal peacetime existence, and I was not yet accustomed to that. I had never seen anything like a Government House except as it were from the other side of the ropes, at Buckingham Palace, when I was a small boy. But I knew how things should look and therefore perhaps how they should feel. The first time I was ADC on duty was at a simple function with experienced people at the other end and with Neville Ussher 'next-in-waiting' and therefore prepared to hiss advice if necessary, a promise he said he would keep only if dire emergency threatened. It was winter and cold and we had a fierce, old-fashioned chauffeur called Southgate, rightly proud of his Rolls-style driving and of his cars. I knew what I had to do when we arrived, which was to run round the car from my seat next to the chauffeur, salute if there was time, and open the car door if there was no one else to do it. We drew up slowly, and I opened my door and started running, skidding slightly on the icy surface and brushing the offside car mirror with my greatcoat sleeve just hard enough to cause it to snap and tinkle to the ground as I breathlessly wrenched the door open and let my (I hoped) unsuspecting employers out into the wintry night. Southgate was not pleased.

To fade into the background but unfailingly appear when required for presentations, to get them in the right order, and to produce notes for a speech, is all an ADC is for. The first time I went out on my own was to look after Princess Alice at a rather simple function, a Chopin recital in aid of the Red Cross by Malcuzynski, a fine pianist then living in Canada. I had learnt very carefully the names of the two people I had to present, the manager of the concert and the Red Cross representative, and we went off to the Château Laurier Hotel in Ottawa. I bounded in my dinner jacket out of the door at the right moment and presented the smart fellow in the white tie who came out of the hotel, only to hear Princess Alice whispering from behind, 'No, no, that's the doorman.' To get the right names for the right people who were in black ties seemed somehow slightly irrelevant after that, though I remember enjoying the recital.

Like most people of experience who have been allowed by circumstances to indulge them, Lord Athlone had one or two eccentricities. At Christmas time, there were parties for the staff where HE and HRH gave out presents – quite an elaborate business based, I imagine, on Buckingham Palace procedures. Senior married staff got a turkey. Neville told me beforehand that the Governor General didn't much enjoy this function, which indeed I noticed made him rather grumpy. This apparently was predictable, as was his choice of suit – brown, with a purple check on it – which he also disliked and wore only for this occasion. He duly emerged gruffly at teatime wearing his turkey suit, smiled over a dozen turkeys at a dozen senior staff and went off to change for dinner, reappearing his usual serene self an hour later. A family quirk? My mother had a brown overall she wore at Harewood only once a year, for decorating the Christmas tree.

There was another story, about soap. HE was balanced and equable and only occasionally did he get cross, usually over something small. Before my time in Ottawa, a party including him and his valet – a nice man called Bennett – and Neville Ussher, flew off for two nights to review troops. After a gruelling day, they flew back in the early evening and had a bumpy and horrible flight, with everyone strapped in, objects thrown about and everybody ill apart from the Governor General, who sat unperturbed through it all. At journey's end, all staggered to their feet and struggled to the cars and home for dinner. Not a word was spoken during the twenty-minute drive; a glass of whisky was drunk, still in silence, and HE went off to change. Bennett, pale and miserable, had unpacked and put HE's clothes out, but suddenly from the bathroom came an appalling bellow of rage. When Bennett went in to see what terrible thing had happened, he found that, though all else was immaculate, the Viceregal shaving kit had been set out by the shaken Bennett with the soap the wrong side up.

Princess Alice was not only a favourite aunt as far as I was concerned and the most entertaining and considerate employer possible, but also I should imagine one of the greatest consorts any pro-consul ever had. She and my mother had become fast friends during the First World War, perhaps because they had the same sort of sense of humour. When I got to know her best she was over sixty, energetic, and very amusing. She always looked splendid, was adored by everyone who met her, official and unofficial, and into her nineties remained a great source of fun, lively and kind to everybody – as we discovered when in Barbados years later Patricia and I dined at Government House to find there three nonagenarians – Zena Dare, her sister-in-law the Maharani of Sarawak, and Aunt Alice herself.

Funny things tend to happen in any Viceregal circles, but Lord Athlone was anything but a figure of fun. We respected him and were devoted to him, and he was a splendid example of a British pro-consul, convinced that whoever he was going to meet would be pleased to see him, confident that nothing untoward was going to happen, and that he could stop anything inappropriate from being said simply by his presence and the force of example. He wasn't an especially learned man, and yet he made a success wherever he went – I believe as Governor General of South Africa, certainly in Canada, where they asked him to prolong his stay. His success was not least because he was the kindest and most generous of men and because, whenever there was any problem towards whose solution he could contribute, he invariably made the right contribution.

I was on duty at the great farewell dinner given by the Government at the

Country Club the night before the Athlones left Canada, and it was an emotional occasion, distinguished by an eloquent (but forty-minute) speech by the Prime Minister, Mackenzie King. When the Prime Minister, who was a sentimental old man, went to see them off next day, he made his little bow, blew his nose and stammered out to them, 'We do love you', and it was of course perfectly true.

In Canada I fell for the first time properly in love, with a diplomat's daughter. Françoise was irrepressible, bubbling with life and fun, a year or two younger than me and apparently as avid for the music and concerts to which I longed to introduce her as I was for the much more sophisticated life I thought she led. Endless small parties and expeditions were the order of that winter, and hardly a day went by when I did not see her. We went skiing, which I had never done before; she had to rescue me from the bottom of a gully, and became known as the *Soutien-George*. We went out in the car on a day I was to accompany the Governor General to Quebec, and I stuck it firmly in the snow with no apparent possibility of meeting my deadline – but somehow we got it out, and I was on duty in the proper clothes at the proper time. Leaving Françoise that summer when I went home to England was not easy, but she was a Roman Catholic, and I did not believe that hurdle could be got over.

When the Governor General and Princess Alice left Canada in March 1946, just before the snow melted, I stayed on to help the Comptroller of the Household, Geoffrey Eastwood, to clear up, experiencing as a result and for the only time in my life the extraordinary exhilaration of a northern spring, when a warmer sun replaces winter's glitter, the ice melts, the flowers and trees mirror the prevailing mood of renewal and hope, and the heart lifts in twentieth-century Canada as surely as in fables from Russia or Scandinavia. It is a quite different sensation from spring in temperate Europe, and no one who has not experienced it can know what a truly northern writer is describing.

Geoffrey Eastwood and I went in April from Ottawa to New York, for me a first visit; I went to the Metropolitan Opera five times in three days, seeing a *Walküre* with Melchior and Helen Traubel (the first live Wagner for me), and we then set off by train across Canada. We left on 10 April and were back in Ottawa by 18 May, staying on the way in Winnipeg, Calgary and Banff, with a three-day side-trip to the beauties of Lake Louise. Then through the Rockies for three days in Vancouver and Victoria Island before setting off for Seattle and San Francisco. On this trip I acquired two notions which have since become convictions: that San Francisco is to me the most congenial of all North American cities, and Vancouver the most beautifully situated.

In Los Angeles we stayed at the Beverley Hills Hotel and dipped our toes into the waters of Hollywood, starting with a tremendous party given for us by Louis B. Mayer. To meet in person the stars one had known apparently all one's life is a peculiar experience, rather daunting for the ultra-shy twenty-three-year-old I found that I was. While engaged on a film, the stars avoided parties and went out hardly at all, work at the studio tending to start at seven or eight and go on all day. On the other hand, for those not working there were parties most nights, lasting well into the morning, and there you tended to meet the same people as the night before with three or four new faces added, so that at the end of ten days acquaintances and even friendships had been struck up.

I particularly remember at those parties Annabella and Tyrone Power, Gene Tierney, David Niven and his first wife, Lilli Palmer and Rex Harrison, and a great lunch somewhere in the country where I met Artur Rubinstein and a Hungarian actress called Ilona Massey. She impressed me by her hot-house beauty and magnolia complexion and by telling me that she had alternated as Tosca with Jeritza at the Vienna Opera; and then in the Californian sun she started to melt, literally, before my fascinated eyes, as her carefully applied mask dissolved on to her dress.

My oddest experience was at a huge party in the house of Darryl F. Zanuck, head of Twentieth Century Fox, intending (and succeeding) with a multitude of stars in outdoing Louis B's of a few nights before. In Hollywood, to be lavish was to succeed, and that night the climax came when the lights dimmed and a great ice edifice with caviar heaped round its base was wheeled in. To my horror I recognized it as a vast muzzled bear's head, the Lascelles family crest, which I rather priggishly felt to be in the worst possible taste, and shrank at first from acknowledging. But what a gesture! What a feather in the cap of Twentieth Century Fox's research department! A friend later assured us that accurate period detail was available to the producer and director of every film made in Hollywood, and that inaccuracies and solecisms were the result of deliberate decisions based on the expectations of the mid-Western American audience, which knew the shape of a British bobby's helmet and would not have accepted him, even in the mid-nineteenth century, wearing a top hat.

My return to England was in the *Queen Mary*, and I was posted immediately

My mother, HRH Princess Mary, aged sixteen.

My parents, Princess Mary and Viscount Lascelles, on the balcony of Buckingham Palace after their wedding, 1922. With them (left to right) are King George V, Queen Alexandra and Queen Mary.

My parents at the Oaks, June 1923

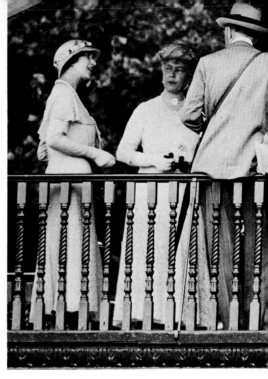

Queen Mary, standing in the Royal Box with my parents, makes a rare appearance at Sandown races.

Queen Mary holds me after my christening, 1923. Seated next to her is my other grandmother, the Countess of Harewood; standing left to right: King George V, my mother and my father.

With my younger brother Gerald.

With Gerald at the seaside.

Walking with our Governess behind my parents and Gerald on the way to Church,
London, 1931.

Out riding with Dick Froude, our groom.

Trooping the Colour, 1934. Riding behind King George v are (left to right) the Prince of Wales, Prince Arthur of Connaught and my father.

Standing next to Queen Mary on the balcony of Buckingham Palace during the celebrations of King George v's Silver Jubilee, 6 May 1935. From left to right: Prince Arthur of Connaught, the Queen of Norway, the Duke of York, my mother, King George v, Princess Margaret, my brother, my father (behind), Princess Elizabeth, me, Queen Mary, the Duke of Gloucester, the Duchess of Kent, the Duke of Kent (behind), the Duchess of York, Princess Victoria, the Prince of Wales and Lord Athlone.

In the middle of a football scrum at Eton, 1936.

Holding Queen Mary's train as she leaves the Chapel at Windsor during the Order of the Garter ceremony, 14 June 1937.

Grouse shooting with my father and brother in Yorkshire, 1938.

Instruction at Caterham, March 1942.

The destruction of Monte Cassino, May 1944.

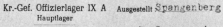

Kr.-Gef. Offizierlager IX A   Ausgestellt Spangenberg
Hauptlager
Zweiglager   am 1. 8.   194 4

Kennkarte für Kriegsgefangene

Nur gültig für den Lagerbetrieb und in Verbindung mit der
Erk.-Marke Nr. 133760

Dienstgrad : Oberleutnant

Name : Viscount Lascelles

Vorname : George Henry Umbert Hubert

Lichtbild

Zur Beachtung !

Die Kennkarte dient als Aus-
weis der Krf. gegenüber den
Organen der deutschen Lager-
kommandantur. Sie ist wie
die Erk.-Marke stets mitzu-
führen u. mit dieser auf
Verlangen bei namentlichen
Appells und beim Verlassen
des Lagers vorzuweisen.
Verlust ist sofort zu melden.

Der Kommandant

My POW identity card.

to Wellington Barracks opposite St James's Park. For most of the last six months of my army time when I was not on duty I lived across the park in my father's apartment at St James's Palace. I had always been keen about racing, which was my father's passion. My keenness was such that on my 1939 summer Long Leave from Eton I chose to go to Sandown rather than to the Eton *v.* Harrow match at Lord's, cricket-mad though I was, and I used to keep a form book of my father's horses' engagements and results, an activity which caused consternation when my Eton housemaster found it open on my desk. Suspecting it was a betting book – to keep which was at Eton almost more heinous a crime than smoking or homosexuality – he demanded a full explanation. He got it, but I don't think he ever completely trusted me again.

It must have been in the summer of 1946 that I was asked to go with my mother to stay at Windsor Castle for Ascot, my father being unwell. I loved the racing, but was bemused by the social activity. The processional drive from Windsor had been restored and I figured worryingly high in the order. I drove either with the Queen or, on one occasion, with the King, which caused another socio-military predicament: did you when in uniform salute when the band played 'God Save the King' or, since the object of the compliment was sitting opposite and acknowledging it, did you sit mumchumps with your hands at your sides?

Military life for me was running out but by no means over. We mounted King's Guard with some regularity from Wellington Barracks, which meant two days' sojourn in comfortable circumstances at Buckingham Palace, if you were the Ensign or junior officer, or at St James's Palace if you were Captain or the other officer. I was Captain more than once, failing the first time to have prepared the drill, so that harsh words were spoken at the practice (I had assumed one learnt it then); I went away and perused the drill book routine, the only time I ever saw that much-invoked, seldom-seen tome. Military ceremony in moderation rather appealed to me, as I suppose would any well-running machine which I could set in motion; and the social side of these guard duties was agreeable. To the amazement of other officers, my guests at dinner on one occasion (men only, women permitted at lunch) were David Webster and Karl Rankl, newly appointed administrator and music director of Covent Garden, met through Tony Gishford shortly before.

Another recollection of Wellington Barracks at that time is of being asked to defend a guardsman accused of being asleep on sentry duty. I did not know the man but traditionally one could not refuse such a request. Knowing virtually nothing of military law, I took advice of a brother officer who was a lawyer and who instructed me to look up certain pages and then visit my 'client', who was languishing in the guard room. He told me that it was true he had been asleep, but simply because he had already been on guard for over three hours when the sergeant came round – they had agreed between them all to double the normal two-hour stints in order to allow the sergeant four hours in bed between rounds. This was totally illegal, and I returned to take more advice from my learned friend. 'Of course you must plead this as a mitigating circumstance, and you should get him off. It's tough on the sergeant, but that's life – and you will be failing in your duty if you do *not* plead it. You must bring it out in the evidence, taking care not to "lead" the sergeant too obviously, and then the routine is that you put on your cap, rise to your feet, salute, and say, "I submit there is no case to answer." Then you march from the room and leave the military judges to make up their minds.'

All went as he suggested it would, although the unfortunate sergeant seemed a little over-anxious to admit his share in the chapter of accidents, and I saluted, made my plea and marched out. But not for long, as the judges in their wisdom decided – correctly, I suppose, everything considered – that there *was* a case to answer, that my guardsman had in effect pleaded guilty and that all I now had to do was to make what was technically I think called a plea in mitigation. I did so; he got a rather small sentence (a week confined to barracks, perhaps) but the unfortunate sergeant and indeed the corporal as well were reduced if not to the ranks at least in rank.

I went to see my client, who seemed not very pleased with the way things had gone, and apologized to the sergeant, who appeared to bear no grudge. It was a rather ludicrous episode – think of putting a well-meaning but legally clueless man up to help another citzen in a situation where skill and knowledge of the law could make the difference between a stiff sentence and nothing much more than a reprimand! On the other hand, I must admit, justice *was* probably done.

CHAPTER FIVE

Inheritance
1946-8

IT WAS IN the summer of 1946 that I went to Glyndebourne for *The Rape of Lucretia*, the first time with my mother, later with an army friend, Denys Martyn. My mother and I were asked to sit in John Christie's box and I remember him saying: 'I do hope you enjoy it. It's a most peculiar piece. I think it's very good, but some of the language is rather surprising. Of course, that *is* how soldiers talk. So you mustn't be shocked.' I don't think my mother was shocked, and we were both enthusiastic about the music and the new chamber opera form which Benjamin Britten seemed to be initiating. The glorious voice of Kathleen Ferrier invested Lucretia with her own form of sober glamour, the sets of John Piper recreated a Roman world to perfection, and the music has haunted me ever since.

On my third visit I took another military friend, and years later I was told that my choice of companions had convinced John Christie I was 'queer'. I always got on tremendously well with his wife, the singer Audrey Mildmay, and sat on various committees with her, but John I felt never liked me.

Thirty years later, staying at Glyndebourne, by now with George Christie, John and Audrey's son, we were talking about his parents. I told him of my fondness for his mother and mentioned that when I had once praised a Glyndebourne Susanna, Elena Rizzieri, his father had reacted by saying: 'Yes, she has improved a great deal, and I think we have done a lot for her since she has been here. Of course, it *is* basically the most hideous voice!' I thought this a curious way of accepting what was after all a compliment, but somebody later said: 'You must understand that John can't accept *anybody* in the roles that Audrey sang. To compliment them is in its way to insult her memory.'

I went on to say to George that his father hadn't liked me because he thought I was queer. 'Oh,' said George, 'I knew he didn't really like you, but

83

he gave me quite a different reason. He said, "Curious chap! The first time he came here in 1946 with his mother, he came in 'ordinaries'" [which meant that I had come to Glyndebourne in a suit and not in a dinner jacket!]. That's why he didn't approve of you.' It hadn't occurred to me, in June 1946, that you went in mid-afternoon *anywhere* in a dinner jacket, but it had also never occurred to John Christie that anyone came to Glyndebourne other than in a dinner jacket. My crime was indeed terrible.

John Christie was of course an eccentric, a very English eccentric, but English in spirit rather than in insularity, because insular he never in my experience was. There was little too that was self-seeking about his eccentricity. On the other hand, there was a kind of wilfulness about his insistence that Glyndebourne virtually alone had standards, that others foolishly, almost criminally, ignored Glyndebourne and its lead, and in this respect he could seem arrogant.

During the 1947 Glyndebourne season, the last for several years as it turned out, Rudi Bing told me that he had persuaded John that they should put in for an Arts Council grant, because John couldn't afford to lose the sort of money now involved. Rudi had talked to the Arts Council and agreed an outline budget, and he took a fuller version to John with a covering letter which he hoped John would sign. John said, 'But you've left out the garden.' Rudi said, 'Yes; we can't ask them to contribute towards the garden.' And John said, 'The garden is part of Glyndebourne. We *must* put it in.' 'They won't accept it,' said Rudi, upon which John decided not to apply for the grant.

I am sure John loved music but it was in a funny, personalized kind of way, for he had no broad musical culture, only a detailed appreciation and knowledge of what had been done at Glyndebourne. In 1947 he was talking about having *Traviata* at Glyndebourne the following year, and we speculated at dinner with Audrey about who would be asked to sing. After perhaps half an hour's discussion, John said, 'Well, I don't really know. I know the music but I have never seen the opera.' That was genuine eccentricity. It wasn't done at Glyndebourne, it hadn't been done in Dresden or wherever he had learnt his Mozart, and therefore he didn't know it. The fact that it had been in every other company's repertory every season throughout his life made no difference to him.

Much later, Glyndebourne mounted the first British performance of Stravinsky's *The Rake's Progress* at the Edinburgh Festival. Ian Hunter was director and later told me that the press conference had produced its crop of Christie-isms. Asked, 'Why *The Rake*?', John had said Glyndebourne felt it its duty and was glad to contribute the work to Edinburgh, though he himself didn't like it. Moran Caplat, Glyndebourne's manager, had interrupted to mention that Edinburgh had of course paid for the production, but John was not to be put off. Why didn't he like it, asked a newspaper man. 'Because it has no heart – like Rossini. Besides, I never think much of an opera whose overture can't be played in concert,' said John. 'What do you feel about the overture to *Tosca* then?' asked Alfred Wallenstein, the opera's American conductor. 'Never heard it! Never seen it!' claimed John, playing his ace.

After the war I went up to Cambridge, encouraged to do so by the only master at Eton with whom I made friends and kept in touch. Robert Graham and his wife Marnie were a haven of civilization in that slightly bleak, male-ridden community, and they admitted to virtues and even foibles which the Spartans and perhaps Eton would have despised. They knew that the young always have insoluble problems which temporarily blight their lives, and they offered refuge from life's storms.

I used to go to plays in London with them (Robert acted while at Cambridge and seemed to know all theatrical London) and stay with them at Datchet. With them I went to an unforgettable *Antony and Cleopatra* (with Edith Evans and Godfrey Tearle) soon after the war. With them I stayed during occasional military weekends, with them I had some of my earliest adolescent-to-adult conversations, and to them I was grateful for it all.

My time at King's did not leave me with the vivid impressions it should have, and my affection for it is muted if genuine. Probably going up to Cambridge at nearly twenty-four, after wartime experience – a fellow undergraduate was a colonel with a family of four – provided too few of the liberating experiences which would normally attach to this stage of life. Mine had already come in the army, in prisoner-of-war camps and in Canada. A bottle of sherry in the cupboard, hard as it was to get, somehow did not represent emancipation; but the talk, the habit of intellectualizing and not fearing to express thoughts and theories however far-fetched, was more suggestive, and for that I have Cambridge to thank – for that, and for reminding me how to read again seriously and sometimes against inclination. I was a compulsive reader when I was a child, but music later took over and where others find their solace in a book I find mine in gramophone records.

I had a first Cambridge term full of discovery, of new friends, of attempts to sit down and *learn* again in an academic atmosphere; and I enjoyed the reactions of slightly younger, non-wartime contemporaries to the 'new' freedoms of university. The Sunday after I arrived, in January 1947, I went for a drink with the College tutor, Patrick Wilkinson, and there met some of my black contemporaries – King's had many contacts with the Commonwealth countries. At one point, the beer ran out and Patrick fetched some more, but there was no bottle-opener. One black Kingsman proceeded to open the bottles with his teeth and, when Patrick exclaimed at how he was able to do this, produced the riposte: 'Rather, Mr Tutor, you should ask yourself how you can *not* do it!', which was unanswerable.

E. M. Forster was an honorary fellow of King's, and I met him at that same party. I asked him about India, which I assumed he knew well, only to find he had just been there for the first time since before 1914, and got an invitation to call on him in his rooms. I saw him fairly often during my eighteen months at Cambridge, dropping in for a cup of coffee or a glass of port after dinner, and was constantly amazed at his accessibility to undergraduates and willingness to talk to them.

In his way he was a considerable influence on my generation at King's. Awe of a great man rapidly vanished and was succeeded by a certain wariness on our part, because he was indulgent to theories and questioning but intolerant of intellectual sloppiness or self-indulgence – an almost perfect recipe, it now seems to me, for a good influence on the young. Once, and only once, I ventured to return his hospitality by asking him to tea, the only meal he would accept from us. This turned out a success, to my great relief, which was compounded when a contemporary told me he had once attempted to entertain Morgan in similar circumstances, only to have his visitor decline to put down cup and saucer or plate with cake but balance the one on the other in uncomfortable silence for the whole hour he stayed.

We found we had in common amongst other things a great liking for and interest in Benjamin Britten. The only thing about him Morgan appeared not to approve was what he thought of as his over-intense Christianity. I did not then know Ben well, though I had met him a number of times; but when I got to know him later, I saw no signs that Morgan was even remotely correct in his conjecture. But I never took it up later with Morgan. When Ben wrote in 1948 while I was still an undergraduate and asked me to be President of the newly-founded Aldeburgh Festival, I was pleased at recognition from someone I admired and liked so much, and it was Morgan's advice I sought as to whether it was appropriate for someone young and unimportant to accept such an honour.

He encouraged me to do it, saying I should not be over-modest and that it looked from the prospectus a real festival and not at all the kind of thing he thought of as 'Put on *Bohème* and *Butterfly*, charge double prices and call it a

Puccini Festival!' As a result, I took a large Cambridge party by bus to Aldeburgh to see *Albert Herring* at the Jubilee Hall, and later went over for a Saturday afternoon concert and had lunch with Benjamin Britten, his sister Barbara, and Peter Pears before a concert in the church – the second performance of *St Nicolas*, which I greatly enjoyed.

I used to see E. M. Forster fairly often after I left Cambridge, occasionally there, most years at the Aldeburgh Festival where, like us, he used regularly to stay with Ben; and sometimes in London, where I remember taking him to some part of the *Ring* at Covent Garden, and to see Boris Christoff in *Boris Godunov*, which he seemed to enjoy – though nothing pleased him more than Boris's extravagant acknowledgment of applause at the end. He did not approve however of Peter Brook's imaginative but less than literal production, and a postcard from him reads:

I often recall the bowing Bulgarian, what a delightful evening – despite the Brook's hell and the Peterkin pendulum clock.

He gave me first editions of his books as a wedding present, which were rare enough for it not to be odd that he had once inscribed them to someone else, got them back, and re-inscribed them to me – though I thought it odd at the time.

Much later, after my divorce was set down, I backed a stage adaptation of *Howards End*, the first of his books I had read (in Africa during the war), losing money on the venture but enjoying the experience and indeed the performance – with a cast including Gwen Watford, Gemma Jones, Andrew Ray and Michael Goodliffe. The play was doubtless wordy and there was a little incidental music – Beethoven and Schumann. Frith Banbury, who produced, told me that the matinée at Eastbourne was filled with old ladies getting in cheap. On the way out he heard one of them say indignantly to her neighbour: 'Just what I should have expected from Lord Harewood. Nothing but music and sex!' A braver epitaph could no man wish for.

Dons were disappointingly predictable, but there were shining exceptions. I remember with pleasure the lay Dean, Kenneth Harrison, who had rooms next to Morgan's and frequently had a few of us for a drink after dinner. My friend Mike Stanley, who stuttered, once addressed him memorably late in the evening as 'You obb-bb-scene Dean', which gave pleasure at the time and stuck for months afterwards. Boris Ord, in charge of music at King's, was another celebrity with whom I made friends and used occasionally to lunch with at a little Belgian restaurant on King's Parade. He was a superb choral trainer, and his English reputation mostly rested on that and on his knowledge of old music. He taught me over a glass of wine in his rooms to decipher ('read' would be a misnomer) lute entablature, and once in a moment of expansion after an operatic discussion admitted that if his life had been spent in Germany he would undoubtedly have gravitated to an opera house and never left it. This bolstered my need to find opera respectable, not uncommon in the English climate of the times, when Puccini was despised by almost all critics and too many musicians, Verdi underrated, and the opera house thought of as a temple in need of a thorough cleansing.

I read English at Cambridge – what else, after six semi-military years since leaving school? – and my greatest Cambridge influence was my tutor, George Rylands. Dadie, as his friends called him, had the inestimable gift of being enthusiastic and conveying that enthusiasm to others. He told us what to read and what lectures to go to, which included those by F.R.Leavis, his great rival in the English school at the time. It was the killjoy in Leavis he disliked, not the constructive thinker, but I am afraid his suspicion communicated itself to me so that the Leavis lectures I attended were too few and too far-spaced: an opportunity missed.

I was demobbed only in December 1946 and so could not go up till January, which meant I missed the first term of my first year. Dadie invoked a concession by which an undergraduate with war service did not have to sit the examination customary at the end of a first year – 'You'd fail it anyhow,' he explained, with the same frankness he had showed at my first tutorial when he said, 'Ah, an Eton boy. Then you'll have read very little.' And he was right, on both counts. He was a persuader, not a disciplinarian, but his methods were not lax and he disliked it if you did not do the work he had asked you for. He communicated enjoyment in his teaching and in his lectures and he expected what you read to delight you, and was disappointed if that spirit was absent from your written reaction to it.

You used to write an essay or commentary (in my case, type – I have always written illegibly and dislike the physical feeling of pen on paper) once a week, and read it out to your tutor. The first time I went, with an essay on some Shakespeare play, I was horribly nervous. But we sat and talked about the play, and then Dadie started to speak with evident pleasure about the pre-war Glyndebourne production of Verdi's *Macbeth*, which he pronounced far more enjoyable and better tuned to the spirit of Shakespeare than virtually any other Shakespearean production he had ever seen. I left in a state of elation, without having read my essay; but Dadie did not forget to make me write a companion piece during the ensuing week and read them both when I next came.

He collected china and was proud of what he had got, and sometimes we would be asked to admire it over sherry in the evenings – spirits were very hard to get in those days. He was chairman of the Arts Theatre, and there was varied and interesting fare there in those post-war years, and occasionally he'd take one or two pupils to the theatre. I remember a French effusion, by I think Mauriac, which we tried to admire until the reiterated description of one of the female characters as 'the girl who couldn't be satisfied' caused us to exchange respect for laughter.

Noel Annan, not much older than me, was another don whom I got to know, and Dadie suggested I should go to his first lectures as they were likely to be not only interesting but brilliant, even though his subject did not concern my Tripos. He was absolutely right; they were a *tour de force* and Noel became somebody whom I admired and towards whose friendship I aspired.

To become an undergraduate with all the attendant rules and regulations, the gowns at lectures and after dark, the proctors, the midnight curfew, was not easy at twenty-four (and many were older) and after war service. University authorities were understanding, and a blind eye was often turned. You had to 'keep' so many nights a term, and obtain leave to be away for the night, but London and the opera beckoned – Covent Garden had reopened in winter 1946 and Italian opera was in full swing at the Cambridge Theatre – and most of us evolved a way of squaring whoever's job it was to check us every morning. In addition, living as I did in King's Hostel (an annexe of the Arts Theatre), there was the advantage of a clandestinely-obtained, communally-held key to the front door, with which we let ourselves quietly in after some metropolitan expedition.

My friends were Mike Stanley, Anthony Lyttelton, and Robin Howard, who lost his legs during the war and whom I had first met falling downstairs like Bader. We were in different colleges but lunched regularly together in the restaurant on King's Parade, where food was cheap (with a five shilling top in the aftermath of the war, and rationing still in force) but where for a time wholly unpalatable whale steak appeared on the menu – once tried, never willingly repeated. You learnt early on to mix your friends with discretion, and another group with whom singly and plurally I made expeditions to London included Michael Jaffé, obviously destined even then to rise high in the field of art expertise; Barry Till, reading for the church and later Dean of Hong Kong and then head of Morley College; Gordon Nares, with whom I went racing, and Peter Bowen-Davies – both now dead – and Michael Edwards, who went into American shipping.

For the whole of my second summer they and I were constantly in and out of each other's rooms, which helped preparation for a Tripos very little. When I went to ask the advice of Noel Annan just before the exam, I confirmed what he suspected – that I had done very little work apart from my tutorials with Dadie – and he advised against staying up all night to make up for lost time. I should rather read my lecture notes and essays again carefully, and then select from the paper only those subjects I was confident of writing about. If I exhausted what I could intelligently tackle, it was best to give the impression of not having had time to finish.

I suppose I took his advice, and at least got a II:ii – nothing to write home about; in those days the only respectable thing was either a First or a Third. Dadie told me I was helped by an essay I wrote about Verdi and Shakespeare, a subject I felt I really knew something about. He gave it back to me after I left, and I unashamedly used the best bits of it four years later when revising Kobbé's *Complete Opera Book*.

In those days we wore our cares lightly, and I am afraid I have never believed that temptation comes only to be resisted. My initial resolve to forego the première of Benjamin Britten's new version of the *Beggar's Opera*, which was scheduled for the Arts Theatre on the evening of the first day of my Tripos Examination (which extended only over four days), was easily dropped – with encouragement, I should plead in mitigation, from the composer and E. M. Forster, whom I ran across on King's Parade the Sunday before my ordeal began.

During the King's absence on a Commonwealth visit, Councillors of State were appointed to act for him on state occasions such as Privy Councils, the reception of new ambassadors and so on. Princess Elizabeth, the Duke of Gloucester, my mother and I were the senior members of the Royal Family, and, with my parents in Torquay trying to give my father an easier than normal winter, and Princess Elizabeth often out of reach, I was frequently called on to act with the Duke of Gloucester.

Off to London I went, as unobtrusively as possible, to receive with my uncle whatever ambassador had newly arrived, to 'prick' the Sheriffs' list (an agreeably ludicrous description of an occasion dating back presumably to pre-literate days), to sign acts of clemency. The Czech ambassador paid his respects, only weeks after the infamous murder of Jan Masaryk, and gossip had it that the ambassador, like other Czech politicians of any persuasion, spent the entire war safely in prison, each opposing political side taking it in turn to 'shop' the other, and the Germans taking advantage of the position to keep opponents permanently under supervision.

When my uncle and aunt eventually got back from abroad, I was asked to lunch at Buckingham Palace. I gave myself plenty of time to motor up from Cambridge in my Morris Minor, fortunately, since, with half an hour in hand, I had a puncture in Regent's Park, ten minutes from my objective. In those days I could change a tyre with the best of them – it was before the days of steam-driven nut-tightening – and I still had fifteen minutes in hand when I drove up to BP, in need of a good wash.

During my Cambridge days and afterwards I used quite often to go to the theatre with Queen Mary. Her choice was catholic, and since the plays started early, we used to go back to Marlborough House for supper afterwards. Sometimes this was in the dining room, with the lady-in-waiting and equerry present; more often we had it together upstairs in her private dining room. She used to worry then and later about the amount of work my mother got through, and how it took toll of her resources. 'You must persuade her to do less,' she used to say, often complaining about the number of speeches my mother made. My grandmother herself had, she told me, made only two in her whole life – one during the First World War and another at Silver Jubilee time. She had often said the words required to launch a ship or open a hospital, but she had not been subjected to the new fad which demanded a speech every time anyone performed a public office. After he died, I found the same worry over my mother's health in pre-war letters Queen Mary wrote to my father.

My grandmother had a wonderfully perceptive eye for objects, and could identify in an antique shop or in a friend's house (hence the mostly fictional stories of her 'claiming' something she recognized) the obscurest likeness of a long-dead member of the family, or the least likely piece which matched something already in the collection. I very much like the story which had her giving a Christmas present of a piece of china to an ardent collector friend, who did not care for it and, after a couple of years, took it back to the shop to exchange. By next Christmas, Queen Mary had seen it, bought it, and sent it to the same friend, saying she had been lucky enough to find the pair to the piece she gave her three Christmasses ago!

It was typical of her practicality and devotion to family that she left her great collection to the Queen with nothing to any individual, although of course she expected things to be shared out a bit, as they were. I remember a courtier's comment: 'Poor Cynthia Colville [her longest-serving lady-in-waiting]! Thirty years of devotion and not even a toque to show for it!'

I wore spectacles at that time, just for driving or theatre or cinema, and my grandmother was surprised to see me in them and insisted I take them off the moment the lights came up, as I would not, surely, want anyone to see me wearing them. She told me too that she herself had always been conscious of having big feet, and tucked them under her chair when being photographed.

I had sometimes in 1939 accompanied the party when she went on expeditions from Harewood to see churches and houses in Yorkshire. I had also been to Badminton to see her during her exile from London during the war, but the relative naturalness of childhood had with me given way to a certain self-consciousness as I grew up, and I could not help noticing the awe and near-reverence with which Queen Mary was generally treated. Even my mother seemed to approach her wearing metaphorical kid gloves, but these evenings together and particularly the times we had supper alone produced a much more relaxed atmosphere than tended otherwise to prevail. I very much enjoyed them and the half-confidences and nuggets of wisdom and family history and insight into my grandmother's sometimes very in-dependent point of view I collected from them.

The fact of the matter was that barriers inside the family were neither stiff nor high, and I easily believe what Aunt Alice Athlone said to me once, when someone had commented in print about the stuffiness of Queen Victoria's court in her later years: 'Oh, but they're quite wrong! She was so funny, she made us laugh so!' I am sure it was true – Aunt Alice was eighteen when her grandmother died and old enough to have a point of view. No doubt Queen Victoria was amusing and relaxed with her own family, since she believed them on her level; but I wonder if she was able to think of anyone who was not Royal as appropriate to share a joke with. Some of this attitude towards non-family had disappeared by the 1930s and more went during the war (that was when I started to be conscious of my mother's birth), but I think the sense of being somehow different dies very hard – and indeed can prove a useful weapon.

Much of my time in the years after the war was spent in one musical activity or another. I got to know E.J. Dent, once professor of music at Cambridge. He was born at Ribston near Goldsborough, where I spent the first six years of my life, and he had an accurate memory for detail of every kind. He could tell you exactly what Busoni had said about Puccini before 1914, who had ganged up on whom at the International Society for Contemporary Music conferences immediately post-1918, what cuts had been made in *The Ring* in performances of the 1920s. He was delighted that my grandfather had his pioneering book on Mozart's operas in his own library at Harewood – 'One of only about 1,200 copies sold,' chortled Dent – and just as pleased when I found a tiny error of fact in the book.

He was a master of the ancient but now dying art of letter-writing, and I have preserved our not very extensive but always illuminating correspondence, full of references to the understanding quality of a school performance of *Freischütz*, to the duplicity of opera houses which preferred inferior English translations to his, to the new Board at Covent Garden (where he once audibly muttered about 'moronic peers in the chair', to the discomfiture of all but the deaf peer presiding over the meeting), and the exciting plans at Sadler's Wells. He mistrusted the social and the grandiose, had in the past inveighed against attempting Mozart in a Sussex hay-field (a not very apposite reference to Glyndebourne), and could be as harsh a critic of the follies of what he thought of as the puffed-up as he was encouraging to those he thought needed a boost.

Dent was rather deaf, in fact rumour had it that he heard at a different pitch in either ear, but he could turn this deafness to account. I had been in Florence and he had given me an introduction to the composer Dallapiccola. Dent and I met in the crush bar at Covent Garden, which brought out the worst in him as he mistrusted that organization's aims and found it hard to hear among so many competing voices. I started to relay Dallapiccola's messages, but he burbled on until what I had said, which he had in point of fact heard, began to seep through, and he interrupted himself: 'What did you say about Dallapiccola?' The deafness was a habit and a refuge (as well as being genuine), also a means of fending off unwelcome interlocutors. I was fond of him and glad to have known him.

In October 1947, Sir Thomas Beecham organized a festival of concert music by Richard Strauss, in one or two of whose events the composer himself participated. One of the concerts was at Drury Lane Theatre, and the programme included the seldom-played *Macbeth*, conducted by Norman del Mar, and the last scene of *Ariadne*, with Maria Cebotari and a strong Viennese tenor called Karl Friedrich, conducted by Beecham. Ernst Roth, of Boosey and Hawkes, a devotee of Strauss and his music, asked me if I would like to meet the composer at the interval. I knocked on the door of the box and Roth put his head out, registered my presence, shut the door again and locked it. A moment later he reappeared and beckoned me inside, where I saw the great man standing at the other end of the little ante-room, with his overcoat over his shoulders. From photographs I had always imagined him to be small and neat and was surprised to find he was tall, even burly. I was

93

taken up to him, presented, and stammered out in my best German how much I had enjoyed the music and the other programmes I had heard. *'Wo haben sie ihre Deutsch gelernt?'** he asked. Searching for an appropriate answer, I said, truthfully but irrelevantly, *'Ich war Kriegsgefangener,'*† whereupon Strauss turned on his heel and walked away. I was hurried out of the box, and remembered that the old man was said to be sensitive about any reminders of his much-discussed and I suspect much-exaggerated Nazi connections, but I thought at the time that this was, to put it mildly, overreacting. After all, I had not *complained* about being in prison, only said (inaccurately) that I had learnt German there; and who had 'suffered' there, him or me?

Some years later, the Swiss conductor and philanthropist Paul Sacher told me that after the war, knowing that Strauss was living in Switzerland in difficult circumstances (German assets were 'frozen' and Strauss couldn't touch his royalties), he had invited Strauss to write a piece for his Basel-based chamber orchestra. Sacher had paid a generous commission and, when *Metamorphosen* was delivered, bought the manuscript as well. A year or two later, he was surprised to get a letter from an intermediary offering him the original manuscript of *Metamorphosen*. 'But I already have that,' he said. 'Ah,' said the man: 'That was a copy.' So Sacher paid again and received another score.

In the 1940s I found Strauss's music immensely satisfying. I luxuriated in Mengelberg's recording of *Heldenleben*, which we had in prison, bought whatever records came out after the war, and never willingly missed a performance of *Rosenkavalier* or *Salome* or a broadcast of one of his other operas. But gradually the taste for such rich textures passed, though my liking remained for the inspiration of much of the pre-*Rosenkavalier* music, and I have to admit I find the influence of his librettist, the poet Hofmannsthal, inflationary and even pernicious.

All the same, I feel grateful to Strauss and Hofmannsthal for having written at least one passage of love music (in *Arabella*) which not only expresses warmly and memorably something that was once a staple of operatic scores (not invariably good, I am the first to admit), but thirty years into the twentieth century did so in a way of which other composers and librettists seemed to have become ashamed. Admittedly, Mandryka's declaration of love for Arabella and her response is exceptional in Strauss's scores; but how perfectly they catch his mixture of unbridled ardour and reverence, her initial half-mocking questioning, and then her abandonment

*"Where did you learn your German?'
†'I was a prisoner-of-war.'

94

to being swept off her feet – and what a notable, whole-hearted, memorable exception it makes when it comes!

At the time I write, I would still investigate the effect in the theatre of those Strauss operas I have not yet seen (remembering the complete change of heart brought about by hearing *Frau ohne Schatten* in 1977 under Böhm in Vienna), but I have developed a conviction that, for me at least, *Salome* is his operatic masterpiece, taut and athletic for all the orchestral virtuosity, pure and powerful in spite of the decadent subject.

During those post-war years, I went often to concerts, hearing Gigli, Flagstad and Lauri-Volpi, Szigeti, Menuhin and Ginette Neveu, Schnabel, Edwin Fischer and Klemperer; I stood godfather to the Usshers' eldest son, Patrick; got to know a fellow undergraduate and opera-lover Pieter van der Bijl (later Rhodesia's foreign minister); went constantly to Newmarket to race meetings or simply to watch my father's horses at work in the early mornings; was at the Arts Theatre to see *The Frogs* of Aristophanes in Greek; and took in at the end of February 1947 my parents' Silver Wedding.

It was the first hard winter of the post-war, and more than once I had travelled by train to Cambridge with a Labour MP and listened to protestations about how unfair it was to blame it on the Government. So the landscape was wintry as I went off to Torquay, to spend almost the first weekend of my life with my parents as an independent adult – something I only thought of later. They were in good form and I enjoyed it inordinately, with a few of their closest friends (the Jimmy Rothschilds, the Bessboroughs and Dick Molyneux) staying with them for the celebration, and shining new silver napkin rings with our signatures inside as presents from Gerald and me.

Within three months, my father had died, on 23 May 1947, a date which well over thirty years later still sends a shock through my system. I had been to *Rigoletto* in London the night before, and did not get back to Cambridge until well after midnight. There was a message to ring Harewood, but I could not do so before morning; but by nine I was in the College office asking for leave to go and see my father, who was ill enough for the doctors to suggest I should go up there. When I saw him, temporarily outside his oxygen tent, I remember him rather weakly laughing at the doctors for having also sent for Gerald from Germany, and saying that I would in future have to take some of his Yorkshire work off his shoulders as he doubted if he would be strong enough to do it all.

Gerald arrived that evening, paid my father one visit before dinner, and afterwards we were upstairs discussing the future when an agitated message came for us. We found he was dead – of heart failure as the doctors said, of asthma as I knew. I have never felt more alone or deprived, and Aunt Madge's attempts to console my mother – 'You and I know that the world can never be the same again' – did not exactly inspire the courage we looked for.

Three days later I put on uniform to meet the King at Dishforth RAF Station north of Ripon, for the funeral that afternoon. I had not before been to a funeral where my emotions were engaged, and then and there developed a conviction that they should properly be held in private, with everyone except those immediately involved held off until the memorial service. Shy, aloof, and worse, I have heard my father called since; but that was not how his friends knew him, how his battalion in 1914–18 remembered him, how those he had helped (including tenant-farmers who could not pay their rent) thought of him, how his family felt about him; and I knew then and know still that when I was twenty-four I lost potentially the best friend and mentor I could ever have – at precisely the moment I discovered this was so.

My father's death started a miserable round of lawyers' meetings in an attempt to face the future. I knew that my grandfather had in 1922 intended to give Goldsborough to my father as a wedding present but had in the end made it over to me direct soon after I was born. Many had been the jokes about it being 'mine', but when I mentioned that saying to the lawyers, they said that my father had enjoyed what was technically known as beneficial occupation of it during his lifetime and that it would come in for full death duties. So much for presents, so much for the law, or at least for its slumbering non-perspicacity.

The rate of duty payable on my father's estate was seventy per cent, so inevitably there were problems. What should we ask to be 'exempted' from death duties, in order that we might retain duty-free the object in question until and if we decided to sell it, when it would attract seventy per cent tax on the selling price? Could we live at Harewood in the future? How much land, mostly farms let to tenants of long-standing, should we have to sell? The lawyers were on the whole pessimistic, but told my mother and me that we should be able together to live at Harewood, where my family had lived for 175 years, probably for my lifetime as well as hers. We sounded out the Treasury about the possibility of their accepting land and chattels against death duties without the need for a sale, but the Chancellor, Sir Stafford Cripps, was not one for that kind of bargain, which might have proved beneficial to all but was somehow in 1947–50 against the Treasury's collective conscience. I see why, I must admit.

Anthony Blunt, Keeper of the Queen's Pictures, was invited to Harewood by my mother to advise about what to keep and what to sell, and I remember my outrage at some of his comments: 'Not a very attractive picture! You should certainly sell it.' How dare he! My father had bought them and it was none of his business to criticize them! Christie's came to value everything, taking a week about their work and choosing the precise period of the first post-war Leeds Festival – my mother missed the Festival's morning events. Christie's did their work with tact, but what a week it turned out to be.

In the end, sales took place three years after my father's death and we got rid of some two-thirds of the land and the chattels. We gave a lunch for the tenants in a marquee in front of the house before announcing the sales. I had in a speech to admit that there was an element of farewell about the party, and shall never forget the collective intake of breath when I mentioned the death duty rate. Many of the tenants were after so many years what amounted to old family friends, and even the prospect of buying their own farms, which many of them did, was hardly enough to reconcile them to the idea of the high rate we were paying and the inevitable results of paying it.

One of the problems we had to cope with was getting the house, which had been a hospital since 1940 and was vacated in spring 1947, back to normal. My parents had, when they came to live at Harewood in 1930, reorganized the main rooms and the ground floor, so that they had a compact, workable private suite of their own. After the hospital moved out, only a few weeks before my father died, we had reoccupied as our main living room the library in the centre of the house, which had during the war been our furniture store, and our spread through the house was not so very different from pre-war. The grand rooms, even before the war only used for parties, were open only so that we could resettle the furniture and the pictures, and for virtually the whole of the year would be under dust sheets.

Everything had to be unpacked and either put back where it had been before the war, or else a new place found for it. The house carpenter, Archie Ambler, somehow pieced together an elaborate chandelier of which there was no photograph and which had been put away bit by bit and not, as tradition demanded, suspended in a barrel. Without our butler, Alfred Blades, reoccupation of the house after the hospital left might never have been finished. He had been with us before the war as under-butler (in charge amongst other things of silver, on which he became nothing less than an expert), had left to become butler elsewhere, served in the war until our butler had very suddenly died, when my father, learning Blades had been down-graded and was unfit for active service, had got him back.

In this position he remained throughout the rest of my mother's life and beyond – in fact until his death in 1972 – a self-appointed (but much encouraged) guardian of tradition. For my own immediate family he was mentor, helper and solver of problems; for my mother a barrier against a sometimes chilly outside world, remembrancer, finder of what she had lost, supervisor of Christmas presents (a major industry with her); the best flower arranger I have known; and withal the most discreet retainer who ever carved a joint, polished a salt-cellar, sorted the post, or gave his employer the benefit of advice or experience.

There was no secret I would not have trusted him with, and he was one of the first people from Harewood whom Patricia ever met, long before we were married. When he died, I wrote to his wife that he had been, family apart, my oldest friend. And it was true, in the sense that I had known no one so long whom I saw consistently, with pleasure, with mutual profit and with complete trust.

Life after 1947 represented for my mother an even bigger change than it did for me. During my father's life, she found it uncongenial to make a move without his support and very rarely did so, and for this reason the first years after his death were for her very difficult indeed. Family and close friends were constantly round her, she hated to be left alone even for a meal, much less for a whole day, and there was almost always a lady-in-waiting of roughly her own age with her – someone younger she would not really have cared for.

All her life, she was an enthusiastic race-goer and this was one of the things she and my father had done together which she kept up after he died. I even went with her to the Derby within three weeks of his death because he had a horse, called Tite Street, running with a chance. Privacy remained an obsession and she would not for instance travel from London to Leeds by Pullman, although it was faster and I thought more comfortable, because it had open carriages and she preferred to take a picnic basket in a compartment. She took pleasure however in recounting that she had been called 'Miss' when shopping in Harrogate and 'Luv' on another occasion in Leeds.

Her preferred method of travel to her various engagements was by car as this ensured genuine privacy. It could however provide unexpected problems for anyone with her who was not used to certain small idiosyncracies and superstitions. When she saw a magpie, she bowed three times and in summer, with whole magpie families still together, this could produce so continuous a bobbing as to cause consternation to any companion not in the know. More disconcerting still was a habit I have met in no one else, which was that when she saw from the car a piebald horse, she maintained strict silence whatever the circumstances until she had seen a dog, which alone exorcized the bad luck that would have ensued had she spoken. In post-war years, Yorkshire seemed to be the favourite resting place for circuses. Their horses turned out temporarily to grass would unwittingly mar a first journey with my mother for an unsuspecting lady-in-waiting who had the night before found her employer anything but the Trappist whose sign language she was now trying to interpret.

In spite of inhibitions and inbuilt barriers, my mother had extraordinary sweetness of nature, and got pleasure from a number of small acts of kindness and consideration. Like her grandfather King Edward VII, as I have always heard, she enjoyed pleasing her friends. Her present list was vast, her Christmas card list little short of encyclopaedic, and she worked very hard at both. Conversely, she had areas of private meanness which amounted to something like mania. The war doubtless taught her to recycle envelopes and to turn off all electric lights in order to save power, and that was something I certainly learnt from her. But her passion for saving bits of string of all lengths started well before 1939, and her keenness to preserve wrapping paper went well beyond the bounds of normality. I always used to say she spent more time clicking her tongue and smoothing out the paper which had wrapped up her own and other people's presents at Christmas than actually undoing them.

I had two foreign holidays during my Cambridge days. The first in 1947 took me back to Italy, with Denys Martyn and Patrick Hedley-Dent. We motored through the heat to Venice, wearing clothes that were too thick, failing to sleep in the hot weather, worrying about money (with a strict post-war holiday allowance of about £70 per annum), but catching opera at Verona on our way to and from Venice. The first was *Ballo in Maschera*, with Mirto Picchi in the tenor lead opposite a soprano called Adriana Guerini who contrived to faint after the great Act II aria and before the love duet. After twenty minutes' gap, they began again where they had left off, which is hard in the Arena di Verona, where there are 25,000 seats, an orchestra of 150, tons of scenery and hundreds of extras, and where the only form of curtain is – or was then – a battery of lights shining in the faces of the audience.

All seats were full for our return visit, when the opera was *La Gioconda*, and the great event the local debut – you might say the mature operatic debut – of Maria Callas. I knew that what we were hearing was quite out of the ordinary: a penetrating, vibrant voice of great power and, when required, flexibility, at the service moreover of a strong stage and musical personality.

We were the guests of the Mayor of Verona, and went with him before the last act to see the new young diva, who had sprained her ankle at a previous performance and was resting on a sofa. She seemed not averse to meeting strangers before the performance had ended and insisted only that we should stay for the last act, as in this occurred her great aria 'Suicidio'. I was photographed with her, and the print disappeared, only to turn up weeks before this book went to press. After the performance, there was a big open-air supper party given by the major and I sat either next to or opposite the evening's heroine; I remember a much older man hovering around her chair – Battista Meneghini, whom a few years later she married.

Denys Martyn, with whom I shared this Italian expedition, I saw often up to his early death in the 1970s and we went on many operatic expeditions together. He stayed at Harewood for Leeds Festivals (and surprised my mother by writing her an 'ordinary' thank-you letter, without the deference considered appropriate for royalty at beginning and end); I stayed with him when Covent Garden was on tour in Cardiff, and again with Patricia between my divorce and our marriage. He was a lively and by no means conventional companion; we agreed about much and argued about some more, enjoyed drinking wine and listening to music together, and his sudden death was a sad shock.

Summer 1948 provided a first expedition to a foreign festival, Salzburg, armed with tickets for the performances, maps to get to the 'Weisses Rössl' on Wolfgang See (the famous White Horse Inn), and letters of introduction from Rudi Bing to the festival's President, Baron Puthon. We went by car, and my companions were Michael Jaffé and Barry Till, the former culturally inquisitive about anything, the latter on a pilgrimage as much to see the churches of Fischer von Erlach as to hear the operas of Mozart. Michael Jaffé had been in the navy, and while I drove the last few miles he succeeded in navigating us in the dark through a pine forest to the very edge of the lake, admitting later that he had followed a stream on the map thinking it a road – on the wrong side of the lake too! The 'Weisses Rössl' was an attractive place to stay but an hour away from Salzburg, and I was inexpert at working the introduction to Baron Puthon. However, we eventually had coffee with him, the tickets were for the right days, we heard Furtwängler conduct *Fidelio* magisterially and Karajan *Figaro* a good deal less satisfactorily (but his *Orfeo ed Euridice* was good), and we experienced Frank Martin's *Le Vin Herbé* in German with Patzak and Cebotari.

Fidelio was the great event that year; I was lucky enough to have been introduced to it at a high level when the Vienna Opera visited Covent Garden in 1947, a year before my Salzburg visit, with Clemens Krauss conducting. It was unforgettably done at Salzburg in the three years 1948–50. Furtwängler had a reputation for slow *tempi* as well as for total seriousness in rethinking each work he tackled – a true festival conductor and the opposite of routine in everything he did, but I suspect the reputation came from Mozart operas, particularly *The Magic Flute*, he conducted at Salzburg, not from Beethoven.

I heard *Fidelio* under him half a dozen times in those three years, and the impression that remains is indelible; it has wholly conditioned my view of the opera. Günther Rennert's production was grand in scale, as was perhaps necessary at the old Festspielhaus. Marzelline was sung successively by three stars – Lisa della Casa, Schwarzkopf and Seefried; the Pizarro was usually Paul Schöffler, not only menacing but somehow internally tortured and almost pitiable. Twice Kirsten Flagstad sang Leonore with an unrivalled golden tone and power but (even I must admit it) less nuance than is desirable, and each year the Florestan was Julius Patzak, a tenor for whose records and public singing I developed great enthusiasm over the years. His Florestan was peerless, and no one has enunciated the words of the great Act II scene with such meaning and pathos, no one has so sharply pointed the contrast between the desperation of the recitative and the resigned nobility of the aria proper, no one has reached such a frenzy of delirium in the fast section of the scena. But it was Furtwängler who was the architect of it all, and Salzburg in those early post-war days, not yet too expensive and still available to music-lovers, was a true place of musical pilgrimage.

We walked (or rather struggled) out of a *Jedermann* performance, which had been transferred due to rain from open-air to the theatre, and motored round the splendid Fischer von Erlach churches, which awoke in me a not yet extinguished enthusiasm for the high baroque – 'camp' if you must, but highly enjoyable to look at; the operetta of church architecture.

On our last evening at the 'Weisses Rössl', we met a very pretty girl from England, just arrived with a Viennese cousin: Marion Stein.

CHAPTER SIX

Marriage to Marion
1949-52

I THINK IT was Ben Britten who introduced me to Marion, probably at the Aldeburgh Festival, and she was at Cambridge in 1948 for May Balls a few weeks before the Salzburg Festival, where we met again. I was in touch with her that autumn and took her out several times before and after Christmas. In February 1949, I went with Covent Garden's General Administrator, David Webster, to Italy, on a mission to persuade la Scala to come to Covent Garden – I always thought he took me as a kind of audition, to see if I knew enough about opera to be useful at Covent Garden. In March, the BBC broadcast a concert performance of Alban Berg's *Wozzeck;* Marion came with me to rehearsals and to the performance, after which we became in effect engaged – to the amusement of her father, Erwin Stein, who said that *Wozzeck* had really come into its own if it could now take the place that *Tristan* had held in his youth!

Back at Harewood, out for a walk, I said to my mother: 'This may surprise you, but I want to get married.' Her reaction was quite simply to say, 'Good God!' and then walk on in silence. In the end she asked some questions, seemed to find the idea less peculiar than she had at first, and eventually said she'd like to meet Marion.

A week or two later, Marion came to stay at Harewood, which must have been something of an ordeal for her as she had never met my mother and had not known me very long. My mother seemed to take to her, but the only thing I remember her asking was whether Marion could cook. She offered to write to the King on my behalf, as by law I needed his permission before I could marry – a crazy anomaly, but George III's Royal Marriages Act, designed to prevent his brothers and his sons from marrying people he did not approve of, laid down that no descendant of George II could marry without the Sovereign's consent. The law stands and until it is repealed no descendant can get married without consent.

In due course I went to see the King, who seemed to think it quite natural that I should want to marry someone with similar interests, even if they were so exotic as to extend to music, but who refused to give me his permission until Queen Mary had agreed. He implied that that would take a little time. Fortunately, I did not then know that she had already expressed herself as vigorously opposed to the whole idea. I was advised to wait, but, though we filled in time by going to performances of Wagner at Covent Garden and Italian Opera at the Stoll Theatre, the weeks seemed to be going slowly by without any positive action.

Towards the end of the summer I went to see Queen Mary, who had always been kindness itself to me. Everybody had been at pains to tell me: 'Queen Mary is in a great state, and she won't talk about it', whereas the fact was that her initially hostile reaction had made everybody, including the King, too frightened to ask her again. I had too much at stake to be scared and proceeded to explain it all as best I could; my grandmother produced no more obstacles, whereupon the King gave his consent and next day (19 July) our engagement was announced.

We decided on 29 September for our wedding. There was only just time to make the necessary preparations, which included arranging a church – St Mark's, North Audley Street, which my family and I had attended when in London before the war; alerting my brother to be best man – he was on a long stint getting to know his sugar properties in Barbados and had to come back specially; giving Ben Britten and Ronald Duncan time to write a wedding anthem, which they had offered; arranging a honeymoon; and making out a list of guests. The church choir turned out to be adequate but did not find it easy to learn or perform Ben's anthem, and Ronnie's words were fastened on by sensational newspapers as having Roman Catholic leanings.

Gerald got back to England fairly soon after getting my message and we set him to work, assigning him everything beginning with P – ranging from Parking of cars to Presents for the bridesmaids, even insisting he on the way look after Ben's score, which we explained was often called Partitura and therefore (as the Scots would later say) was within his remit. Gerald laboured like a Trojan to get all the details of our wedding to run smoothly – and in those days, weddings were complicated productions – and we owed him a lot.

During the summer, Princess Elizabeth and Prince Philip stayed at Harewood for a tour of Yorkshire, and my mother of course went round most of the time with them. So, for at least part of it, did I, and I remember the procession of cars and the miles and miles of cheering crowds through which we crawled. The crowds tended to close in after the Princess's car had gone by and the effect was startlingly claustrophobic, a condition to which I reacted by an attack of sleepiness. I was sitting between my mother and her lady-in-waiting, Gwynedd Lloyd, who woke me up once saying she had just seen a woman by the side of the road waving a goose at the royal car. Gwynedd was later reduced to telling Welsh stories in order to keep me awake.

Everything comes to an end sooner or later, even waiting, and we were duly and with rather a lot of fuss married at the end of September. Having always loathed speeches at other people's weddings, I managed to avoid them at mine, and nothing more untoward occurred than that Morgan Forster found himself bowing to the wedding cake thinking it was Queen Mary – that, and the solecism which I committed when I got into the car first after leaving the church, thinking it would be easier that way for Marion to manoeuvre her dress and train. (I had not lost my knack of misjudging the ceremonial occasion, and remember while kneeling at the altar being appalled at the idea that the soles of my clean shoes might have a number chalked on them, as happened at school or in hotels in the days when hotels cleaned shoes.)

We spent the first days of our honeymoon in Paris. The hotel gave us what they said was Marlene Dietrich's room, and the bed was so short that I found my feet hung out over the end. But to complain about the bed on one's honeymoon did not seem quite the thing. We viewed the Dior collection, still too self-conscious to enjoy the experience as much as I have subsequently enjoyed sorties into the fashion world, and managed to shake off a persistently-tailing journalist only to find that he was the French detective assigned to us.

From Paris we went to Venice, where we stayed in the same hotel as had my parents on their honeymoon twenty-seven years before, and where for four days we toured the sights. When I cashed a traveller's cheque, by an unlikely coincidence the teller was the son of the composer Gian Francesco Malipiero whom I had got to know on holiday in 1947. He told his father, who took us that evening to a rehearsal of a concert at the Fenice Theatre, whose conductor, he said, was a new talent. When after the rehearsal we expressed little enthusiasm, he said, 'I agree. He was listening to the orchestra and not letting the music flow. It will be different tomorrow.' It was; the conductor was Carlo Maria Giulini, then a radio conductor, within four years the best man at la Scala and within ten one of the best in the world.

Rome and Naples were stepping stones to Capri, where for twelve days we had been lent a villa. There we were entertained by Axel Munthe's son, and there we met Cecil Gray, the composer and writer. Some of Cecil Gray's acidulous, penetrating writing I was already acquainted with, and so was unprepared for the bulky, slow-spoken, kindly, amusing man I met and made friends with – the vinegar pen and the good-hearted gossip seemed curiously at odds. We used to eat, or more often drink, with him, and Marion warned me that his reputation as a toper was considerable. His marital life had been more eventful than successful, and he lived on Capri with a Scandinavian singer who seemed, by his own account, to make what would otherwise have been a bleak life bearable.

He took us to see the aged Norman Douglas for lunch one day, an experience so beguiling that we stayed until eight o'clock in the evening, the hours spent partly admiring the constantly changing view, partly listening to the great man talk – about Capri, about music, about the England he mistrusted, about the writing he did not do. The night before we left, Cecil gave a dinner with traditional music and dancing afterwards. As we sat drinking, we reminded him we had to pack and catch the morning ferry to Naples; he said that many a man had come for a visit to Capri to forget some misfortune and had remained there, unable to get up in time to catch the early morning boat, and too comfortable with drink to catch the ferry at night.

I knew my new parents-in-law relatively well by the time I married, and had come to love Erwin Stein as a person and admire him as a professional – he worked for the music publishers, Boosey and Hawkes, and was a much respected member of London's musical life. The accumulated wisdom of the central European, in his case Jewish and sophisticated, was in him combined with humanity and compassion, which is not to say that he could not be sharp about what he disapproved of.

By the time I met him, just after the war, he had identified himself totally with England in a way that Sophie, his wife, couldn't. He wrote idiomatically and to the point in his adopted language, whereas she had never really learnt English properly. Erwin identified himself with English aspirations to the extent that when he talked about 'our' music he meant English music; he was no longer an Austrian musician. Sophie's 'we', in contrast, might have meant anyone. All the same, she had charm and warmth and for that we all loved her. She never truly recovered from the loss of her sons in the war, and if she had been a different type of woman, this would have been more apparent. As it was, her vitality and ability to appreciate everyday life enabled her to put some of the very real horrors behind her.

Erwin and I made an expedition to Salzburg together in 1950, when Marion was expecting David and could not travel. He was a rewarding travelling companion, suffering with no apparent impatience my musical naiveties and able to share in my enthusiasms – for Furtwängler's performance of *Fidelio* and for Patzak's singing of Florestan, for some (but not all) of *Capriccio*, then being heard for the first time since the war ended, and for aspects of the performance of Ben's *Rape of Lucretia*. I went with him to the pre-dress rehearsals of *Lucretia*, and he noticed that Josef Krips had misread a metronome mark and was taking the Act II lullaby at a jog-trot. He predicted that Krips would never be prepared to admit the mistake to the players but would be able by sheer technique to mitigate the solecism by the time it came to performance – and so it turned out.

We talked a lot about pre-war Salzburg and what it stood for, and there was a nostalgic moment when a man came up to Erwin in the Gardens of the Schloss Mirabell (the Archbishop's Palace) and addressed him as *'Herr Chormeister'*. The man had been a member of the choir in Vienna which Erwin had taken over in the 1930s – fifteen or twenty years earlier – from Anton von Webern, who had resigned in a fit of pique over some slight, real or imagined. Erwin was quite moved by the re-awakened association, and his talk of Schoenberg, Berg and the circle of Schoenberg's pupils was more illuminating about a great period of Viennese musical history than most of what I have read.

From the musical point of view, Erwin was perhaps Ben Britten's closest friend, the man with whom he was prepared to discuss in technical detail what he was attempting to do and whose advice he most often sought. He was too one of the most sympathetic verbal interpreters of Ben's work. When he died in 1959, I wrote about him for the magazine *Tempo*, and tried to pay tribute to his constructive, precise, and open-minded musical wisdom.

Marion had – still has, I don't doubt – a real talent for travel. She used to find out new places to go to and know about them from books by the time we got there. In contrast, I find it hard to enthuse in advance about places I have not seen, hard to read about them beforehand, and I used to be better at revisiting somewhere I had come to love than at discovering it in the first place.

If Erwin taught me to be at home in the musical world, Marion taught me how to travel, so that even on our first prolonged journey together, our expedition to Salzburg six weeks before we were married, I was discovering things unsuspected during my holiday there a year before. We stayed not at the grand Schloss at the Salzburg end of Lake Fuschl but at the other end, in a comfortable but unpretentious *Gasthaus*. The owner's wife had the Austrian habit of promoting her guests so that I was *'Hoheit'* and Erwin was 'Herr von Stein'. We went in the evenings to performances and by day were indefatigable in our exploration of the lakes of the Salzkammergut and their incomparable scenery. I even overcame my rather tepid feeling for mountains – brought up in the Yorkshire Dales, I was unused to the towering Alps of Switzerland or Austria, and it has taken time to widen that perspective – and I certainly added to my knowledge and enthusiasm for the baroque churches of the area.

If you have a talent, you must exercise it, and by the time we went to India in 1958, nine years after we were married, Marion and I had made only a few less than fifty journeys out of England. Little more than three months after our marriage, we were off to Vienna, which I did not know but where Marion was born. In 1950, there was still something left of the Vienna of *The Third Man*. It took six hours to get there flying from Northolt, and war-scars were by no means all healed, so that one would eat, often very well, in patched-up cellars. Moreover evidence of the three occupying powers was everywhere apparent. We spent a fortnight there and saw performances of *Turandot* with Roswaenge, *Aida*, a new large-scale production of Britten's reworking of *The Beggar's Opera* at the Volksoper, and a splendid *Meistersinger* with Hans Hotter maintaining (in my experience of him, uniquely) fresh voice throughout Hans Sachs. Julius Patzak and Elisabeth Höngen in *Aida*, two of the most intelligent and musical singers in Europe, produced in their Act IV scene the effect of lawyers arguing an unanswerable case – a major confrontation – but on the B flats of 'Celeste Aida' I swear that the tenor's whole body shook with the physical effort.

Performances by the Staatsoper in those days were given at the medium-scale Theater an der Wien, but the singers were still those of the Vienna Opera's post-war boom, with its exemplary Mozart ensemble and a company that had yet to disperse throughout the world. That year the only blots on our operatic map were a disappointing *Figaro* and the fact that there were no performances for the last four days of our visit because of a strike – I had never then (poor innocent!) heard of a strike in the theatre.

Ljuba Welitsch was uncrowned queen of the Vienna Opera at that time, and she to a considerable extent took over our visit. I had come to know her during the visit of the Vienna Opera to London in 1947, and she had sung the Verdi *Requiem* at the Leeds Festival immediately afterwards, coming out to Harewood for lunch after the rehearsal. I had occasionally entertained her when she was in England, and had once, greatly daring, taken her to a performance of Rimsky-Korsakov's *Snow Maiden* at Sadler's Wells. She and I had quite early on (rather inappropriately at dinner in my mother's apartment at St James's Palace) made a formal decision to call each other by our first names, a declaration which seemed then to be required by Central European protocol, and had sealed the compact by drinking a kind of *Blutbrüderschaft* with interlinked arms – a more complicated manoeuvre, I would have you know, than it sounds.

She introduced us to the Viennese practice of *Heurige* at an inn at Grinzing, where we ate the tender and delicious boiled meat and drank the delectable new white wine – the point of the expedition – to such effect that I had to insist to Marion we sober up with a walk in the snow before going to bed in our Pension Schneider near the Theater an der Wien. Marion of course talked fluent German (or rather Viennese), but by half way through our fortnight said she was getting a sore throat, due, she thought, less to the cold weather than the unaccustomed effort of rattling the gutteral Viennese 'r' round her throat so often!

I felt the fortnight had been thoroughly worthwhile. We had heard Furtwängler conduct the Vienna Phil at a Sunday morning concert; we had gone after breakfast to hear the Sängerknaben at the Hofkapelle; we had been to the Philharmonic Ball; we had looked at paintings at the Kunsthistorisches Museum and Breughel and Dürer drawings at the Albertina. But it was the intimate glimpse of a wholly foreign way of life that had intrigued me most: intimate because with Marion's relations and Ljuba Welitsch we were not in the simple tourist category; foreign because everything, from the overheating in the buildings to the *plumeaux* on the beds, from the plants in the living rooms to the formality and hospitable warmth of the inhabitants' behaviour, from the cosiness of restaurants to the central position occupied by the Opera, was foreign to my English upbringing – foreign but by no means unattractive.

A central position was occupied too by la Scala in Milan's life and that was where we went from Vienna, partly for the sheer joy of hearing *Falstaff* and *Samson and Delilah* conducted by de Sabata. An unexpected pleasure came from a journey to Brescia's ornate and not too large theatre for *Bohème* with Tebaldi, in 1950 at the very peak of her form and in glorious voice; but the abiding memory of that journey was to fall in love with la Scala, a love which the passing of thirty years has done nothing to diminish.

Never was a building and its ambience better calculated to ensure that a visit to the theatre would be a special occasion (and I agree with John

Christie that it should be something out of the ordinary). I am not sure whether this is because of that unforgettable dimming of the lights until only the soft crimson of the boxes is still illuminated, because of its frock-coated ushers with their gold chains of office, because of the theatre's un-Italian punctuality of starting time, or simply because of the sense of honoured tradition that pervades the place. By luck I met and got to know la Scala at the time of Sabata's ascendancy and heard many of his performances, and cemented the feeling of friendship during Callas's hegemony in the 1950s. It is therefore not surprising that I quickly accepted it as the theatre with the highest standards I knew.

I already knew de Sabata as a symphonic conductor from his London appearances with the LPO (an unforgettable *Enigma Variations*, among other things, which I heard with my mother), but little had prepared me for first hearing him in opera. This was at the dress rehearsal of la Scala's revival of *Otello* with Tebaldi, Vinay and Bechi in February 1949. David Webster and I were safely tucked away in a box and the lights were out when we saw a couple of shadowy figures come in at the back of the stalls, one of them holding a torch with which he appeared to guide the other, who wore hat and cloak and limped badly. They progressed rapidly up the centre aisle to the rail of the pit, where a door was quickly opened, the limping figure shed hat and cloak with something of a flourish and had picked up the baton and, still seemingly in the same movement, launched the orchestra into the most exciting opening bars ever written. It was as if a sorcerer had taken over, and the impact was tremendous.

Sabata was reputed to have the keenest ear of any conductor before the public, and to be moody, even destructive, in his rehearsal techniques. Tito Gobbi told me years later that ten minutes of 'You are flat! Now you are sharp! Behind the beat! Flat again!' demoralized him so much in the preparation of his first Scala Ford that he had to throw the role in, and other singers testified to awkward changes of tempo between rehearsal and performance and between one performance and another.

But he was a sovereign interpreter, whose tempi for virtually everything I ever heard him do stick in my mind to this day. Certain passages were taken very slowly, like Iago's 'Brindisi' or the little march with which Falstaff celebrates (*'Va! vecchio John!'*); others, like the brass following Amneris's imprecation to the departing priests or the end of Act III of *Otello*, were of unparalleled brilliance. Everything was very clear, the accents weighty, fairy music sharp for all its softness, nothing ever smudged. When la Scala came on its first visit to Covent Garden in autumn 1950, they were to open with

Otello, and I went to the stage rehearsal. As de Sabata came into the pit, there was some delay on the stage and he filled the time by rehearsing the cataclysmic opening bars again and again: One, two, three, four – crash; One, two, three, four – crash. The effect on anyone hearing it for the first time must have been devastating.

In Milan we made friends with Wally Toscanini, the great conductor's daughter, and with another member of la Scala's committee, Guido Vanzetti, of whom we became fond. We usually saw Wally, always Guido, whenever we went to Milan, where their hospitality was warm and welcoming, and Guido once went with us and Denys Martyn to a Salzburg Festival. Neither Guido nor Wally quite approved of our unconcealed admiration of de Sabata, and Guido explained that he like Wally had been brought up in Milan in the 1920s during Toscanini's last and perhaps greatest Scala period, and that the mere idea that anyone could take his place had to them something not so much of *lèse majesté* about it as of the improbable – most of all, I suspect, to Toscanini himself. When they heard that tapes had been made of Furtwängler's *Ring* at la Scala and in Rome, they simply could not understand what the fuss was about. Or at least Wally couldn't. But I think of her, with her guttural 'r' and her invariable *savoir faire*, as the height of international chic, and am grateful to her for much kindness in Milan and occasionally at her house in Venice.

Marion and I were at la Scala again in May 1950, and again risked what we had come to call 'Scala neck', a crick derived from sitting in a box and peering round the side. We saw a rather run-of-the-mill *Don Pasquale* (with the veteran Pasero in the title role) and some rehearsals of a new *Ariadne*. Dobrowen who conducted told us he was in despair, as he could not persuade Victoria de los Angeles in the title role to sing out; either she maintained it was too early in the day for her to get to rehearsal, or else she had been having an afternoon rest and was not ready to sing in the evening – but she refused to offer full voice until the first night.

Alda Noni was very different. We saw and heard her rehearse Zerbinetta one hot afternoon in a smart summer frock, dancing engagingly up and down a complicated set of steps near the front of the stage, singing all the while with immaculate precision perhaps the most difficult coloratura music ever written. Well might the Scala's orchestra give her an ovation at the end for a virtuoso display, and so too might they have for Mariano Stabile, rehearsing a year later at la Scala in similar heat the scene between Ford and Falstaff, with Ford unexpectedly absent from the rehearsal and no understudy called.

Every inflection, every gesture, every nuance was in place, in spite of no one to play to – all this in a role he had first sung at la Scala almost thirty years before, then with Toscanini, now with de Sabata.

The real point of going to Italy in summer 1950 was to experience the Maggio Musicale Fiorentino, and Florence that year rewarded us not only with its own incomparable riches, its Michelangelos and Masaccios, its Pitti Palace and Uffizi Gallery, but with my first *Elektra* under Mitropoulos, Spontini's *Olimpia* with Tebaldi under Serafin, the world première of Dallapiccola's fine *Prigioniero*, and a five-act *Don Carlos* under Serafin good enough to please the gods themselves.

The Dallapiccola we heard four or five times in rehearsal and performance and came to like very much. On the first night it was fun to listen to a single dissentient whistle throughout the curtain calls, and then to watch Dallapiccola at his last solo call acknowledge him personally – not unlike Bernard Shaw who said in a first night speech in the same situation: 'My dear fellow, I quite agree with you, but what are we two against so many?' Caniglia, Stignani, Mirto Picchi, Silveri, Boris Christoff and that blackest of dark basses Giulio Neri, made up Serafin's cast for a truly great revival of *Don Carlos*, of which we heard enough rehearsals to send me away convinced that this might become my preferred Verdi opera, a view since confirmed. Not only has it the profusion of dramatic situation Verdi always demanded from his librettists, not only a host of engrossing political and human motives running throughout, not only amongst his operas a unique feel of 'place' and period, but it conjures up from the master a rare quality of invention with which to clothe its differing characters, as well as deploying them on perhaps the widest canvas on which he ever ventured.

From Florence in 1950 we went to Siena, which that year departed from tradition by having in early June an extra Palio – that extraordinary mediaeval horse-race round the Piazza del Campo which does not forbid wrestling, bumping, boring and every kind of iniquity outside the rules of the Jockey Club. We went as guests of Count Chigi, who explained all to us beforehand but would not himself attend something so far outside tradition as a Palio in the wrong month. The race lived thrillingly up to expectation, and we watched in fascination the attempts on the downward slope to run opponents over the barrier and into the crowd, the whip-lashing and the fisticuffs, and it was won by a riderless horse encouraged with a shrewd clout from behind by his dislodged jockey; at any rate, that's my memory of it – that, and sleeping with a Botticelli above the bed in the main guest room – a 'school' picture, explained our host.

Italian expeditions of some length continued for a couple of years. In 1951 we were in Milan for a performance of *Traviata* scheduled for Tebaldi with de Sabata conducting but in the event cancelled a couple of hours before the curtain was due to go up. We consoled ourselves by going to Brescia for *Adriana Lecouvreur*. Magda Olivero, who had the title role, had even then enjoyed a curious career. Making a highly successful debut in 1933, she had married during the war and announced her intention (to her husband's dismay, we were told) of retiring then and there, although still in her twenties. After ten years she changed her mind, and we were hearing her just after her triumphant reappearance in *Bohème* in Rome. The intensity and brilliance of her singing and acting in *Adriana* sufficiently explained her renewed success, which continued unabated for virtually another thirty years, taking in a whole American career at an age when most sopranos have retired.

I had not heard opera in Naples since 1944. We arrived punctually at our matinée of *L'Amico Fritz* to find so few people there I thought I must have mistaken the time. I hadn't, only the Neapolitan sense of it; the opera got under way over an hour late. We were unlucky as Beniamino Gigli, scheduled for one of the few middle-aged roles in his repertory, was ill and a very young tenor sang in his place opposite his daughter, Rina. Only the impassioned playing of the orchestra for the last act interlude – and its enthusiastic encore – remains in my mind.

Cecil Gray came over from Capri for *Sonnambula*, and we supped together, after a mediocre performance, at Papagallo in the Via Chiaia, walking home in the not so early hours after much musical gossip and much wine. We met for lunch next day at Cecil's hotel, sitting silently in an almost deserted bar over an aperitif before wandering off to eat. On the way Cecil asked us if we had noticed the threesome in the corner, also sitting quietly; one of the two ladies had been playing with a little dog. 'That was Lucky Luciano!' said Cecil, and I realized that the respectable-looking man in a dark suit had indeed been the Mafia big-shot.

Milan that year and the next brought us pleasant surprises and rarities in the shape of Verdi's first opera *Oberto* and Piccinni's delightful *Buona Figliuola*. We heard de Sabata conduct an orchestral rehearsal of *Aida* without the scheduled but still suffering Tebaldi but with a stand-in in the title role, although he promised to surprise us with another singer by the time of the dress rehearsal. This turned out to be the handsome, lithe South American soprano Constantina Araujo, not a dominating voice but a suitably exotic and youthful heroine to put alongside the pillar of a Radames that was (vocally) del Monaco. Sabata's conducting and the orchestral playing amounted to a revelation but, oddly, a performance of the prelude at the rehearsal which was nothing short of sublime turned on the night into something rather more conventional – a perfect example of what singers had always told me, namely that nobody varied more than de Sabata between rehearsal and performance.

It was around this time that we became enamoured of the excellent restaurant Giannino, rather out of the centre of Milan, a large, posh affair, seating far more people than a good restaurant can normally accommodate without loss of quality. I would have no hesitation in putting it with Harry's Bar in Venice as the most consistently excellent of any I know in Italy. To walk in past the tanks of trout and the great glass windows giving on to the super-active kitchens and, if you are lucky, to be ushered to your table by a waiter who, even if you have not reserved, can remember where you sat last year and what you ate – this is to anticipate culinary perfection.

A year later, the 1951 Florence Festival offered a revival of Verdi's *Vespri Siciliani* under Erich Kleiber, of a quality fit to set beside the previous year's outstanding *Don Carlos*. Boris Christoff was Procida, and if neither tenor nor baritone was outstanding, to renew acquaintance with Maria Callas in the theatre was worth any journey – more of that elsewhere.

We went to a number of rehearsals and knew Kleiber and his wife from London – he was an old friend of Erwin Stein's and used to say Erwin was the only man small enough for him to borrow shirts from. Kleiber was an autocrat of the old school; *Vespri* is a long opera, and he had stipulated that there be no rehearsal for other repertory on the day of the dress rehearsal, and naturally none on the day of the first performance. The dress rehearsal went better than traditionally these affairs are supposed to, but afterwards his American-born wife Ruth seemed determined to get under his skin. 'Papito, did you look at the orchestral notice board after the rehearsal?' 'No. I had no need to.' 'Well, I think there were some rehearsals put up *after* you had gone into the pit. Now, I wonder why they would do that?' 'Perhaps to stop me seeing them.' 'I was thinking that too' – and, sure enough, a rehearsal had been slipped in before the first night, contrary to promise. Kleiber fulfilled, as in my experience of him at Covent Garden he usually did, his threat – which was never to visit Florence again, in spite of a success at this 1951 Festival that was nothing short of sensational.

Cecil Gray was in Florence that year, and told us he was sitting on a small international committee which had been charged with giving away a large sum of money to 'the greatest musician alive'. I said I was convinced the choice would be between Stravinsky and Schoenberg, and I hoped the latter would get it as he at least needed the money. Cecil revealed next day that they had made their decision and it had indeed been between the two composers I had mentioned. He had been alone in voting for Schoenberg.

In Florence, the painter Derek Hill took us to visit Bernard Berenson at Villa I Tatti, and we sat rather formally exchanging platitudes about Florence and painters, on which subject he was omniscient, and music, which he did not seem to care for or know anything about. We were taken too through San Gimignano to Perugia, where I had not been since 19 June 1944, when I had preceded by a few hours the advancing Allied forces; and we saw something of the composer Luigi Dallapiccola, who was hospitable, provocative (like apparently all Italian composers), and analysed unforgettably for me after dinner one night the music of Debussy's *Le Martyre de Saint Sébastien* which we were to hear next day at la Scala. That was an interesting experience; d'Annunzio's vast, hollow play reminded me of the composer Alfredo Casella's cruel dismissal of the same author's *Pisanella, ou la Mort parfumée* which he paraphrased as 'Mortadella, ou le Pis parfumé'.

As the lights dimmed at la Scala for the *Martyre*, a girl of quite outstanding beauty slipped into the seat next to mine. For the next ninety minutes we sat listening to de Sabata and the orchestra but unable to concentrate on the windy hyperbole of d'Annunzio, so that I found myself now and then sleeping soundly with my head on my comely neighbour's shoulder. Embarrassment was only slight at the time, but grew when we were taken at the interval to have a drink with Signora de Sabata and found that the girl was their daughter.

I was in Venice with Marion for the première of Stravinsky's *The Rake's Progress* in September 1951, motoring there from Salzburg with Tony Gishford, who worked for Boosey and Hawkes, Stravinsky's publishers. We stayed on the Lido but went into Venice for rehearsals and whatever the festival offered at night. I had that summer written in the magazine *Opera* about performances at Glyndebourne, and had made one or two slightly critical remarks about details of staging; but I had always looked upon Carl Ebert (who, as well as presiding at Glyndebourne, was producing *The Rake's Progress*) with reverence and awe. It was therefore a little disconcerting to find him and his wife cutting Marion and me as we walked about Venice; it was quite a feat, too, in those narrow alleyways. By the time of the première, his natural *bonhomie* had returned and we were forgiven.

Ferdinand Leitner prepared the cast and conducted, apart from the première and two of the final rehearsals, when Stravinsky himself presided.

Once, not too accustomed to the Opera House, he asked the orchestra to go back to a certain Figure only for Elisabeth Schwarzkopf, who was the very accomplished Ann Trulove, to complain that that meant she had to begin in the middle of a word!

I now know that I undervalued *The Rake's Progress* at the time, and I remember my disbelief when the pianist Nikita Magaloff, sitting just in front of us at the Fenice Theatre, picked out the cemetery scene, with its dominating harpsichord,* as a dramatic high spot. He was right and I was wrong.

I also remember the shemozzle that surrounded the première. Ralph Hawkes, chairman of Boosey and Hawkes, had as soon as Stravinsky started to compose agreed with him that the work should have its first performance at Covent Garden, in whose establishment Hawkes himself had played a considerable part. David Webster, in New York with the Sadler's Wells Ballet, flew to Los Angeles to discuss details with Stravinsky only to have the great man react with apparent surprise and delight to the idea that Covent Garden should 'also' give the opera. But 'the première will be at la Scala,' he told a by now disgruntled Webster.

It was found that he had sold Venice the world première, and la Scala (who assumed it would be first done in America) the European première. A law suit was avoided by the expedient of la Scala giving the première at the Fenice during the Venice Festival and taking the production back to open the Milan season a couple of months later. But both paid Stravinsky in full. As we went out to the Lido by motorboat, we passed David Webster going towards the station; he had warned me he might not feel like staying for the première, and in the event his spleen proved stronger than his curiosity.

Late summer of 1954 brought another première to Venice – Ben Britten's *The Turn of the Screw*, with which we felt ourselves very much bound up. Again, we motored out with Tony Gishford, and stayed on the Lido. The opera had been carefully prepared before leaving England, and there remained only to put the final polish to it in Venice, whose Festival had paid for the production. Because we were so much involved, the first night was a nerve-racking affair, and I well remember my indignation at a by no means young Italian couple sitting immediately in front of us, who appeared to whisper to each other throughout the first act. At the end, the man burst

*In the notice I wrote for *Opera* magazine, I referred to the *piano* in this scene. Was I right and had they made the substitution (an amazing notion nowadays), or could there have been an unaccountable slip of pen (or ear)?

into enthusiastic applause, and we realized that he had merely been keeping her up with the drama as she knew no English.

In 1952 we had paid another visit to Vienna, staying at the Embassy with Harold and Nancy Caccia, on our way to a ski-ing holiday. This time we caught the first night of a new production of Heuberger's *Der Opernball* at the Volksoper, and a fine *Meistersinger* conducted by Clemens Krauss, with Sena Jurinac as Eva. Sena told us afterwards that it was her first performance after a couple of weeks' holiday, and that Clemens Krauss was notoriously hard on any soprano (the Vienna Opera did not engage his wife Viorica Ursuleac, and for him anyone else was a mere substitute); she was more frightened of the quintet in this opera than of anything else she sang – so it was a hard evening for her. She was excellent notwithstanding.

We paid a memorable visit to Helene Berg, the composer's widow, for tea. She had, Erwin told me, been a proficient linguist in her youth, but the shock of Alban's death had been so great that every accomplishment of that sort had deserted her, and she now understood no English. Before tea, she offered us cigarettes from a half-empty box, adding that she hoped they were not stale but they had been left like that at 'his' death; and after tea she paused for a moment before assuring us that 'he' was pleased we had come to see her.

She seemed to believe absolutely in her continuing communication with her dead husband, which she referred to when discussing her ban on the completing of *Lulu*. Subsequent revelations about Berg's emotional entanglement at the time of Lulu's composition cast doubt on the genuineness of her reasons for the ban; but she was a touching figure, with her bird's nest of hair still blonde, her gentle face and manner, and her obvious affection for Marion, whom she had known since childhood.

On that Viennese visit I discovered a source of old gramophone records, and came back with a pile of Slezak, Schmedes, Lucie Weidt, Demuth, Hesch and other singers of the Mahler era, together with newer ones by Rose Pauly, Patzak, Piccaver and so on. The man who sold them, a collector as well as a dealer, told me he kept a complete set of the rarities by Gutheil-Schoder permanently parcelled up and ready to take away with him 'against the inevitable day of a Soviet takeover'. This would be his capital abroad and, at the kind of inflated prices they would have fetched even then in America, he was probably being prudent, although he never happily needed to put his fail-safe device into action. He even gave me a cracked but just playable Gutheil-Schoder as a present to add to the pile which I laboured to carry on to the aeroplane.

CHAPTER SEVEN

New Responsibilities
1949-59

NOT ALL THE life Marion and I led together was spent travelling. After we married, we were living in the rooms that had been my father's at St James's Palace, trying to find a house. In the end, through Keith Falkner, the singer and by then the British Council's music officer in Rome, we heard of something which sounded what we wanted. Two Orme Square belonged to Anthony Tuke, chairman of Barclay's Bank, and in 1950 we bought it from him, moving in late July – I remember the night before drinking champagne at St James's, sitting with Richard Buckle and Lincoln Kirstein on the last of our packing cases before a performance of the New York City Ballet, of which Lincoln was director. The new house had once belonged to Lord Leighton, the painter, and there was a big drawing room, which had been his studio, as well as a dining room and sitting room on the ground floor; there was ample bedroom and kitchen space, and a small cottage over the garage, where we were told his models used to change.

Much of our time was spent in Yorkshire, with Harewood very much a preoccupation. Harewood is large, and after I married there seemed little problem in my mother as well as Marion and I continuing to live there. Large, yes – but not planned for flexibility. It was my aunt who finally suggested to my mother that she should relinquish her downstairs rooms to Marion and me and move into the largest of the visitors' bedrooms upstairs, complete with dressing room and bathroom. She quite rightly retained her downstairs sitting room, a lovely south-facing room originally designed as the grandest of the visitors' bedrooms, and Marion converted what had been my mother's dressing room into a sitting room, with writing table, armchairs and a piano.

At Harewood we spent up to half our time walking, inspecting timber, crops and the repairs wartime restrictions had denied the estate, shooting (I had inherited my father's keenness though not all his expertise), and occasionally indulging in the traditionally useful though diminishingly demanded pastimes of opening playing fields, visiting shows, attending regimental dinners and so on. Marion performed her share of these duties gracefully, though she was no doubt more at home at the Huddersfield Choral Society's annual *Messiah* or perhaps the Harrogate Flower Show than at an Agricultural Show.

She found time to practise the piano – Franz Osborn who taught her had told her to work on the Liszt Sonata as suitably 'stretching' – and prepared to be a mother. I was an assiduous attender of Leeds Festival committee meetings, of which I was a member from 1946–7, and began to form a number of local Yorkshire connections, while resisting any idea of automatically taking on the bulk of my father's very large list of commitments. It seemed to me then and still does now little short of ludicrous that inheritance should give one the right or the obligation to meddle in public affairs, on which one could not automatically be an authority and need not necessarily be an ornament. My mother did not wholly agree with these views, which were alien to her upbringing two wars before, but exerted little pressure to get me to change them. To the affairs of the musical world on the other hand, whether in Yorkshire or in London, I was as keen to contribute where and whenever I was asked as my mother was over her own public duties, which themselves had started to proliferate after my father's death.

It is possible that Marion never felt she truly 'belonged' at Harewood; not primarily because she was by upbringing and nature a townswoman but because Harewood to her was my mother's house more than it was mine or hers – a point of view which to her credit she never articulated to me but which she implied by treating the house in Orme Square as 'home', home being something she must have longed to identify since she came to London as a child before the war, and then moved about from one apartment to another until marriage. Her parents used to come frequently to Harewood, often for quite long periods, and she showed no reluctance to spend time there nor to invite her friends and mine.

Life I think was made no simpler for her by having nobody but my mother as an example for living in the country in a big house. In many ways and for obvious reasons my mother was an unsuitable model. She saw the cook and ordered the food, but she had a lady-in-waiting, and assumed that others did, as they always had, the household chores; she lived in a way that was not essentially different from before the war. So her example taught Marion little about life as it would be lived, only as it had been in certain circles in the past.

I was in some ways at the other end of the spectrum, loving Harewood and having from the time I was seven thought of it as home, the place I felt most at ease in, the refuge I resorted to, animal-like, in times of stress, the place I have most wanted to identify with and hang on to. I was brought up in a grand pre-war style, but had known it in the simpler circumstances of wartime, and would have adapted or attempted to adapt to any pattern which would maintain Harewood as my home.

David, our eldest son, was born in London in October 1950, an experience I found scarcely less formative for the father than it is necessarily for the mother. I could hardly believe afterwards that I was the same person, that the change was not visible to all I met, although there seemed little gain in labouring the point as others seemed to think a father was no more than a necessary adjunct to birth, a kind of drone whose function for the Queen Bee had stopped at some easily measurable time before the crucial event. It did not feel like that to me, and the mixture of pride, responsibility and a sense of something close to awe was very potent indeed.

Queen Mary came to see David eight days after he was born, and I came close to a bloomer by going that afternoon to a concert at which Benjamin Britten's 'Diversions for Piano Left Hand' was being performed for the first time in England (an important occasion I thought), and seeing as I turned my car into Orme Square the door closing behind my grandmother who had arrived early. Queen Mary either did not notice or pretended not to mind, an achievement she repeated in July 1952 when we took David at her suggestion to Marlborough House for her to see him. He was well short of two, but seemed in very lively mood as we went up the great central staircase on our way towards my grandmother's sitting room. The page opened the door and we saw her standing by the open window, silhouetted against the bright afternoon. This proved David's undoing as he screamed and started to climb up me in his efforts to get away. It was possible somehow to grab him and we went on talking as if nothing were amiss, while my grandmother offered him various toys which he rather reluctantly accepted. By the end disaster seemed to have been averted, but it was a fairly awkward forty minutes.

A fortnight after David was born, Sophie and Erwin came to lunch to see Marion, and I walked back afterwards to their flat in Kensington, only to find on getting there an incoherent message from our housekeeper at Orme Square to say I must hurry back as some very important visitors had arrived during Marion's rest-time and had insisted on being shown up to her room. I got back to find Princess Alice and Lord Athlone sitting by the bed, and soon Aunt Alice and I were deep in Canadian reminiscence while Uncle Alge (so spelled; pronounced 'Algie') and Marion were going strong on a subject he had introduced by saying, 'How do you manage? *She* has great difficulty but sometimes borrows from her, and *she* has no trouble at all. *She's* on a different system altogether.' Marion's mystification was resolved only when Princess Alice said, 'Oh, Alge! You haven't explained you're talking about ration books!', although I knew from my past experience that one 'she' was sure to be Princess Alice (who was having difficulty) and the other to be Queen Mary (whose Marlborough House was for rationing purposes treated as a catering establishment).

If Marion was an excellent mother, the description 'proud father' applied I think to me and could have been renewed with each of the three sons I have subsequently had; although an 'L' plate would have been in order where David was concerned, it was progressively less appropriate with the other three. For David, James and Jeremy we had nannies, which precluded neither of us from doing quite a lot for the children but removed us from the front line at strategic moments – no need to find baby-sitters when we went to concerts or the opera, no need to park the children on grandparents when we went abroad. The presence of a nanny I believe causes at least half a remove of parent from child, though nothing like the barriers my brother and I had known as children; and no parent likes the sight of a child running first for comfort to nanny, nor forgets the moment when nanny comes second.

My own children were a source of infinite pleasure to me from the time they were born, and their physical proximity something I not only accepted but, except when trying to write, welcomed. David turned out to be accident-prone, breaking his leg at just under two by falling at a standstill over a balloon, acquiring housemaid's knee at six by falling over in long grass, escaping by a bee's whisker a detached retina from a blow in the eye from a tennis ball at school, and breaking a grown-up front tooth crashing into a wall a year later. All this by the time he was twelve!

James and Jeremy who, sixteen months apart, hunted as a pair from an early age, missed this disadvantaging characteristic, and grew up in spite of their proximity with quite different qualities. David like me always did reasonably well at school, but James found most learning quite alien to his way of thinking. Jeremy on the other hand was unusually bright at school and had no difficulty in passing exams or indeed in pulling the wool over schoolmasters' eyes in a whole host of ways. When he was fourteen he broke his wrist playing football. I was no longer living at Orme Square and rang up to commiserate, hearing next morning when I checked that it was hurting a good deal less. I telephoned again some days later and asked if he could by now write at school, only to be told that he could write left-handed but was not back at school. 'Why not?' I asked; he said the school had indicated he was not to come back until he had had his hair cut, which he did not want so he had not returned. It was not so easy in my day.

Jeremy had a confidence, often justified, in his ability to 'get away' with things, and when I became forty-two he congratulated me on being forty-three, which I believed, so that for a whole year I thought of myself as a year older than I truly was, and only at my next birthday rumbled the con trick he had successfully played, to Jeremy's not inconsiderable satisfaction. James was more retiring as a child, perhaps suffering from being a second son in that his exploits surprised us less than David's at the same age (as *déjà vu*). His enthusiasms and excitements over whatever caught his fancy were touching in their whole-heartedness: though he was a rather specially shy child he was never afraid to commit himself. School he thought a mystifying waste of time, a view he eventually took no pains to hide, particularly from schoolmasters, and his reports were as negative as his own reaction to them when I tried unsuccessfully to remonstrate. He took early to the piano and I was amazed (though I should not have been) when one day later on Marion told me he was having improvisation lessons from the composer John Tavener.

Just before I left Cambridge, I was asked by Eric Walter White of the Arts Council to lunch with him to meet Richard Buckle, whose admirable magazine *Ballet* I already knew a little. We were to lunch at the Etoile in Charlotte Street; my train arrived late (thus establishing an unvarying pattern, said Dicky later), but by the end of lunch Dicky had asked me to contribute on a more or less regular basis to *Ballet* with a view perhaps to turning the magazine into *Ballet and Opera* later. I began to get press tickets from Covent Garden and Sadler's Wells and to write about what I saw and heard, including several impressions of opera abroad, and in mid-1949 agreed with Dicky that the proper thing would be to arrange an amicable divorce of *Opera* from *Ballet* at the end of the year and found a new magazine.

I asked Harold Rosenthal, who had been contributing a round-up of news from abroad since early the previous year, to become assistant editor, and he, after not too much cogitation, decided to leave his schoolmastering and join us – a decision I suspect he has hardly ever regretted, whatever the problems, since he has been passionately devoted to opera since boyhood and to work in the field must have been as much his ambition as it was always mine.

Harold and I put together the first issue, with much help from Dicky over the layout, and celebrated with a party in Dicky's Pimlico house to which came a whole host of operatic celebrities.

I had already mastered proof-correcting and its cabalistic signs and now started to become familiar with the mysteries of layout and paste-up. *Opera*'s second number came to me for final checking with the big 'formes' still intact and not cut up into individual pages so as to provide a consecutive whole, which baffled me, not least because I did not know whether I was allowed to cut them up to facilitate the check. I didn't, but spent a couple of hours around midnight crawling over and around the huge sheets laid out on the floor, getting more and more confused and frustrated as time went by and still uncertain at the end whether I had completed the check.

The early numbers of the magazine were brought out against a background of rather constant change, and naturally when I joined the Board of Covent Garden I ceased to write about performances there, leaving those to Harold. A bigger problem arose in 1953 when David Webster asked me to work at the Royal Opera House. I decided to hand the magazine over completely to Harold, who eventually assumed financial as well as editorial control. He brought *Opera* to a position of real authority, and it is to his credit (as well as perhaps to mine) that, whatever *Opera* has written about performances I have been connected with, and even when we crossed swords, we have remained close friends.

I continued to contribute occasionally with news from abroad – I covered the opening of the new Met in New York in 1966 – more often with features on the recordings of individual operas. But my contact with Harold was by no means confined to the magazine, and we met then and meet still at performances and often privately for that best of all reasons, an operatic gossip, which can range from current iniquities at home and abroad to the reasons why this première in the distant past was held in Venice and not in Rome, why that singer was preferred to another in Mahler's or Strauss's Vienna, how and why one's own operatic tastes and criteria changed gradually over the years.

In 1950 in *Opera* I reviewed in a rather caustic manner a reissue of Kobbé's *Complete Opera Book*, ending with the words: 'For the next reprint, let us have a collaboration between Kobbé . . . and someone sufficiently enthusiastic and self-effacing to rearrange all the material and rewrite such of it as was not from Kobbé's pen.' I had let myself in for more than I knew when the chairman of the publishers, Putnam, turned out to be an old school and university friend, Roger Lubbock, who wrote to invite me to undertake the task myself.

I agreed. I slaved on every railway journey at the task, cutting, revising the existing chapters, writing a great deal of new material, and in 1954 the new edition appeared, with the warning in my preface that any revision 'still cannot hope to achieve anything like a truly "complete" collection.' The reviews were good, Kobbé sold well – it always did – and I reaped satisfaction but little financial reward for my labour. We afterwards worked out that I had written about half of the nearly half a million words of which the book consisted.

My Kobbé entry would not itself be 'complete' without reference to an even more extensive revision and rewrite of it that I undertook in the late 1960s. Though the book was to be completely recast, the first idea was to reprint as much as possible from the existing type. With this in mind, I had the whole thing pasted page by page on to large foolscap sheets, so that I could write (or, better, type) my alterations and additions at the appropriate places. When I cut, I made sure in order to avoid resetting that I cut complete lines; when I added, I tried with the same object to get the new sections into line-lengths. I took the pages with me on a trip to Australia and worked on them spasmodically either on aeroplane or in hotel, and every opera reheard in the theatre or on record provided the cue to reread the appropriate section. Imagine my chagrin when I heard one day from the publisher that the idea of reprinting from what existed had long since been abandoned; everything was going to be reset anyway.

Nevertheless, I wrote and rewrote – having always enjoyed the latter process more than the former – checked and rechecked, and was lucky enough to have a musician as secretary when it came to the music examples, which I chose and she copied with exemplary clarity. Section by section, we got the whole thing to the printers, and gradually galleys started coming back, fortunately at a time when I had little better to do than correct them – I remember a daily stint on a holiday spent at Marbella in Spain. The publishers enlisted the help of a musically-minded person who read it all through at proof-stage and seemed to go back to source for everything; he not only uncovered misprints and mistakes but pointed to grammatical errors and solecisms of style. The publisher and I debated hotly over what to change, what to leave – his work was done after I had finished the proofs – but I have little doubt that the result of his labours had a good effect on the book as a whole. The only snag was that it enormously added to my corrections bill – I had forgotten that all publishers' contracts contain a clause limiting the publisher's liability to ten per cent of the total print bill. My bill was bigger than that – but then so this time were my royalties; and nothing I did to the book seemed to stem Kobbé's sales.

In the 1950s, Ronnie Duncan and his wife Rose Marie were constant visitors to Orme Square, and early in that period rented our cottage as a London *pied-à-terre*. Marion and I went to stay with them in Devon, and I was connected, for a time as its chairman, with the Devon Festival which Ronnie had started. I found him always a most congenial companion, as lively with words as anyone I have met, with a sense of the ridiculous that coincided with mine and convictions that often did too. He despised journalism, which he was very good at, preferring to think of himself as poet and playwright. For me, he has been a friend in a thousand, rejoicing when things have been going well, prepared to listen and help when they have not. Together we went on expeditions to Salzburg, Munich and Bayreuth in 1953, just before James was born, and a year or two later to Paris when literary business of his coincided with Covent Garden business of mine; and he came with Marion and me on holidays to Yugoslavia and Spain.

Our Salzburg/Bayreuth trip was memorable for a number of reasons. We heard an outstanding *Don Giovanni* conducted by Furtwängler, the first time (friends told us) that his opening night had been better than the dress rehearsal; and went on to Bayreuth to see Wieland Wagner's production of *Götterdämmerung*. The journey was not without vicissitudes. We reached the station early, joined a short queue for tickets, but so slow was progress that, by the time I had paid for them, we could only watch the train – the last to arrive in time for the performance – leave for Bayreuth as we rushed helplessly for the platform. There was nothing to do but hire a taxi for the journey, and we agreed a price to include the night and the return to Munich. It was a good performance but, for us, not inexpensive.

Emotional entanglements of one kind or another were not something Ronnie could avoid, or perhaps even wanted to avoid. I have watched and tried to help him through several, but on one occasion the blame for a matrimonial row was mostly mine. It was after we had been to Salzburg, where I knew one could buy leather things very cheaply. We went off to the shop I knew from previous visits, found fine briefcases for ourselves and then started to look round. There was a beautiful bag in the window, but when they brought it down to show us we found the sun had caused one side to fade to a lighter colour than the rest. Another was found and Ronnie decided to take both, one at a reduced price, saying it would not be hard to get the rest of the bag to fade to match. Weeks later, Ronnie and Rose Marie were at Orme Square for drinks when I remembered the bag, and asked Rose Marie if she had succeeded in getting the two sides to match. She was nonplussed by my question and I realized I had made a bloomer of the first order, as she had not been the recipient of Ronnie's bounty. There was no way of allaying her suspicions which had been, quite justifiably, alerted.

Aldeburgh Festivals were a regular part of our calendar. After I started to work at Covent Garden, Marion would go with the boys for the whole festival and I would go up and down for weekends but still with sufficient time to savour the particular and peculiar festival flavour, and occasionally to contribute a mite to the feast Ben Britten and Peter Pears served up to their visitors. In later years they came to feel that anyone who picked a plum or two from the festival cake and did not come for the whole slice was not quite playing the game and therefore ineligible for tickets, which were quite soon for certain weekend events very hard to get. Staying with Ben first at Crag House on the sea front and later at the Red House half a mile inland was a privilege and a joy, and I look back on those visits in and out of festival time as happy and treasured times.

The Holland Festival was another regular haunt, and the brilliant summer weather during our first visit in July 1949 persuaded me that Holland was, like Florence in summer, hot and dependable, a view that it took years of experience to erode. The Holland Festival was built round the personality and musical aspirations of Peter Diamand, Schnabel's secretary before the war and not only a man of taste and knowledge but someone with his finger constantly on Europe's musical pulse. Year after year he devised a festival programme to attract the *cognoscenti*, and there I first heard Klemperer in the glory of his later days (with Mahler's *Second Symphony*), there I first heard Janáček's *Jenùfa* and *House of the Dead*, Stravinsky's *Oedipus Rex* and *Rossignol*, Falla's *Vida Breve* (with de los Angeles), Giulini's Mozart.

Peter Diamand and his first wife, the Italian pianist Maria Curcio, became close friends, often visiting us in London and occasionally at Harewood and Edinburgh. Throughout this time, Maria illuminated so much music and showed such wisdom in more worldly matters as to become the kind of friend whose advice I often sought and listened to; and it was Peter to whom I turned in several moments of crisis in my life, Peter who recommended me when a group from Leeds came to invite him to take over the Leeds Festival: 'You have the right man on your doorstep!' (as they were honest enough to tell me a month later).

In the 1950s, I was also invited to sit on the jury of the famous singing competition at Toulouse. The first year, by the time I was due at the first session I realized I was in for Asian 'flu. I staggered through the streets in dark glasses and was glad to end up sitting in the dim theatre. Lola Rodrigues de Aragón from Madrid had already dropped out with the same illness and was being nursed by a pupil in the hotel, but I could not think what to do except sit still where I was.

From lunchtime to half past midnight, with forty minutes for dinner, we listened to singers, all female (there were vast numbers that year). To make matters worse the preliminary round had us sitting in the front of the circle with a screen stretched before us so that we might not see the participants.

I sat next to Giorgio Favaretto, the Italian accompanist and teacher, which was illuminating as, though we were not allowed to see the contestants, we were not forbidden to talk amongst ourselves, and we discussed whoever seemed worthwhile. We awarded no first prize that year, a fact which was borne in on me six years later when in Brno I met Nadezda Knipplová, who had received the top soprano award we were prepared to make.

The whole competition was made memorable when Lola Rodrigues asked on the morning of the final day if we would like to hear her pupil, whom she strongly recommended. We agreed, and a pretty Spanish girl came out on stage with Favaretto, who had volunteered to accompany. She had no music and he played from memory while she sang the *Cenerentola* Rondo, *'Voi che sapete'*, half of *Frauenliebe und Leben*, and a couple of Mahler's *Lieder eines fahrenden Gesellen* – quite a feat for an Italian who might not be expected to meet Mahler every day of the week, and a feat of vocalism on the part of the singer too. Marion and two friends had come in to the back of the theatre to listen, and one of them afterwards asked me: 'Are auditions usually like that?' The singer was Teresa Berganza, who had not yet sung outside Spain, and I assured him that they were not. The moment I got home I invited her to make her English debut at the 1958 Leeds Festival. Two months later she had the good manners to beg me not to insist on a debut as she had been asked to sing the title role in *Cenerentola* at Glyndebourne that summer – Carl Ebert too had been on the Toulouse jury.

Toulouse that year brings another agreeable memory. Marguerite and Neville Ussher were on holiday at her family's home at Saint Marcet, at the foot of the Pyrenees, perhaps fifty miles away, and we went over for the day. The drive was in perfect autumn weather and the view from the château of the greatest beauty. The family planned to sell the property, which none of them had visited since the war and which looked as though Miss Havisham was the caretaker. We toured the farm, where we were given a bottle of the delicious marc that we had drunk after lunch to take home with us.

For two months this was drunk at Orme Square only on special occasions, and although I knew it must be coming to an end it was hard to see how much was left in the opaquely green bottle. Ronnie Duncan was at dinner with us one night and I offered him the last drop – only on up-ending the bottle to see in his glass nothing but a dozen pickled flies, which had been there since just before it was corked and were all that remained of the noble and potent drink.

I was again in Toulouse a few years later. This time the jury members included a provincial Russian conductor, Janine Micheau the singer, and a Jugoslav bass. The Jugoslav talked only Italian or Serbo-Croat and I seemed to have the job of translating the French language proceedings into Italian for him. The standard among the men was not high, and we named a couple of slender-voiced tenors as first and second, putting a stentorian but much-applauded baritone lowest of the six men who reached the final.

The choice among the women was harder. Two Russian high-voiced coloraturas and a Romanian were outstandingly good. I found the Romanian more interesting, and watched the *viva voce* voting with mounting disbelief. We awarded marks out of twenty, and the scores for the Russians varied between sixteen and twenty, as did the Romanian's. The Russian juryman was sitting on the chairman's right; voting started on his left, and when it at last came to the Russian's turn, he gave the Romanian only twelve and so ensured victory for 'his' candidate.

I had never seen anything so bare-faced, but the others seemed to take it in their stride. My fellow juror Janine Micheau at any rate had different misgivings. 'I shall go in next to you; you're the biggest!' she said. I asked what she was afraid of, and she said she knew Toulouse audiences of old. They fancied themselves as vocal connoisseurs – Toulouse was the Parma of France – and would not like the male prize-winners, having opted themselves, she was convinced, for the loud baritone, whom she had seen drinking in the cafés and drumming up support.

We stationed ourselves with the mayor in the great room of the Capitole on one side of a huge table, with the spectators and competitors on the other side. The names of the women were received with equanimity, but when it came to the men, there was a roar of protest and a storm of booing. Gabriel Dussurget, who founded the Aix Festival and ran the competition, sprang bravely forward and berated the mob, insisting that they wanted people who yelled and the jury was looking for *singers*. It was a splendid scene, slightly marred for me when at the party afterwards a young Greek soprano looked at me venomously and spat!

Hostility was in the air, and when I was ready to leave I looked round to see who else of the jury remained and would be going my way. There was no one, so I set off by myself, walking along the side of the building towards the cafés at the end of the square. There, tables were full and from one of them I could hear: *'Voilà l'anglais! A bas le jury! A bas le jury!'* The abuse was heartfelt and I remember thinking: Keep walking at the same pace, don't look round; there's always the chance that if you walk tall nothing will happen, and even if it does, you may run faster than them. Nothing happened, so I never had to put my speed to the test.

Years later, when Slava Rostropovich told me that Richter, press-ganged for jury service at the Queen Elisabeth Competition in Belgium, gave every pianist a zero, I told him and Galya about this competition, naming the Russian singers and asking what had happened to them since. Galya said they had got on all right; the winner was already at the time of the competition the girl-friend of the Russian conductor who had given the Romanian a poor mark!

CHAPTER EIGHT

Benjamin Britten
1943-76

I FIRST MET Benjamin Britten through Joan Cross at the New Theatre in St Martin's Lane during the interval of an opera in 1943. I had known his music since the beginning of the war, mostly on gramophone records – the 'Hymn to St Cecilia' with Auden's words, the Frank Bridge variations, the two pieces for piano four-hands recorded with Clifford Curzon, and, above all, the Michelangelo Sonnets. One day on guard at Windsor in late 1942 – a chore which entailed a day of rounds from a small room in an outer tower of the castle, the sentries wearing rubber boots at night so as not to disturb the King and Queen – my eye lit on a review in *The Gramophone* of two newly issued records by Britten. There was a gramophone in the officers' room, and we were allowed to send out for what we needed. I played the four sides, one twelve-inch and one ten-inch plum label HMV, again and again with mounting enthusiasm until by the end of my twenty-four-hour stint I knew the words and the music of the Sonnets more or less by heart, and was hooked. I knew too that this was a prospective operatic composer.

The première of *Peter Grimes* was the highlight of my first summer after the war, *The Rape of Lucretia* and *Albert Herring* of the two following summers; I had off-the-air recordings of the two chamber operas which I returned to repeatedly until I could be said to know them too by heart. The original version of *Lucretia* (1946) contained some passages, mostly of recitative, which were much improved in the revision of the following year, and also an aria for Collatinus on quite different lines from the revised version. The point of the revision of this section was to remove what Ben and particularly Peter had come to feel as a softness in the musical portrayal of Collatinus; but I found the original aria a wonderfully beautiful, tender tune, an example of Ben's ability to conjure up sympathy for his characters. But it disappeared, and when in 1980 I approached the Britten Estate (effectively,

Peter Pears and Donald Mitchell) on behalf of an American foundation that wanted to reissue the tape of a 1946 performance as a historical document, I was told that it would have been against Ben's wishes. The existence of the printed original score did not seem to affect the issue; only those parts in which Kathleen Ferrier sang (her Lucretia was otherwise not on disc) were considered suitable for reissue – a pity, I thought, and an example of how to miss an opportunity.

I saw Ben occasionally at Glyndebourne, and again after the first night of the new *Peter Grimes* mounted at Covent Garden in winter 1947, after the great break-up at Sadler's Wells – itself partly the result of the choice of *Peter Grimes* to reopen the Rosebery Avenue theatre.

Ben asked me in spring 1948 while I was still at Cambridge to be President of the Aldeburgh Festival, and I went to the EMI studio in Abbey Road that summer when bits of *Peter Grimes* were being recorded with Joan Cross, Peter, and Covent Garden forces. From then on I saw him more and more often, soon with Marion at whose parents' Melbury Road flat he and Peter used to stay when in London.

I heard him memorably accompany Peter in Schubert, play beautifully for Peter and Joan in an opera concert at Cambridge, and by spring and summer 1949, unofficially engaged to Marion, we were visiting Aldeburgh for the day to see him, and then staying at his home, Crag House, for the Festival in June. We went to Holland for the première of the *Spring Symphony* in July, and Marion and I revelled in getting to know it through rehearsal and performance. The new work seemed fresh, moving and delightful, wholly worthy of its ambitious title. The première was a very grand occasion – with white tie and full evening dress, rare enough at that time – and Ben made no bones about rather resenting his thunder being partially stolen by the presence in the audience of Lord Montgomery, invited presumably as a tribute to his military achievements rather than because of any musical sympathies.

For me it was a period of consolidation of a friendship that I valued highly, partly because of my admiration for Ben as an artist, partly because of my growing sympathy for him as a person. He wrote an anthem for our wedding in September, was one of the first people we saw after returning from our honeymoon, and I saw him regularly for the next fifteen years.

Watching *Billy Budd* grow scene by scene and then finding he wanted to dedicate it to Marion and me was my first important experience with Ben. I had listened to him deciding on the subject and discussing it with Erwin Stein, who had raised the difficulty Ben might have in finding contrast with only male voices involved. 'I think you can trust me for that,' Ben said. We discussed the libretto, which E. M. Forster was writing with Eric Crozier – Eric was an experienced theatre man, Morgan had never written for the stage, and Ben, for all his operatic expertise, liked the challenge and the inherent possibilities of collaboration.

I got to know the opera's shape very well as work progressed, and I remember discussing with Ben one day a particularly tricky scene – the confrontation of Billy and Claggart in Vere's cabin, and the ensuing trial – and him saying, 'I know the shape I want; it's just a question of finding the notes.' Time and again he would sit down in the evening and play through another scene, always from the manuscript, which was written in faint pencil and was quite hard to decipher, let alone read if you were turning pages, as I often did. The excitement of watching the growth of what I was already convinced was a masterpiece was intense. But it was not plain sailing all the way.

To begin with, Ben had thought of writing the opera for Sadler's Wells, with whose aspirations he and Peter were in greater sympathy than those of Covent Garden, on whose Board I was invited to sit a year later. But Norman Tucker at Sadler's Wells got cold feet about the subject and seemed not to believe that Ben could bring it off, so it went to Covent Garden. Ben wanted as good a conductor as he could get and had struck up an understanding with Josef Krips, the Viennese. Krips conducted *Lucretia* in Salzburg in 1950 – had indeed insisted that it figure in the programme of that chauvinist festival – and Erwin and I had heard it there. Ben had already invited him to conduct it again with the English Opera Group at the Festival of Britain in summer 1951. I remember Krips's indignation that a young English conductor concerned with the other operas did not come to his rehearsals – 'When I was young, I went always to Weingartner's rehearsals. I may not be *so* good a conductor, but I am more experienced than he is. Why he not come to mine?' – but the performances went well, and Ben asked him to conduct *Billy Budd* at Covent Garden in December 1951.

All seemed to be going smoothly until Krips got the full score of the first act, which he said was impossible to read; he did not think he would be able to study it well enough to have it ready to rehearse in early November. We were asked to intervene and persuade Krips to change his mind, and he and his wife came to lunch at Orme Square on 18 October – the première was to be on 1 December.

Krips and Erwin and I pored over the manuscript. Erwin assured him he would have a beautifully legible score within a week but that he should study the work from this manuscript in the meanwhile, and he left wreathed in smiles and promising that from now on he would work at *Billy Budd* day and night, and would communicate with us first if he foresaw snags; Covent Garden and Ben could go to bed assured of his collaboration. We felt pleased with our work, and were amazed to hear next morning from David Webster that he had received Krips's irrevocable resignation; he must have gone home from Orme Square and written the letter straight away. We only gradually came to understand that it was a genuine case of cold feet; Krips had hardly ever conducted a première before, certainly not one of such importance.

In the event Ben conducted, however reluctantly, and the first night was something of a triumph; but the critics were considerably less friendly than the audience. I don't know whether this critical reception turned Ben against the big theatre and the big audience, but there was much talk of metropolitan and micropolitan, a phrase Kenneth Clark had used in a lecture at Aldeburgh that summer. Ben was in fact an outstanding conductor, of his own and other composers' music, and his concerts at the Aldeburgh Festival were unforgettable events.

Contact however tenuous with other composers of eminence did not always suit Ben, although he made great friends with Shostakovich after the 1962 Edinburgh Festival. He and Erwin told me separately that during a recital tour of the United States in 1949 he met Schoenberg and Stravinsky with near-disastrous results. Schoenberg came to his dressing room at the interval of a concert that Ben was conducting, something which away from Aldeburgh always crippled him with nerves, and was turned away from the door by an attendant who assured him – correctly, I am certain – that the maestro was in the bathroom being sick. Schoenberg put it down to drink rather than nerves and, the least charitable of letter-writers, conveyed as much to Erwin.

With Stravinsky the contact was more personal but little more fortunate. Ben was, he told me, from early days a fervent admirer of Stravinsky's and he had looked forward to meeting him while he was in Los Angeles on this same recital tour. Stravinsky talked a bit about the music of Britten's he knew – *Peter Grimes* from the score only, *Lucretia* from local performance. When was Stravinsky himself going to write a full-length opera, asked Britten. 'I have one in progress even now,' said the old master; 'But opera, not music drama, is my interest – and I shall write in closed forms.' 'Just as I did in *Lucretia*,' said Britten. 'Not at all,' said Stravinsky; 'My opera will have *secco* recitative accompanied only by piano, not by orchestra!' Britten was dumbfounded. Had he not done exactly that in *Lucretia*, which Stravinsky claimed to have heard? Either the master was a liar, or a fool.

His relations with great contemporaries were not always thus. He agreed to play the accompaniment to Shostakovich's 'Eleven Jewish Poems' at the 1962 Edinburgh Festival, then fell ill so that we had to replace him, with results that initially displeased the composer. Later, they became firm friends when Ben visited Russia, and I enjoyed the producer Colin Graham's account of an exchange between the two. Shostakovich: 'What do you think of Puccini?' Britten: 'I think his operas are dreadful!' Shostakovich: 'No, Ben, you are wrong. He wrote marvellous operas, but dreadful music!'

Erwin and I together concocted the idea that Ben could be persuaded to become Music Director of Covent Garden, where his influence could turn the promising ensemble into something far more important, and where he need conduct only his own works, a Mozart opera every year and perhaps one other that he really loved – *Traviata* or Gluck's *Iphigénie en Tauride* or Tchaikovsky's *Eugene Onegin*.

David Webster liked the idea but was a little diffident as to how to get it through his Board, on which sat not only sympathizers like Eddy Sackville-West and myself, but also men like William Walton and Leslie Boosey, who might for quite different reasons be less happy. David and I from time to time talked about whether or not to make the unofficial approaches official, both to Ben and to the Board. One evening before dinner, when I had suggested, rather dogmatically perhaps, that only a powerful personality of this kind would advance the company, David disagreed. The company would advance anyhow, he said, because the opportunity existed, and opportunities, like voids, cry out to be filled. I began to think he was right in his argument; but he remained in favour of getting Ben.

The difficulty as always was to persuade David to act, but eventually it was agreed that he should come up to Harewood for the night at a time when Ben was staying and, so to speak, pop the question. Ben was warned, David duly arrived in the early evening, and allowed the talk to remain general until we all went to bed. He was leaving by a morning train, but just had time after breakfast to take Ben aside and say that the idea was in the air. How would Ben react? Ben sketched a few difficulties, but said he was sympathetic to the company and its aims (which were then not dissimilar, apart from the admixture of ballet, from English National Opera's now) and hoped they might talk again about it. With that David was off to the station and we were left wondering if that was all he had planned to say.

Nonetheless, he put the idea to a Board meeting at Covent Garden, at which I was present. Reactions were fairly predictable. There was some general good will, and then Willie Walton asked whether Ben was really a conductor, in the sense that he would conduct Willie's own *Troilus*, which was now finished and would be due for performance in a couple of years' time. 'Yes,' I said boldly, 'he would.' Leslie Boosey insisted he was primarily a composer, not a performer and, though the discussion ended inconclusively, I do not think there was ever again any official talk about the project. I suspect Ben, who had a sense of duty as well as of his own mission, was relieved; and perhaps it was a misconceived scheme from the start, as Ben was too professional and regular a composer for time away from composition to be other than wasted.

All the same, Erwin, with Ben's interests very much at heart, had been one of the plan's begetters, and when we eventually appointed Rafael Kubelik, Erwin begged me to tell Ben myself and not let him read it in the newspapers. I have little doubt that for four or five years Ben could have inspired an ensemble and indeed a public, that outstanding performances of his favourite works could have been mounted. Strongly as I was in favour of the scheme, being wise after the event I doubt if as much was lost for Covent Garden as was gained for Ben's peace of mind and indeed his work.

After *Billy Budd*, whether because of critical reaction or from inner conviction, he started to plan his next opera for Aldeburgh, the Jubilee Hall and the audience he thought of as 'his'. William Plomer was to write the book and it was to be based on a Nôh play. In February 1952 the King died. In March we were in Vienna, where Ben and Peter had a recital, and from there we went with them for twelve days to a ski-ing resort called Gargellen. We had a little room where we dozed or read or worked after ski-ing, had a drink before dinner, and where we sat around after, gossiping and planning for the future. What was 'national' expression in opera, we asked ourselves; what were the 'national' operas of different countries? *The Bartered Bride* obviously for the Czechs, said Ben, *Manon* for the French, *Boris* and all that for the Russians. We weren't so happy about the Germans – had it to be Lortzing, whom we none of us liked, or must it be *Meistersinger*, which Ben thought ponderous and against which he had a grudge. For the Italians undoubtedly *Aida*, said Ben. 'It's the perfect expression of every kind of Italian nationalist feeling, national pride – but where's the English equivalent?' 'Well, you'd better write one.'

The next three or four hours were spent discussing a period – the Merrie

England of the Tudors or Elizabethans? – and a subject – Henry VIII? too obvious, and an unattractive hero. Queen Elizabeth? highly appropriate! What about a national opera in time for next year's Coronation?

We talked into the night, agreed that Lytton Strachey's *Elizabeth and Essex*, which I had recently read, would make a good starting point, and then started to face the difficulties. Peter played devil's advocate, reminding Ben of his opera for Aldeburgh with William Plomer, of their autumn recital tour, of another commission, none of which could be jettisoned and all of which prevented the new, madcap enterprise. But Ben was intrigued, and by the time Peter left for England for concerts without Ben, we had decided Noel Mewton-Wood might be persuaded to accompany Peter in the recitals, the commission could conceivably be postponed and William diverted on to the new opera – provided only, Ben insisted, that his Coronation opera was made in some way official, not quite commanded but at least accepted as part of the celebrations.

We went from Gargellen to Zürich, from where Peter flew home and where next day we took Ben to see *Eugene Onegin*, an opera he had loved from the score but was, like us, seeing for the first time. The performance was not ideal, but it was musical and unpretentious, and Ben's enthusiasm was as great and uncritical as ours. We buzzed with shared pleasure throughout dinner afterwards, and Ben commented on the touching and striking dramatic effect made by the disappearance of Olga after her disastrous provocation of Lensky in the first scene of Act II, which he compared acutely and accurately with the unexplained but equally convincing removal of the Fool from *King Lear*.

From Zürich we went to stay with my cousins Peg and Lu Hesse (the Prince and Princess of Hesse) near Darmstadt, as Ben wanted to see *Billy Budd* in its first German performance at Wiesbaden. It wasn't very good, with a clumsy translation and hefty cuts; when we got home Ben had a lot to drink at supper and then gave a hilarious performance of the opening of the Tchaikovsky concerto as rendered by an inebriated pianist.

Next day we discussed the opera again. If William Plomer refused to be diverted from the Nôh play, then the only man to write the libretto quickly enough would be Ronald Duncan. But Ben felt he had had too many tussles with Ronnie over the shaping of an opera in the past to trust him on his own; would I collaborate and assist Ronnie to shape the new work?

As soon as I got back to London, I bought a paperback of *Elizabeth and Essex* and started to divide it into operatic scenes (I still have the copy), and got in touch with my cousin Tommy Lascelles, the Queen's Private Secretary, to tell him the great idea and to ask his advice. He was enthusiastic and said he would put it to the Queen so that it should get the positive reaction we now all wanted. William Plomer quickly agreed to write the libretto and I went to see Tommy again at Buckingham Palace on 23 April. Later that afternoon I told a meeting I was attending at Covent Garden of the possibility – David Webster of course already knew.

Among recitals that Ben and Peter were maintaining were some in July 1952 at the Aix Festival and at Menton, planned in effect to provide and to finance a holiday, which both Ben and Peter always sorely needed after an Aldeburgh Festival. We drove down in procession, Ben and Peter in Ben's Rolls, Marion and I in our Austin Princess, and stayed with Tony and Thérèse Mayer (he was the French cultural attaché in London) at Ménerbes some twenty-five miles from Aix.

From there we sampled the unparalleled excellence of the cooking of Baumanière at Les Baux; there we talked again about the new opera. Peter had taken up a glum position over the whole thing, hating the cancellations, disliking the disturbance of his routine, the official nature of the affair, the risk involved in the venture into international waters, and perhaps too of playing a young, ardent lover in the shape of Essex, which Ben of course planned to write for him. He preferred to sing Cecil; let Ben find another Essex! When the others had gone off to the market one day, Ben and I stayed behind and he poured out his woes. Might Peter's suggestion be right, and should we look for another Essex? What about Boris Christoff – or the new bass star, Nicola Rossi-Lemeni, who had taken London by storm as Boris a few weeks before; did he speak English? But his heart was never in this new tack. He had Joan Cross for Gloriana, he wanted Peter for Essex, and he was accustomed to getting his own way.

The one thing that worried him was the possibility that he might fall ill, which he could do disconcertingly easily, recovering on the whole quickly. Marion and I used to say that some of his illnesses were psychosomatic (he agreed, but maintained that knowing it didn't make him feel any better), and that he was tough, like a reed which bends easily but springs up the moment the wind drops. Any interruption would now be fatal and the opera not ready in time. In the event preparations, and not least the inspiration for composition, went swimmingly and to schedule.

We arranged with the Salisburys to take Ben down to Hatfield to absorb Cecil and Elizabethan atmosphere; we took Ben to see Callas and Stignani in *Norma* at Covent Garden. (He was quite smitten with Callas and the magnitude of her performance and wanted her for the projected Scala performance of *Gloriana* next season; it never materialized, as de Sabata got cold feet after reading the notices.) After Christmas he and Peter came to spend some days at Harewood, where he played the opera to my mother, William Plomer after Peter had left joining us so that he and Ben could work.

We had some gloriously sunny, frosty weather and went over to Plompton Rocks not far from Harewood. Plompton has an echo, and to try it out we found ourselves, hopefully alone, yelling with less than total conviction 'Henry James!' to the answering rocks.

Ben was writing the title role for Joan Cross in almost mezzo range, but after he had left Harewood I listened to a broadcast of Bartok's *Bluebeard* and heard so pure, so easy a top C from Joan that I was tempted to ring Ben and tell him that he need not worry about at least an occasional top note for her. Lucky that I didn't, as a few weeks later, when I complimented her on the performance, Joan giggled and asked how I had liked the C. 'I haven't got one any more and Robbie [Stanford Robinson] asked me what my best top note was; I said probably B flat, so they recorded that on its own and stuck it in over the broadcast, screwed up to sound like a C!'

During the whole period, we were constant visitors to Aldeburgh and Ben to Harewood and Orme Square, sometimes with, sometimes without Peter. Ben told me that he had had to give up the section of the Coronation service which had been commissioned from him, a March to go with the Entry of the Princesses. He had decided this should be for my mother and was planning to introduce the note of her much-used dog whistle, which he said he associated inevitably with her!

In March, with all but the Ballad scene of *Gloriana* finished, we went together for a couple of weeks' holiday in Ireland – Dublin, Cork and the Ballylickey Hotel, Bantry Bay. After it was over, I was to meet David Webster to decide when precisely I would join the staff at Covent Garden, which I had long hankered to do; but Queen Mary died while we were away and we had to cut everything short to get back for the funeral. It was said that my grandmother had expressed great concern in case the Coronation might be postponed on her account – the papers were full of it – so that particular worry over *Gloriana* was laid quickly to rest. Three weeks before the first night, the Queen and Prince Philip dined at Orme Square with my mother and William Plomer, to hear some extracts from the new opera performed by Ben, Joan and Peter, who also dined, and this seemed to go well, with what felt like an appreciative audience; the right seeds, we felt, were sown.

The première of *Gloriana*, six days after the Coronation, was one of the great disasters of operatic history. The audience, so far from being a gathering or artistic Britain to honour the Queen (as we had naïvely hoped) consisted of Cabinet, Diplomatic Corps and official London first and foremost, and the rest apparently nowhere. They applauded if at all with their kid gloves on and the press, critics as well as journalists, gathered next day to castigate composer, performance, and choice. Ben was criticized for his music, I was criticized for pushing such an obviously poor choice for such an occasion; it was clear that some sort of simple-minded glorification was what had been expected, not the passionate, tender drama inside the public pageantry that Ben had contrived.

I remain convinced that he chose a serious subject, that he had the ability to write for the large public without in any sense writing down, and that the audience had in fact proved unworthy of an event they should have felt it a privilege to attend. It may not have been the right audience, but would the Queen's ministers and the diplomats and court of Gloriana's day have proved so unreceptive to a grandiose new work as their counterparts in our second Elizabethan age? Subsequent and repeated impressions have confirmed that *Gloriana* is a skilfully contrasted, well laid-out opera, exactly calculated to provide listeners with a challenging but ultimately seductive evening in the theatre. What were those first audiences – and those first criticisms – about?

Ben was clearly mortified by the whole fiasco, and a few weeks later, when we were changing before an opera recital at the Devon Festival, confided to me that he had received a broadside from Peter – did not the reception confirm his worst fears? Should they not in future stick to the public that wanted them, the loyal Aldeburgh friends, and not get mixed up with something that was none of their concern? Ben was in the mood to take his advice. In point of fact, it was probably the last time he got a 'bad notice', in the sense that the press as a whole was against him, but I think it very materially affected his view of his own work and of its likely reception, as also the influence of those of us who hoped he would gradually assume a metropolitan as opposed to a micropolitan stance.

Curiously enough, his next operatic première, *The Turn of the Screw*, was anything but micropolitan in ambience, taking place in September 1954 at the Teatro Fenice in Venice – because no commission was forthcoming in England and the Venice Festival had offered to pay for a new production. Ben had started to talk about the new subject well before *Gloriana* was finished, and I had read the Henry James short story for the first time on our way down to Ménerbes for that July holiday in 1952. I found it so suggestive and creepy that, when I discovered the room Marion and I were to occupy was separate from the main house, I could only read it by day.

Ben and I argued about the haunting; had it to be explicit, or could it be the product of the governess's paranoia – *she* was convinced that something was wrong, but was it really? I insisted on ambivalence, he on the need for the composer to make a decision – and he *had* taken one: that the haunting was real. Staying months later at Aldeburgh when Myfanwy Piper had finished a final draft, Ben let me see it, and asked William Plomer to read it too. The next day was beautiful and we went for a walk. When William did not mention the new project, Ben could not contain himself and asked his opinion. Unexpectedly, William said that, having been born and brought up in South Africa where the supernatural was part of everyday life, he could not take Henry James's gingerly northern hauntings truly seriously. His imagination was not engaged, for all his admiration of the technique with which it was put across. Ben was disconcerted, even indignant, and needed much reassurance.

Whatever my reservations about the interpretation of the theme, I followed the opera's composition with just as much fascination as I had *Billy Budd* and *Gloriana*, though not quite so closely – I was already working at Covent Garden and had less spare time – and looked forward just as eagerly to the Venice première. This was a lower-keyed event than Ben's last new operatic exposure to the public, with an interested audience and a genuine success at the end of the evening. Ben had the knack of inspiring performers; he was himself one of the greatest performers either as conductor or pianist I ever encountered, and his preparation of *The Turn of the Screw* was exemplary.

Back in England, he asked me to introduce the new opera at the Wigmore Hall, and it was an education to me to try to guide a prospective audience through the intricacies of a work that would be schematic if it were not so inspired. Ben would not allow them a preview of the end of the opera with its heart-breaking repetitions of 'Malo', so we ended with my spoken word, not as I should have liked with his music.

I do not remember him playing through the smaller operas, *Let's Make an Opera* and *Noye's Fludde*, as he wrote them, only when finished; and perhaps the composition of these took a short period, and was in fact confined to a single inspiration. But his ballet *The Prince of the Pagodas* was a grander undertaking, and we heard about it as it went along.

Originally, John Cranko had been asked to do a full-length ballet for the

Sadler's Wells branch of the Royal Bellet and had asked Ben to write the music. Ninette de Valois, when she heard about it, would not allow the second company to have so prestigious an event, and Cranko was asked to make the ballet for the big group of the Royal Ballet, to David Webster's delight. Ben found composing a ballet meant entering curiously uncharted, even alien territory – he once referred by a slip of the tongue to the 'Pas de Six' as the 'Pas de Quoi' – and he tended at first to misjudge the lengths dancers could sustain, so that Cranko had to correct him. When it came to scoring, he was disconcerted by the need for a full or fullish orchestra so much of the time, unlike in opera. He told me he referred constantly to Tchaikovsky's *Sleeping Beauty*, not only as the touchstone of balletic quality but also as a kind of ballet-music dictionary, and from it he got ideas for length, for the kind of variations dancers would respond to, for the variety and contrasts which, with all those short sections, would make up a satisfactory whole. I find the result, with its Gamelan effects (the result of his stay the previous year in Bali), one of the most delightful and certainly one of the least-recognized of all his works, and the records give me constant pleasure.

The first night seemed to go down well enough, even if Cranko's choreography was less than universally admired. The ballet was mounted at a time when Covent Garden was short of money and the Board decided against having a party afterwards, as they had done a couple of years earlier for Walton and Tippett premières. My cousin Peg Hesse, in an access of indignation, had arranged we combine with her and Lu to give one ourselves, so that Ben might not feel neglected.

If short operas caused Ben little trouble, there was much discussion of *A Midsummer Night's Dream* and how to compress the play to operatic length without losing any of its essence. In the end, he and Peter, whose immensely skilful cutting of the play was what Ben set, decided that the Wood was what the play was about, and that the mortals should only figure once its mood was established, a decision which provided perspective, focus and scale for the entire opera, just as one of Bottom's boasts has provided me with a title for this book. *Midsummer Night's Dream* was planned for the Jubilee Hall at Aldeburgh, but Ben agreed almost from the outset to design it so that it could be staged the following year at Covent Garden – where I was working – with a larger body of strings and with the children's chorus augmented by unseen grown-ups. Peter would not be cast as Lysander and insisted on Flute, which he played and sang exquisitely, and Ben allowed one or two Covent Garden singers to augment the Aldeburgh regulars – Joan Carlyle shared Tytania with Jenifer Vyvyan, for example.

In 1956, I was asked to revive the Leeds Festival for its centenary year in 1958, and of course turned to Ben to write a choral piece. He was reluctant, promised to write something that would probably not be choral, and eventually turned out the strangely beautiful *Nocturne*, a setting of poems each with a different instrumental obbligato. Because Ben disliked the playing and personality of the BBC Symphony Orchestra's leader, Paul Beard, he wrote his obbligati for wind instruments only!

With the *Spring Symphony* to his credit, a choral piece from Ben was still something I hankered after and I obtained some kind of half-promise that, if he wrote one, it would be for Leeds. It was disappointing therefore to hear he was contemplating writing a *Saint Peter* for York Minster (it came to nothing), and worse still to learn quite by chance that he had accepted a commission to write for the opening of Coventry Cathedral in 1962 – the *War Requiem*.

If I were to point to Maria Callas as the most musically ambitious and musically most completely realized of any singer, perhaps any performer, in my lifetime, I should be hard put to it, if looking for a second, to name any other singer above Peter Pears, whose name must recur in any discussion of Benjamin Britten.

Whether he sang Schubert or Schütz, Pérotin or Purcell, Bach or Berg, Verdi or Britten, he was the kind of artist who made the music on which he was engaged seem his only preoccupation. Nothing sounded haphazard, but nothing ever sounded calculated or cold. The voice was not sensuous as is the voice of an Italian, and yet the intensity of phrasing, the delicacy of *portamento*, the musical imagination, which could not help but be engaged in the production of sound as much as in the overall shaping of a piece, ensured that nothing less than a sensuous effect came from Peter's lips if that was what the composer desired. All of us who revere him as artist would, if asked to embark on a panegyric, praise his peerless musical intelligence and taste; and yet we should, if we were to quote from an anthology of his performance, be quoting *sounds* which are as beautiful in their way as any heard from Gigli or de los Angeles and preserved on their records. From *Grimes*, it would be the unique tone quality at 'Who, who, who, who can turn skies back and begin again' and the exquisite colouring as well as the intonation of the resolution of the ninth at 'What harbour can embrace'; the rich fullness and confidence of Captain Vere's 'And listen to them singing below decks! Where there is happiness, there cannot be harm', and the silky cantilena of 'And this is the man I'm told is dangerous'; the withdrawn, inner quality of Essex's 'Happy,

happy were he'; the insinuating colour of that first, other-worldly 'Miles' in *The Turn of the Screw*; the relaxed *piano* security of the final 'Does beauty lead to wisdom, Phaedrus?' in *Death in Venice*. How else, except in terms of the sound quality, could one describe them?

Ben wrote constantly for Peter, and Peter's career could not have been the same without Ben; but his repayment of his debt was rich, and the world was the beneficiary in a whole host of performances that were literally beyond compare. Two days before I wrote these words, a foreign conductor friend asked me, 'Who can sing Peter Pears's music now? Peter has just cancelled and I must replace him' – and I could not from a host of good British tenors suggest a genuine replacement.

He was unique in our time, the successor of Karl Erb and Patzak amongst Evangelists and tenors of style and subtlety, the peer of Callas, de los Angeles, Boris Christoff, Jurinac, Stabile, Schwarzkopf, Hans Hotter and the other great singing interpreters of our age. He was the inspiration of Benjamin Britten from the time they met in the late 1930s to the gestation period of *Death in Venice* thirty-five years later. He would have been King Lear if Ben had written it, he will be the quoted voice for succeeding generations of tenors who tackle Britten's music, operatic or otherwise, whose name – like 'Trial' or 'Martin' or 'Falcon'* – should by rights be applied to a particular vocal category: in his case one whose tenor range lies low for most high tenors, but whose '*pp*' soarings defeat all but those with supreme technique and imagination.

During the 1950s and early 1960s I thought of Ben as one of my closest friends. He was godfather to my eldest son, I consulted him about decisions great and small, we were in and out of each other's houses – partly because Marion was the daughter of two of his best and oldest friends and herself close to him, partly because we had I think developed a considerable sympathy over the years. We met his friends and he met ours.

We went every summer to Aldeburgh for the Festival, and Ben used even to ask us for suggestions for programmes. The unique quality of the Festival came from the personal nature of its planning and performance; the personalities were Ben's and Peter's, but other people might suggest ingredients which would become part of the blend. On those days when he was playing the piano as a solo performer, we would sit with him for a drink

---

*French singers whose voices, respectively a character tenor, brilliant baritone and dramatic soprano, came to describe the type of voice needed for particular roles and were even used by composers in their scores to denote what they wanted.

before lunch and then eat without him – he usually felt the need to practise before the performance, and to feel sick with apprehension on his own. Apprehension came out too in his concerto playing, which was always beautiful but sometimes hurried. I was glad when he took to conducting and left the solo playing to others.

When we stayed at Aldeburgh in the summer, cold bathes were the order of the day. Ben had always preferred the bracing cold to the Mediterranean alternative and would plunge blithely into the icy North Sea, whereas I saw him leave the sea shivering at Monte Carlo precisely because of its tepid quality (and the sun oil he said he saw floating on top of the water). I remember before one Festival driving with him and Peter some little distance to a wood where one could hear nightingales – a hare-brained expedition, I suspected, until I actually heard the magic sounds and was converted to enthusiasm in a single evening. (Apart from in Aldeburgh and its neighbourhood, I heard nightingales in the gardens of both the houses Patricia and I had in St John's Wood, where in one of the hot summers of the late 1970s we once spied the bird sitting on the TV aerial of the house next door.)

Sometimes we went to stay at Aldeburgh in late summer during school holidays, and played cricket – Peter had been a useful cricketer at school and Ben loved the game, declaring, when I once asked him where his preference lay, that he was really a keen fielder rather than bat or bowler. Tennis was very much one of Ben's games and both he and Peter played well, Ben with immense tenacity and more than a little of the 'will to win'. Later, he started to get bursitis in his shoulder and this not only interfered with playing the piano, which we said (and he did not deny) was psychosomatic, but also with his games, which disappointed him almost as much.

Ben's habit, as I always understood it and observed, was to get up early and write till lunchtime, often, at least if he had people staying with him, going out after lunch for a walk (or in summer playing tennis); then before dinner he would revise what he had done in the morning, or sometimes score if he had reached that stage. He believed strongly in the benefits of routine, of sitting down regularly at his desk, and tended to mistrust composers who could not get down to things until they were 'in the mood' and somehow gripped by inspiration. He knew as well as anyone that the value of what he wrote every day could vary in quality and indeed in volume, but this in no way diminished his belief in regular work. All composers get blocks, he said, but you work to get out of them and mostly you succeed. If you are obliged to manufacture the music to fill the shapes you know are necessary at a given moment in a composition, you must do it as conscientiously as if it were the 'inspiration' you hope will come when the creative juices are flowing. One of the reasons, he used to say, why he could not take music critics seriously was because not once had one of them singled out for adverse criticism one of these 'manufactured' passages in any of his works.

Morgan Forster used to stay at Crag House, sometimes for quite long periods, and once when he was recovering from an operation. We would go up to his room to talk to him, and he and Ben became very close. Ben professed to like nursery food, by which he meant good, plain English food, and his housekeeper was expert at keeping him and his guests happy on this kind of fare. She was a good cook and we ate well though seldom richly. But one day a new pudding appeared, so sticky and stiff-textured that we all struggled with our helpings while Ben took some up to Morgan. Comparing notes next day before Marion and I left, Morgan said he had been quite unable to cope and had left his portion of toffee apple, as he called it, on his plate, only slightly mangled. Two days later, we got a postcard from Aldeburgh saying no more than, 'Would you believe it, toffee apples have been re-presented, topped with cream. I ventured on a pip only. E.M.F.' Morgan was at Aldeburgh once for the Festival and seemed not to have tickets for *Albert Herring* that night. 'Would you like to come?' asked Ben, who had a spare. 'No, thank you,' said Morgan. 'I've seen it already' – so little the reaction Ben had expected that he even told me about it.

Ben cannot have been in any doubt that my own feelings about his work were only just this side of idolatry, that I would have done anything to further his, and its, cause. He asked me once to introduce one of the operatic recitals that he, Joan Cross and Peter Pears used to put on, and I later introduced similar operatic programmes, with different singers – at one time or another, Joan, Peter, Arda Mandikian, Nancy Evans, Anna Pollak, Bruce Boyce, Otakar Kraus, Trevor Anthony – but always with Ben at the piano. These became quite a feature not only of Aldeburgh Festivals but of English Opera Group life. Several times we did short tours, either to keep the Group's name in front of the public or else to raise money. I have the happiest memories of some of Ben's operatic discoveries, and particularly of his playing of the dance music before 'Un di felice' in the first act of *Traviata*, and the delicacy and bounce with which he would break into the little march before the canon quartet in the wedding scene of *Così fan tutte*; and listening to him rehearse with singers was an education. Often I lent him vocal scores to play from, and still come across pages of *Masnadieri* or *Due Foscari* or *Oberon* with his pencilled phrasing marks on them.

Photographed at Innsbruck after our release from prison, May 1945. The Prominente are (from left to right): Max de Hamel, myself, John Elphinstone, (Werner Buchmüller, attaché of the Swiss Red Cross), and Michael Alexander.

My parents,
October 1946.

With Maria Callas and the Mayor of Verona, 1947.

Escorting Queen Mary at Southwark
Cathedral, 1949.

With Marion on the lake at Fuschl, August 1949.

Marion and I leaving the Church after our wedding, 29 September 1949.

Peter Pears, accompanied by Benjamin Britten. With them are Ronald Duncan (centre) and Arthur Oldham.

Benjamin Britten (right) and E.M. Forster walking over Aldeburgh's common, October 1949. Forster was writing the libretto for *Billy Budd*.

Talking to Benjamin Britten and his sister at the Aldeburgh Festival.

My mother and her brother, the Duke of Windsor, March 1953.

With Marion, my mother and Gerald after Queen Elizabeth's Coronation, June 1953.

Participating in the blessing the stage ceremony which took place before the appearance of the Azuma Kabuki dancers and musicians at Covent Garden, September 1955.

LEFT Arriving at the *Observer* exhibition of film history with Marion and Dicky Buckle (left), June 1956.

RIGHT In conversation with Maria Callas, who was in London to take part in the centenary gala performance at Covent Garden, June 1958.

Patricia in Italy a few days before I met her.

Dancing with Patricia in fancy dress at the Opera Ball, February 1959.

My three elder sons bicycle along the terrace at Harewood, while their cousin looks on, 1963. From left to right: David, Jeremy, James and Henry Lascelles.

Harewood House, north front by T. Malton, *c.* 1788.

The north front of Harewood House in 1981.

A dream I had was perhaps partly the product of these operatic recitals. In it, Ben was to conduct *Don Giovanni* with Tito Gobbi in the title role and, with Gobbi ill, had asked me to take his place. I donned the costume with some misgiving as I felt I did not really know the music by heart, but was slightly reassured by the fine figure the looking glass outside my dressing room suggested I should cut. Together with Maria Cebotari, the Donna Anna, I walked out across the sands of a great arena, in the middle of which stood a grand piano at which Ben was sitting, and braced myself to sing. *'Grazie per tanto onore'* came from my throat, mellifluously I thought but with a certain irrelevance – since the phrase belongs to Don Ottavio and does not occur until the finale of Act I!

During these years, we imbibed the joy and wisdom of his Festival, and in return took him to the Olivier–Vivien Leigh *Titus Andronicus*, the Berliner Ensemble, *The Trojans* at Covent Garden, and the Bolshoi Ballet on their first visit to this country. I well remember the pleasure he got from the *Falstaff* that la Scala brought to London in 1950, and his rage when the notices emphasized slips and were generally patronizing in tone. He wrote to de Sabata afterwards. He took us to hear Ravi Shankar – our first taste of Indian music, which soon became little short of a passion – and I remember the grace with which Peter introduced that recital, which was at Friends' House in Euston Road, a far cry from the packed Festival Hall that Ravi was to command a few years later.

It was to Ben that Marion poured out her heart in 1959 when she knew that I had fallen in love with Patricia, and Ben was my sympathetic listener when I tried to explain it all to him a day or two later. However much he regretted what had happened, he knew it was not the kind of thing people exactly invite into their lives, and he even used the phrase to me: 'Do you think you could ever make the break?'

Marion and I separately and together saw him regularly for the next few years. I went to Aldeburgh as often as I ever had, including to the première of *Midsummer Night's Dream* in 1960, but in 1964 it was he who decided to make a break with me.

I had gone to the Holland Festival at a different time from Marion, and was at a concert in Scheveningen which Ben was conducting and which included his *Cello Symphony* with Rostropovich. At the end I went round with Maria Diamand and the conductor Alberto Erede to the dressing room to see Ben and Peter, only to watch them push out past the queue and go off into the night. I sensed that their precipitate departure had to do with me, and somehow got through the party which followed (in their honour, and their absence). I was told by Maria next day alone at lunch that Ben had asked her to drive with him to the port to catch his ship and had had to stop to be sick on the way to relieve his nerves.

I was distressed to have been the cause of scandal, however private, at Peter Diamand's festival, but even more distressed by Ben's new attitude towards me. When I got back to London there was a curt note from him saying that my behaviour to Marion had alienated him so much that he was putting an end to our association. That seemed to be that, and of course he was entitled to behave as he chose, however much at variance with his professed determination not to take sides it might seem. But it was a little surprising a month later to open the visitors' book at Harewood and find that he and Rostropovich had stayed there with Marion just before the Holland Festival, in my absence and without a word ever being said.

Ben's 'corpses' were notorious throughout his career. He hated to be lumbered with someone whose friendship or collaboration he no longer wanted or needed, and many who had been close to him found themselves no longer asked to Crag House or later to Red House. If you know the poetry of Ronald Duncan and look carefully at the libretto of *Peter Grimes*, you will make some connection between Ben's falling out with Montagu Slater and the fact that Ronnie was the librettist of *The Rape of Lucretia* (which saw the light of day one year after the première of *Peter Grimes*), and see that some lines in *Grimes*, such as 'Since the solution is beyond life, beyond dissolution', could have been written by no one but Ronnie. In his turn Ronnie suffered when Ben wanted to revise some idiosyncratic elements of the libretto of *The Rape of Lucretia*, and enlisted the hand not of Ronnie but of another writer.

The 'corpses' hated their demise – Ben was a celebrity and a genius, but also a man of great charm and warmth in his friendships – and I was no exception to the rule. I genuinely loved the man and the musician and for years could not hear his music in performance, on radio or record, without a deep sense of sadness for what I knew I had lost. Occasionally a friend – Joan Cross, Donald Mitchell or Jack Phipps – would say that he or she felt Ben regretted the break he had brought about; one once told me Ben had admitted that he had broken with the man he supposed was his most single-minded and devoted supporter.

I wrote him a note when he was to conduct a concert in early 1967 with the New Philharmonia Orchestra (with which I was then working) and said I would not come round to see him if he preferred it that way. He wrote back to say he would find that ridiculous but that it might be better if I came alone

– which may have been tactful in the circumstances as Patricia and I were not yet married.

The breach was never healed, though we corresponded a little and talked on the telephone about practical problems after I started to work at the Coliseum in 1972. We revived *Gloriana* for a few performances when Britain joined the EEC, and invited Peter to sing Essex. He could not because of conflicting engagements, but they agreed to attend a performance – unfortunately choosing one which Sylvia Fisher was not singing and eventually deciding that she would be hurt if they went. So another meeting was avoided, on purpose or by accident.

Later still we heard from Joan Cross and Bill Servaes, the manager of the Aldeburgh Festival, that there would be no umbrage taken if Patricia and I came to performances at Aldeburgh or the Snape Maltings, and we ventured down to see *Death in Venice* and later *Paul Bunyan* and talked to Ben for a few moments; he was already very ill and could not get about except on the arm of his nurse. A year later we were there for a Scottish Opera performance of Gluck's *Alceste* and were on instruction taken by Joan Cross, with whom we were staying, to see Ben. He came for a few minutes to a party being given for the performers and talked very amicably to us there, but of course it was too late to renew friendship even if he had wanted to – which he never said he did – as he tired quickly, and saw only a few friends.

When he was made a peer – a curiously unnecessary honour I felt, but doubtless he was under pressure to accept because Olivier had done so and music needed a peer as much as the stage – I wrote a slightly ribald note of congratulation and got a postcard in reply, on which he had taken pains to write that he thanked us both for our good wishes. Well, there it ended, and perhaps it could not have been otherwise – since Joan had caught sight of Marion and her husband Jeremy Thorpe coming up the stairs behind us after that *Alceste* and then, on seeing us with Ben, turn round again.

Ben despised the ivory tower for the artist, and yet he was shy in the face of the world; he could not bear its censure and longed for its praise. Increasingly, he came to resent the intrusion of others. We once arranged to take Ben and Peter out to dinner after a performance of *Billy Budd*, but Ben got Peter to cry off when he heard that Richard Buckle was coming with us. When Ben was staying at Harewood soon after Marion and I were married, we went without him into Leeds for a lunchtime recital by Natasha Litvin, Stephen Spender's wife, and asked them out to Harewood for dinner. Ben was in a lather of nerves at the prospect of seeing Stephen, whom he inevitably associated with Wystan Auden and the past – Auden whose poetry he had set before the war, who was a prime influence in persuading him to go to America in early 1939, and of whose artistic colony he and Peter had for many months been a part. He disliked being reminded of that period of his life, but together he and Stephen looked more like long-lost friends than anything else. Ben was the life and soul of the party, and it was amazing to hear him say, after the Spenders had left, 'Well, it was not *quite* as bad as I had expected!'

I have little doubt that the initial public and critical failure of *Gloriana* was a turning-point for Ben. It shut him in on himself and he became even more private. He had made a great public gesture and the public had, so to speak, rejected him. He had risked writing for other than 'his' audience – in a sense, all composers have written for 'their' audience – had given instead a hostage to fortune and had forfeited it. The experience confirmed his suspicion of what one could expect from the great public, and he was determined not to take that kind of risk in future – hence the keenness to write for Sadler's Wells Ballet, not for the Royal Ballet at Covent Garden, hence the chamber-scale concept of *A Midsummer Night's Dream* in a micropolitan context, rather than the metropolitan one it could so easily have had.

He did not take that risk again until the time of the *War Requiem* in Coventry in 1962, and I suspect this was just as traumatic an experience for him as the other, only this time it was the *Gloriana* situation in reverse. Then he had given the 'popular' audience all he had; this time he was making what he felt was a private statement in a bigger but still serious context – and he suffered nothing less than revulsion at finding the press acclaiming a 'universal masterpiece' and so on. He had carefully chosen poems to indicate an ambivalent attitude to war, and had set up the cast to express the tensions of the times – Peter Pears the Englishman, Fischer-Dieskau the German, Galina Vishnevskaya the Russian as the healing angel – and he got the response proper only for an 'easy' piece. I don't believe it was a case of recognition coming after ambition had gone; I think he felt the easy success was an outrage and an invasion of privacy. Every creative artist who goes before the public takes something private with him, something vulnerable that can be crushed and wounded, only with Ben it turned out sometimes to have been too private to risk.

All his life part of Ben felt, I am convinced, that it was him against the world. An American commentator has recently diagnosed the struggle of Peter Grimes as a symbol of this feeling of Ben's, and I find the analysis hard to refute. He had too strong and too English a sense of humour to allow himself to feel positively persecuted, but I do think he felt more and more threatened by anything and anyone outside his own world. Quite early on, he started to react against anything approaching a new interpretation of one of his works, and he confessed once that he tended to think of his operas in terms of their original staging, which he himself had supervised, and to dislike anything else. As for the unfortunate tenors who took over the roles Peter Pears had created – and Peter could not sing *all* performances – they tended to get a very reserved reception.

Ben was not only a sensitive but a complex person and his basic humanitarianism was often contradicted by harsh actions; but, however much a thinker and a man of striking intelligence, he was very much a man of the heart. As he grew older younger composers did not appreciate his music – 'It says little to me,' they said – but I know that he brought a feeling of renaissance to English music, that there is no contemporary composer of any country who speaks to me so immediately, so regularly, so deeply, not even Michael Tippett.

His was an attractive, even a mesmeric personality, hence the disturbed feelings that his ending of our friendship left behind. That this hurt me abominably I do not deny, but I could never feel that he was on that account wholly in the wrong; and my belief in him, my admiration for what he achieved, and my affection for him as a human being remain quite undimmed.

CHAPTER NINE

To Covent Garden
1947-60

DAVID WEBSTER MUST have known almost from the time we first met, just after the war's end, that I would like to work at Covent Garden. I was twenty-eight and had already started the magazine *Opera* when I was asked in 1951 to become a member of the Board of Covent Garden, and had indeed written about performances there for much of 1949 and 1950. By then I knew David Webster quite well; I became an active member of the Board and was, I think, quite useful in those early days – the new opera company only gave its first performances (many months after the transferred Sadler's Wells Ballet) in late 1946 and early 1947.

Lord Keynes, chairman of the Arts Council and of Covent Garden at the outset, was responsible for bringing Webster to the Opera House. He had known him when he was chairman of the Liverpool Philharmonic during the war, and Webster was running one of the larger branches of John Lewis stores, report has it very efficiently indeed, but his great love was music and the theatre. Nonetheless, when he started to work in London, the musical profession decided that he was a draper and certain to make nothing but mistakes. He inherited no personnel except the heating engineer, a chief stage machinist and a pre-war secretary of Beecham's, but succeeded in founding an organization that within ten years of its foundation had performed the *Ring* a number of times, to say nothing of *Wozzeck* and *Elektra*, could mount an *Otello* of real quality, and had put on several important world premières of British operas, including two by Britten and one each by Tippett, Walton, Vaughan Williams and Bliss – one up (at least) for the draper, it would seem to me.

The first few years of Covent Garden's existence as a permanent institution offering opera and ballet on a year-round basis must have had its frustrations for those who ran it, as for those who sponsored it. They had expected I believe nearly as instant a success with the opera company as with the ballet, taken over fully-fledged as it were from Sadler's Wells, but things did not work out like that. The chorus was very fine but Karl Rankl, the surprise appointment as Music Director, wrought no miracles with the orchestra and many of the early performances were pedestrian.

David Webster seemed to have adopted an Asquithian attitude of 'wait and see'; he never criticized the forces he could regularly command but basked in the occasional warmth generated by guest appearances of Kirsten Flagstad and Hans Hotter, of Schwarzkopf and Seefried, of Erich Kleiber and Clemens Krauss, Patzak and Eva Turner. Not all the company performances were negligible and I remember a Pamina from Schwarzkopf – not one of the roles for which she was most renowned – which produced a G minor aria to treasure, much notable singing from the tenor Walter Midgley, enjoyable fluting from Virginia MacWatters as Manon, a sound *Rosenkavalier* to which I returned again and again, Sylvia Fisher's first operatic steps as Fidelio, Countess and Marschallin, *Turandot* with Eva Turner and Midgley, and much else besides.

During the two years I was on the Board, I went with Marion on a visit to Milan and Florence with David Webster in summer 1952 to see *William Tell* and to have discussions with Gobbi. On the way back, I asked David if he thought he would ever find room for me on the staff at Covent Garden. He had developed a masterly tactic when he didn't want to commit himself to something, and was one of the very few people I have ever met who was able in any situation to say and do absolutely nothing. On this occasion, he looked intelligent, sipped his drink and made no response whatsoever. It seemed somehow indelicate to question him further.

But later that year he did ask me to go to work there. I asked, 'What as?'; he said, 'I think you had better come in a general kind of capacity and find your own level.' We agreed that I should start in his office soon after the Coronation. David told me that I must see Sir John Anderson (Lord Waverley as he became), a great pro-consular figure who was by then chairman of Covent Garden, at his office at the Port of London Authority in the City. The only advice he gave me was that the chairman hated anyone to be late. I asked what he wanted to talk about, and David said, 'Oh, I think he wants to convince himself of what you and I know to be true – that you mean to work and don't want to have long weekends and that kind of thing.'

I arrived at the chairman's office exactly as ten was striking. He asked precisely the kind of question David had predicted: 'Do you realize that everyone else in the organization will work a full day and a full week; are you prepared to do the same? I am sure you wouldn't want any special treatment.' It would have been insulting if it had not been done gently and seriously, and I reassured him.

To work in an opera house had been my ambition since I was fourteen or fifteen, and, in spite of my wartime debt for performances and general feeling of allegiance to Sadler's Wells, the post-war bust-up there following the choice of *Peter Grimes* to reopen the Rosebery Avenue Theatre, and the consequent departure of Joan Cross, had combined with the opening of Covent Garden to cause a shift in my loyalty. Both companies were based on the principle of opera in the vernacular performed by an ensemble – an all-round versatile team such as once existed in every famous opera house of the world, reaching heights for instance before and after 1914 under Mahler or Toscanini, in the 1930s under Clemens Krauss in Munich, in Vienna just after the war, later in Hamburg under Rennert and Liebermann. The possibility of an alternative system did not occur to any of us, although it was assumed that the existence of an ensemble did not at all preclude guests from being invited from time to time to take part in performances.

I have always believed in an ensemble as the basis for opera, in other words in a company. Of course, any ensemble must attempt to grow its own stars and these stars must be encouraged to move around the world a bit. I used to believe it ought to be possible to cast *The Magic Flute* entirely from the company, as we usually did while I worked at Covent Garden (apart perhaps for the Queen of the Night, a voice I think we never had in residence). The temptation to vary the policy came when we gave a work such as *Meistersinger* in German. A guest or two was desirable in principal roles, but then one began to question whether Pogner, for instance, should be sung by an admirable company bass like Fred Dalberg or by a great guest such as Ludwig Weber. To deny your own man opportunity and kudos was unkind; to deny the public a performance such as Ludwig Weber's, and the company the splendour he could bring it, was perhaps also unkind. Not a simple decision.

A singer like Geraint Evans, who became a star in the international firmament, could never have developed if the policy of a home-grown ensemble had not obtained at Covent Garden when he joined. The voice was not at first specially beautiful, he was not always a 'smooth' singer (although from the outset an excellent artist), but he was cast as Figaro within a year or two of his début and he maintained his hold on that and comparable roles throughout a period when there were better singers of those parts in other

European houses. Under the ensemble policy, he received one chance after another which served to develop him until he himself, partly through his appearances at Glyndebourne, became a star and in demand abroad. It would not have happened without the ensemble system.

David Webster himself was a remarkable chief to work for, easy to criticize because he wore his faults on his sleeve, more difficult to praise as his greatest virtues were plainly visible only to those who worked with him. His reluctance to commit himself made people think he was indecisive. I once told him, 'People say you won't make up your mind', and he replied: 'You should never have to *take* a decision. The right course should be obvious. If it isn't, you may be committing yourself the wrong way.' Himself scrupulously loyal to his subordinates, he had little trouble in inspiring a reciprocal loyalty, even devotion – rare emotion! – inside the company.

I worked at Covent Garden from 1953 to 1960, and it was one of the happiest periods of my life. I was doing for the first time what I most wanted to do, and the work involved something that almost anyone would find exciting – a conscious effort to build, primarily, an ensemble within the theatre, and second, a public to appreciate what the ensemble was doing. That audience had to be won and we battled hard to win it. By the time I went to Covent Garden, the war was eight years behind us, and the spirit of the times had thrown down challenges that we were all prepared to take up. Everyone in the company enjoyed the sensation of helping to create a new tradition, and it was a very happy house to work in.

I was conscious at the start of a certain amount of suspicion to overcome. Did this young aristocrat know anything about the business? Would he work? Was he a snob? I remember the tenor James Johnston coming to see me in my office (when I eventually got one) and asking exactly what I was going to do. I tried to satisfy him, and he said: 'Anyway, what are we going to call you?' I said he was to call me George – what did he call Pat Terry (the company manager)? 'Ah, that's different, he's Pat! But you . . . I don't know.' But after a bit George I became to all and sundry.

During these early days I was also introduced to someone who was described as a very promising young singer, by name Joan Sutherland. I knew she was under-studying Penelope Rich in *Gloriana* and was to sing the role later, and I asked her (rather fatuously I suppose) if she was looking forward to it. I got an emphatically negative answer, but some weeks later, to her credit, Joan told me she had quite changed her mind and was finding the role very rewarding. Very good in it she was, too.

The company went that summer of 1953 to celebrate Rhodesia's fiftieth anniversary, but I stayed in London with instructions to go to Salzburg to discuss with Igor Markevich plans for *Le Coq d'Or* which he had agreed to conduct around Christmas time. To be involved in the planning of a new production from the start was of course a special excitement. Frederick Ashton was to produce and Mattiwilda Dobbs to sing the Queen of Shemakha.

Igor Markevich wanted Owen Brannigan for the King; we had Howell Glynne in the company and part of my job was to persuade him that Glynne would be good,which I did – and he was. For the Astrologer, with his weird, unearthly high notes, I suggested Hugues Cuénod, whom I had heard at the première of *The Rake's Progress* a couple of years before, and Igor, who was not specially versed in opera, fortunately knew and liked him. In the end, Ashton ducked out and Robert Helpmann took his place, making a fine job of the production, which was a considerable success. On the first night, I felt very proud of it all.

While the company was on holiday after Rhodesia, there was a short season of opera from Munich, and I was to act as host for the event, David Webster having to be in America on ballet business. I met the company at the station, looked after Rudolf Hartmann, the Intendant and chief producer, dined and wined him and singers like Lisa della Casa and Hermann Uhde, and established a relationship with Hartmann which proved valuable a dozen years later, when at short notice I invited the Munich Opera to bring two operas from the Cuvelliéstheater to the 1965 Edinburgh Festival. Munich in 1953 offered three Strauss operas – *Arabella*, *Capriccio* and *Die Liebe der Danae* – and I attended more than half the performances, delighting in the sounds of della Casa and Uhde in *Arabella*, and of Leonie Rysanek and Ferdinand Frantz in *Danae*, an opera I have sometimes since thought was underrated.

Our own season that year opened with a new *Carmen* and Anthony Asquith, the film director, was producing it. David had warned him that he must not fall into the trap of thinking there was unlimited time, 'as if it were a film' – to 'Puffin' Asquith's considerable indignation: 'Doesn't he realize that in films we work to a strict schedule?' But ten days before the first night he had failed to finish the last act, which was put into shape in a few days by Tyrone Guthrie, brought in like a company doctor to save the day. Guthrie was enormously practical, but not always kind; and I remember him going up on stage during Act II and saying loudly to Joan Sutherland, the Frasquita: 'What we want here, darling, is sex. Know the facts of life?', which was less than comforting to a somewhat gawky, if vocally talented, beginner. It all came right on the night, the Wakhevitch sets looked stunning, and we were left regretting that Puffin had not tried out his operatic hand on something like *La Traviata*, where personal relationships and not crowd scenes would have been the heart of the matter.

In those days, Covent Garden used in spring to go on tour, and in 1954 I set out with them, starting not far from home at Croydon. To begin with, I followed every move throughout the day, which was exhausting but interesting, and got to know a lot of people I had hardly met in London. Two of them were Liz Latham, a marvellously authoritative and knowledgeable stage manager, and Ande Anderson, her assistant, later for many years resident producer at Covent Garden and as warm-hearted a man as you could meet in the theatre. It is axiomatic that friendships grow on theatrical tours and one of the pleasant moments on arriving to work at the Coliseum nearly twenty years later was to find Bernard Collings, chief electrician for those tours, now a member of the Sadler's Wells staff.

I had known Reginald Goodall since early days after the war, when he conducted *Peter Grimes* and *The Rape of Lucretia* for Benjamin Britten, but he had made no great impression in Massenet and Verdi in Covent Garden performances. On that 1954 tour, Goodall was in charge of *Walküre*, with a strong cast including Anny Konetzni as Brünnhilde, Sylvia Fisher, Edith Coates, Hans Beirer, and Ludwig Hoffmann as Wotan, and the result was little short of a revelation. In Manchester, we had the opulent-voiced Hilde Konetzni, Anny's sister, instead of Sylvia Fisher who had gone off to get married, and the performance was perhaps even better. After the 'Ho-jo-to-ho', whose top notes were by now beyond Anny, Hilde waited behind the rock and put her arm round her sister to comfort her while she waited for the next entrance.

The Goodall 'revelation' – much written up subsequently by critics such as Andrew Porter, who heard the Croydon performance – coincided with the arrival of Kempe at Covent Garden, and the *Ring* became Kempe's for several years. Goodall did not even get a look at the orchestra for the preparatory work, as Kempe did not feel him in sympathy with his own approach. This hurt David Webster, who admired Goodall greatly; he looked upon Goodall as 'his' man – but Kempe too was 'his' find, and the international reputation was Kempe's. After Kempe came Solti, also a Wagnerian, and after a bit Goodall seems somehow to have lost heart or at least sympathy with the rehearsal possibilities Covent Garden had to offer.

It was not until Sadler's Wells, through the intervention of Edmund

Tracey, gave him *Mastersingers* in 1968, and in 1970 *Valkyrie*, that we came to know what we had been missing all those years. Or, in actual cold fact, *had* we? *Could* Goodall have worked satisfactorily without the unusually extensive, time-consuming, expensive, infinitely rewarding rehearsal offered him at Sadler's Wells? We shall never know – but I shall long remember those tour *Walküre* performances of 1954.

I recently came across a press-cutting from that tour which referred in characteristically flippant style to my presence in Manchester as a working member of the Covent Garden Company. This seemed to astonish the reporter, but David Webster dealt with his questioner in equally characteristic dead-pan fashion: 'Like all my employees,' he was quoted as saying, 'he gives every satisfaction.'

In my second full season at Covent Garden, we achieved two world premières of important British works: Walton's *Troilus and Cressida* on 3 December 1954 and Tippett's *Midsummer Marriage* on 27 January 1955 – madness by any reckoning but achieved somehow, what is more with the same tenor, Richard Lewis, in the lead in both operas. The works could not have been in greater contrast. Walton's is the operatic equivalent of a 'well-made play', modelled carefully on what he personally liked best in the operas he knew well; Tippett's a long, occasionally sprawling compendium of the many philosophical ideas and trends which he found appealing at that time. However hard we tried to avoid it, for many of us it was impossible not to take sides.

Opposition to *Midsummer Marriage* was led by David Webster's deputy, Steuart Wilson, which precipitated a difficult situation. This group maintained that the opera was much too long, very awkward to sing, in fact nearly impossible to perform – and there was an element of truth in their view. Christopher West, its producer, some of the younger members of the music staff, and I were David Webster's strongest supporters in his successful attempt to maintain it in our programme. In the end, we made quite a success of both ventures, but those of us in the Tippett camp found it more and more difficult to maintain interest in *Troilus*, while the Tippett-knockes were able to point to the work's length, its apparently contradictory dramatic themes, and the less than satisfactory box office.

It was a good lesson as far as I was concerned in how hard it is to avoid being drawn into controversy, even when, as in this case, the controversy is artificial and unnecessary. In my time at Covent Garden, I was accused of being pro-Callas and anti-Tebaldi, for Boris Christoff and against Rossi-

Lemeni, favourable to Britten and hostile to Walton; and it was certainly not easy to preserve detachment.

Looking back, I am quite sure *Midsummer Marriage* is the masterpiece we then sensed it to be, a work for all time. It has never stopped fascinating me, so that with every repetition I find certain awkwardnesses of phraseology, certain clumsinesses, mattering less, and the whole an even more rewarding experience than before. But a subsequent revival of *Troilus* has convinced me that this too is a rewarding work, on any terms a successful opera, and a bit unlucky perhaps in its initial timing in that it was born under what amounted to a low-brow star. I think incidentally that Walton's decision to revamp the soprano role of Cressida for the great mezzo Janet Baker was a cardinal error. The original high tessitura gave the role a nervous vitality, which at the same time brought to Cressida a certain attraction and, in its intimation of nervous strain, suggested the highly-strung girl whose too-frequent disappointments would manoeuvre her into a false position. With a mezzo tessitura, this strain is less apparent, and I hope the composer's decision to allow no other version is not final.

We were not satisfied that we had a contralto able to take care of the awkward but rewarding role in *Midsummer Marriage* of Sosostris, the soothsayer. I felt that I had heard just the voice, Oralia Dominguez, a Mexican mezzo, who sang much in Germany. She auditioned for the role just seven weeks before the première, on the morning of the first night of *Troilus*, and we took her. Living dangerously it undoubtedly was, and I cannot claim that her words were audible at rehearsal or on the first night. But I doubt if anyone else's voice has fitted the role so well since then, just as I doubt if any subsequent production has come as near to fulfilling Tippett's unconventional scenic and production demands as that original staging by Christopher West, with Barbara Hepworth's remarkable sets and John Cranko's inspired choreography.

A week before the first night, the BBC's TV *Panorama* programme asked for a short discussion with the composer. David Webster himself would not do it and asked me to go instead. I talked on TV for half an hour with Michael and John Pritchard, who was conducting, taking the opportunity of having the enchanting Adèle Leigh (the original cast's Bella) sing a short excerpt for the viewers – a rather rare example of an operatic preview before the large audience that a TV programme could provide. Michael became shy in the middle and would not say 'live' what he had told me beforehand – that he had originally asked T. S. Eliot to write the libretto – and I remember him at supper afterwards with his hair still sprinkled with gold-dust make-up. The newspapers wrote mainly about the 'first member of the royal family to appear on TV', which left me with only one hand clapping.

In my innocence, I had never imagined that my arrival at Covent Garden could threaten anybody. On the contrary, I felt that my passion for opera would be apparent to all and justify my presence on the staff. The morning after I started work, I was therefore more than a little surprised to receive a Private and Confidential note from Sir Steuart Wilson, David Webster's deputy and a distinguished man I had been on friendly terms with for several years, saying in effect: 'Your arrival causes many misgivings. What do you expect to do? David has told nobody about it, not even his deputy. That is the kind of trust he puts in us all.'

David advised me to take no notice, but a few weeks later a memo from Steuart went the rounds following the assumption of the roles of Queen Elizabeth and Essex in *Gloriana* by Constance Shacklock and John Lanigan respectively: 'Last night's important changes of cast seemed to me eminently successful and the bigger voices told well. It will not help matters if members of the staff are heard telling people in the audience that they should have come another night and not to hear "the second cast".' Another palpable hit; I had myself heard Marion say just this to friends in the interval, and they must have repeated the remark to Steuart.

War between us was never open – he was one of the senior musical administrators of the country and had been a most distinguished singer, and I could hardly have been more junior – but his constant sniping at David Webster was barely concealed and it came as a relief to know that he had reached official retiring age in summer 1955 and would not return the following season. At the last performance of 1954–5, on a Saturday night, David showed me a copy of the *People* containing an interview with Steuart, who said that, now he was no longer a member of Covent Garden's staff, he proposed to expose the way it and other British musical institutions were riddled with homosexuality, which he was determined to eradicate from the arts. There was never a follow-up, and it all came to nothing – but what a farewell!

I last saw Steuart in 1962 as I queued as a sightseer to get into the newly completed Coventry Cathedral. There stood Steuart; we greeted each other as old acquaintances, which is what we were. It was good to have a last glimpse of someone whom I had come to think of as an enemy in such mellowed circumstances.

Respect for the stage area itself was something I had acquired early. Once the stage is prepared for the performance, no one, I believed then and believe still, should walk on it in case footmarks show, the stage cloth gets wrinkles, or anything occurs to interfere with the main purpose of the day. That feeling of something approaching reverence was agreeably reinforced when a touring Kabuki company, brought from Japan by Sol Hurok, came for a short season in September 1955 to Covent Garden. It was explained that nobody could walk on their stage – a raised platform covering perhaps half our stage and elaborately groomed and polished every night – without removing their shoes, which was after all standard practice in any Japanese house, and that after it was fitted up at Covent Garden a ceremony would be necessary to 'bless' it for the season. Webster being away with the Ballet Company in America, it fell to me to do the honours. The role was not hard; one went on stage at the appropriate moment, sat on a plain hard seat without a back, drank ceremonially with the principals of the company a cup of *saké*; they executed a couple of manoeuvres, and all was done. Ian Hunter, who had done it in Edinburgh, assured me the only prerequisites were to have socks without holes in them and not to spill the *saké*, but I knew my own propensities where public ceremonial is concerned and was glad when all was over and nothing had gone wrong.

Sol Hurok, who had assembled the Kabuki company, was the most exuberant and confident impresario of any I ever met. I hardly knew him then, but later, in New York, I met him with David and found that his stories of the past – 'Once, when I was in Paris with Ysaye, Busoni was going after dinner to accompany Melba and Chaliapin in some songs . . .' – however unlikely, were all true. Hurok had known everybody, and had represented half of them. He had become an institution in New York, and David told me he was once there when Hurok said, 'Can't you stay on a day? On Thursday I have my annual party for the critics – champagne and caviar and all that.' David asked him why he bothered; he could hardly expect them to give him a good notice rather than a bad one merely because he gave a party for them. 'Of course not,' said Hurok. 'But there are two ways of writing a bad notice.'

The quality of performance is what the public and indeed the critics must judge an ensemble by. Rafael Kubelik was responsible for an *Otello* during autumn 1955 which caused virtually a change of mind in public and critics about the possibilities of the young company. Admittedly we had Ramon Vinay and Gré Brouwenstijn as guests, but the remainder of the cast was from the ensemble, and the results were very good indeed. Gré was regally magnificent and Vinay's Otello, as it had been the first time I saw it in Milan in 1949 and at Covent Garden in 1950 with la Scala, an incomparable assumption of one of the greatest roles. The grandeur of Act I and the poetry of the love duet was his, and no one else threatened physical danger in Act II like he did, no one else produced so frenzied a reaction to betrayal. Not only was he master of telling detail but everything he had had stature, and he was the most co-operative and magnanimous of colleagues. Years later, I went to see him in Venice when he had resumed the baritone roles with which he began his career, and his Falstaff, vocally nothing to write home about, was just as full of musical and dramatic nuance as had been Otello. And *big* too.

We followed with a new *Magic Flute* in January 1956 to celebrate the two-hundredth anniversary of Mozart's birth, a serious and beautiful production by Christopher West with sets by John Piper and of course conducted by Rafael himself. In January, Elsie Morison and Richard Lewis were fine as Pamina and Tamino, but by autumn we had Joan Sutherland and Peter Pears in these roles and the whole thing had ripened. The German producer Günther Rennert used to tell me that every serious producer ought to do a new *Magic Flute* every five or six years, rethinking his approach to the subject; it was the touchstone of humanity and of invention.

After two or three years, I had become useful to David Webster, as he knew that I believed in what he was trying to do and was discreet. We talked endlessly of the future and, quite soon after Kubelik arrived, discovered that he shared the enthusiasm David and I both felt for Berlioz's *The Trojans*, of which we resolved to make a production. David wanted John Gielgud to produce; Gielgud insisted on Mariano Andreu as the designer, and we eventually mounted the mighty work in 1957 with only a single guest in the long cast – Blanche Thebom, a handsome American mezzo, as Dido.

David had decided we must bring in new singing blood from Canada, and he held auditions there in early autumn 1956, returning to tell us that he had found two good young tenors: one a lyric of real quality, Richard Verreau, and another, Jon Vickers, a strong, youthful, all-purpose kind of voice who might take the place of the no longer young but still invaluable Jimmy Johnston.

Vickers was first cast in an English revival of *Masked Ball*, and I went to Cardiff for his début. The personality was full of energy, and the singing powerful and brilliant. His arrival solved the problem of casting Aeneas in *The Trojans*, and indeed he made a wonderful success in this role, the whole production turning out to be one of the most worthwhile at Covent Garden during the decade.

We did not in those days do much to understudy our leading roles, and my later work with Sadler's Wells makes me see how frequently we went nearly naked to the battlefield. There was a scare in the later stages of preparation of *The Trojans* when Jon Vickers came one day to tell us that the doctor had that morning diagnosed measles in one of his two children. He himself had never had the infection and the risk was therefore great. We urged him to say nothing to the Music Director, who needed no such worry in the final stages of his assault on this mountain peak, and in the end decided to get two different tenors to learn the different halves of the opera. Fortunately we never needed to put this piece of panic-planning to the test as Jon survived and sang all the performances.

For some seasons Rudolf Kempe had been a regular guest, and the *Ring* was his each year. There is no point in pretending he was not disconcerted when Kubelik became Music Director, although he had himself been offered the post, but he came down with jaundice in autumn 1957 and was never quite the same force again. In any case, we felt we needed another ingredient amongst our guest conductors, and for some time had been trying to persuade Carlo Maria Giulini to conduct for us. We were told that he would not conduct anything but a new production, but we persisted in offering him important revivals, to be informed each time by the agent that he would not agree. I saw him one year in Edinburgh, when he was conducting *Falstaff* for Glyndebourne, and told him how sorry we were that he had not accepted the offers we had made. He looked rather mystified, and I later learnt that he had never in fact received any offer from Covent Garden!

The problem was not difficult to solve: the agent had never made the approach, convinced (correctly, I suspect) that Giulini would anyhow have refused. But we felt this reluctance to pass on Covent Garden's offers, quite apart from being less than straightforward, weakened our hand in the sense that an approach for a new production would come to him, not as we thought as the culmination of several invitations, but as an offer out of the blue.

In October 1956, Giulini, David Webster, Rafael Kubelik and I lunched at the Savoy Grill, where he agreed to our suggestion of a new production of the five-act version of *Don Carlos* for summer 1958, with Luchino Visconti to produce. *Don Carlos* celebrated the centenary of the opening of the building, with a magnificent production and a splendid cast. Only Jon Vickers among the leading singers was a member of the ensemble, but the performance was of a quality to break new ground in its field, and to establish Giulini as the leading conductor of Italian opera anywhere, a reputation on which his temperament did not allow him to capitalize. For my part, I had the satisfaction of knowing that I had played some part in the planning and casting of the great enterprise.

Ironically, the success of that international cast presaged the end of our ensemble policy, as the Board, already pressing for an element of internationalization, was quick to twig that this brought success much more certainly and easily than did our efforts to develop native talent. From then on the cry was for more and more international singers. David asked me to 'cost' the forthcoming season as if we were engaging everyone from outside, as he believed this might convince the Board that the cost of the change of policy would be too great.

Kubelik himself said that he felt our *Don Carlos*, though a fine achievement, was a much easier one than other things we had attempted, simply because we brought in the top singers and then put them on display. This was too simple an explanation, as it is quite possible to engage the best talent and make less than ideal use of it, but it contained a grain of truth. I think the episode soured Kubelik and was one of the reasons why he would not renew his contract after that initial three years, even though David Webster tried to persuade him to do so. It was sad that there was some bitterness in his leaving, as he was much loved inside the building. Hindsight suggests there was insufficient steel in his character to enable him to carry through the job of musical direction.

Personally, I was devoted to him and we had splendidly rumbustious evenings together, at Orme Square or at his house in Hampstead, when we laughed and drank, and made light of the difficulties and rejoiced over the successes. I remember an evening at Orme Square when he played through with mounting excitement most of the score of Tchaikovsky's *Mazeppa*, and another at his house when he lectured several of us, including Ramon Vinay and his wife, late into the night on the iniquities of Schoenberg (whose music he incidentally conducted splendidly on record) and the dodecaphonic method, which he described as against nature and natural harmony.

I also remember early in his association with Covent Garden taking him and his violinist wife out to dinner in Soho. She was sitting at the end of the table, with Rafael on one side and me on the other, when she dropped a boiling snail down her cleavage. The division of labour was obvious: I sustained it from below in case it fell any further, Rafael retrieved it from above, she shrieked. I can't think what our fellow guests thought was going on but it all seemed quite scientific at the time, unlike the positively undergraduate assault Rafael launched on a fellow Czech, the designer Jan Brazda, as we made our way through Soho Square to where we had parked the car. This produced such a riot of noise that a policeman intervened and we had to explain that it was the high spirits of opera and not a developing Soho crime.

Kubelik was a committed and splendid colleague who identified himself totally with the work and his collaborators. I remember we were once discussing the producer for a particular opera and he did not like whoever had been suggested. 'No, no! I think it should be someone of *our* age!' David looked at me and later said, 'I wonder how old exactly he thinks you and I are?' We worked out that we were ten years apart – David fifty-four, Rafael forty-four and I thirty-four – but we were colleagues and therefore to Rafael coevals.

Kubelik was a conductor of, at his best, a fine abandon, with an ability to conjure sound and inspiration from his ensemble and his orchestra. I always found him a patrician musician, unwilling to take the easy way out, very well prepared, and only inclined sometimes to schedule too much rehearsal so that he risked grinding the ensemble's freshness into the ground. David Webster felt he had done this with *The Magic Flute* in January 1956, when the critics complained of a certain lack of spontaneity, but the rehearsals paid dividends the following autumn. In this new production Kubelik took immense pains over Papageno, reducing strings dramatically at his entry in Act I to suggest distance (two desks only of firsts, I remember) and digging out from the vaults a remarkable affair of jangling bicycle bells for his chimes in the Act I finale and 'Suicide' aria, which was hated by our orchestral manager (because of its tendency to be out of tune) but was undeniably effective.

Some of what we did during that period was carefully planned, like *The Trojans*, some had unexpected results, like *Don Carlos*, some was quite accidental, like performing *Boris* in Russian. This was after Kubelik had left as Music Director but was still with us as conductor. We had asked George London to sing the title role, naturally in English. He eventually turned it down, and we decided the only other appropriate person to do it would be Boris Christoff. Christoff refused to sing in anything but Russian, Kubelik would not contemplate a mixed language performance, and it was therefore settled that we should teach the whole company Russian to perform this narrative epic to an audience which was basically English-speaking – a solecism if ever there was one, but applauded as a proper solution by the Board. Another accident was the triumphant début of Leontyne Price as Aida in summer 1958. Anita Cerquetti, a very large woman with a big voice, had been contracted, but had had to have her appendix removed ('How did they find it?' asked Maria Callas), but Price's triumph was of a rare order and heralded the start of her international career.

Excitements while I was at Covent Garden were often in connection with our attempt to develop stars within the ensemble. Amy Shuard had been originally scheduled to sing Elisabeth in *Don Carlos*, but Giulini heard adverse reports of her Aida and asked us to change the casting. We then made plans to put Amy forward in the title role of *Turandot*, with a new tenor beside her as Calaf, Hans Kaart, a Dutchman who started life in Holland as an actor but had a splendid and untiring dramatic voice with a brilliant top. The revival of *Turandot* was an exciting occasion and both Amy Shuard and Hans Kaart came out of it resplendently, the former established as a true dramatic soprano with the proper brilliance and stamina at the top, and the latter as an excellent potential member of the company.

That was the kind of evening which gave me most satisfaction; that, and such things as the early appearances of Joan Sutherland in leading roles. We had cast her as Agathe in the second team of our new production of *Freischütz* in 1954, Sylvia Fisher being the first Agathe. Joan's singing of the role was remarkable, and I used to go back night after night specifically to hear her in the slow aria in the last act, in which for beauty of sound and purity of *legato* it was hard to find her equal. She was excellent as Antonia in *Hoffmann*, highly promising as Micaela and Desdemona, and David Webster and I among others were convinced from the start that, even though she always looked a big girl on stage, she possessed so rare a vocal talent that we should set about putting her forward in something special.

She and her husband Richard Bonynge favoured *Lucia*, maintaining that she was going in this direction rather than towards Wagner and the dramatic Italians. David and I agreed that Lucia would be the role that should establish her once and for all – not so easy then, with most of the repertory of that period of operatic history still quite out of favour and no production of *Lucia* in Great Britain since 1926.

First of all we seemed balked by an Italian production of the opera with Virginia Zeani in the lead at the Stoll Theatre, at about the time we were making up our minds, and, worse still, when the Board did not look with any favour on the suggestion. We had already asked Christopher Hassall to make a translation (which still exists in draft), when they said we should have second thoughts. The music staff agreed with the Board and suggested we should revive instead *Louise*, whose soprano lead is first among equals. In the end, we got the Board to accept that we should mount *Lucia* for Joan if we could engage the great Italian conductor Tullio Serafin. She sang for him, he professed himself delighted, and said he would conduct the new production – but only in Italian. The rest, as the books say, is history; Joan triumphed in the role – and I have not the slightest doubt that there is no member of that Board and very few members of the music staff who would not now maintain that they had discerned her potential for it from the start!

The funny thing is that this 'fame in a night' – that is what it amounted to – was anticipated by most people in the theatre and in the audience. Joan's ability, not yet proclaimed, was sensed by everyone from her previous roles. There is a postscript to this triumph. Joan's career developed through roles in operas by Handel, Bellini and Donizetti; but Serafin, when we asked him to advise on how to build on the success of *Lucia*, suggested she should next sing Verdi's Lady Macbeth. This is true dramatic stuff, and I have often asked myself how differently that admittedly great career might have developed if Serafin's advice had been taken by Joan and Richard. As it was, she followed it up with Amina in *La Sonnambula* – quite another kettle of fish from Lady Macbeth.

In November 1957, we had scheduled a revival of *Elektra* for Kempe with Christel Goltz in the title role. Goltz fell ill only a few weeks before the première, but by pure chance I had only recently read a rave review for one Gerda Lammers in the role, and had noticed that this singer was due to give a recital a day or two later in London at Mahatma Gandhi Hall. I went along with Freddy Dietz, the agent, and found her rehearsing. She was free, she sang for Kempe who approved the choice, and we realized as rehearsals were going on that we had a marvellous Elektra on our hands. The performance was one of the greatest individual successes I ever remember in London, and the rave notices I had read were repeated.

Gerda Lammers was a Dutch woman, living since the war in Germany, and she was rare at that time in portraying Elektra as a princess, not a raving lunatic, and singing the whole role as if it were an exercise in *bel canto*. During rehearsals we observed at one point a particularly effective, twisting fall. Christopher West, who was in charge of the revival, asked her if that was what she was going to do on the night. 'Oh yes,' she said; 'It is very astonishable for the publikum!'; and she was right.

In 1957, the fabled Lotte Lehmann came to London as the guest of Joan Cross and her school to give some master classes. These took place at Wigmore Hall and turned out, as I have since found all such affairs, of more value as display cases for the master than classes for the students. All the same, I shall not soon forget Lehmann taking two talented girls through the scene of the Presentation of the Rose from *Rosenkavalier* – she had, after all, in her time played Sophie and Octavian as well as Marschallin – and demonstrating to the Octavian how to make the presentation. I don't know if Lehmann had long arms; but I do know that nobody ever made a more gracefully rounded gesture with the rose and then stretched further than she did on that occasion. From *that* something could be learnt.

Before she left, she came to lunch at Orme Square and we asked David Webster as well. She told us that she had a young mezzo-soprano pupil, a coloured girl – one said 'coloured' in those mealy-mouthed days – in whom she believed and whom she wanted to audition for us with a view to taking her first steps on the operatic stage as a member of the Covent Garden company. She recommended her highly, and we readily agreed to the only condition the great lady made, that we should report to *her* first on what we thought about her pupil, and, if we wanted her, make an approach through her teacher.

The girl duly turned up a week or two later, looking handsome and singing like an angel – the best audition (with Nell Rankin's three or four years earlier) I ever remember; we bubbled with enthusiasm – but, honouring our agreement, not to the singer herself, to whom I made complimentary but non-committal remarks afterwards. David cabled Lehmann to say we were keen to take her on. We waited for acceptance and then I received an anguished letter from the old lady to say that, without telling her, her pupil had auditioned in Zürich and had accepted an engagement there. Her name was Grace Bumbry.

CHAPTER TEN

Covent Garden: Personalities and Politics 1953-72

IN HIS BOOK *Double Harness* Lord Drogheda writes of discord at Covent Garden on the ballet side in the late 1950s, specifically of complaints by Ninette de Valois that she was not kept properly informed about what was going on and frequently had her scheduled ballet dates changed. At the time I should doubtless have resisted the suggestion, but now I have little doubt that there was truth both in the story that she complained – Ninette was not disloyal but certainly not one for keeping silent if she felt her rights infringed – and in the burden of the complaint. This was probably one of the areas in which David tried to play his cards too close to his chest, trusting in his ability to play the conjuror and keep everyone happy.

Our method of planning was quite simple. Ninette decided when the new ballets or major revivals were to take place and space was made for them on the plan, for which I was basically responsible, and on the stage. She and I hardly ever communicated directly, perhaps because for most of the time I worked at Covent Garden I had no defined position; to have talked to her myself might have simplified things but would have gone against David's habit of non-delegation (one of the things Lord Waverley warned me about when I went to see him). David's custom was to give me the dates, and I then built them into a plan.

The arrangement was that there should be the same number of opera and ballet performances; and David believed that ballet, coming from the company and relying on virtually no guests, was rather more flexible than opera. Ballet needed less scenery on the stage than opera, because they wanted the space to dance in (this was before the days of mammoth ballet productions like Nureyev's 1977 *Romeo and Juliet*, which could anyhow never have existed in that form in repertory). Ballet also needed less rehearsal time on stage, because dancers could rehearse in a studio of appropriate size – or so David led me to believe, and so I still think in essence it was.

But of course, not *quite*, and certainly not *always*. Sometimes he would ask for the plan to be changed to suit the Ballet Company, and this was always done when humanly possible, which was most of the time. Doubtless there were times when it was not done, and then the Ballet would be left with a grievance, on the whole legitimate – there is nothing so maddening as someone else's unalterable plans which cannot be so convincingly explained as one's own legitimate demands. David preferred trust to explanation and often got away with it – but again, not always.

Truth to tell, I think we were all a little frightened of Ninette and her sometimes brusque manner, and it is maybe a pity contacts were not developed to remove this obstacle. Perhaps David felt direct communication would weaken his control of the whole complicated apparatus of the Opera House, but had Ninette and I discussed the position and come to him only in an *impasse* (as might have happened had I stayed, and doubtless obtained after I had gone), most friction could have been avoided – unless perhaps Ninette was like the conductor Erich Kleiber who, greeted on arrival by David with, 'Mr Kleiber, I hear you sometimes have trouble in the theatre. I hope you won't while you're here', growled back: 'When there is no trouble in a theatre, I make it!' But I think, with her Irish sense of humour and my sense of her position, it would not have come to that.

I have to admit that, in spite of seeing hundreds of performances here and everywhere, I have never become a balletomane, much as I love many individual ballets and some individual dancers. After I started to write for *Ballet and Opera*, I used often to go with Dicky Buckle to see visiting ballet companies – Roland Petit, and the 'fringe' companies that proliferated after the war, as well as Sadler's Wells – and I listened to what he had to say; he was expert and wide-ranging in sympathies which extended far beyond those of the average critic.

The great musical ballets of the Sadler's Wells Company – *Tricorne* and *Sleeping Beauty* and several Ashton ballets – I saw again and again. Margot Fonteyn I admired without reservation, but the musical side of the dance as it was practised at Covent Garden I often, perhaps priggishly, deplored. Scores of importance were badly played and poorly conducted, much totally inferior music was allowed into the theatre via the ballet, and I longed for a musical policy as serious as the planning of the ballets themselves. I had read that Diaghilev came to ballet via music, and certainly the list of his commissions makes impressive reading. I could not understand why Balanchine's New York City Ballet could produce weeks of dance to serious music while we had to wait for occasional solace from *The Prince of the Pagodas* or Stravinsky's *Agon*. The introduction of Prokofiev ballets was to me a delight, but the general musical policy seemed haphazard and hard to accept.

In the world of ballet my own greatest experience while I worked at Covent Garden came at the time of the first visit to London of Moscow's Bolshoi in autumn 1956. We already had the opera season planned and had to go to considerable lengths to unravel or postpone what had been scheduled, because the finalization of arrangements for this Russian season came late in the day. The reality made the waiting and the alterations worthwhile. Those of us who worked at Covent Garden were allowed to buy four tickets for each of the ballets, and competition was fierce. The opening *Romeo and Juliet* (to Prokofiev's music) will not quickly be forgotten by those of us who were there. It could be argued (and was) that it was all taken at a rather leisurely pace, and that the dance seemed rationed to accommodate the drama rather than the other way round, as we in the West had become accustomed to. Galina Ulanova was the Juliet, already forty-six but a genius of technique and stage resource; none of us found her incongruous. In one of the intervals David Webster commented on how, when she had to make an exit, she went first towards the other side of the stage and then ran very fast with very short steps so as to enlarge the possibilities and prolong the magic.

One of the ballets the Russians brought was a rather meretricious piece called *The Fountain of Bachshisherai*, whose action involved among much else an effective conflagration on the stage. To a matinée of this effusion came Prince Charles, then aged about eight. A few days later, a message came from Buckingham Palace to the effect that the Queen would like the Royal Box for this ballet during the last week of the season. Consternation! Ulanova was not billed for that performance; she did not perhaps even dance the role any more (though she created it twenty years before); and Ulanova *must* be on when the Queen came – Bolshoi protocol, nay, decency and common sense, demanded it. In place of *The Fountain of Bachshisherai*, it was suggested, she would dance *Giselle* that night for the Queen.

The message came back from the Palace that Her Majesty did not want to put anyone out, and anyhow wanted to see *The Fountain of Bachshisherai*. David Webster pleaded with his contacts, the chairman wrote officially to see what could be done, the Foreign Office made representations, I was bidden to do what I could behind the scenes. I don't know what tipped the scales, but I do know that in the end the Queen saw Ulanova in *Giselle*, and that I was rewarded with an extra pair of tickets for that night on the grounds that I had earned it.

During those Bolshoi weeks I came nearer than at any other time to becoming an *aficionado* of the ballet. The music was taken seriously – under the principal conductor Yuri Fayer, *Giselle* sounded the masterpiece Dicky Buckle had always assured me it (in ballet terms) was – and the company's resources of talent seemed limitless. Because the Opera had eventually to begin, the Bolshoi could not extend their stay at Covent Garden even though they offered to, but it was found that for the week following the Covent Garden season the Davis Theatre, Croydon, was free.

There, on her last night, I saw Ulanova in *The Dying Swan*. I don't remember her dance as spectacular, but I do remember her final curtain. The calls lasted much longer than the short ballet itself, and she came back to bow again and again. Then, she seemed to go further over than before, delayed a little, and I suddenly knew this was her last call, that this new-found idol was about to vanish from my life for ever. I was unlikely to go to Moscow, and even if the Bolshoi returned to London within five years, she would be too old to dance. I hate goodbyes more than anything else in the world, even those more personal and less final than this one, but at that moment the world seemed to stop still. Then, with her fast, short steps she was gone, and I had lost something I never before knew I wanted.

Life at Covent Garden during these years may have been enjoyable but it was not all plain sailing, and during the late 1950s there were rumblings. Frank Howes of *The Times* once started a music leader about Kubelik's resignation and the fact that there was no announcement of a successor with the words, 'The news from Covent Garden is bad.' We felt we could hold the fort well enough with guest conductors like Kempe and Giulini until we got the right man; Howes and *The Times* disagreed.

Then Garrett Drogheda took over first as acting chairman while Lord Waverley was ill (Waverley died in early 1958), and subsequently as chairman. When he heard of the plans to mount a Handel work initially at the 1958 Leeds Festival, he blew up a tempest of a fuss. The Board had been told nothing of the plan, he said, they were being railroaded into it, and anyhow it was ridiculous to do Handel for the first time at Covent Garden in the year preceding the bi-centenary of Handel's death which was to be celebrated, together with the ter-centenary of Purcell's birth, in 1959. In the end, it was found that the project had been minuted in Opera Committee reports, and calm and reason prevailed. But the episode could be seen as a symptom of the way Garrett's chairmanship might develop. Decisions would be queried, judgment constantly questioned. By autumn 1958, David Webster was telling me in all seriousness that he was doubtful whether he should continue under pressure of this kind. He certainly saw certain developments, such as the appointment of Walter Legge to the Board, as deliberate threats to his authority if not his position, and the correctness of his suspicion is confirmed by the statement in Garrett's autobiography that the Board considered putting Walter Legge forward as Artistic Director.

Events of those years highlighted a quite legitimate point of debate: to what degree should unpaid Boards, in whom control of many state-supported British institutions is vested, interfere in the conduct of the institution? Ultimate responsibility is undoubtedly theirs; but day-to-day planning and work must be carried out by the appointed officials, provided everything is within a pattern of policy and a budget laid down and approved by the Board. No Board can attempt to make decisions that demand speedy action; the spectacle of busy men and women from the City and other corridors of power suddenly summoned to an emergency session to decide who to invite to conduct or sing *Traviata* when a Giulini or a Callas drops out is too ludicrous to take seriously.

It would be equally ludicrous, I would suggest, if an Intendant were required to have a producer's choice of designer ratified by the Board, and yet something of that kind is postulated by Garrett Drogheda's memorandum about the choice of designer for *The Trojans*, a condition (as I understood it) of John Gielgud's agreement to produce at Covent Garden. Committees, David had said in a note, were 'mainly advisory and consultative'. Garrett felt that David was being obstructive and, revealingly, his memorandum contained the following passage:

> . . . all major decisions relating to the employment of artists should be discussed by the Sub-Committee before action is taken by the Executive. The minutes of the Opera Sub-Committee . . . are always circulated each month in time for the Board's monthly meeting, so that any proposal can be questioned if any member of the Board so wishes. This cannot be so if decisions are taken by the Executive without reference to the Sub-Committee. I fully recognize that there are occasions when a swift decision is necessary, but on such occasions it should be possible for the Executive to refer to the chairman of the Sub-Committee, particularly when the decision proposed is contrary to the sense of the Sub-Committee's discussion on the matter in question.

I could never have subscribed to such a view, which seems to me to a great extent to beg an important question. Is an Intendant fully executive, or is he mainly the mouthpiece of a Board or a committee, to which he must refer decisions? Should he visit Rome to see Giulini and Visconti and then refer their choice of designer and singer to a committee? The mind boggles. Not in Edinburgh, not in Leeds, not at Sadler's Wells or English National Opera, have I ever been put into such a position, nor could I ever have accepted it – and I speak as an admirer of the Board system. The chief executive of such organizations is to my mind appointed to carry out the Board's *policy*, and he in his turn accepts it as an implied condition of the job that major failure will lose him that job, and failure on a lesser scale will endanger it.

The system, unwritten like the British constitution (though there is case law in the Arts Council's upholding of an Artistic Director against the Board of a theatre company), is sophisticated, rather like democracy itself. It demands acceptance of unwritten provisions, understanding, considerable give-and-take, above all trust between a Board and its chief executive. Garrett at heart to my mind rejected such an arrangement, which he felt left the Board impotent, and he believed that he had cause not to trust Webster. Webster however was a senior and experienced executive used to running his own show and taking responsibility for his actions. There was a clash of personality here and, but for the advent of Georg Solti as Music Director, who brooked no questioning of the artist's absolute authority and in whom Garrett believed, the outcome of the clash could have been unpleasant.

It would be wrong if I left the impression that I thought Garrett Drogheda a poor chairman. It was sometimes a bit hard to work with him, mainly because of his insistence on being involved in everything, but in many respects he was first-rate, with the interests of the organization at heart, his considerable energies and influence constantly at its disposal. His achievement at Covent Garden was to change the whole concept of the Royal Opera House's subsidy, even perhaps the Government's attitude to subsidy of the metropolitan artistic institutions. Moreover, whatever his gadfly tendencies as chairman (and in his book he goes some way towards acknowledging them), he was a staunch and loyal friend when one was in difficulty, as I have cause to know and have tried elsewhere in this book to acknowledge.

David Webster on the other hand was a deeper influence on Covent Garden and its post-war development. It is much easier to dub a man 'great' than to substantiate the claim, but most who worked for David at that time would have poured scorn on anyone who doubted his right to the adjective. He half-unconsciously contributed towards an atmosphere within the house that most of us, myself unreservedly amongst them, found congenial. It was not so much the conviction that we were all working towards the same end, that we would whatever happened pull together – though these factors were present – which provided the 'happy atmosphere' on which we prided ourselves. Rather was it a sense of balance, a conviction that we stood for something worthwhile but had to earn our right to recognition and, having earned it, could never rest on our laurels. While David was in his heyday, to belong to the staff of the Royal Opera House imposed a duty to live up to ideals that we had all worked to see generally accepted. David's own mixture of genuine humility and deep pride in what he had accomplished, of hopeless shyness and absolute confidence in the rightness of his case and his ability to put it over – these qualities affected those who worked for him and helped to give the place an aura that I believe was conducive to good work and honest thinking.

Not every facet of his professional make-up was to be emulated, but ever since I left Covent Garden (more than twenty years ago as I write), I have kept David's example constantly in front of me, have asked myself what his attitude might have been in present circumstances, and have used his splendid blend of idealism and pragmatism as a standard by which to measure my own approach to the problems of theatre. There was, for all the skirmishing, in the Drogheda period as chairman of Covent Garden, no suggestion of a showdown between Board and management; but, if there had been, the Board might have been astonished at the deep roots of loyalty that David Webster unassertively commanded.

In 1959, I was made Controller of Opera Planning, a title which exercised the Board no end – nobody except the head of music and Ninette de Valois could be called Director – and which was suggested by Isaiah Berlin, one of its members, mainly I suspect because he liked the sound of the initials. By now I not only attended meetings of the Opera Committee, of which Isaiah was chairman, but, at Garrett's suggestion, of the Board as well. My job had changed subtly over the years and I was responsible for most aspects of operatic planning, co-ordinating and sometimes initiating casting of roles, negotiating with artists and their agents (David Webster kept a few favourites to himself), arranging performance dates and rehearsal schedules – everything to do with planning except fees. Even that was starting to creep in, and the success of the 1958 Leeds Festival, which I had run, seemed to suggest I could be trusted in areas with which I had not previously been concerned.

Within a few months of the creation of a title for my job, I had been offered and had accepted the artistic directorship of the Edinburgh Festival, and a few months later, before the advent of Georg Solti as Music Director (though his appointment was already agreed), had left to take up the position. Before I went, Garrett as Covent Garden's chairman made a characteristic and generous gesture – he presented me, on behalf of the Board, with a beautiful mechanical singing bird. He talked then in terms of my coming back to Covent Garden. The new man in my office, he said, needed time on his own, but, after I had been in Edinburgh a couple of years, he would ask me back as a co-opted member of the Opera Committee, not as a member of the Board. He was as good as his word, and I enjoyed those meetings and particularly the sensation of being again attached to what I thought of as my parent company.

But there were surprises in store. I was a member in my own right of the governing body of the newly-formed London Opera Centre, which had been set up by the Arts Council to replace the Opera School founded years before by Joan Cross and Anne Wood. After a year, it became clear that things weren't working out, but the Board lobby for Humphrey Procter-Gregg, the director, was strong, and even when the Centre's entire staff resigned in early summer 1964, this was represented as a plot on the part of Joan Cross and Anne Wood. Procter-Gregg nonetheless wrote to resign and, when it became plain that Joan and Anne were to be made, as I felt, scapegoats for the whole affair, Tony Gishford, Lois Sieff and I resigned from the governing body. I was a little surprised a couple of weeks later to get a letter from Garrett thanking me for my services on Covent Garden's Opera Committee, the term of my appointment having come to an end. It was maybe less surprising that I had never been told the appointment had a particular term.

A year or two later, when I had finished in Edinburgh and rumours that David Webster would soon leave Covent Garden were becoming audible, I was with David one day at lunch and told him quite straightforwardly that I had heard he would be retiring; did he think I might be a candidate to succeed him? He was evasive, and it was not hard to deduce that the succession was already promised – presumably to John Tooley, his second, whom I had got to know and like during my time at Covent Garden – and that David agreed with the decision. I could not but feel disappointed, but of course I had no claim to the job other than the qualifications I could show, and I knew how David had been relying on John those past years.

A year or so later, as chairman of the Music Panel of the Arts Council, I was an observer from the sidelines when the job actually came up. Lord Goodman, the Arts Council chairman, told me that the Council's Music Director had recently been asked to leave a Board meeting at Covent Garden while the matter of David Webster's successor was considered. Arnold

Goodman was indignant since he felt the Arts Council should know what was being discussed, and insisted that the post must be advertised. He was told this was not to be. 'Those Bourbons!' he exclaimed. 'They are besotted with their own power and don't see that people from outside may come to question it!' In the end, a compromise was reached: the refusal to advertise was maintained, but anyone who felt he had a claim to the position was allowed to write to the chairman for an interview.

Before long, Garrett asked me to lunch and suggested that, though he would of course have no right of official nomination, I should join the Covent Garden Board as a potential successor to himself as chairman. David Webster's successor had not yet been finally chosen, but I saw this as perhaps the only chance I had left of again being connected with a British opera company. I wrote to him, accepting to go back on the Board, and welcoming a resumption of at least some operatic activity.

Those were the years of Peter Hall's ascendancy at Covent Garden, with the prospect, once Georg Solti's directorship had ended, of a triumvirate heading the Opera Company's activities: John Tooley at the top and Colin Davis and Peter Hall as dual artistic directors. A new production of *Figaro* was planned with the two of them in charge, and a strong cast had been engaged when they decided that the performances, to make maximum impact, should be given in English. This went against the Board's policy of having everything in the original language (nothing I fancy has yet been given in Czech, nor, a cynic might argue, truly in Russian), and Garrett went into battle the moment the idea came up. At a Board meeting, I had said I was in favour of the English-language suggestion and Garrett asked me to write him a letter setting out the arguments. I did so as fairly as I could, suggesting that Covent Garden had reached the happy position of having the best of both worlds in that it was precluded by habit neither from original-language productions nor from translation, but I came down firmly in favour of translation for this particular opera in this particular case. Lord Robbins, similarly appealed to by Garrett, reached exactly the opposite conclusion.

As so often, principle in the end had little to do with the resolution of the argument. Sadler's Wells, with Charles Mackerras as the new Music Director, suggested they should perform *Il Trovatore* in Italian; this was seen as a riposte to a challenge, and it was with some nervousness and reluctance that the Covent Garden Board decided in favour of what the artistic directors-to-be wanted, with the rather heavy proviso that the singers who had been engaged accepted the decision. One of them refused; Colin Davis and Peter Hall accepted the new position, although Peter's resignation from the job before it had started put him out of the picture before *Figaro* reached the Covent Garden stage.

Peter Hall duly produced the opera two or three years later at Glyndebourne – in Italian! I have subsequently become convinced that a Covent Garden *Figaro* in English and a Sadler's Wells *Trovatore* in Italian could have provided quite educative and salutary experiences for all concerned – audiences, Boards and maybe the Arts Council as well. Too entrenched a position benefits neither audience nor performers.

In early 1972 I was asked to take over at Sadler's Wells Opera from Stephen Arlen, who had died very suddenly, and I had no compunction in accepting. I can't say I was really surprised to get a letter from my old friend Covent Garden's chairman within thirty-six hours of mine to him telling him I had got this new job; doubtless, he wrote, I would want to resign immediately from Covent Garden's Board.

My time as an employee at Covent Garden (1953–60) was a period I look back on with pleasure for the work it entailed and with affection for the institution as I knew it. It was a happy time and we felt we were a happy team. Garrett Drogheda was chairman for only part of the time I worked there, though for all of the short period when I was again, after fifteen years, a member of the Board. On a personal level I have considerable regard for him, but on policy I cannot pretend we have always seen eye to eye; and I have often wondered if I could have shown David Webster's patience, at least in public, if I had continued working at the Garden and not gone to the Edinburgh Festival.

CHAPTER ELEVEN

English Stage Company
1954-75

THE IDEA OF the English Stage Company (on the analogy of the English Opera Group, which was not a permanent ensemble but relied on festivals for its main outlet) came from a conversation in 1953 between Ronald Duncan and Oscar Lewenstein, who found it anomalous that there was no theatrical group prepared to mount offbeat plays for special occasions. In music and opera, it was easy to find such organizations, but not in the straight theatre. There was a whole range of stage works, including the kind of poetic play written by T.S.Eliot, Christopher Fry and Ronnie Duncan himself, which was seldom staged; when Ronnie and Oscar came to talk to me, they mentioned others then almost wholly neglected, like Beckett's *Waiting for Godot* and everything by Brecht from *The Threepenny Opera* to *The Caucasian Chalk Circle*. The idea seemed to me admirable; the problem was to turn it into practical terms.

The best thing I did for the English Stage Company was to refuse Ronnie's invitation to become chairman. The chairman, I argued, must be prepared to do much more than preside at meetings; he must be a fund-raiser. Edward Blacksell, a neighbour of Ronnie's in Devon, made the suggestion which solved the problem. He had a friend who had recently sold his business and was now working only part-time, but still brimming over with energy. Ronnie saw Neville and we lunched together on 29 November 1954, and he seemed prepared to come in, provided we found a theatre as a 'home', and provided we could get an artistic director to run the show under his chairmanship. Our choice lit on George Devine, who was coincidentally producing *Troilus and Cressida* at Covent Garden where I was working, and George accepted – not surprising, since we found he had put up an almost precisely similar scheme a few years before but had found no backers.

George and Neville made an odd team and it took the efforts of at least three of us to keep them and the company together over the ensuing years. George was something of a legend in the theatre, content to maintain a low profile but possessed of extraordinary determination. He was perhaps ruthless in that he was quite prepared to 'use' a company that had Ronald Duncan as a key figure, even though he disliked the kind of play Ronnie wrote and indeed put them on at the Royal Court only from a sense of duty – an attitude that Ronnie disliked with an intensity that rapidly turned to bitterness, at first at meetings and in the end in print.

Neville Blond was quite a different kind of man, with no particular knowledge of the theatre but great feeling for what makes things work, for success, and above all for people. He had always been successful and one of his assets was a very considerable charm, which he did not mind putting to use. We were confident he would put his energy behind the English Stage Company and would identify with it, provided we could formulate a set-up which satisfied him, and could make the books balance or at least feed him constantly with figures to show why they didn't. He found out that the Kingsway Theatre in Great Connaught Street was to be rebuilt and we had a lien on it until Alfred Esdaile, who was on our new Board, offered us the Royal Court Theatre in Sloane Square.

We started with a feeling of real purpose, even adventure. Neville early on suggested that Robin Fox should join both the Board and the Artistic Committee (of which I was chairman from the outset as well as being a Board member), and Robin proved invaluable to the whole enterprise – partly because of his rare theatrical knowledge and judgment, partly because he could retain passion while remaining above the fray, partly because he could seemingly without effort manage both George and Neville – no mean feat.

Neville announced that he would accept any plan put forward to the Council by the Artistic Committee, and George insisted that our little group read all the plays that he was seriously considering putting into the bill. I had never read plays before but quite soon got the hang of it, and most train journeys to and from Harewood or on behalf of Covent Garden involved devouring a couple of scripts. An early example came from John Osborne and was called *Look Back in Anger*. We knew it had already been rejected by several other managements but George was keen about it and I read it with mounting excitement on the way up to Harewood one evening. Dicky Buckle was staying with us over the weekend and I told him we had had a script from an unknown playwright, brilliantly written and enormously exciting. Would he like to read it – in confidence? He took it away and said next morning that he had found it a thrilling experience, but that we could never put such a thing on in the theatre. One could not insult an audience in this kind of way and, though he very much liked it himself, he could not see it being any kind of success. Nevertheless *Look Back in Anger* was the comet to which our wagon during that first season was hitched, the success that transferred to the West End, balancing the English Stage Company's books in its first year of operation and incidentally making fortunes for those connected with it.

In March 1956 I had been with George Devine to the Lord Chamberlain's Office after we heard that they would not give *Look Back in Anger* a licence. We asked them at the meeting what aspects of the dialogue they objected to, and they told us they could not accept the great speech in which Jimmy Porter, not knowing Alison is pregnant, charges her with nurturing inside her a growing lump of prejudice against him, while his friend Cliff squirms in misery not only at what he is saying but because he, unlike her husband, knows Alison's condition. What's wrong with that, we asked. 'It goes too far.' What should we cut? They would specify nothing and, in the end, we said: 'What you're saying is that it's *too good*!', and they agreed. John Osborne's solution was to halve the speech and send the script in again. They passed it this time.

I always had rather more time for the Lord Chamberlain's Office than some of my reforming friends. They had to administer a rule, which none of us liked, and on the whole did it not too badly. Don't believe the stories which specify their idiotic choice of alternative wording; they never made specific suggestions, though they would discuss alternatives. They also had a corporate sense of humour. Just before I started to work at Covent Garden, the administration realized they had forgotten to send in the libretto of *Gloriana* which, since it had never been performed, they were required to do as if it were a play. Within a day a message came through that all was passed apart from the explicit stage direction which had the Housewife in Act III empty a chamber pot over the heads of some of Essex's followers who were drumming up support for his cause. A chamber pot could not be shown on the stage. The solution was easy but the ruling rankled with me, and, on being met by the Comptroller of the Lord Chamberlain's Office, Norman Gwatkin, one day when I was going officially with my mother to St Paul's, I whispered to him as we walked side by side up the nave: 'What possessed you to censor that scene from *Gloriana*?', and got the deadpan reply: 'Oh, the Lord Chamberlain has always set his face against pots!'

The success of *Look Back in Anger* showed how, with subsidy from the Arts Council, which was important but insufficient, we could still make the operation into a success, and Neville was quick to cotton on to it. We needed nearly full houses all the time at the Royal Court if we were to make ends meet, and such returns were highly unlikely if we were to choose plays that were adventurous and in accord with our policy. Any transfer, any move to put the plays on to television, brought us extra income, and it was not long before Neville's first reaction to every programme we presented was, 'Which of these pieces you're offering me is going to transfer and make us some brass?' George didn't really like that, but it was the difference between survival and extinction; it was one of the issues between George and Neville which Robin Fox and the rest of us had to persuade each not to ram down the throat of the other.

It was not long before we heard that John Osborne was writing another play, *The Entertainer*, and we knew Laurence Olivier was interested in playing it. We read what John had finished – an act or a bit more – and were asked as the Artistic Committee to make a recommendation to the Council in order that the production with Olivier could be set up and contracts drawn.

We had an evening meeting at 2 Orme Square, at which Ronnie Duncan, Oscar Lewenstein, George Devine, Tony Richardson and I were present and, after very lengthy discussion, it emerged that Ronnie and Oscar were against doing the play, George, Tony and I for it. I said, 'Well, that's three of us for and two against. I will tell the Council.' 'But only you, Ronnie and I are members of the committee,' said Oscar, 'and that makes two against and one for. So we *don't* do it!' He was of course technically right, but I am afraid I told Neville the story forthwith and suggested that he and I should overrule the vote. Democracy went out of the window, we took a step towards a balanced budget, and incidentally put on one of the best plays we ever sponsored.

George was no hogger of the limelight – Tony Richardson had produced *Look Back in Anger* and, in spite of his own close friendship with John Osborne and the obvious financial advantages of being connected with his plays, George always insisted Tony should produce each new one as it came up. He was essentially a backroom dynamo, keeping everything going, prodding, cajoling, criticizing, helping out, sometimes producing, occasionally himself taking a part in a play. I remember him particularly with Joan Plowright in Ionesco's *The Chairs*, and in what must have been one of his last roles, as queen of a drag ball in John Osborne's *A Patriot for Me*, in which he was both funny and touching.

The subject of *A Patriot for Me* – a homosexual Austrian Chief of Staff in the years before 1914 being blackmailed by the Russians into betraying his country's secrets – fell foul of the censor, one of the last plays to do so, and we decided to turn the theatre into a club for the duration of the run. The process was uncomplicated, though we thought it against our 'principles', and the twenty-four hours which legally should elapse between joining the club and being eligible to buy a ticket were frequently ignored. We were had up before the court and it was decided that Laurence Olivier and I should be called as, so to speak, character witnesses for the company.

We waited side by side in court for some time and Larry was called first. His recital from the box of the oath had so musical and dying a fall on the final cadence – 'and nothing but the truth' – that you could hear the gasps of sympathy before he had started on a short recital of the company's virtuous enterprise. He was there for five minutes and there was no cross-examination. When it was my turn, I found it easy enough to express confidence in the company's claims and to testify to its ultimate probity, but much harder to deal with the gruelling cross-questioning that followed. I was president of the English Stage Society (the club that presented the play privately); how many meetings had I attended? None. Was I conversant with its rules? Could I tell the court approximately how many members it had? How long had it been in existence? How long must elapse between joining and being allowed to buy a seat? I must have made a poor impression and gone some way inadvertently to support the contention that the Society was a mere device to get round the law. But we were fined only a small sum and little leeway was lost.

The whole prodigious effort proved in the end too much for George Devine, who resigned, burnt out with the strain, and died not long after. I found him an engaging human being, sometimes direct to the point of near-rudeness, but a remarkable talent-spotter and protective of the talent that he discovered. He was slow and methodical in manner, frequently taking refuge behind a pipe which not only billowed forth protective smoke but took ages to fill and draw; but there was something confident about his recommendations and his decisions, and his loyalty was unassailable. The whole period with him is one I look back on with pleasure and real affection for all those who 'made' it.

After George was gone, we continued with a number of excellent directors – Bill Gaskill, Lindsay Anderson, Tony Page – and did good work from time to time over the years. But then Neville died, to be followed, after a brief period as chairman, by Robin Fox. Robin was a rare mixture of buoyancy, like an amateur's, and total professionalism. He was a joy to have as a colleague, with his knowledge and his discernment and his conviction (which I fully share and partly learnt from him) that you ought never to prevent your work and your beliefs from being fun.

Neville Blond's qualities were not dissimilar, and his was so invigorating a personality that I never failed to look forward to meetings with him in the chair. Whatever the issue under discussion, whether it seemed likely to be positive and forward-looking or negative and dangerous, the liveliness of his mind, the constructive quality of his ideas, kept us somewhere near the crest of the wave and stopped us fearing that we might eventually sink. With him, we were sure we would not.

With hindsight, I suppose we ought some time in the late 1960s to have adopted a suggested of Ronnie's – made I'm afraid at the time more in anger than in sorrow – to the effect that the Council should give notice of its intention to resign *en bloc* and make way for a new Council and a new artistic direction, young and with a fresh approach to the problems. I wish now that we had done that, and not risked the accusation (never made, I fancy, which was odd in a back-biting profession like the theatre) that we were hanging on in the hope of finding a policy, as I believe we essentially were.

I later became president of the company until, after I had been working a while at the Coliseum, I decided that all my energies had to go into what I was trying to do there, and resigned. But I did so with a pang because of the remarkable work with which in the past I had been associated, however much at a distance, and because I would not have liked any action of mine to undermine however slightly the work of George Devine, Neville Blond and Robin Fox.

CHAPTER TWELVE

Edinburgh Festival
1947-65

THE EDINBURGH FESTIVAL was founded on quite a small financial investment, mostly on the know-how and capability of Rudi Bing and the vision of the Lord Provost of Edinburgh, Sir John Falconer. They aimed to provide a kind of post-war rallying point; differing ideologies would be forgotten in a celebration of the arts and in the idea of the international, particularly as expressed in music. That ideal was still voiced when I started working there in 1960, thirteen years after the first Festival.

When in autumn 1959 I was invited to become Artistic Director, I realized I had been to every Edinburgh Festival since 1947 except two. I had quickly become something of an *aficionado*, partly because the setting is splendid, partly because I'd usually been there with people I liked and often stayed with the Roseberys at Dalmeny, partly because the programmes regularly provided excitement.

In October 1959, I was recovering from a sinus operation when the City Treasurer, Duncan Weatherstone, and the man tipped to be the next Lord Provost, Jack Dunbar, visited me to see if I would be interested in taking over from Robert Ponsonby who had just resigned. I asked the advice of John Denison, then music director of the Arts Council and later director of the Festival Hall, and he recommended a careful scrutiny of the relationship between subsidy and box office earnings. If reliance on the latter was too great, artistic risks would be hard to take and emphasis would be on balanced books rather than on an exciting programme.

The annual balance sheets were not very reassuring. The next thing was to meet the Council, presided over by the retiring Lord Provost. Beforehand, I tried to take stock of my attitude towards the Festival. Its assets were enormous and all it lacked, I felt, was the feeling of expectancy that had been there at the start and that could be recaptured provided one could regain the

183

regard of the critics – by putting forward a programme that everybody would recognize as festive. To regain prestige was all-important, because if the press looked forward to every Festival, so would the Festival public.

As I got into my sleeper to go up to meet the Council, I knew I had to say something positive if I wanted to get the job. Programme building is a matter of detail, but I had already decided that Edinburgh's was so large that it needed some focal point. I had the idea that the obvious thing was to choose a composer each year and mount what would be effectively a retrospective exhibition of his work. This I decided to say to my interrogators, taking two figures as examples: Schoenberg, who was dead but wrote in all forms, and Villa-Lobos, who was alive, versatile, and known as conductor and pianist. I got off the train and was reading the newspaper at breakfast when my eyes fell on an obituary of Villa-Lobos!

Interviews with prospective employers are commonplace, but few are with so big a group as faced me at the Edinburgh Festival – the first time I had been through this kind of ordeal. But all seemed to go well, and later in the day I was invited to take the job. I accepted, and Harry Rosebery, a contemporary of my father's at school and in the army, said we would celebrate with something worth drinking. His father, the Prime Minister, had bought a cellar-full of wine when he went to Dalmeny and we had a magnum of, I think, Château Lafite of 1867. It was a wonderful wine and lasted us through dinner and indeed lunch the next day, the other guests at Dalmeny turning out to my great delight to be almost teetotal.

Edinburgh ran its business from two offices – administrative in Edinburgh, artistic in London. Like my predecessors, I was called the Artistic Director, and there was an Administrative Director in Edinburgh – until 1965, called the Secretary. For my first Festival this was John Reid, who had held the post from the start, thereafter Willie Grahame, who had been his deputy.

Administration covered the detailed arrangements for the renting of theatres, halls, rehearsal rooms; printing of tickets, box office arrangements, hotel bookings, press, publicity, and everything else apart from daily programmes, the souvenir programme, the arranging of events and the contracting of artists. The Edinburgh staff was not small, but it was badly paid, everyone being on a municipal scale by which war service seemed almost to have counted against you. One of my last contributions to the Festival was to make an impassioned plea that Willie Grahame's worth be recognized for what it was to the Festival, not calculated by his position on the municipal ladder.

The address of the London office was in St James's Street, though the entrance was on the other side of the block, near Wilton's Restaurant. When I started to work there, I anticipated there would be a problem about space, but there were across the passage from the main office two spare rooms separated by a bathroom, which were unoccupied until I came. Before he left, Robert Ponsonby and I often wondered what the rooms could originally have been; with the bathroom, rather grand working space for tarts from nearby Jermyn Street, we surmised.

Michael Whewell as my deputy was my first appointment. He was a practising musician (a bassoon and basset horn player) and had worked at the BBC, where I had got to know him years before. He was a man of imagination and flair, efficient and painstaking, and he quickly became a friend as well as colleague. He left to run the Arts Council in Belfast, and my colleague for my last Festival was Alex Schouvaloff, a man of the theatre who was prepared to face decisions, even unpleasant ones, on his own, and later went to run London's new Theatre Museum.

Nineteen sixty-one was my first Festival, and Schoenberg was the central figure. We grouped together a representative selection of his *oeuvre* – the four string quartets for instance, but unfortunately none of the operas – and opened the Festival with the *Gurrelieder* conducted by Stokowski. We got together as good a cast for this greatest of post-*Tristan* essays as has, I believe, ever sung the work, with Gré Brouwenstijn and James McCracken at its head. I have heard in real life or on record or tape most of the ambitious *Gurrelieder* projects since the war and, prejudiced as I know I am, have found no performance to compare with my memory (and my tape) of this one. The ripely romantic music was very much to Stokowski's taste (as it is to mine; a proof if you want it – and I often do – that Schoenberg could, as they used to say about Picasso, draw when he wanted to). So too were the possibilities of the huge orchestra, with which Stokowski worked his usual magic.

He was then around eighty (his real age always a matter for conjecture), and he had a few months before broken his thigh playing passage football with his sons, and was worried it might let him down. He rehearsed meticulously with chorus, orchestra and soloists, saying little but repeating what he was dissatisfied with until it reached his standard (orchestral legend of the period had it that he would suddenly cup his hands, single out an individual member of the orchestra and say meaningfully, 'You, sir! You can do better!'). Alvar Liddell, a musician as well as a famous BBC wartime newsreader, was the speaker in the *Gurrelieder*'s last section and had not been able to get to the penultimate Edinburgh rehearsal. At the final run-through

185

THE TONGS AND THE BONES

Stokowski somehow with ten minutes left managed to give the impression
that he was going to omit the finale and indeed thanked his forces before
tackling it. Alvar Liddell's apprehension showed and he begged the conductor
to go through the tricky section which precedes the choral finale. 'Mr Liddell
would like to practise his solo. Will you please stay a few minutes longer to
help him?' he asked – a reaction which was not only deflating but also, one
must add, disingenuous.

The performance went splendidly, Gré Brouwenstijn and Nell Rankin
sang their great solos with authority and the vocal beauty I was looking for,
and James McCracken, not then well-known as he became later, sang
untiringly through the exacting role with a battery of top notes which were
not only highly impressive in themselves but vindication of what Erwin Stein
had years before told me – that Schoenberg insisted the prime requisite for
the role of Waldemar was a constantly effective top register. McCracken had
it and was the perfect Waldemar.

At our press conference the morning after the performance of *Gurrelieder*,
an Edinburgh habit I disliked but could not lose, Stokowski talked endlessly
of his passion for brick-laying and house-building and little about music; but
for all his posing, phoney accent and nonsense, I admired him immeasurably
as a musician, and am convinced the world has never heard his superior as a
wizard of orchestral sound. Years later, with the New Philharmonia, I
engaged him whenever he would come. He was one of the few conductors
Klemperer admired.

Arnold Schoenberg's widow and her two sons were our guests throughout
the Festival, and her waspish comments and vacillation over what tickets she
wanted provided the kind of needle you didn't require at a first Festival. But
we managed fairly well, the Schoenberg theme interested the critics, and there
was no evidence that it put anyone else off – after all, it was perfectly possible
for there to be twenty-five works of a single composer in the Festival
programme and for a visitor to fill a week without hearing one of them; that
was the advantage of a Festival of this size.

Exhibitions had always in the past been a Festival feature and, at the
suggestion of Dicky Buckle, we had a retrospective of Epstein in 1961.
Epstein often worked on a big scale, so we needed space. We secured the
Waverley Market and filled it with corridors and vistas, temples and
grottoes, in which to display the sculptures and bronzes. It was all done with
scaffolding and inexpensive window-dressing material, with much help in
kind from Jack Lyons, a prominent businessman and a friend from Leeds
Festival days, who chaired our special Epstein committee. We got the cost

back in admission money, which was unprecedented, and it was one of the things I was most proud of during my time in Edinburgh, and I am still grateful to the imagination of Dicky Buckle and the generosity of Jack Lyons.

Drama, I quickly found out, was considered the poor relation in Edinburgh programming. Yet in my time and before, there were three drama theatres working throughout the three weeks, with a minimum of seven performances a week in each theatre – at least sixty-three performances of drama altogether. Seven concerts a week in the Usher Hall and seven chamber concerts at the Freemasons' Hall made a total of forty-two specifically musical events. Add in three weeks of opera – sixteen to eighteen performances – and you have something like an equality in the number of *performances* under the two headings. But the real difference lay in the number of *events*, each play counting as a single event, with repeated performances; whereas each concert, each recital offered something different, and there might be anything from three to ten operas at the King's Theatre. Music critics had the equivalent of two first nights every day of the week, often three; drama critics only on Mondays. So drama was quickly accepted as second to music at the Edinburgh Festival.

Drama critics felt less involved than their musical confrères, and went for consolation to the famous Fringe, where the *ad hoc* groups, the amateur and university performances, came into their own. The fare they offered was undeniably more varied than the official Festival programme (in quality too), but word quickly got about as to which Fringe event was worth seeing, and there was always the hope that something exceptional would turn up. I had no grudge whatsoever against the Fringe, but when I arrived it was officially very much frowned on, as taking away money that could be spent on Festival tickets.

The Festival brochure had, by the time I came on the scene, acquired something of the status of the sacred cow. It *had* to be ready for printing by the first day of February, it *had* to contain everything we were trying to sell. I rather enjoyed the discipline of the deadline, even though there was often a hustle to meet it. During early January we sent the Festival programme to the printers, leaving blanks or putting in hypotheses to make up the right format. This would then be proofed, and on 31 January I would go to Edinburgh for a meeting, with the late afternoon and evening given up to a meticulous reading of final proofs, and telephoning to the London office for confirmation of last-minute programme or cast changes. I corrected the proofs with our Press Officer, a delightful Scot by name Graham Cowie.

After the work, we used to celebrate with a rather bibulous dinner before I caught the night train back to London.

During March, the head of the Scottish Tourist Board, Bill Nicholson, would invite a bevy of journalists, including a few music critics, for a tour of some aspect of the beauties of his native country, always ending with a day and night of roystering. Then they came to Edinburgh for the serious business of unveiling the programme, which had by 1961 acquired quite a ceremonial routine. There was a great lunch given in the City Chambers by the Lord Provost. My first year, the Lord Provost was considerably exercised over protocol but agreed in the end to seat me precisely where my predecessor had sat – just below the salt, so to speak. After lunch, we repaired to another great room, the leaflets were handed out, and I talked about the programme. This was not unenjoyable as by then I knew it by heart and was able to emphasize whatever seemed particularly innovatory or challenging.

Hospitality in Edinburgh always presented problems. Twice a week during the Festival the city entertained in the magnificent City Chambers, but on an exiguous scale. Buns and cheap white wine were the order of the day, and the faces of Yugoslav and Russian visitors, let alone Americans, faced with this fare had to be seen to be believed.

For my own part, I used to give a couple of parties a week, which was relatively easy if you had the good fortune to have, as I had, a cook. A party each Sunday seemed essential because the restaurants tended to shut early, which was tough on artists who were performing that night and could find nowhere to go afterwards. We very often gave them haggis, explaining that it was 'una specialità di casa' or 'specialité de la maison' or whatever we could manage in the appropriate language, and we provided a good gravy for it laced with whisky – better to my mind than washing the bare haggis down with whisky from a glass.

I have introduced gourmets of every nation to haggis with complete success, amongst them Shostakovich the Russian, and Fritz Wunderlich, the remarkable German tenor who could cope with more alcohol in a short time than anyone I have ever known. At these parties we dealt with situations of every kind, from the dietetic problems of Indians, a group of whom once asked for fresh orange juice and then ignored the vats we had squeezed in favour of whisky, to the appetites of impecunious Czechs who saved up over the earlier part of the day for their evening meal, knowing that it would be copious and free. Stokowski came to my first party, toiling up three flights with his broken thigh, and at another that year, Kathleen Epstein, spying late in the evening Herbert von Karajan and Albert Finney standing back to back, attracted their attention and then said enigmatically: 'Just look at you! Each of you has what the other lacks!' – and walked away.

I rented a different house or flat each year. In some of them, the beds were too small, and one of the houses had a pink plastic bath that sagged in the middle when you stood up to soap yourself. That was our Indian year, and Ravi Shankar and Ali Akbar Khan, brothers-in-law and once fellow students, came several times with their wonderful tabla accompanist, Alla Rakha, not only to eat and drink (only Wunderlich rivalled Ali Akbar in this capacity), but also to improvise with Western musicians, Julian Bream and Larry Adler in particular. I have a tape of a kind of Indian jam session in that house, when they improvised until late in the night on the theme of 'Greensleeves', which Narayana Menon and I had suggested to them. My mother came for each of my first four Festivals, staying with Eva Rosebery at Dalmeny, and I have memories of her at that Indian party, sitting with Robin Fox late into the night.

Our London office, indeed the whole Festival, underwent the ordeal of an investigation by Time and Motion experts. It happened, I was informed, because the Town Councillors on the Festival Council were tired, when asking for money from the Town Council itself, of being told that the Festival wasted money, and wanted to reassure their colleagues that this was not so. Even though I neither wasted money nor cooked the books, I faced it all with a certain feeling of apprehension.

Our interlocutor was to spend three days in London and then go for a week to Edinburgh; he duly arrived, dapper and dark-suited, professing to be a lover of the arts and a frequenter of theatre and concert hall – this presumably by way of reassurance. We opened the books, discussed expenses, compared the fees we paid to different artists (on his promise that these would not be quoted in any report), talked about other festivals as we knew them, and he eventually left us to start his investigations in Edinburgh.

After a couple of days, I heard from Willie Grahame that he was being grilled on every conceivable subject, half of the questions apparently designed to check if we had told the truth in London. One evening, I had an urgent question on which I needed Willie's help – it involved getting some decision from the Lord Provost, whom I knew to be going abroad next day, and I thought Willie could find him before he left more easily than I could. It must have been the only time I ever rang him at home, but although it was ten-thirty in the evening, I was told he was still at dinner at the Caledonian

Hotel with our Time and Motion man. I telephoned him there, asked my question and was reassured. The following day I was told that Willie had had thirteen solid hours with our tormentor, as we by now felt he was, who was so insistent that they continue their discussions that he even missed his last train home.

Some weeks later the report came. It was not in the slightest degree hostile or damaging, but it contained some rather odd comments. One was that the artistic direction appeared not to follow accepted business practice in its dealings with artists; it should not, for instance, let a musician know that he was the first or only choice for a particular engagement, but should leave him with the impression that others were being sounded out, so that a more competitive price might be obtained. Another was that there appeared to be little co-ordination between the London and Edinburgh offices; there should be set times at which telephone conversations might be held with a list of queries from each side already prepared, thus cutting down wasteful time and effort. The London office even seemed to need to pursue the administrator as late as eleven at night in order to query something which had doubtless been forgotten during the day! My comment on the first suggestion was, 'Try that on Klemperer or Karajan'; and on the second, something rather less parliamentary.

What do I remember best of those five years of hard and rewarding labour?

At the 1961 Festival, Giulini conducting Britten for the first time and the composer's euphoria on listening to a virtuoso direct his music; planner's pleasure at witnessing audiences react positively to Schoenberg's music, and planner's horror at having persuaded Alex Gibson against his better judgment to conduct a programme including Schoenberg's *Violin Concerto* and Liszt's *Faust Symphony*, which added up to a meal of plum pudding; a theatre programme with Western Theatre Ballet and Scottish National Orchestra, based on Weill's hybrid *Seven Deadly Sins*, a favourite work of mine; my discomfiture when Lotte Lenya telephoned to say she was leaving for New York in protest against Kenneth MacMillan's choreography for it, and my luck in getting Cleo Laine at two weeks' notice to replace her. I remember too the near-triumph of Patricia's friend, the Australian pianist Maureen Jones, who was greatly admired playing the Britten Piano Concerto with the Berlin Philharmonic but whose career never seemed to take off as from that performance I judged it sure to; the friendliness of press notices; and how incredibly tired you could get once the Festival was under way – I relied on twenty minutes lying down before the evening's performance, and a *very* hot bath at seven-forty-five in the morning before embarking on the new day's chores.

In 1962, the special feature was Shostakovich's music, with a wealth of Russian specialists performing. I shrivelled watching Shostakovich himself flinch through the official aspects of his visit, and was pleased when he enjoyed a little of the remainder, including the haggis and its gravy. We opened that year with Beethoven's *Missa Solemnis* conducted by Lorin Maazel, with Vishnevskaya as soprano soloist. She and her husband Rostropovich had been staying at Aldeburgh, and she accepted Peter Pears's offer to go through some of it with him. He found (and warned me) that she had a very inaccurate idea of it, but she calmly came up inadequately prepared to rehearse with Maazel. He restrained his indignation in the interests of international accord, but that could not be said of her fellow-soloists when, having hogged all the rehearsal time in order to get it nearly right, she proceeded on the night to steal the honours of the performance with a nearly flawless display.

We had twenty-five Shostakovich works in the 1962 programme and another highlight was Rostropovich playing the six Bach solo cello suites in St Cuthbert's Church off Princes Street – magical performances with the great cellist giving his services free as a gesture to the Festival. I wonder if I ever heard a greater musical executant.

We had commissioned a new work from Luigi Nono, Schoenberg's son-in-law, who as a communist applauded the Russian participation but as a modernist hated the Shostakovich he had to hear; we had an exhibition of Yugoslav primitive painters which attracted some attention; and we had a Writers Conference, which had its disappointments as well as its rewards.

A novelty was the elaborate ballet-spectacle, *The Four Sons of Aymon*, which Béjart had devised for circus presentation in Brussels and which we brought for a fortnight to Murrayfield Ice Rink. We filled the building with tiered seats at one end in order to increase the accommodation provided by the normal rows around the rink. All went well and several audiences enjoyed the show until one evening, sitting in another theatre, I got a message that the performance had had to be abandoned as the hall had slowly filled with something like tear-gas. Apparently ammonia is an important ingredient in keeping an ice rink in shape, and some stored for the forthcoming season had escaped that evening, making the hall quite uninhabitable. Fortunately, it only happened once.

Nineteen sixty-three for me was an Indian year, with delicate chamber concerts in the Freemasons' Hall, the first British appearance of

Subbulakshmi, the Callas of India, and dance appearances by Balasaraswati, the greatest living exponent of *Bharatanatyam*, the South Indian Temple dance. I was asked for a couple of sentences with which to introduce Balasaraswati in our programme brochure and said spontaneously, 'It has been said that she is one of the three greatest living dancers.' Someone asked me who said it, and I said, 'I did.' It was true, too, the others being Margot Fonteyn and Ulanova. Bala was unique in insisting that she could not dance on a springy, wooden stage; the nearer it could be to the stone temple floors she trained on the better.

We paralleled the performers with an Indian exhibition, which never quite caught the public fancy as it should have, in spite of some superb Indian miniatures (I was asked to censor a couple of them as too sexually explicit). Narayana Menon, whom I had got to know well in 1958, not only helped me persuade various Indian artists to come to Edinburgh but stayed with me throughout the Festival, introducing several recitals, playing Bach on the veena at one, and acting as host and trouble-shooter for our Indian guests throughout the Festival.

In 1963 Isaac Stern, Leonard Rose and Eugene Istomin brought remarkable trio performances, Szell came with the Concertgebouw, and Colin Davis conducted Berlioz's *Fantastic Symphony* and 'Lélio' in one programme as the composer intended. We had exemplary performances of Britten's version of *The Beggar's Opera* and *The Rape of Lucretia*, and I got John Ogdon and his wife Brenda Lucas to repeat the Bartok Sonata for two pianos and percussion, which the previous year had encountered disaster when, quite early on, her carefully coiffed hair started to fall – a process that was complete by the end, unlike some of the music. It went much better in 1963.

That same year we took the Empire Theatre, which had gone over to Bingo, and put into it successively the Hungarian State Opera, with the Bartok triple-bill (*Bluebeard*, *The Wooden Prince* and *The Miraculous Mandarin*), as the composer had later in life hoped it would be performed; Martha Graham's company; and the Stuttgart Ballet under John Cranko on its first visit to the United Kingdom. The theatre in spite of cleaning was in horrid condition, and an anti-communist saboteur after the dress rehearsal of the Hungarians turned on a top floor tap so as to flood the company out. I heard about it only after the first night was over – and so learnt that Iron Curtain companies can sometimes give the West a lesson in manners.

The 1963 Festival ended in high comedy or tragedy, depending on how you looked at it. During the last week we had a Drama Conference and John

Calder, who organized it, had much difficulty in squeezing out the juice he had hoped for. I had allowed myself the rare liberty of going to sit in on the last afternoon session with Patricia, when to our amazement we saw a lady who seemed to be unclothed trundled on a lighting stand across the organ loft at the back of the stage of the McEwan Hall! It certainly woke the audience up.

There were long faces at the final concert that evening, none longer than the Lord Provost's, who said to me (and was quoted in the paper on Sunday and Monday): 'Three weeks of glorious Festival ruined by one squalid little episode.' After the Festival was over, John Calder admitted he had staged it all. Everyone seemed to think that I knew about it beforehand, but in fact I didn't.

In 1964, the Opera came from Prague and provided one of the greatest successes of the five years I was in Edinburgh. I had an instinct that they had a lot to offer, and went to see them for myself in the winter of 1963. Standards in Prague were on the whole high, but constantly vitiated by anomalies which could only be described as historical – singers long past their best kept in great roles simply because that was how it had always been. With the agent, Lies Askonas, I worked very hard with the direction during the ten days I was in Prague and managed to get some old blood relegated and some new included in the cast lines. By the opening night we had achieved a very impressive line-up, and the company had possibly its biggest foreign success to date.

An agreeable postscript to that visit came when, years later, I met Schuyler Chapin, then General Manager of the Metropolitan in New York, who reminded me that we had met before, in 1965, when he was in Europe to prepare a festival for the first session of the Lincoln Centre in New York. He had come to consult me in my Edinburgh Festival office about the desirability of the Czechs forming part of the programme. I reported favourably and he engaged them, only to have them lay the theatre's proverbial egg. He was angry at what he felt was my cynical advice and mentioned it to a friend, who said: 'But didn't you know? Harewood vetted the casting down to the last member of the ensemble and cut out the dead wood; that's why they made their great success in Edinburgh.'

Janáček, a composer whose music I love, was featured at that Festival and we successfully included two of his operas and much of his orchestral and chamber music. When in 1963 we were planning the 1964 Festival, the Council decided that times were hard and that less money was available; would I plan accordingly? I said it was perfectly possible – but for one year only; do it twice, and parsimony would become apparent. I loaded the programme with celebrity recitals, which were cheaper than orchestral concerts, and had three chamber orchestra concerts with Serkin (including no fewer than seven Mozart concertos); these sold as if they were symphony concerts but cost less. The rest was as normal – but perhaps no Festival could be described that way which had Serkin playing Schubert's late A Major Sonata on Sunday and Richter his B Flat Major (Op. Posth.) the following Wednesday – the most wholly successful tribute I have ever been able to organize to the genius whom over the years I have come to know as my favourite composer.

That 1964 Festival was in many ways a fraught period. Patricia, to whom I was not yet married – indeed I was still married to Marion – had had Mark in the summer, and word had reached the ears of a member of the Festival committee, quite a close friend of mine. That friend thought it necessary to convey the information to the Lord Provost, to whom it came as a great surprise. I went to see him to avoid what could have become a ridiculous situation; moreover, though I wasn't going to advertise Mark's birth at that juncture, it was also something that I was not anxious to deny. If the Lord Provost was embarrassed, it was up to me to get him out of his embarrassment – and I did not forget that, at the time of my appointment, I had been told that the Council was worried as to how they would go about it if they ever wanted to get rid of me. They were reassured then, and I could not let an impossible situation develop now.

I told Lord Provost Weatherstone that I had a child by someone other than my wife and that divorce was in prospect though not imminent. He said he thought this could have very serious effects on the Festival; he didn't feel that he could keep this confidence to himself if divorce were to arise, or if indeed anything came out in the press. I went off to see my friend Lord Cameron, who was a senior judge in Scotland and also the senior non-Town Council member of the Festival Council. I made the point that I didn't want to be pushed out of the job for what was after all an external consideration when there were perhaps people feeling that I had brought something to the Festival it needed. I was probably overplaying my hand. He took my point but thought that the kind of publicity which could eventuate might have an adverse effect on the Festival, which was what I had told him I wanted to avoid. Perhaps, he said, I should write the Lord Provost a letter of resignation that he could keep in his safe, so to speak, and use only when the moment came.

I wrote the letter, and the Lord Provost kept it for some months. It was agreed that I should not only carry on with the 1964 Festival but plan and execute 1965; the Festival meanwhile would put out feelers to find a successor who would take over by 1966. In point of fact, they went, I think wisely, straight to Peter Diamand in Holland; but we delayed any announcement of my resignation until he was actually in a position to say he would take over.

For me that last Festival in 1965 was rather special, partly because I didn't have anything to lose, partly because we offered some things which were in themselves unusually exciting. It was Michael Tippett's sixtieth birthday and we ran quite a lot of his music through the Festival – he had composed a Festival commission for 1962, his *Concerto for Orchestra*. We also had, perhaps more challengingly, a week of Boulez in the middle of the Festival, as composer and conductor and pianist. This was the kind of 'festival within a festival' I had always envisaged, and I suppose it was the biggest assemblage of music by Boulez that had yet been put together anywhere. I am sure audiences enjoyed the opportunity; I believe Boulez did, and we have remained friends ever since.

Within a few days of each other that year, we had in Edinburgh the two greatest woodwind players I ever heard – Heinz Holliger, the Swiss oboist, and Bismillah Khan, the Indian *shahnai* player. Bismillah had only once been out of India before, and within a day of his arrival in Edinburgh war broke out between India and Pakistan. He is an Indian and a Muslim, and his fear was that religious fervour would inflame patriotism in India and endanger his family. But he played like a god, or like a magician, and he did things as impossible it seemed to me on his instrument as Holliger on his. Such a conjunction is perhaps what festivals can bring about better than can be managed in other contexts.

For 1965 we had agreed on a co-production of *Don Giovanni* with the Holland Festival. Giulini was to conduct, Virginio Puecher to produce and the designer was Luciano Damiani. I went to late rehearsals in Holland, and the first night; and there were aspects of the production with which it was easy, to put it mildly, to disagree. Giulini quite early on said that if we persisted with the production, he would not conduct in Edinburgh, and I embarked on a lengthy and rather acrimonious correspondence with Puecher and Damiani, offering to pay their fees (but not fares) for their non-services in Edinburgh, but only on condition they stayed away. We did away with all the scenery and costumes that had been used in Holland, commissioned new and sumptuous costumes from David Walker and decided to do it all with lights and props, and no scenery apart from Donna Elvira's balcony and a table for the supper scene.

I got David Webster to agree to 'lend' us Bill Bundy, Covent Garden's lighting expert, and we spent the night after the last Amsterdam performance conferring with Giulini until five-thirty in the morning. The Edinburgh performances duly went on with a success that was almost, but not quite, complete. There was not quite enough technical time in the King's Theatre to achieve the full possibilities of such an approach, but I regretted nothing of our attempt.

Late night shows – ten-forty-five to midnight – had by the time I arrived become a feature of the Festival and, as they had started with the incomparable *Beyond the Fringe*, the standard set was high. During my time we had a number of entertaining Scottish shows, but the glamour came from the two or three foreign visitors we persuaded to undertake these evening spots. In 1961 it was Juliette Greco, who said flattering things about me to the press and brought style and panache to the Lyceum. The following year, Amalia Rodrigues came from Portugal with her *fados*, enchanting someone like me who was already a lover of her records, and astonishing some others who did not know that 'April in Paris' started life as 'Coimbra'.

In 1964 we were offered Marlene Dietrich, which seemed to me a most exciting prospect, and she came with musical backing from Burt Bacharach and played to full houses. Off-stage, things were not quite so rosy; in fact, I can safely say she was the only visitor to the Festival while I was there whom I would happily have consigned to hell.

Nothing we did was right for her, and her capacity to express her displeasure was versatile and unrivalled. To cap it all, we were offered her services for the following year. Festival weal overcame prospective private woe, and I re-engaged her. Again the houses were full, and we could but admire the total professionalism of her performance. But she had not changed. I even thought I would try to get some of my own back by circulating the rumour that reports about her age were greatly exaggerated; she was in truth only just over fifty ...

There is one *canard* that I must scotch: that the Festival Council and the Town Council are the bane of an Edinburgh Festival Director's life. I have often had it suggested to me that it must have been misery working with them. It was not. Edinburgh's Festival was in chronic need of money – and usually managed to get most of what it needed, even though it was sometimes a struggle. The Festival Council, for all its rather stuffy deliberations, did its best to make the Festival run well, and I never knew it strew thistles or even the odd bramble in the director's path.

The Town Council as such I never met, though I knew those of its members who belonged to the Festival Council. When Jennie Lee, as minister responsible for the arts, came to Edinburgh, the Lord Provost, the Festival's chairman, decided to fly the kite of government aid for the Opera House. The matter was discussed for about an hour, with the minister making wise statements about planning for the future even when finance was currently short; and then I had the pleasure of hearing her rebuke a member of her own party, who insisted that other priorities would always rule out an Opera House, particularly from a Labour point of view, with the words: 'I never heard a greater piece of political illiteracy in all my life.'

During those five years, I succeeded I think in what I had at the outset told the Council was my aim – to recapture the press's interest. In fact, looking at the press cuttings, I am astonished at the generosity of what was said. The truth is I think that it was much easier then than now to devise programmes that were not only fresh but positively innovatory; substantial areas of music by great composers hardly got a hearing in those days. What was then novel has by now become old hat, and the Festival Director's job is correspondingly harder.

During my Edinburgh time I inevitably fell foul of one or two local interests, and my proud claim is that throughout one whole Festival, of which the *Scottish Daily Express* seemed to disapprove, a banner head was kept permanently set up:

GODLESSNESS AND DIRT
HAREWOOD MUST GO!

Peculiar things were sure to happen in an occupation which was not only far-flung, in that one went all over the world in search of attractions, but also intensive, in that it all happened in three packed weeks each year.

In my first year, to get a programme, or rather a pair of them, out of Karajan was difficult and, until he had chosen, the others could not have their say. No amount of writing or telephoning seemed to get us anywhere, and, in summer 1960, André von Mattoni, his ubiquitous assistant, suggested I should come out to the Salzburg Festival; I need only telephone for a pair of seats when I arrived.

On arrival I asked for an appointment with Karajan and a pair of tickets for that night's concert which Böhm was to conduct. Mattoni rather reluctantly produced the tickets and said I should find him at the interval and he would take me to Karajan. At the interval I was told Karajan had decided to go home. Tickets for tomorrow? Very difficult, since it was *Rosenkavalier* and quite sold out ... but he would try. About the appointment, why not telephone in the morning? The telephone call produced nothing; Karajan liked to rest on the morning of a performance and would not be in Salzburg. We went to *Rosenkavalier* that night, and heard a fine first and second acts, then felt we had had enough; we would dine at the Goldener Hirsch. We were having our drinks when another diner entered the otherwise empty restaurant. It was Mattoni, to whom we felt we could but wave in faintly embarrassed salutation.

Next morning on the telephone came the news that Karajan would see me that night – in the interval of *Don Giovanni*, whose première it was and which he was conducting. I was duly led to the great man's dressing room to find Karajan reclining on a sofa in a large room, talking to the conductor Mitropoulos and the impresario Walter Legge, Elisabeth Schwarzkopf's husband and the architect of Karajan's post-war career. He waved them out, and I sat at his side to discuss what he and his orchestra would play in one year's time in Edinburgh. The theme would be Schoenberg, I said; had he featured any in the Berlin Phil. programmes? 'I have never found the necessity,' he answered, but finally relented, only however to the tune of including Webern's Opus Six. He was a difficult man, to say the least.

As part of our Literary Conference in 1962, we had a discussion on censorship and, to accompany that, an exhibition of banned books, from *The Well of Loneliness* through Frank Harris and Henry Miller to *Lady Chatterley's Lover*, with several others on the way. Imagine our horror when I heard that the police had staged a raid on the bookcase in which they were exhibited, and that it was at the instigation of a member of the Lord Provost's staff. They did not prosecute – the exhibit cannily had only the covers, not the books themselves. It was Willie Grahame who pronounced the informer's epitaph when he said, with some feeling, 'The man's so insipid his idea of a wild night is to go to bed at ten and turn the electric blanket up to medium!'

My last Festival had quite a few jokers in its hand. Slava Rostropovich, an incomparable musician and executant, I first met with Ben Britten at Aldeburgh, and he had become a friend; but there was no doubt about his taking sides in my matrimonial problems. As it was, he said he was coming by train the day before he rehearsed, then by plane the night before, then on the early plane on the day, and finally by the night train. I would have met him if the time had been normal but seven-thirty was asking, I thought, too much, and I was happy that Victor Hochhauser's Russian-fluent assistant Anthony Phillips would undertake to be at Waverley Station when the train got in with Slava and the conductor Rozhdestvensky. At nine-thirty Anthony telephoned me in my office to say the two Russians had disappeared. He had taken them to the hotel only to find the rooms not yet ready, but had pacified their not inconsiderable displeasure by taking them to the dining room for a big breakfast. He then went upstairs to shave and had come down to find the Russians not in the dining room, indeed not in the hotel; the hall porter had seen them leave in a cab.

I mobilized my three secretaries, told them what had happened and, knowing that when in a tantrum Slava often worked it off in a shopping spree, sent them off to the big shops along Princes Street. What on earth else was there to do in Edinburgh at ten on a September morning? Some time after eleven they were back, having drawn a blank, but a few minutes later a foreign gramophone executive came in to say that he had met Slava as he left the hotel and had promised not to reveal where he was going – but the thought of the professional enormity Slava was committing in cutting his rehearsal had made him decide to tell me. I delivered the shame-faced but still complaining Rostropovich twenty minutes late for his noon rehearsal.

Russian Roulette in its Edinburgh version was not quite over for the year. Richter was ill and arrived a week late, and one of the programmes he was playing was of the five Beethoven cello sonatas with Rostropovich. The BBC asked if they might telerecord the recital, and have a run-through in front of the cameras on Monday afternoon. I gave the Slavas lunch and had a car waiting to take them the length of Princes Street, but they waved it away and said they would walk. We waited for half an hour beyond the appointed time and were beginning to despair when they rolled in, delighted with the warm weather. But rehearsal and the hot BBC lights bored and irritated them, particularly when they discovered it was not just one sonata the BBC wanted rehearsed but the whole five. Suddenly they embarked on one of the noble works super-*pianissimo* and about treble speed – it sounded like the buzzing of purposeful gnats – and the BBC technicians retired in total discomfiture.

Edinburgh might-have-beens? I was sorry that the Music Committee would not wear an idea I had for 1965. I had discussed with my ever-constructive deputy, Michael Whewell, the possibility of using three different aspects of twentieth-century music to make a comment on improvisation and its place in modern musical creation. We had Indians already scheduled – Bismillah Khan, Vilayat Khan and Palghat Mani Iyer, a wonderful South

Indian drummer – and all Indian classical music relies for its energy on the spirit of the moment. We had Boulez and the limited amount of choice he allows in his music; we also had Nielsen's *Fifth Symphony*, in which the percussion is asked to improvise a great cadenza. I thought we could extend the idea to include jazz, have John Ogdon improvise cadenzas to Mozart piano concertos and make a feature of it, but Hans Gal's classical training was against this kind of idea and we failed to get it through.

I think that was the only thing I ever failed to put across, apart from my idea that we should do Liza Lehmann's 'From a Persian Garden' song cycle at a morning concert. They found that too much of an Edwardian good thing – but I got it done, with very good singers, at the Coliseum sixteen years later.

And the Opera House? Oh dear . . . that never seemed to get far beyond the status of the never was.

CHAPTER THIRTEEN

In Russia
1961

MY SECOND YEAR at the Edinburgh Festival, when we concentrated on the music of Shostakovich, I talked to the cultural attaché at the Russian Embassy in London and received a lot of co-operation. It would have been odd if I had not, as we were in a way doing his job for him; a cultural manifestation is the most genuine propaganda there is. Whether you like it or not, it represents a people, perhaps untypically but, within its limits, truthfully. If you hate the rest, the culture at least you may love and grow to understand – and such an understanding may lead to other things.

When I went to Russia in March 1961, I was the official guest of the redoubtable Minister of Culture, Madame Furtseva, who was as formidable as she was cracked up to be but, in the flesh, not without something less usually associated with communist officialdom – charm. I was invited in order to take a look at the Russian scene and to meet the people whom I wanted to invite to perform at the 1962 Festival; Russian performers – Oistrakh, Richter, Rostropovich, Vishnevskaya, Rozhdestvensky, the conductor Mravinsky if we could get him, and a quartet called the Borodin, whom I had been told were exceptional – were to form the core of the Festival. I also wanted discussions with Shostakovich to see if his ideas on what we should present coincided with mine.

It was hard, indeed impossible, to get an itinerary out of my hosts. I was in their hands, not only as a guest but because they alone knew where all these people were. Early on, the British Embassy said it would be something of a diplomatic solecism if in Moscow I stayed anywhere but at the Embassy; after Moscow, I should be in hotels, but in Moscow I should start off with British hospitality and British advice – so Kenneth James, the charming first secretary, whom I saw in London, conveyed to me.

I went out alone in early March 1961 on a Russian flight, was met by the

Ambassador, Sir Frank Roberts, and taken by him to the Embassy, a large, handsome building to one side of the Kremlin – that's what you see out of the window – which had once, he told me, belonged to a shipping magnate but had been the British Embassy since the Revolution and the move of the capital to Moscow. Frank Roberts I found a delightful man, and he and his wife made marvellous hosts.

The first evening, he told me about the problems of an embassy in Moscow, with the certainty of bugging and the likelihood of infiltration of staff, about the difficulty of maintaining morale amongst British staff isolated as they were from Russian life, about Russian opposition to almost any other than the barest official contact. He welcomed Edinburgh's cultural approach and indeed my appearance, as he hoped the relatively uncontroversial nature of what we were to discuss could open a few doors. Information, he said, about internal Kremlin moves, about the hardening and softening of attitudes within the *Politburo*, was exchanged among foreign missions, and the uncommitted nations like Egypt and India were disposed to pool their gleanings. They had all come to believe that murder was no longer one of the crimes of the *Politburo*, and that demotion and exile were what were now mostly to be feared, not death. Only one politician, Beria, had been killed since the death of Stalin, and that had been the result of an incredibly complicated piece of political and military manoeuvring.

Beria, like Stalin, was a Georgian, and, after Stalin's death, certain aspects of Russia's military power were loyal primarily to Beria. When his colleagues decided that his removal was essential to Russia's future and their survival, they had not only to keep their intention secret from him but also to achieve Moscow's insulation from the armies which supported him and which normally maintained an inner military circle round Moscow, with other troops always in wider circles and further from Moscow's centre. Somehow, during the annual military manoeuvres, they contrived that all Beria's forces were positioned in outer circles at the same time, and then gave the word that he should be arraigned before the Praesidium found guilty of plotting against the state, and shot within the hour – all before any word could be sent to the distant troops that supported him. The diplomats had no idea what was going on until one observer, who had his own theory about where Beria lived (which was a secret), saw that there were no longer sentries outside the building. Either he was wrong, or Beria had moved, or he had fallen from power. No enquiry could raise Beria, and after a while his death was confirmed. What a subject for a thriller that military manoeuvre would make!

When the great Ernest Bevin was Foreign Secretary, he defined true international understanding as a situation in which anyone could go anywhere without a passport or visa, and my father told me that in the years before 1914, when he first travelled, you needed a passport only for Russia and (I think) China – or was it Japan? Every other country accepted people for what they were and not for what was written in a little book they carried. What we have come to think of as post-revolutionary suspicion is as much Russian as communist. Russia was completely new territory to me; I knew no Russian person, emigré or Soviet, and my mother's cautionary remark when I told her I was going – 'Remember, those are the people who killed your grandfather's first cousin and all his family only forty-odd years ago' – did not much affect the general feeling of goodwill I felt.

Even the short three weeks I was there revealed the warmth and open-heartedness of the basic Russian character as well as confirming the quite abnormal recalcitrance of official barriers. The barriers seemed to arise partly from genuine incomprehension, partly from a rather low average level of competence, partly from a deep-seated belief in the principle of the buck stopping elsewhere. If you asked whether something would be possible tomorrow, you tended to get the answer 'Oh yes, of course', but it usually didn't happen. There was probably nothing sinister behind this failure, just ignorance and the fear that the suggested course of action might not come within that man's area of decision. The Westerner, in the meanwhile, would be nettled by the aura of mystery. At one point, Frank Roberts asked me how I was getting on and, irritated at constant failure to secure appointments and even news, I said that I felt I was floundering, was even being put off. 'Make an official complaint to Furtseva then,' he said; and this we did, through an embassy official, with the result that some obstacles at least were removed, although not so fast that it might not have been a coincidence.

During my time in Russia I was taken regularly to performances – of *Sadko*, *Onegin*, Prokofiev's *Story of a Real Man* – at the Bolshoi in Moscow; to a new ballet and Prokofiev's *The Stone Flower* at the Kirov; to Georgian works in Tbilisi. In a rather ponderous way, they were all well done – it was not much liked when I said I thought *Sadko* the slowest-moving opera I had seen since I last saw *Parsifal* – though the singing tended to be less memorable than the dancing.

I also made official tours of the sights; above all I visited seats of learning, usually starting rather too early in the morning for comfort. The car would come at eight-thirty and we would be received at nine-fifteen by the director of some conservatory, who might be an official or might be an eminent musician – it was once the pianist Gilels, whom I already knew from London and who talked German. We would then tour the establishment for forty minutes, looking in at classes, glancing at libraries, peeping at rehearsals, talking occasionally to staff or students. At the end of our tour we would go back to the board room, and there the staff would be sitting round the table in order of seniority, ready, after brandy and cakes (or with luck, but too seldom, coffee), to answer questions.

We would start with a little lecture by the director on the objects or history of the institution, and I would then have to think up sufficient questions to keep us going for an hour – hard work at the best of times, since I am no musical educationalist, and very hard indeed on the occasions when question-time came before the tour. I remember well the balalaika class in Tbilisi, when the room seemed packed to the rafters with the great triangular things, varying in size from portable to colossal, from as it were violin to double bass – and always the dreaded hospitality, the brandy, the comestibles and the over-heated rooms.

The Kremlin itself of course I saw, with St Basil's Cathedral and the various modernized sections of the great citadel – including the extraordinary museum of carriages, starting with the unsprung vehicle, little more than a decorated farm cart, presented by Queen Elizabeth to Tsar Boris Godunov as a token of her esteem at the time of the first exchange of ambassadors between England and Russia.

Food in Moscow was not very good, not least because of the absence in winter of fresh vegetables of any kind – when I went to Tbilisi, the Robertses begged me to bring back vegetables and fruit. The Ambassador grumbled a bit because his French colleague, with whom we lunched while I was there, was enabled by Air France, who brought it in free, to have twice-weekly deliveries from Paris and so maintain a superb table for his guests.

The Ambassador gave a dinner at which I sat between Madame Furtseva, with whom I could only communicate through an interpreter, and the female professor of English at the university. The professor was a big, handsome woman, not only fluent in English but infinitely more knowledgeable and articulate about our literature than I, and with an open quality unusual amongst Russian officials – the result, I was told, of having been cured of cancer and so treating life as if it were lived without the usual constraints. At lunch another day, I sat next to the composer Kabalevsky, with whom I think I spoke French and who upbraided me for not speaking Russian, since after all many Russians spoke English. He liked Britten's music, he said, but did not much care for his *Turn of the Screw*: 'Much too morbid a subject for my taste.' Had I then read Shostakovich's *Testimony*, with its description of Kabalevsky's effort to get a colleague's name on to the 1948 black list instead of his own, I might have felt a little less sympathetic towards Kabalevsky.

Moscow is not a particularly attractive town at first sight, apart from such obvious features as the Kremlin. Much of the old town, which was solidly residential, had by then been pulled down to make way for new housing, and what was left, with its yellow-washed buildings, looked rather like the less impressive parts of Vienna, respectable and bourgeois but not distinguished. New building, apart from the disruption of the skyline by half a dozen distinctive skyscrapers in New York style – a real solecism prompted by Stalin's desire to keep up with the Joneses – was solid and uninspired.

While I was in Moscow I was invited to the Union of Soviet Composers, where Tikhon Khrennikov waited with some of his committee to receive me. This was a formal occasion, and when I was asked if there was any particular piece of Soviet music I would like to hear, ignorant and unwilling to be diverted from my main Shostakovian aim, I asked to hear something of his which was not yet on disc. They did not find it, and instead we heard among other works Khrennikov's own violin concerto, which sounded to me like an elaboration of the material of Weber's *Euryanthe* overture. It was not until later that I learnt he hated Shostakovich with a loathing only rivalled by Shostakovich's for him, Khrennikov having been in 1948 the instrument of denunciation of both Shostakovich and Prokofiev.

Later, in Leningrad, I went to Shostakovich's apartment and with my interpreter saw him alone, discussing with him aspects of the Festival – what music he would like played, whom he would like to play it. He was a bundle of nerves; he had recently broken his leg falling downstairs at his son's wedding (the only surprising thing, people said, was that he *did* break it; with his drinking, one would have expected him to fall soft), and cigarettes sprayed from his case as he tried with fumbling fingers at every moment to extract one and light it. But I felt a sympathy towards him as a human being as I always had as artist, and this persisted through the Festival, when he stayed three weeks in Edinburgh.

In Leningrad I also met Mravinsky, whose records I have always revered and whom I heard rehearsing his incomparable orchestra. Madame Furtseva told me that Mravinsky and Richter were the only two artists she could not influence, let alone control; whether they came to Edinburgh was between them and me – and Mravinsky never agreed to come.

I went to Leningrad by night train. It was colder while I was there than Moscow had been, but with its splendid buildings, its great vistas, a revelation to the eye. Though it was bombarded to death in the war, its restoration had been meticulous and it looks undamaged. Peter the Great's house escaped the destruction, and it stands now as a tiny monument to the city's vast and unattractive founder. It is the size of a summer house, which it rather resembles, except that among its curiosities is the Tsar's writing desk, at which he liked to work standing up. As he was nearly seven feet tall, the desk looks more like someone else's wardrobe.

To go round the Hermitage in a day, as I did, is hardly possible and can only be done at the price of a severe case of museum fatigue. The pictures in themselves would repay a lifetime's study, have probably often done so, not least by the then deputy director, Levinson Lessing, the successor of Alexandre Benois, who had been the last curator under the Tsar. He showed me round, taking to a wheelchair for the last few hundred rooms and pointing to the Rembrandts as his special joy. *Jupiter appearing to Danae in a shower of gold* (in reality, the painter's wife or mistress in a uniquely imaginative surround) seemed to bear out his judgment, but the morning spent downstairs among the Scythian gold, topped in its field only by the museum at Bogota, and the Fabergé collection, was scarcely less rewarding.

We visited Tsarskoë Selo, the Tsar's summer palace built for Catherine the Great rather in the style of Adam by the Scottish architect Cameron, and now called Pushkin, and here a transformation of heroic proportions was taking place. The Germans had filled the rooms with petrol-soaked straw and set fire to them so that nothing remained intact. Subsequently the paint, gold leaf and everything else that survived had been analysed, and workmen were now threequarters of the way through restoring it precisely as it had been built – the most amazing and determined piece of restoration ever known, and a curious comment on the present-day Russian attitude towards the past.

We went too to see a great monastic foundation with a central, rather decayed but beautiful cathedral church, which our guides needed a little coaxing to show us. It was then, perhaps still is, an active monastery, and the cathedral on Sundays always full of worshippers. They were on their knees, bowed to the floor, and looked round as we entered the ice-cold interior, perhaps just to see who we were, perhaps to wonder if these three or four men wearing hats were KGB and hostile – much as the worshippers at Sant'Andrea della Valle might have looked round at the entrance of Baron Scarpia in 1800.

From Moscow, later, we flew very early in the morning to Tbilisi, which the West once called Tiflis and is the capital of Georgia, a thousand and more miles away. 'It will be like summer,' they all said in the Moscow mid-March, but it wasn't, though the sun was out most of the time. This is the Middle East, not Russia at all, and you might fancy yourself in Turkey; I started to understand the difference between Russians and the inhabitants of the other, non-Russian republics that make up the Soviet Union. Stalin came from Georgia, and it was disconcerting to see his statue still in the streets, and to find some of the famed female beauties of the locality with more than a rudimentary version of his moustache. Most of the Georgians could talk some Russian, but none of the Russians could talk any Georgian, and when I wanted to get my shoes cleaned in the hall of the hotel my interpreter had to enlist Georgian help.

We went the usual round of conservatories, enlivened mainly by the singing classes and by the consort of balalaikas, and it was late before we got back to the hotel for lunch. There was Georgian brandy (rather like Spanish) to warm us, vodka with the *hors d'oeuvres*, and then wine throughout the meal. We were perhaps twenty people that first day, and they had invited a quartet of young composers who at the slightest provocation – such as that they had been silent for the past ten minutes – would raise their voices in short snatches of song traditional in character, beautiful in effect, remarkable for precise intonation and sheer musicality. I attempted to invite them to Edinburgh, but somehow the whole thing fizzled out.

Our host was the head of the Opera, an old bass singer by name Chedlidze, with quality still left in the voice as I heard when he sang unaccompanied and also when he made a short speech ending with a toast, which we were all required to drink in Georgian fashion. This consists of draining a full glass and up-ending it over one's head to show that it is empty, whereupon, at least if you are a guest, it will immediately be refilled in readiness for the next toast. A dozen toasts and a dozen glasses later, I found myself singing a verse of 'The Ash Grove', which David Thomas from the Embassy capped by singing the next verse in Welsh. At the end of the meal at around five-thirty there was no escaping the fact – but could I still disguise it? – that I was completely and totally sozzled, able to stand up, perhaps able to walk in a kind of straight line, possibly not publicly about to disgrace Queen and Country, but sozzled nonetheless. The evening would be spent at the Opera House, with a Georgian opera, but before that a cold bath seemed the likeliest way back towards a state of relative grace.

I am not one for cold baths, but there was a great tub in the middle of the huge bathroom, the only snag being the absence of a bath-plug, customary in Russia where, as in the Middle East, they think bathing in your own washed-off dirt a filthy habit. Before the bath, other needs had to be attended to and, with this in view and in something of a hurry, I slammed down the lavatory seat, only to find that it was not anchored at the base and, being made of rubber, bounced merrily round the room like a child's hoop with a will of its own, and I had to pursue it before reducing its recalcitrance to a mere seat for my pressing needs. The cold bath did the trick; I was sober when I went to an enjoyable, rather well-sung performance of Paliashvili's *Absalom and Etery*, an opera of early twentieth-century provenance, Italianate in style rather than Russian, and of about the cut and sophistication of Balfe's *Bohemian Girl*. Paliashvili must have been Georgia's latter-day Smetana; he is not to be ignored, though I think not to be exported either.

During this visit to Georgia, I sampled contemporary Georgian music, and my report to the Edinburgh Festival contains the sentence: 'The Tbilisi Symphony Orchestra played two long orchestral works to an audience consisting of myself and the small party from Moscow, a few local officials and their wives, and the respective composers, perhaps 25 all told.' One of the composers I remember was Andrei Melitonovich Balanchivadze, George Balanchine's brother. That night we went to the ballet, having in Moscow been promised a new work based on *Othello*. This was choreographed and danced by the man whom many Russians told me was the greatest male dancer of his generation in the Soviet Union, Chabukiani. But, though I met him at a party beforehand, we were told we could not see the ballet as the conductor was away and no one else knew the score. Rumour had it that Chabukiani was considered too independent to be reliable, and that Western admiration of his ballet was not encouraged.

On my last day in Tbilisi we drove to Mtskheta where we saw the cathedral and lunched with the mayor. Lunch followed the previous day's pattern, except that my speech seemed something of a triumph under prevailing circumstances; but the drive home along a winding road proved my undoing, and the cold bath was quite insufficient to compensate for the excesses of lunch. Attendance at the ballet that night was apparently mandatory but for me confined to the middle act, after which we went rather wanly home, exhausted by Georgian hospitality – bottles of brandy and records awaited us in the hotel room – to catch the early plane next morning and be back in Moscow for a second breakfast.

That night I went eagerly to the Bolshoi to see *Yevgeny Onegin* in which Sergei Lemeshev was singing Lenski – a pre-war recording star, and now pensioned (but still occasionally singing) on the same rate, Madame Furtseva told me, as a Marshal of the Red Army. Kipkalo was the excellent Onegin, Boris Khaikin conducted with total commitment, and the production, though not old, was old-fashioned in the sense that it included, one felt, every leaf on every tree and took every stage direction literally. It was very effective in the way it unerringly caught the mood and atmosphere of this subtlest of nineteenth-century operas.

I have used the expression 'old-fashioned' about these Bolshoi and Kirov performances, but the word now has overtones of choice and this is not the sense in which I mean it. Since the 1914–18 War, and in many areas for generations before that, Russia has been to a greater or lesser extent isolated from the West, which it once intellectually aped and was once partly *of*, though never *in*. In terms of singing, the era in Russia when Battistini was a regular visitor, when the great Edmea Mei settled and married, the era of Sobinoff and Neshdanova and Smirnoff (before he emigrated) – this was the last generation of performers and listeners to have regular contact with Western singing style. Since then Russians had only themselves to listen to and copy in terms of style and its evolution.

In this performance of *Onegin* the great name was that of Lemeshev, displayed in larger letters on the poster outside than the name of the opera. With him, nothing was thrown away. He did little that could be described as acting, and yet he conveyed more about the role than many who would superficially have seemed more inside it, and he contented himself for the first act with accurate, small-scale singing in a rather small, white voice. In the early part of the second act, he stood around at Madame Larina's dance, fiddling with his white gloves and seeming to have little part of the action. True, his invitation to Olga to dance was delivered in honeyed tones, but it was only after the challenge to Onegin and with the revulsion of feeling with which he tries to apologize to his hostess that he started to dominate. 'Yes, in your house' he sang in long, wonderfully expressive phrases, all at about half the speed at which the great ensemble itself was to go when it had a chance to get under way.

This performance was arguably over-expressive, with its drooping tendrils of melody, its expressive *rubato*, and more like de Lucia than Caruso; but it was beautiful and grandiose in a way (and in a bygone style) I shall never forget and probably never again hear; and at the end (of his solo phrases, not the complete ensemble) the theatre exploded. Naples for Gigli could not have revalled those Muscovites in their applause for Lemeshev, and they screamed as bobbysoxers screamed at Johnny Ray thirty years ago. In a way, it would for me have made the whole visit to Moscow worthwhile to hear a man sing like that, and I was fascinated to find that this is precisely how he sings in the last complete recording of *Onegin* in which he figures. It was as if the style of another century had been preserved, like a fly in amber, the style of an era when great licence was allowed to stars and they could use it to great effect. And to find it in Moscow ...

I had to leave after the second act, as the Ambassador was giving a party and had told me Malik, the deputy Foreign Minister, had accepted an invitation, the first time he had agreed to come to the Embassy, and this was a good sign. But the party was no different from other parties, and Lemeshev had been different from other tenors. On the other hand, Lenski is dead after Act II.

My interpreter was Mrs Afonina, middle-aged and expert, indefatigable, and when I asked her if she would not get bored at so many musical affairs, she said there was little possibility of that as her husband was a cellist in the radio orchestra and music was her passion. She was so expert that she could keep conversations going and their temperature fluctuating as if they were taking place with the speed of real talk, not through translation, and only once did we nearly come to grief. That was when I had already made a number of short, jejune speeches and was in the middle of another – 'I'd like to thank the chairman and other members of the committee for their invitation. ... And I want to say what a marvellous morning I've had looking round ...' – and suddenly realized in the middle of her Russian sentence that there was I on my feet with no idea what I'd just said or indeed where I was. She saved the situation, which must have been a matter of some dexterity as I tremble to think how many speeches vowing undying friendship she must have translated.

Russia kept surprises to the very end. The day before I left I went by invitation to say goodbye to my hostess, Madame Furtseva, at the rather inconvenient time of one-fifteen. Behind her when I went in was standing her permanent Under Secretary, Mr Stepanov, and something told me that, in that country of formality where even the eleven o'clock brandy was drunk as a toast, an informal farewell would not be quite the thing. Nobody had briefed me, but I launched into a little unpremeditated speech of thanks about the interest and value of the trip, and the co-operation and help I had had from everybody and in particular from the Under Secretary I saw standing before me, from Mr Boni, the ex-second trumpet of the Leningrad

Phil. who was at the ministry and accompanied me everywhere, and from my interpreter. I sensed a thaw of the atmosphere and saw that the permanent Under Secretary was now wreathed in smiles. The accuracy of my hunch was confirmed when Madame Furtseva half-turned and said, 'Well, I'm very glad to hear this, because I had understood that you had some difficulty at the start of your tour and I was distressed about it. I am very glad that you have had the co-operation you needed from the people whose job it was to give it to you.' I thought: 'My God! That poor unhelpful bugger is breathing again – and only because by fluke I sensed an atmosphere and launched into my panegyric.'

I had asked my hostess if I could take some caviar home, perhaps a couple of the large tins I had heard so much about, and she said she would arrange it. When I got back from my afternoon, she said they had got the caviar but there were no big tins that day, only quantities of small glass jars, which held as much caviar but would weigh an awful lot in my luggage because of the extra glass I should be carrying. With the butler's help, I wrapped them all up in newspaper to avoid breakage, gave him my Georgian brandy to make extra room in my luggage, and set off for the distant airport hoping my inevitable overweight would cause no trouble.

One of the idiosyncracies of official Russian invitations (which as yet I knew nothing of) is that they expect you to get there under your own steam but pay for the return half of the trip. Never before I suspect in the history of Anglo-Russian relations had so much unexpected overweight been incurred.

Two postscripts. Madame Furtseva came officially to London some years later, and I went to a lunch given in her honour and was allowed to entertain her to dinner at Orme Square. We collected a little party of sympathetic people, caught her in a relaxed and confident mood and, with the aid of an interpreter, had what started as an agreeable evening and ended after much story-telling as something almost riotous.

Later still, when the newspapers had carried stories of her disgrace, the Bolshoi Ballet was at the Coliseum. Marius Liepa, perhaps the biggest star among their splendid male dancers, brought me Madame Furtseva's greetings and best wishes for the season, assuring me he had seen her two days previously and in the best of spirits. The disgrace? 'A story only – she is indestructible,' he said. Then he leant closer and his voice took on a confidential note: 'May I ask a favour?' I recognized with a feeling of something like sickness that he was about to defect and ask for asylum. What could I say? The season was already hedged around with Zionist protest, we had been hoping to break into the Bolshoi's foreign touring circuit and get them to come to the Coliseum in future; how would this affect that hope? But here was a human being in trouble and about to ask for help; how could I refuse? He went on: 'Last time I was here, Queen come to see me dancing. I have little gift for her, but I am afraid she may not get it if I send it through Embassy. Will you send for me?' Never was anti-climax more welcome. I hope the gift was appreciated.

CHAPTER FOURTEEN

Patricia
1959-67

IN EARLY JANUARY 1959, I was sitting rather disconsolately at about lunchtime in the Air France terminal in Milan, eating a bar of chocolate. My mission over the past day or two – to persuade Maria Callas to sing a second opera in London that summer – had not been a success. I had cancelled my place on that day's flight to London in order to see Maria again and, knowing Milan's propensity to fog, was going halfway and spending the night in Paris in order to be sure of reaching London the following morning.

When the flight was called I offered to carry the violin of the only other occupant of the waiting room, and was allowed instead to pick up the less precious bag she had in the other hand. She told me she was an Australian, Barry Tuckwell's sister, and on her first visit to Europe. I had met Barry, already well-known among musicians, and this seemed sufficient introduction; we gossiped about music here, there and everywhere as we flew in a nearly empty plane to Paris, and I gave her dinner when we arrived.

Patricia had been staying with friends in Trieste and was booked for a week in Paris before going on to London to stay until spring with her brother. As I was due to hear a singer in Paris a few days later, I asked her to come with me and so, for her first opera in Europe, Patricia saw *Salome* at the Paris Opéra, with Jane Rhodes excellent in the title role supported by Ramon Vinay and Rita Gorr, the singer I had come to hear. Weeks later, I discovered the accidental nature of our meeting – not only had I stayed on in Milan quite by chance, but Patricia had been due to leave Trieste days earlier and had changed her plans because the friend with whom she had been staying, the Australian pianist Maureen Jones, had fallen ill between Christmas and the New Year.

I told Marion about my chance meeting with Barry's sister, and Patricia came several times to opera or plays with us. A photograph even appeared of

Patricia and me dancing together at the annual Opera Ball in March –
Patricia in a sari that Marion had lent her, I for the only time in my life in
drag, as a rather tall, bonneted Ellen Orford! I had seen Patricia several times
in London before that but, soon after the Ball, my feelings for her had
become too strong to conceal any longer and I felt obliged to tell Marion
about them.

This was the start of a very difficult period for all three people concerned,
and perhaps for others who found themselves dragged into it. Marion told
me she was convinced that Patricia would quickly become bored and the
whole thing would pass over. But I knew I was deeply in love, I believed
Patricia was too, and the second possibility seemed therefore a bit remote. I
saw Patricia frequently during the hot summer of 1959 and it was inevitably a
time compounded partly of the sheer joy of being in love, partly of the
miseries of deception (since Marion knew what was happening but obviously
not the details), partly of despair at the uncertainty of the future.

Patricia comes of a musical family and was a musician from infancy,
joining the Sydney Symphony Orchestra when she was sixteen and playing in
the first violins until she married. Her first husband was a photographer and
she became well-known in Melbourne as a fashion model, though years later,
when our involvement became public, she intensely resented being described
as that; modelling was a sideline, but music was her profession.

By the end of summer 1959, she decided she should not remain in England
but would take up her life again in Australia, where she had a small business.
She might return to Europe, she thought, some time the following year, but
in the meanwhile we prepared for her to continue her long-interrupted
round-the-world trip which would take her through the United States and
Hawaii. I have always hated goodbyes and the element of finality they
contain – even if planned to be short, they are in their context absolute – and
I could not imagine how to steel myself for this one; whatever gloss we put on
it, I felt as if I was planning my own execution. Patricia and I had dinner
together, and I saw her leave for the airport, then went back to spend the
evening alone, numb and desolate, as realization flooded in on me that I had
just knowingly and with my eyes open said goodbye to someone who seemed
to embody my greatest hope of happiness.

The separation gnawed at me. Though we had talked about Patricia's
return the following year and I was clinging to this as to a lifeline, we both
knew the parting was meant to be final and, though I tried to hide it, once
Patricia had gone she filled my thoughts night and day. Marion and I had
been invited long before to stay with Topazia and Igor Markevich near

Positano, and we went there together. When we got back, rehearsal was about to start for the new season at Covent Garden. Patricia had agreed to write letters to me there and I had already received two or three describing her travels when, arriving at the theatre around ten one morning, I found one saying she had made up her mind that it would be folly to return to Europe as this was sure to reopen something between us that could not fail to be painful to everyone; she was therefore giving up any idea of coming back.

The desire to throw myself under a bus has come to me only this once, but it was replaced by the more practical realization that it was still early evening in Australia and I could telephone her from the Post Office before bedtime there. I half-expected to find her in the middle of a party celebrating her marriage or something equally final, but she was alone, and sounded her old self. She assured me she had felt that her letter, hard as it was to write, contained the sensible solution, but that she had no plans and was prepared to wait to hear from me. This felt like some sort of reprieve, and confidence of a kind returned.

I wrote and told her what a devastating effect her letter had had, and said I found the future impossible to contemplate without her. A week of suspended animation meandered by until one day in the train from Harewood to London, my head whirling with so many unspecified worries that rational thought tailed off into chaos, I fell asleep and woke ten minutes later with a quite new sensation of confidence. In my mind I had no doubt that Patricia had had my letter and decided to come back to England, that the future however great its problems was no longer quite bleak, that life could be resumed with vigour and purpose. Three or four days later, a letter arrived saying that she had brooded over what I had written, that she would resolve her business in Australia and would come to England around the New Year.

My ideas were nebulous, in the sense that I had no detailed course of action mapped out, but I had no doubt that my future was with Patricia and that I must somehow resolve the situation. It was plainly going to be very difficult and I was under no illusion that the pain it would cause Marion was not the least of the obstacles I faced. Our children, David, James and Jeremy, were around nine, six and four years old, and David at least was old enough to understand. What to tell them and when worried me more than almost anything else, and to this major problem I could think of no solution. In early autumn, I told Marion the situation and tried to discuss things with her, but she seemed to find it hard to take what I said seriously, even to believe that Patricia would return to England. In fact, it was not until the following year and after Patricia was in England that I asked Marion if she would give me a divorce.

For a variety of reasons of which we were only partly aware, Marion and I had been drifting slowly apart. Close friends whom I think of as wise and therefore not just concerned with being knowing after the event, told me around the time of our divorce that they had sensed unease amounting to serious friction between Marion and me long before any element of break was visible, some time before Patricia came into my life. One suggested that we failed too regularly to overcome the small misunderstandings and breakdowns of communication that occur in any married life but allowed them to grow into issues where no true issue should have existed, and that this failure was not confined to one or other of us but was mutual. Marion herself accused me (not perhaps totally without justice) of Sunday after Sunday sheltering behind gramophone and typewriter and (less fairly) of using them to form a barrier against the real world and particularly against her, refusing to communicate on the vital issues or talk them through. Another friend later told her, to her indignation, that she had run neither Orme Square nor Harewood with the efficiency I was unconsciously demanding of her. A third said that we (and particularly I) had never been sufficiently tested by life, and had had it too easy too long to be properly equipped if anything were to go wrong in so outwardly untroubled an existence, and followed this up by saying that I had always looked for a partner from a background unlike my own, and that Marion had adapted so completely that I had subconsciously begun to look for someone else to fill the role I had assigned her.

These things were, perhaps not surprisingly, by no means apparent to me, nor, I must in honesty admit, did they immediately emerge from my long and (I felt) successful sessions in the 1960s with a psychoanalyst, to whom I had recourse, urged on by those who thought this would help me to see my position with greater clarity and persuade me to give up Patricia. This he did not attempt, nor did he urge any sudden change in a situation which he may have felt – even though he perceived it of necessity entirely through my conscious and subconscious reactions – not yet ready to be resolved. I can't tell, and he is dead and can't, and doubtless wouldn't, say.

When I started to see the analyst, I had a powerful feeling of guilt about my whole situation, and could not believe it was right to eliminate this feeling. My talks with him put it into perspective, until I was nearer to accepting it. 'In this life you pay for everything, for every happiness,' he said. I believed that, and virtually nobody I talked to at this period of maximum strain other than my analyst ever suggested that, though the 'guilt' was inevitably mine, the 'blame', which I felt indistinguishable from the guilt, could possibly be shared.

The analyst was right to suggest that the instinct for love cannot readily arise unless there is room, even need, for it. I felt that my love for Patricia was strong and abiding – I had never in my heart doubted it, but the contrary view was rather persistently urged on me – and I persuaded myself that the passing of time could bring Marion to accept the break I felt had become inevitable. I somehow hoped this might be made more acceptable, and she might be cushioned against the hurt, if the process were not too quick. With hindsight, I cannot understand how I was naive enough to misjudge the situation as I did – and it is of course no use emphasizing, as anyone who embarks on this kind of explanation is in danger of doing, the difficulties involved in seeing clearly in a misty situation. I did not succeed when it was my obligation to do so, and for that the blame is mine, not someone else's – nor the situation's.

Friends helped. To be, as I was, seemingly condemned on all sides as 'the guilty party' is an educative experience, partly because it helps you discover who your friends are – a true friend may be tough with criticism but will be generous with support – but also because the intensity of the experience of rejection helps you sort out your own values and priorities. I do not believe that you can have dozens of friends – you may know and like hundreds of people but only a few count as friends. I was lucky in my friends, but sometimes surprised to discover those who were turning out to be no more than acquaintances and so, from my point of view, falling by the wayside.

I found myself able to talk to very few people about the problem, as neither self-pity nor recrimination seemed useful, and there were few who could do much even by way of palliative. Ben Britten was an early and sympathetic listener, but it was soon apparent that his old ties with Marion and her family impelled him towards a one-sided and therefore to me unhelpful view. Ronnie Duncan on the other hand was a constant refuge from the storm, partly because its buffetings were not unknown to him, partly because he is a man of humanity and kindness who would not take sides in an issue where he knew both parties well and which he felt was a matter for the two of them to resolve.

Patricia and I unburdened ourselves to Dicky Buckle, an old friend, and to Ken Tynan, a new one, who did not, unlike the others, know Marion. It was some element of comfort to receive understanding from my neighbour and friend in Yorkshire, Everard Radcliffe, who was a Roman Catholic and might have been expected to be the last to sympathize. It was good to find long-term acquaintances, as were Howard and Margaret Hartog, becoming close friends, and I relied as always on Neville and Marguerite Ussher, the staunchest of allies (but it was disconcerting to hear years later from Neville that a mutual 'friend' had urged him to leave Harewood in an effort 'to bring me to my senses').

The sessions with the analyst, designed to help me straighten out my life, might quite possibly have turned out negatively; Patricia went to another at the same time, from whom she derived only hostility and muddle. With mine however I eventually saw that divorce was not only the right but the only course – and I doubt if it is possible to exaggerate the horror with which I initially looked upon the idea of divorce, which was less prevalent in England in those days and seemed to me at first, inasmuch as I had thought about it, the refuge of despair. But my analysis at least taught me to contemplate the idea, though nothing could have prepared me for the horrors the whole inexorable process inflicts on everyone concerned.

Not everything about those years was the hell that some of it felt like at the time. I was very much in love with Patricia and we travelled about a certain amount; it was one of the few ways we found of being together for any length of time, and we got to know Spain a bit in the process. Together we plotted the programmes of Edinburgh Festivals (through which Patricia then solitarily suffered) and we took holidays afterwards. By no means least important, we found we could laugh at the same things. Marion persisted in refusing me a divorce and Patricia and I inevitably wondered about the future as well as bemoaning the present. Finally, we made up our minds to have a child. Patricia had been twenty-two when Michael, her elder son, was born; we had often told each other that it was an intolerable waste of love and affection not to have a child together and we had begun to feel that time was not necessarily on our side – she was nearly thirty-seven. We were delighted when she became pregnant soon after we made our decision.

When they heard about Patricia's pregnancy, 'friends' urged me to recognize that I had been 'trapped'. As I knew that this was not so – Patricia and I had made a joint decision as a result of prolonged discussion, and believing that Marion would not then or in the immediate future contemplate divorce – I did not take this line of thinking very seriously. We had half-expected a girl, but were delighted when Mark was born in July of 1964.

During what were often difficult days, I used to return to Harewood on my own, partly to attempt to think things out but more in search of refuge. These visits carried with them something of the joy of rediscovery, of the knowledge of certainties that I had perhaps never doubted, mainly because I had never had cause to question them. Harewood and more generally Yorkshire was that certainty, the surrogate family to which I found I was able to retreat in times of stress. Respite from the fray is all you can hope for at such moments, not the solution of problems, which don't go away just because you stop looking at them. I never doubted my love for my three older sons but could not help telling myself I was betraying them, and no amount of rationalization along the lines that a marriage from which love has departed is worse for its children than a broken one could remove that insidious ache. The possibility that I might lose contact with them was acutely painful, and at times the mental stress seemed to permeate every waking and sleeping hour.

I had clung on to some idea of Marion agreeing amicably to a divorce before I left Orme Square but I should have known earlier that this was an illusion. Accordingly, the night before they were due to go off with her on holiday abroad, I steeled myself to tell David, James and Jeremy that my intention was to leave Marion, and next day I waved them good-bye as they departed – for some reason, I had built up a mental and psychological block about the notion of watching the boys wave to me as I left and this seemed slightly less impossible; *all* choices in this area were basically unacceptable. Marion had – it seemed to me, very generously – the evening before made some reference to having enjoyed much of the time we had spent together but my response had entirely failed to satisfy her. Since I was leaving her, it felt altogether too easy, even glib, to reciprocate whole-heartedly, and I only thanked her for what she had said. I think she resented this, and of course the truth was that I too was grateful for a number of happy years we had shared. We had had a lot in common, had shared love and affection as well as children, and logically even divorce could not entirely eradicate these things, however much a part of the past subsequent events had made them become. I wish I had said so more convincingly.

After I left the Edinburgh Festival in 1965 I started to work for the New Philharmonia Orchestra, and the work and the contacts it brought me provided distraction from my worst preoccupations. So did the by now constant presence of Patricia, who was adept at lessening the pressures I felt, partly perhaps because she had herself undergone some of them before.

In the end, some eighteen months after we had finally broken – perhaps five years later than we should have – Marion agreed to divorce, and the case was set down in January 1967. I had earlier been advised by Ronnie Duncan, and had the advice confirmed by an astute lawyer, that press interest (the harassment had sometimes been hard to accept) could be focussed and defused by a single all-embracing statement and the pressure on everyone thereafter considerably lessened. Accordingly, at the same time as the divorce was set down and became public, I instructed my lawyer to send the following to the press:

We have recently, on Lord Harewood's behalf, accepted service of divorce proceedings, whereby Lady Harewood petitions for divorce on the ground of her husband's adultery with Miss Patricia Tuckwell. Lord Harewood will not defend these proceedings and he and Miss Tuckwell would wish to marry if and when they are legally free to do so.

Lord Harewood has lived separately from Lady Harewood for the last sixteen months at his house in St John's Wood, London. A son, Mark, was born there to Miss Tuckwell in July 1964, of whom Lord Harewood is the father.

I hoped and believed that one explosion would finish the whole thing off, ending speculation about Mark's existence and Patricia's and my intentions. To a considerable degree it worked, and I am sure, in spite of her protests at the time, that Marion benefited from the ending of speculation. Nonetheless, press spies continued to lurk round the house in Hamilton Terrace which Patricia and I had shared since before Mark was born, and a friend assured us that the *Daily Telegraph*, for which he then worked, was maintaining a close watch in the person of one of its most eager reporters. He had personal proof of this since the individual concerned approached him for news as he left us after a visit.

A couple of months after our divorce had been set down, Marion agreed that my three elder sons could meet Mark for the first time. He was two and a half and had become very excited at the prospect of seeing them. David was already a very tall sixteen and the others must also have appeared like giants to Mark when they came for lunch to our house in Hamilton Terrace, but he turned to us in amazed delight: 'Are these *all* my gruthers?' From the time they played football together in the garden that day, David, James and Jeremy, whatever resentments they may subconsciously have had, were always marvellous with Mark, as later was also Patricia's elder son, Michael Shmith.

The divorce came through in early July 1967, and Patricia and I were determined to be married quietly and without fuss. There would if we could help it be no repetition of what had happened in January, when we had been bullied into making a bad slip. When my divorce was set down, the press said they had no picture of Patricia and told her lawyer they would leave her alone if she would allow one to be taken. The lawyer arranged this with the Press Association and the photograph appeared with, in certain papers, references to shameless posing for publicity purposes, which seemed rather tough in the circumstances. The *Daily Telegraph* had taken pains to publish Mark's birth certificate, in which the father's name was left blank; the *Sunday Telegraph* had followed this up with a reasoned article about the decline of moral standards in Britain, of which we were a prime example. Privacy seemed a very definite requirement of any arrangements we might find ourselves now able to make.

My lawyer found out that the Queen's consent to my remarriage, which I had asked her for, would be given at the Privy Council on 28 July, and that we could be married at any time after that. A skilful formula had been devised to avoid as far as possible offending religious susceptibilities, with the help I have always imagined of Harold Wilson, then Prime Minister, and perhaps too of my friend Lord Goodman, who was then his lawyer. The Privy Council's announcement read like this:

The Earl of Harewood has sought the Queen's consent, in accordance with the Royal Marriages Act of 1772, to marry Miss Tuckwell. The Cabinet have advised the Queen to give her consent and Her Majesty has signified her intention to do so.

Nonetheless, things were not yet simple. The British Act of Parliament making it legal to be married in a registry office in its wisdom specifically excludes anyone covered by the Royal Marriages Act; banns and a church wedding were therefore necessary for us in England (but for divorcees unavailable), and things were not much easier in Scotland and Wales. We discovered that notice of some length was needed in France, Germany and Scandinavia, that only Roman Catholics seemed to be legally wed in Italy and Spain, that in Lebanon only Muslim or Catholic marriages existed (why not turn Muslim? asked the Lebanese Ambassador, Nadim Dimechkié).

Our best bet seemed to be America, where lengthy notice could be waived without difficulty and where a civil marriage was perfectly in order for anyone. The foreign currency allowance was then set at £50 a year, so, having checked with our lawyer that in America it could be worked quickly and without fuss, we asked a kind friend in New York, Nancy Lassalle, if we might stay with her in her apartment on Fifth Avenue.

We had been invited by Lies Askonas to stay with her in Menorca, as a ten-day pre-honeymoon, so to speak, and arranged with an airline to get us out of England under assumed names. We smuggled first our luggage and then ourselves out of our house in Hamilton Terrace, Patricia hiding under rugs at the back of the car, leaving the press to watch the house while we were away (a lethargic kind of surveillance, which sprang into life only if both of us left the house together, when they followed us, even to the theatre or a restaurant). We spent a night with Garrett and Joan Drogheda at their house at Englefield Green, not far from London Airport and out of reach of reporters – a refuge for which each of us will long be grateful, which they offered without hesitation and which enabled us to get away unobserved.

The holiday was fun, except that we had decided I should in the interests of anonymity wear some headgear, which I never do, so that to our friends' amazement we turned up in Menorca in dark glasses and, in my case, a blue summer hat. Our flight to Menorca from Mallorca had been with a party from Manchester, which we had not anticipated, and the sea round Menorca seemed to be full of people from Yorkshire, including, as we heard him say, a man from Knaresborough, not far from Harewood; but we stayed anonymous during those ten days. Once on board an aircraft at Barcelona bound for New York, we felt entitled to think the worst was over. We had arranged with our lawyer in London that he would alert a New York firm to arrange formalities – we needed an uninquisitive registry office somewhere close to New York (in which city divorced people could not be remarried within a year of divorce), someone with a knowledge of American law to tell us what was required before the ceremony could take place, and a discreet Justice of the Peace to make it all legal.

On arrival, I telephoned the firm to find that the partner I was told to ask for was on holiday, and no one else seemed to know anything about us. But our arrangements lumbered on, few of them made by the lawyers and most of the information gathered by Nancy Lassalle. The formalities had to be lodged a few days beforehand with the registry office, and a Wasserman test (to see if you have syphilis) had to be undergone and a certificate produced before any marriage could be legalized. A nurse took samples of our blood (and $10 from each of us), the lawyer contacted a friendly Justice, and we went off to register our intentions at New Canaan, Connecticut.

The July heat and humidity were sweltering; we found the office and in it an old gnome of a registrar, looking, as Patricia said, like Guy Kibbee of film fame. He sat in his shirtsleeves and a green eye-shade at his desk with a typewriter, and asked for my name. He managed to get it all down, with some muttering about a real live Earl and confusion between Lascelles and Harewood as surnames (which were after all on my passport); but when he asked for my mother's maiden name, I felt unequal to the struggle. Patricia weighed in unperturbed and dictated while he typed in spluttering disbelief. Patricia's details were simpler, and eventually we left, having arranged to pick up the licence after the weekend.

Back in New York there was little still to do, except pick up our

Wasserman certificates. (The American lawyer took us to lunch and said he had never understood why, with modern medicine, if the test proved positive, the two parties could not work it out together!) And we invited a few discreet friends to celebrate with us the following night. It was hot, and we never in those six or seven days succeeded in getting attuned to the time change. To wake at five was therefore normal, and I used to get up and watch the first joggers in Central Park. I was doing this one morning with nothing on, when to my left, through another window, I saw on the roof a floor below some nuns, eyes discreetly cast down, gathering for their dawn orisons. Nancy told us it was a convent school – the Sacred Heart – ironically enough in the top floors of the old house of Otto Kahn, the banker and onetime backer of the Metropolitan Opera.

On the day itself, Patricia's brother Barry flew up from Daytona, where the London Symphony Orchestra of which he was a member was in residence for the summer. The lawyer had turned up trumps with the day's arrangements, and we were married in the garden of a client of his, which to some extent offset the blistering heat and humidity of Connecticut in summer. The words were read over us by a tall judge, who spoke beautifully but split his trousers from knee to crutch as we opened the champagne. Back in New York, several friends came for a drink, including Lincoln Kirstein, who whirled in on a shuttle from Boston, stayed half an hour during which he gave us wedding presents – including a netsuke which turned out to be a *memento mori* – and then whirled out again on the next shuttle.

We had problems finding two seats together on the morning flight to London, but Pan Am helped, and in the end got someone to change. So we flew home, having run the gauntlet of a lounge where everyone was deep inside a paper on the cover of which our photograph appeared – a journalist had rumbled the names put down at the New Canaan registry and had queried it with our lawyer, who gave the photographer exclusive rights provided he kept his mouth shut. The photographer came to the wedding ceremony, bringing, as Barry found out, only two plates with him; but the *Daily News* duly carried the photograph and so did the English papers, as we found when we got to London Airport.

Next day we drove up to Harewood. Mark followed a couple of days later, and we spent the week driving round the woods and going for picnics as if things had never been different, feeling grateful to our friends in Englefield Green, Menorca and New York, who had helped us out and made us feel so welcome – but less grateful, perhaps, to the New York lawyer who sent in a bill for $5,000, of which on advice taken in London we only paid half.

CHAPTER FIFTEEN

Maria Callas
1947-76

GIANTS IN ANY walk of life are usually easy to recognize in their own time, certainly in retrospect; and when I was asked to talk about Maria Callas at a public lecture for the British Institute of Recorded Sound rather less than a year after her death I suggested that she was in her sphere as dominant a personality as in theirs had been Churchill, Roosevelt and de Gaulle; Hitler, Mussolini and Stalin; Chaplin and Garbo; Toscanini and Furtwängler. Their names were household words, and so in opera was hers, as had once been Patti and Jean de Reszke, Melba and Caruso and Chaliapin. After 1945, she was the one operatic performer known to the majority of the Western world.

I first heard her quite by accident at the Arena di Verona in August 1947, in *La Gioconda*. It was the second or third performance of her Italian début role and she was no more than twenty-three. But even I, only a few months older, could tell then that her voice and her style already demonstrated some of the characteristics which one was to associate with her for much of the rest of her career. There was a very strong attack, and a power that was almost steely when she sang at full throttle, which in that vast amphitheatre she had very frequently to do. She displayed considerable flexibility and a smooth and expressive *legato*. The Arena di Verona holds some 25,000 spectators and for this *Gioconda* it was full. The conductor was Tullio Serafin, who was to become Callas's mentor, and there was a strong cast – Elena Nicolai was the mezzo, Richard Tucker making his Italian début was Enzo, Tagliabue the Barnaba, Rossi-Lemeni was Alvise, and the production, as it had to be in that great space, was grandiose. Much of Venice seemed to be on the stage, ships hove into sight and burst into flames, and the audience reacted with enthusiasm.

When I listen to the recording she made five years after that Italian début, I

224

find the same power and dominance that I remember, and the brilliant and what people came to call 'tigerish' quality, which was one of her characteristics. Callas was always an individual and the shrillness, which some found disturbing in her singing, and an element of unsteadiness on high notes, were already apparent at her début and can be heard in the recording. But I nonetheless prize it for the memories it brings back.

The next time I heard her was purely by chance, as she had been performing at Verona. I was twiddling the radio one winter evening and caught the last act of *Tristan* in a broadcast from Venice. It was in Italian, and the voice of the soprano immediately sounded familiar, though I could not put a name to her. At the end of the last act, which was all I heard, I found that the tenor was Fiorenzo Tasso, the bass Boris Christoff, and the soprano Maria Callas. As in Verona, Serafin conducted. Eighteen months later she recorded the '*Liebestod*', with a sweetness of sound uncommon in any singer of this role and perhaps even in Callas at this period. The intensity and fire which develop on her recording seem peculiarly apt to the role, and it is one of the sadnesses of recording history that tapes of the complete opera have disappeared.

Rumours of this new portent in the operatic land began to circulate widely, but I didn't hear her again in the theatre until 1951, when Marion and I went to Florence to hear Erich Kleiber conduct a splendid revival of Verdi's *Sicilian Vespers*. The night we arrived we dined in our hotel, and saw, sitting alone, someone whom I was convinced was the young soprano I had met in Verona three and a half years before. She had put on a lot of weight, and indeed the buxom soprano of 1947 was now a very large lady indeed; but, when we came to hear rehearsals, we found the vocal qualities hadn't changed, although I found them better integrated than before. The technique and assurance seemed to have grown enormously, and what had formerly been an obvious aptitude for operatic tragedy had turned into nothing less than a sovereign dramatic authority.

I had little doubt I was listening to a great artist and of course talked about her to David Webster when I got back to London. He was aware of her growing fame and I was delighted, as a member of the Board at Covent Garden, to learn that negotiations immediately started to get her to sing in a new production of *Norma* at Covent Garden in 1952. I went to some rehearsals and must have heard three out of the five performances given; their effect was overwhelming. *Norma* is not an easy opera to stage, and the garb of a Druidic priestess, consisting as it does mostly of white sheets, is unflattering to all but the possessor of a svelte figure. Neither Callas nor Ebe

Stignani would then have been described as that, and these two big ladies could, had they not been consummate artists, have proved risible stage figures. But of course they were not, as they sang superbly, and I remember their first duet (*not* the more famous '*Mira o Norma*') being encored.

I saw a little of Maria socially during that visit and was invited to a party for the four principal singers at the Italian Embassy where all were expected to perform. Callas, the Greek, was the only one who turned up, and she did indeed sing for her supper – the first act aria from *Traviata*, which was magnificent if inordinately big-scale in the relatively small space. I took her and her husband Battista Meneghini out to lunch at the Musicians Club in South Audley Street, and Marion offered to take her shopping. The weather was warm and Maria had a short-sleeved dress on; she looked at her arms with disdain and said she didn't think she had the energy to go shopping: 'Who would want to drag all this around?' she said. It was true that she was then so fat that her elbows appeared to be dimples rather than bones.

After that same lunch, a French mezzo soprano called Renée Gilly, whom I had met and who was a lady of formidable presence, strode towards our table and demanded to be introduced in order to compliment the diva. She started to talk, whereupon Callas, whom I knew to be extremely short-sighted, whipped off her glasses and put them on the table, gazing in a generalized sort of way at the other singer who was lecturing her in an admittedly complimentary manner. When she had gone, I asked Callas why she had taken her glasses off, as I thought she couldn't see without them. She said that that was precisely the reason: 'She seemed so ferocious it was the only protection I had!'

Next summer, the Coronation year, she came to London to sing *Aida*, *Norma* again (this time with Simionato) and *Trovatore*, which were perhaps the most successful performances during that celebratory season. *Trovatore* I remember was conducted by Alberto Erede, and she and he never reached agreement on how to phrase the last act aria.

I felt I really got to know her voice at this time and became a whole-hearted and devoted admirer, unprepared to hear ill of her (and in those days one often did), and keen to spread appreciation of what seemed to me a phenomenal talent. The previous winter I had taken Ben Britten to hear her and Stignani, and Ben had come away overwhelmed by the talent and the sheer size and majesty of her voice – he didn't always react that way to 'star' performers. I don't think I overtly tried to analyse what was going on, but I was conscious that she was quite a different kind of singer from other people, and was delighted when many years later in the splendid book on the singer

226

by John Ardoin and Gerald Fitzgerald I came across a quotation which they felt relevant to Callas, but was in fact from something written by the French composer Camille Saint-Saens on the subject of Pauline Viardot. Saint-Saens said that Viardot's voice was 'a little harsh and it was likened to the taste of a bitter orange'. I find this extraordinarily appropriate to Callas, and it was no doubt this unusual quality which caused some people to find her voice too different from their expectations to give them genuine pleasure.

At Covent Garden, where I was by then working, we tried to get her for the summer of 1955 but were told she was unavailable; we might succeed in persuading her rival Renata Tebaldi to come instead. Accordingly, I went in early January to Naples to see Tebaldi and, my visit over, repaired to Milan where Callas was appearing, at very short notice, in *Andrea Chénier*. I knew she had been dieting, but the slim, lissom girl I saw on the stage came as something of a shock. In a sense her whole personality had changed, though the lightness of movement and new feminine beauty had not been won at the cost of the powerful, dramatic personality we already knew. This was not however the type of role in which she had won fame and I believe there was considerable disagreement with her interpretation, at least at the première. By the time I caught it, she was completely assured and what I saw and heard was revelation.

When we met, my surprise and delight gave her obvious pleasure, and I think this must have been one of the first times she said to me something she was to repeat more than once: 'If you want to appreciate me, you must hear me often. I know I vary, that the voice varies, but I am always trying to *do* something and only sometimes will it be successful. If you don't come often, you won't catch the good performances.' I thought this at the time rather arrogant, but I came to believe that it was the literal truth. She knew perfectly well that what she was trying to do could not be fully achieved more than occasionally, given the type of voice she had – and without that kind of voice she could not have embarked on the attempt.

People became accustomed to saying that she was besottedly ambitious, and ambition is something most people would associate with her – with the way she bestrode the operatic world for a decade, the way she slimmed from a heavyweight soprano to a front-page beauty, the way her several attempts at a later comeback were partially defeated by the sheer load of fame she carried to each performance. I would myself accept the description solely in the sense that she was *musically* ambitious, that she never by any chance allowed herself to shirk anything which seemed to be implied in what the composer had written. Of course she seldom achieved perfection, whateve that may be, but always she aimed at something far beyond the normal: not just an absence of faults but the full achievement of what she believed the composer had in mind.

What this kind of ambition could produce I discovered perhaps most completely the following year, when there was a revival at la Scala of the famous 1955 production of *Traviata* by Luchino Visconti – she sang it no less than seventeen times that season. The production was itself of quite astonishing beauty, updated to 1880 but with an attention to detail and, from Callas at least, an expressive freedom that would have been worth going half-way across the world to see and hear. Everything she did seemed to me perfection, and some of it was very far out of the ordinary. At the end of the first act, she looked in a great looking glass over the chimney piece before beginning her aria then, at its end, kicked off her shoes, swept glasses and crockery off the front of a table and leant back on it to sing her *cabaletta* – a quite wonderfully convincing dramatic accompaniment to wonderfully convincing singing. Years later, she told me how she had worked to perfect the moment of Violetta's death. The point, she said, was that she was dead *before she actually hit the floor*; that this is how somebody with consumption would have died; and of that dying fall she remained very proud years after she and Visconti had rehearsed it.

If I had to nominate my own favourite among her roles, I suppose I should choose Violetta, partly because it is a very favourite opera, but also because I think it is not fanciful to suggest that she identified with the character more fully than with perhaps any other; she found in it parallels to life that bit deeper than those in her beloved *Norma*. Was not Violetta someone whose past could never be forgiven, whatever the purity of her present – a woman whose attempts to subdue her illness because of the depth of her love for Alfredo somehow paralleled Callas's own attempts to subdue her voice because of what she wanted through it to give the world? Above all, whatever her faults, was not Violetta more sinned against than sinning, and might God not judge her, like Callas herself, more charitably than have her fellow men? She played the role more often than any other except Norma, and perhaps that Milan production for her by Luchino Visconti was the high watermark of her career.

In early 1957 she came again to London, to repeat *Norma*. In one sense, even though far from Violetta, Norma was the essence of Callas, the epitome of the grand, tragic figures she was born to portray. It was this heroic brilliance that her voice and one aspect of her art aspired constantly towards. She used to sing the great opening aria, '*Casta diva*', on the grandest scale, always with poise, powerful enunciation, and command of the voice (perhaps not invariably the same thing as control). At a dress rehearsal at Covent Garden in January 1957 I heard her sing it much more quietly and in a uniquely imaginative way, which I felt suited the introspection of the prayer better than her more usual manner. I complimented her afterwards, but she explained that to sing it like that would not be in any circumstances permissible in front of the public, and she had only done it that way at the rehearsal because she was assured that there were only students and management present. In Italy, she said, a heroic approach to the music was mandatory, and that evening she repeated the comment after dinner when I had played her some records of Lilli Lehmann in the role, which she enjoyed with the comment that she only wished one would be allowed to sing it that way nowadays in Italy.

'Norma resembles me in a certain way,' Callas said to me in Paris in 1968. 'She seems very strong, very ferocious at times. Actually, she is not, even though she roars like a lion.'

In the summer of 1957, I went to see her to persuade her to sing in London in 1958. I believed I had got her to agree to do two operas, one of which would be *Traviata* and the other perhaps a revival of *Norma*. She disliked tying ends up securely, and preferred to ponder decisions; and indeed she enjoyed the process of being wooed more than that of final agreement, although that too would eventually come.

As I was leaving, I said that Marion and I were going up to Edinburgh to hear her in *Sonnambula*, and she said, 'I am singing on August 19, 21, 26 and 29.' I remembered that I was going to her last performance, but thought the date was in September; when I got home, I looked it up in my diary and found I was right. This was the year of the great hullabaloo, because she did not sing this fifth performance and was held to have 'cancelled' and let down la Scala and public alike. There was of course little truth in the whole thing. She had been asked to sing all five performances, had told la Scala she would sing only four, and was determined to leave at the end of August because she needed a holiday. La Scala refused to accept her refusal but took care to engage no less a singer than Renata Scotto as her understudy. Scotto duly sang the performance and Callas was made to carry the can, nobody having the courage to admit that she had never agreed to do more than four.

In early December of 1957 I heard her sing quite splendidly in *Ballo* at la Scala, a performance that has been issued on record by Cetra. A few weeks later, she was to cause another scandal when she was due to open the Rome season in *Norma* on 2 January. She had informed the management that she, like two other members of the cast, had a throat infection; they replaced the two colleagues but refused to have an understudy ready to take over in case she couldn't go on. In the event, she refused to continue after the first act and all hell was let loose. The President of Italy was in the audience, which was kept waiting for nearly an hour before the management realized it could in no circumstances get her to continue.

As it happened, after that ill-starred evening in Rome Callas went to America and did not sing again in Italy until early April, when *Anna Bolena* was due to be revived at la Scala in connection with the Milan Spring Fair. The tension before that revival could be felt all week and, when I lunched with her the day before, there were graffiti of a by no means complimentary nature on the pavement in front of her house. It was startling to an outsider to find at the performance what one would have thought of as 'her' audience in Milan – to whom she had given so much for the past five years – greeting her at her entrance in total silence, and then proceeding to rapturous applause five minutes later for the admittedly admirable Giulietta Simionato.

But Callas was not to be outfaced. In the opera, Ann Boleyn is wrongfully accused and the king threatens to arraign her before the court. '*Giudici ad Anna!*' exclaims the queen, and the magnificence of the diva's musical and vocal attack combined with the appropriateness of the stage situation to her own to give her complete victory. Applause grew throughout the evening and at the end it must have lasted for a full half hour after the curtain had fallen on the opera.

The drama was not yet over. I was going to have dinner with her, but she was not ready to leave until an hour and a half after the curtain calls had finished – and then we found that the streets were lined with hundreds of enthusiastic Milanese waiting to escort an exhausted prima donna to supper – at three in the morning! That had really been a battle won – and the conductor Giulini, who worked with her often, pinpointed this element in her career in a tribute he paid to her in the magazine *Opera* a month after her death: every performance, at least in Italy, was something of a battle between her and the audience.

That summer of 1958 we failed to persuade her to sing two operas at Covent Garden but she appeared at the Gala which celebrated a hundred years of the theatre's existence. Callas accepted our invitation to sing the mad scene from *Puritani* – to my mind, vocally perhaps the most perfectly shaped and enunciated of anything she sang – and this was the centre-piece of the evening. By 1958, everything Callas did, if the media had their way, had to be surrounded by controversy – there had to be cancellations or threats of cancellations, other singers had to have their noses put out of joint, managements to be grey with worry about what would happen, the diva herself to be cajoled into making some controversial pronouncement or other. None of these things did they manage to provoke that summer, but they contrived one piece of dirt – fictitious, though based on uncontroversial elements of fact.

A number of leading theatrical performers were taking part in the Gala, headed by Callas and Margot Fonteyn – the resident prima ballerina and a world star. All of them, we felt, could defer to Callas in the matter of the Number One dressing room except Margot, who had dressed in it for every performance she had given at Covent Garden since the reopening of the theatre.

I had a brainwave. My office, one floor above stage level with which it was connected by lift, had originally been a dressing room, and there was a wash basin in the corner. Could we not rig up a nicely-decorated dressing table and lamps, put in a sofa and chair, and ask Maria to change there – as an honour rather than an expedient? I was to ask her – I always seemed to get the awkward jobs where she was concerned, much as David Webster loved her – and her reaction was a simple one: 'How kind of you! That would be lovely!' But the press's version was that she had insisted on something special and eventually succeeded in turning me out of my office as the only place appropriate to her status. When she read it, she only laughed, but a trifle wryly.

Much more interesting, if the press had only known, was another episode. After a press conference, I was taking her through the theatre where a rehearsal happened to be taking place on the stage. It was Joan Sutherland singing, superbly I may add, 'I dreamt that I dwelt in marble halls' from *The Bohemian Girl*. Maria instantly stopped to listen, raised her eyebrows quite high as she remembered the beginner who had sung Clotilde at her own début performance of *Norma* six years before, said that Joan sounded pretty good these days – and then added, 'She has learnt very well how to copy me!'

It was neither unkind nor untrue, and Joan was delighted when I told her later in the day. Perhaps I should have told the press too, but they would no doubt have sensationalized it into a scene of hysterical jealousy and cast us in the roles of frantic management persuading Maria to go on in spite of her tantrums. No; on the whole, better to have left them to the purity of their invention.

We had supper together after the Gala, which I remember, but I had forgotten something that, as I recently read, she told a later collaborator, the accompanist Robert Sutherland. When the artists who had appeared at the Gala were presented to the Queen, she had something to say to all of them except to Callas. Maria asked me afterwards why that was so and my answer – that the Queen had said she couldn't think of anything to ask her or say to her – has the ring of truth about it.

The business of that season was five performances in June and July of *Traviata*, and these constituted perhaps the last time I myself saw her relaxed and confident in an operatic performance. Some critics detected a falling-off in her powers, but I found her art so expressive and complete that these performances remain in my memory as among the most enjoyable I ever heard her give.

Early in January 1959 I was in Milan to talk to her again, in particular to try to persuade her to sing another role beside the Medea, which she had already agreed to sing at Covent Garden later that summer. I had concluded the business, not wholly satisfactorily – she declined to sing another role – and was due to leave next morning for London when she rang me up to suggest we should meet again next day around noon. This we did, and I remember strolling across the square in front of la Scala arm in arm with her, while she smiled at the people waving at her from in front of the theatre, all the time making it quite clear to me, not for the first time, that Covent Garden had been treacherous in arranging to mount *Lucia* later that January for Joan Sutherland rather than for her. We had discussed it all the previous day, and it was this very opera we were trying to persuade her to sing for us in the summer. She smiled through the battle of words, eventually saying she did not want lunch but we would have coffee together in the Via Monte Napoleone on her way to try on a dress at Biki's. It was later that afternoon that I met Patricia for the first time – but that is another story.

So too is the production of *Medea* at Covent Garden that summer. She had told us that she thought what they had done with this opera in Dallas was exactly what she wanted to do in London. The production had been by Alexis Minotis, a celebrated Greek actor and producer, the husband of Katina Paxinou. We were to repeat that, with Minotis rehearsing the new people into the opera and she herself arriving only for the last ten days of preparation. She expected them to be ready for her just as she would be ready for them.

We engaged Minotis and he came to London to discuss the details, insisting, when we offered him a small group of dancers from the ballet, that he wanted the chorus themselves to dance in the opening scene. We said that they were unlikely to be very expert at this kind of thing, but he would not be put off; he himself would teach them.

The rest of the cast, which included Jon Vickers, rehearsed for ten days, and then Maria herself arrived. After the first rehearsal, I went round to see her in her dressing room and found her in a towering rage. 'How can you do this to me? Poor Alexis says you would not allow him the ballet, in spite of all his pleas, and we have these clumsy louts for the opening dance!' Meneghini had already been thrown out of the dressing room and was standing outside (this I realized only subsequently), and Maria would listen to no explanation. I don't know if she ever discovered what actually happened, but I liked Minotis distinctly less after this episode (though my affection for his wife continued), and of course the tension which Maria then showed exploded later that summer when she left her husband for Onassis, who threw a huge party for her in London after the first night of *Medea*.

Two weeks later she gave a concert in Amsterdam as part of the Holland Festival. Rescigno conducted, as he had *Medea*, and this was the last time I heard her in her finest form. Her arias from *Vestale, Ernani, Don Carlos* and the great scene from Bellini's *Pirata* sounded with the old fullness of tone, the full expressive panoply.

I never again heard her in such good vocal condition, and the few later performances I caught – isolated concerts at the Festival Hall, *Poliuto* and *Medea* at la Scala, the latter her last in Italy, even the final appearances as Tosca at Covent Garden – all bore out Tito Gobbi's perceptive verdict in his autobiography:

. . . people demanded the impossible of her so that she forever carried the burden of having to reaffirm her supremacy or else be regarded (by herself as well as by others) as in some sense failing. Such a unique position creates a great loneliness and a sense of responsibility so crushing in its weight that it is almost more than a human being can bear.

Few of those later performances came off in the same way as did her *Tosca* at Covent Garden in 1964 and 1965. To begin with, she had complete confidence in Zeffirelli who created a well-observed production round her. Within this frame she was uniquely expressive, whether as the mock-innocent prima donna of the first act, the suffering tigress of the second, or the lover who had been through fire in the third. Patricia and I thought it one of the experiences of a lifetime; and yet dining afterwards with two theatrically involved professionals, all they could talk about was two sour top notes. What was all that artistry to them – though one of them was himself a supreme theatrical practitioner? It was only 'the taste of a bitter orange' that they remembered and held against her.

I suggested after Maria had died that much of her career was paradoxical. Her range of musical interests was limited but her musical ambition boundless; she raised vocal display to a quite new level of expression for our times, and yet had a vocal method that was never quite secure. She would occasionally refer to, and indeed treat, her own voice as if it were a force belonging to her but somehow outside her; as if it were waiting with some reluctance to do her bidding as it had before, but always essentially a force to be tamed. I think that was why she often gave the impression that she felt admiration was her due on the occasions when she succeeded in taming it and creating what her imagination impelled her towards.

Was the change that came over her around 1959 first and foremost vocal and physical, or was it primarily emotional? Had the super-human discipline and dedication been the result of a denial by circumstances of any other emotional focus than her performing art? Did the appearance of Onassis in her life reveal to her what she had been missing, and by providing her with other outlets remove the single-mindedness? I do not believe her decline was entirely physical and vocal, and I have always felt that the Callas of the 1950s could somehow have conquered the problems that arose for her in the 1960s if only she had retained the ambition and the dedication.

Determination she had not lost, which was perhaps why she denied us those mezzo roles she might have sung – Carmen, which she recorded so beautifully but used to say she disliked as a character; Charlotte in *Werther*, whose Letter scene she recorded better than anyone else; some Rossini; some Berlioz. She sang scenes and arias on records and even in concert, but she would have felt that she was in some way betraying an ideal if she had abandoned the taxing soprano roles she had learnt with Serafin, and compromised – as she would have felt it – with the mezzo roles which were for her an easier option.

I don't of course for certain know the answers. In early 1968 John Culshaw of the BBC rang me up to say that they wanted to make a television film with her and that she had asked that I should do the interviewing. I was naturally delighted, both as admirer and friend, and I played through a mountain of recordings in preparation for the interviews. I was nervous, not having seen her for a couple of years; she had never met Patricia (except for a minute on stage after *Medea*), and she had known Marion.

In the end, there was no need for nervousness. She talked easily and enjoyed the challenge of the questions and trying to formulate theories from her own practice. She took immense trouble with her make-up and the selection of dresses, and on the second day we sat with her in her huge dressing room while she was prepared for the camera. She gossiped and joked and reminisced and I think rather surprised Patricia by saying, 'You know, George, if we had fallen in love when we first met, our son would now be twenty!'

I had warned her that I would ask her first about her early study, her teachers, her work with Serafin, then next day concentrate on how she approached the preparation of a new role, and finally go on to the great roles themselves – Norma, Violetta, and the rest. We sat down on a comfortable sofa in her room and I asked her something like, 'People talk about the importance of training for a musical career; do you think that's exaggerated, or that how one starts work on a voice is crucial?' – and she burst into helpless giggles and said: 'How can we after so many years sit on a sofa and ask each other questions like this?'

But she soon warmed to it and our first session must have lasted three hours. Quite soon she became involved in explaining the inexplicable, lauding those who had helped her, formulating practical advice for people who might try to emulate her own serious approach. In attempting to emphasize points, she started to pat a cushion on the sofa, and the technicians had to stop her as they said noises were coming over the microphones like pistol shots. We dined with her at home after one of the sessions, and invited her to come out to a restaurant after we had finished shooting, but when the time came she said she would stay at home. Onassis was coming back next day from America and she did not want to be tired when he returned. It was very domestic and rather touching.

In winter 1973, Maria embarked on a series of operatic recitals with Giuseppe di Stefano, an ill-starred venture one felt from the outset, as there seemed little likelihood of either being in good voice and operatic excerpts with piano accompaniment in large halls seemed a curious vehicle for her comeback. In the event, little went right, except that the audiences were everywhere large and cordial; the singing of each was threadbare and there was only occasional evidence of the unique force Maria had once been. Patricia and I decided that the crush to see her after the performance effectively let us off the hook and that we need not go round and attempt to hide our unhappiness.

When I rang her up the next day she said that our names had been among the very few she had left 'on the door'. So the hook bit a little, as, if we did not much want to lie to her, still less did we want to appear as rats leaving a sinking ship.

Later still, in New York, Lincoln Kirstein gave a party for us to which she came. It was an enjoyable affair, at which, perhaps because she did not know so many people, I inadvertently succeeded in almost monopolizing Maria's attention. By then, she never gave performances but she had not retired – in fact, she never did – and she was still in every way a star, if after a series of reverses a rather more subdued and, curiously enough, more relaxed version of what I had once known.

I don't expect ever again to hear anyone like her, and when I listen to her records, and my tapes of the many performances which were never officially recorded, I continue to wonder at the heights towards which she aimed and to be moved by the degree of success she achieved. I was lucky to have met her early in her career – to have heard her during her initial weeks in Italy in August 1947 and in her last Italian operatic appearance in June 1962 – and to have followed her in different capacities, but always as a devoted admirer, for the rest of her life.

She took her art and therefore herself seriously, and she was humble only insofar as the composers and the problems they had set were concerned. It was there that she suffered, there that her humility was total. In the world of the theatre, with its fickle, sensation-seeking audiences, its uninvolved, selfish managements, her too-easily satisfied colleagues, the ignorant and irresponsible critics, she also suffered – but for this world she reserved what was little less than scorn. Legend has it that she was a tigress; but the tigress inspired envy and emulation on the part of her colleagues, belief and surrender and nothing short of love on the part of thousands of listeners, to a degree that is given to few artists.

Hers was not a long career, but during it she recreated by herself the idea of the prima donna that had obtained in the nineteenth century, when the writer Turgenev was in love with the singer Pauline Viardot, when Malibran and Pasta held sway. If opera was able in our time to raise a star of such brightness that the whole world followed her every move, whatever Maria suffered – and suffer she undoubtedly did – was not entirely in vain.

CHAPTER SIXTEEN

Melomania
1934-81

I AM A MELOMANE. This doesn't mean I take black pills or am enamoured of melancholy; rather, that I love sounds and in particular the sounds of singing – good singing, naturally. From boyhood, I have used the gramophone avidly; one of the first presents I asked for and chose with that care only adolescence can find time for was a large EMG horn gramophone; I had heard that among serious gramophone-users it was looked on as the best.

Within a few years, I was not only adding my favourite operas and, not quite so often, symphonies and piano music to my collection, but starting specifically to collect those singers who gave me most pleasure. All their names are household words within the collectors' world, many outside it as well – Melba and Tetrazzini, Martinelli and McCormack, Bonci and Anselmi, Amato and de Luca, Pinza and Kipnis, Meta Seinemeyer and Elisabeth Rethberg. A new *Lucia* recording issued just before the war gave me great pleasure, as did the appearance of excerpts from *Otello* with Martinelli, and the acquisition of the complete *Das Lied von der Erde* of Mahler, given to me with other records which had belonged to a cousin killed at Dunkirk. The horizons that appeared with a first playing of the Mahler showed me that there was a whole world of music available for my delight which I had previously thought of as highbrow and inaccessible.

I think it was listening to Tauber sing Schubert in a romantic film about the composer's life that first turned me firmly towards music, or at least towards singing. I came back from the cinema in a daze of pleasure at what I had heard, and Tauber's records, particularly of Schubert, were very often to be heard at Harewood when I was about ten or eleven years old. On the radio a little later I listened to him singing '*Durch die Wälder*' from *Freischütz* at a Prom, and it was rare in those days that a month went by without a new recording from Tauber. I believed then that he sang them all beautifully, and listening to them again I don't think I was far wrong. Tauber had as sure a touch with popular music as had McCormack, and his singing of the finest music was, like McCormack's, of the highest quality – if he was not quite the Irishman's equal as a vocalist, I find his taste more positive and his recorded repertory more versatile. That he never recorded a complete opera or an entire song cycle is one of the peculiar gaps of gramophone history. In opera, I heard him only once, in *The Bartered Bride* at the start of the 1939 Covent Garden season, but the occasion, however enjoyable, so overawed me that my memory is now coloured by his recordings from the opera rather than by the performance itself.

Tauber's constant characteristic was the ability to catch the lilt of a tune, the balance of a phrase, so that it haunts the listener's memory as if it had never been properly sung before. When he was young, his nutty, baritonal voice conveyed a quite unusual exuberance – listen to any of his records of Puccini arias or duets, to '*Im chambre separée*', to Schubert's '*Ungeduld*' – there are not many German tenors who give such consistent pleasure.

Acquaintance with singers via the gramophone could be made before the war for a few shillings, which was not too difficult even though pocket money was far from unlimited, but the greatest pleasure of all was to be found in opera house or concert hall. Joan Cross was the first singer in whose performances I thought I recognized greatness. It was as Pamina at Sadler's Wells early in the war that I encountered her subtle, balanced art, and this was followed by an occasional Countess in *Figaro*, Dido, Violetta in *Traviata* and a whole series of performances of Butterfly, a role which others in the touring Sadler's Wells company left alone. Joan's ability to caress a phrase, to sing softly, to suggest emotion rather than insist on it, to use words for colour and for emphasis, to sink dramatically into the role so that the often down-to-earth person I soon got to know disappeared within the characters she was portraying – these characteristics seemed to me to match descriptions of the acknowledged great I found in old copies of *The Times* in the Eton library, and to match the singers whose recordings I treasured and pored over as if they were old manuscripts made audible.

Youthful memory is a treacherous thing, but I don't think I was wrong in my early affection for Joan Cross as performer. I tested it again when I got back from the war with her subtle Ellen Orford in *Peter Grimes*, her melting Fiordiligi in *Così*, and then the Britten creations that followed *Peter Grimes*, culminating in her touching, multi-faceted Queen Elizabeth in *Gloriana*. Quality was what I found in all her singing and acting, and that was not too common in wartime and post-war music-making in England. Of Peter Pears I have written elsewhere. The great Wagnerian tenor Walter Widdop was another of Joan's partners with Sadler's Wells, and I heard him in Harrogate (of all non-operatic places) singing Pinkerton – for the first time? – with a wealth of generous and rich sound which gave me a quite particular pleasure.

Years later, I tried to analyse what Joan had and the others hadn't, and something Erwin Stein said to me seemed to apply to her. 'One of the most difficult things for all musical performers is to suggest the precise future duration of any sustained note the moment he or she starts it. To succeed in this is one of the marks of the artist.' I came to know that was true, and Joan was I realized one of the first who *in propria persona* demonstrated it to me.

Broadcasts and records had acquainted me with the formidable voice of Eva Turner, but I had not heard her myself until I caught her at the Albert Hall in a Prom one Saturday in 1942 while I was at Sandhurst. The great voice rode massively into the hall, carried easily to a top c in '*In questa reggia*' from *Turandot*, and I was thrilled with the scale of her singing, and just as thrilled six years later when I heard her a number of times late in her career as Turandot at Covent Garden. Eva's recordings remain unique and I have heard no one since to rival that generosity of sound, unless it be Kirsten Flagstad and Birgit Nilsson – no one at all with that blend of opulence and 'blade'.

Flagstad was quickly on the scene in England after the war, the voice not young but still in good condition after several years of rest. She was a rare Brünnhilde in performances at Covent Garden, from which her dark golden, rich, enormous tones emerge as a prime memory. I heard her too as Dido in Bernard Miles's garage – one of the oddest post-war London operatic occurrences – and as Leonore in *Fidelio* at Salzburg; and when I met her at dinner with Karl Rankl, Covent Garden's first post-war Music Director, I was as nonplussed by the deep contralto speaking voice as by the genial, motherly personality which had a few days before – somehow convincingly – been my first Isolde.

With Flagstad, the memory is always of richness of sound, vast, rolling size of voice, and only secondly of a rather placid personality, of *portamenti* which were little short of scoops, of an unvarying depiction of character which could have been uninteresting had not everything been supported by this Rolls-Royce of a voice, which brooked no obstacle or difficulty. She overrode them all as if she belonged to another race.

Soon after the war had ended, there was established in London something which turned out to be an almost unique phenomenon in the post-war world

– a privately-subsidized opera company. This was at the Cambridge Theatre and was paid for by Jay Pomeroy, a businessman whose affairs had prospered and who put on *La Bohème* for Darya Bayan and *Don Pasquale* to alternate with it. Dino Borgioli was engaged as artistic director for the season, which lasted for a couple of years with a growing repertory, and was repeated at the Stoll in 1949. Bayan had a certain charm, vocal and physical, but the season's major pleasures for most of us came with the foreigners, mostly Italian, it brought to London. At one time or another, we had Alda Noni as Norina, Margherita Grandi as Tosca, Eugenia Zareska as Rosina, the tenor Antonio Salvarezza, the baritones Taddei, Stabile and Rothmüller, the bass Andrea Mongelli, and of course from nearer home, William and Murray Dickie in *The Barber*, Martin Lawrence in *Don Pasquale* and Ian Wallace in a variety of bass roles.

Mariano Stabile was the revelation of the season. Already by then nearly sixty, he had sung Falstaff in 1921 at the start of Toscanini's last period at la Scala. His reputation was for vocal and musical subtlety and dramatic effectiveness, for athletic urgency rather than for the golden throat often expected of an Italian. Even that reputation did not prepare many of us for the delicacy and strength of his Dr Malatesta when *Don Pasquale* opened at the Cambridge Theatre. Certainly there was no special vocal beauty, but to hear him phrase Malatesta's opening aria, '*Bella siccome un angelo*', was a revelation of the singer's art; a triumph of mind over matter it may have been, but that was forgotten the moment he showed the expressiveness latent within a scale or a turn, the contrasts of *piano* and *crescendo* possible within the space of a couple of phrases – the musical weapons available to a singer who has never been able to rely for a career on outstanding vocal attributes.

All in all, I don't know that I ever saw a more involving male singing actor than Stabile, whom I heard time and again in London and in Edinburgh, and came to enjoy as few other singers, certainly none with so little gold left in the voice. No one else was so menacing or so purposeful as Scarpia – I remember he bore down on anyone he was questioning and crowded them until they had scarcely room to breathe – never can there have been another Malatesta of such relaxed elegance, nor an Alfonso with so strong a sense of that character's blend of bitterness, irony and the mixture of indulgence and indignation with which an older man greets the follies of his juniors.

Falstaff was his greatest role by the time I saw him (Rossini's Figaro no longer vocally credible), and there was not a semiquaver out of place, a phrase exaggerated or a liberty taken, a climax wrongly calculated. In this he was perhaps an Italian counterpart of the great professionals of the German

'Homage to Harewood' – drawing by
Coia, Edinburgh Festival, 1962.

To the Artistic Director
who has won the
wholehearted admiration
of
COIA

' Homage to Harewood '

Talking to Georg Solti (left) and Harold Rosenthal (right) during an interval at the Royal Opera
House, Covent Garden, 1964.

On holiday in Spain with Patricia just after Mark was born, September 1964.

In conversation with conductor Pierre Boulez during a press conference at the Edinburgh Festival, 1965.

Neville Ussher (right) and my brother Gerald at Harewood, 1964.

My mother pruning roses at Harewood shortly before her death.

With Rostropovich (left) and Rozhdestvensky (right) at the Edinburgh Festival, 1965.

LEFT Escorting the Queen during a visit to York University, of which I was Chancellor, October 1965.

RIGHT Entertaining Dr Klemperer (left) and Barry Tuckwell (right) at my home, 1966.

Mark meets his brothers for the first time.

Posing with the Judge who married us after our wedding in Connecticut, 31 July 1967.

Our first appearance after our wedding with three-year-old Mark at the Harewood Show, 9 August 1967.

The Bird Garden at Harewood. Patricia and Mark with a macaw.

LEFT Garlanding at Kalki, Madras, 1970.

RIGHT Patricia and some Nepalese children pose for the camera with the Himalayas in the background, 1970.

The Queen and Patricia before a dinner in Leeds Silver Jubilee, 13 July 1977.

At a Leeds United match at Elland Road.

Partridge shooting with Neville Ussher and Jack Charlton (right).

Walking with Patricia in the grounds of Harewood, May 1981.

and Viennese schools, of men like Ludwig Weber, who appeared to be able to reproduce without any risk of staleness the performances they had been giving for the past thirty years. Stabile was such a one.

I was told by William Dickie, who sang with Stabile for those unforgettable months at the Cambridge Theatre in London in 1947–8, that a group of his colleagues once got together to give a dinner in his honour. During its course, Bill Dickie mentioned that he had managed to find some of Stabile's early gramophone records, only to get the rejoinder: 'If you want to do me a favour, smash them!' 'Why?' asked the Scot, 'they're very good.' 'I'm not saying otherwise,' said Stabile, 'but I want people to go on thinking that I *once* had a fine voice, and the truth is that it was always like this!'

Stabile once told me that, after a late *Falstaff* at la Scala, a critic had written a panegyric, ending up by saying that the performance was the more remarkable coming from a man of sixty-eight. Stabile took him to court next morning, determined to establish that he was only sixty-three. 'In three years' time I shall sing just the same; they won't trust a Falstaff of seventy-one but they would be prepared to risk one of sixty-six!'

As soon as I was back from the war, I started to hear about a new and prospectively 'great' voice – people were talking about Kathleen Ferrier. It was not long before I heard her in concert but the revelation came in 1946 with *The Rape of Lucretia* at Glyndebourne, and the following year when her Orfeo was urged towards greatness by the conducting of Fritz Stiedry. The fashion was to say that her singing of Mahler with Bruno Walter was her highest achievement but I always felt that she was at her best in Britten, because he understood her qualities so well that to meet the music's demands she needed only to approach it instinctively.

Kathleen always had an enormous voice but it sounded best deployed at *mezza forte* and not *forte*, when she tended to lose quality. She was a true lyric contralto, not happy at first even about the A flat of Lucretia's outburst in the last scene. In other music, she caressed the phrases like a great singer, but shyly, as if for the first time, and with less authority (though often more charm) than other great singers. There was little contrivance about her singing, no guile; the style was direct and the voice could ring out with something of the golden clarion quality of Flagstad's, but on a smaller scale. In Britten's *Spring Symphony* and his chamber cantata *Abraham and Isaac*, both written for her, nobody came near her for the quality of 'rightness' that denotes a great performance.

Among the delights of the years after the war were the visits to Covent

Garden of an Italian company from the San Carlo, Naples, in 1946, from which the names of Margherita Carosio, Paolo Silveri and Luigi Infantino stand out among the singers; and in 1947 of the Vienna State Opera with Clemens Krauss and Josef Krips as its conductors. A host of great names adorned those momentous Viennese performances of *Don Giovanni*, *Figaro*, *Così*, *Fidelio* and *Salome* – Hilde Konetzni, Ludwig Weber, Paul Schöffler, Hans Hotter, Georg Hann, Julius Patzak and Maria Cebotari, already known pre-war and from records; Elisabeth Schwarzkopf, Irmgard Seefried, Elisabeth Höngen, Sena Jurinac, Hilde Gueden, Ljuba Welitsch, Anton Dermota, Erich Kunz, Peter Klein, Marko Rothmüller, all new. It is said that Krauss, who came to conduct the non-Mozart operas, joked about Cebotari, Schwarzkopf and Gueden, the ladies of the opening *Don Giovanni*, as in vocal weight three Zerlinas; but it seemed less like the truth than the disappointed jibe of a man relegated to a supporting role because of his supposedly murky political past (an unjustified suspicion, according to Patzak, who said Clemens Krauss was the most helpfully, if discreetly, anti-Nazi of any of the leading conductors who stayed in Germany). The Viennese ensemble was magnificent, perhaps the best permanent company any of us has known since the war.

For me, the most individually exciting among them were Ljuba Welitsch and Julius Patzak. Patzak sang Florestan and Herod – in the latter role suggesting something I have come to believe: that in art evil must be seductive, prospectively beautiful. With what musical relish Patzak offered the wine-cup and the ripe fruit to Salome, how erotic became the anticipation of the shared sip and bite into the fruit! This I felt was great operatic singing, a conviction I was able to apply to other fields when I later heard him sing *Lieder* (including an outstandingly impetuous *Schöne Müllerin*).

Ljuba Welitsch was something else – a voice, a force, a musical energy such as I had never heard in quite this form. Most singers need the same time to attack as is required by a horn or clarinet player: Welitsch's voice 'sounded' as quickly as a violinist's bow on the strings, and she could articulate with the same rapidity, soar as easily – indeed the voice itself had something of the sound quality, the immediacy and purity of a great string player, with the brilliant articulation of a Szigeti, the exultant soaring at climaxes of a Ginette Neveu. I loved her as Donna Anna with her red-headed beauty, her nervous energy and the fluent, fast phrasing – too fast on records, it often seems, even in those made in her heyday – but her Salome was nothing short of a revelation.

Hans Hotter told me years later that she sang Salome far too often for the relatively light quality of her voice and her slighter natural resistance to physical wear and tear. But in those years of her ascendancy, audiences were greedy for her in the role, which became her physically to perfection (unless you prefer thin women) and which her voice adorned as if Strauss had written for her.

Welitsch came up to the Leeds Festival in 1947 to sing the Verdi *Requiem* for Barbirolli, and I started to get to know her then, loving the warmth of her personality, slightly alarmed by her sexy reputation. She was Musetta in the first post-war Covent Garden production of *La Bohème*, which used the old sets – copies of the Italian original, and none the worse for that – opposite Schwarzkopf, Rudolf Schock and Silveri, and I took Joan Cross to the first night. The first act went well, and we looked forward to the appearance of Musetta. Ljuba as we had expected stormed on to the stage, smiling fit to bust, but we were hardly prepared for the diamond brilliance of her singing of the Waltz song; nor apparently was the audience, which went pleasurably mad. Joan and I yelled with the rest of them and we were still applauding when the act came to an end, fully four minutes after she had finished the solo proper – and were properly castigated next morning in *The Times* by Frank Howes for muffling 'one of Puccini's most subtle curtains', or words to that effect.

Ljuba's was a ridiculously short career, lasting internationally – she was a Bulgarian based in Vienna – from mid-war until only about 1953. But with that sound and that energy she permanently affected any of us who heard her in her prime. The voice was silvery rather than golden, but wonderfully sensuous, and always individual. When she came after a year's absence to sing Tosca at Covent Garden (which she did, unforgivably, in German, rather than the contracted Italian), I felt tears in my eyes with the first offstage 'Mario! Mario!', and I told myself it was because I had not heard her for some time. Years later Patricia gave me the Karajan Gala recording of *Fledermaus*, in which top Decca artists contributed to the second act cabaret, Ljuba among them. When the first notes of her '*Vilja-lied*' came from the speakers, my eyes again filled with tears; I shall always be captive of this sound and what it suggests to me.

In the 1970s, with Patricia in Vienna after many years' absence, we saw her again, and at supper she was the same Ljuba as ever, warm and physically hardly changed, but now appearing only as a pensioner and in walk-on parts at the Volksoper. Nonetheless, she left a party early because she had a performance next day – Praskovia in *The Merry Widow*, virtually a non-singing role. She was applauded at her entrance as if she had been Jeritza herself back from the shadows; and when we went to see her afterwards, she hardly accepted our compliments before rushing us in to salute the evening's excellent Hanna Glawari, the handsome Mirjana Irosch, whom she wanted us to admire. That wasn't hard, and we admired equally the warm-heartedness of the possessor of a major voice of the past towards someone who was, however you looked at it, a lesser star of the present.

You can generalize about a singer and a voice only with care, and reactions must be personal and particular. Mine to Sena Jurinac were immediately positive. I did not hear her during the Vienna Opera's 1947 visit to London but caught her in Salzburg a year later, as Cherubino and as Amor in *Orfeo*. Strikingly fresh vocal quality seemed combined with unusual authority and unfailing vivacity, and the same qualities were apparent when she was Dorabella in Florence and later Fiordiligi at Glyndebourne. The music was executed with such accuracy and articulation as to make the bravura as exciting as a coloratura soprano's, and with such sensitivity as to make every phrase apt, expressive. I thought her a great singer then, and her recordings confirm my impression. So does my tape of her Butterfly at Covent Garden in January 1959, when she proved the most honest, most heroic, and in the end most touching interpreter of the role I had ever encountered.

The voice itself is uncommon in that for a relatively high lyric soprano it is unusually low-based, very rich in the sounds of the bottom register. With it all, the exultant, free-sounding quality implicit in the upper fourth of a lyric soprano (G to top C) is very much in evidence and seldom more beautiful than in Sena Jurinac's at her prime.

I used to try without success to get her to sing *Lieder* in England. She said she knew nothing about them, a statement contradicted by a recording made in the early 1950s of Schumann's '*Frauenliebe und Leben*' and the greater of his two *Liederkreis* (the one containing '*Mondnacht*' and '*Waldesgespräch*'). Eventually, she capitulated, and at Harewood in the 1970s gave us a programme of Brahms followed by this *Liederkreis*. My own delight was unbounded, and I was happy to find that two admirers had come all the way from Vienna just because they did not want to miss the chance of hearing her sing *Lieder*.

Thrilling: producing a sudden wave of excitement or emotion; piercing the feelings. So the Oxford English Dictionary; so too most singing which aspires to the quality of greatness. The listener may find thrilling some wonderfully long, expressive phrasing – Fischer-Dieskau's in Schubert, Martinelli's '*Riposa, o madre*' in his record of '*Ai nostri monti*'; or easily taken yet vibrant top notes – Caruso's or Destinn's or Eva Turner's; or very difficult things done apparently easily – records of Selma Kurz's trill and Tetrazzini's elaborated coloratura flourishes, Ivogün's buoyancy and infectious joy in 'The Blue Danube' and as Zerbinetta, Karl Erb's or Elisabeth Schumann's or Pears's *diminuendo* at the end of phrases in *'Du bist die Ruh''*; or great intensity which cannot but seize and hold the imagination – Björling in *La Bohème*, Patzak in the quick section of Florestan's aria, Callas in the *cabaletta* of Elena's entry in *Vespri Siciliani*; or the controlled relaxation which is used to produce the same effect – Pears in 'Since she whom I loved hath paid her last debt', Hotter in *'Der Augen leuchtendes Paar'*. Or it can be a unique sound – Welitsch's as I have described above, Rita Hunter in full cry in the last act of *Trovatore*, the burnished mahogany of Gwynne Howell's bass in Gremin's aria, Vishnevskaya in Russian song, Janet Baker in Purcell or Berlioz, Valerie Masterson soaring in the Presentation of the Rose.

The reaction remains personal and no one else need feel it, but it may sometimes sweep over a number of people at the same time. The advent of Victoria de los Angeles on the international scene sent more than a ripple of interest round the melomanes. This singing was something rather different: the scale intimate, the sound as individually seductive as Vermeer's blue, the detail as exquisite as a piece of fine Fabergé. She is Spanish, and all the music she sings is invested with qualities which by association at least we have come to think of as Spanish; they were to be found again ten years later with hardly less intensity in Teresa Berganza and Monserrat Caballe. Victoria de los Angeles was to the post-war generation the first of a line, and those turns and skirls, those *pianissimi*, that rainbow range of vocal colouring, the immaculate sense of pitch – these qualities and the Spanish repertory she brought into the concert hall (not new to those who knew the records of Conchita Supervia, a great but totally different artist) gave her an aura all her own.

In opera she has sometimes seemed the miniaturist writ large, unlike Hotter or Schwarzkopf when they turn from *Lieder* to opera; but her large-scale miniatures have often seemed more important and more relevant than other singers' big canvasses.

Wagner was necessarily for me a post-war discovery. Before long-playing records, there were many individual Wagnerian excerpts but few complete recordings, so Wagner in the theatre came as an overwhelming experience. So too did my first contact with Wagnerian singers of the calibre of Flagstad and Hotter, of Ludwig Weber and Set Svanholm, Astrid Varnay, Gottlob Frick, Windgassen, Mödl and Ferdinand Frantz.

For nearly twenty years, Hans Hotter was Covent Garden's regular Wotan. As Kurwenal he was immense – all man's devotion to man gathered into one huge frame; as Hans Sachs I only once (in Vienna in 1950) heard him fully stay the course – singing of Hotter's generosity seldom maintained equilibrium throughout an evening, and even as the Grand Inquisitor he tired before the end. But as Wotan he was supreme. This was not conventionally beautiful singing; he did not seem to mind forcing, he could sound harsh and out of sorts, he regularly went through the tone and recovered to sing magnificently a few phrases later. The whole performance was on a vast scale, but so grandiloquently expressive that criticism of detail evaporated in face of such stature.

No other Wotan seemed able to stretch his spear-bearing arm to such godlike length, and it was essentially the *size* of the impersonation, dramatic as well as vocal, matching the gigantic figure of the King of the Gods, that put Hotter on a pedestal amongst the Wotans of his generation. Brünnhilde was never more exultantly urged to her war-cries than by Hotter's '*Reite zur Wal!*', nor more commandingly conjured from her hiding place than by his reiterated '*Keine wie sie ...*'; and his Farewell quickly and with reason became legendary.

And yet the mighty thunder could be subdued, so that in *Lieder* he was scarcely less compelling than on stage. To *Lieder* he brought the authority of a Jehovah in repose, whether in a much-transposed '*Winterreise*' late in his career (he sang it once at Harewood) or in Schubert's '*Im Frühling*' on a record of rare subtlety, in Loewe ballads or Hugo Wolf's 'Michelangelo' sonnets. A unique force.

If the dominating spirit of the Italian singing scene of the immediately post-war period was without doubt the Greek-American Maria Callas, I believe it was another Italian-based singer of foreign extraction, the Bulgarian Boris Christoff, who came nearest to her in an exact and subtle realization of Italian music. Italians have told me that his first few appearances on stage suggested to them that this was no more than another well-voiced High Priest, an Oroveso, a Padre Guardiano; they were amazed at the transformation that came over Christoff when he sang Russian roles like Boris and the contrasting princes in *Prince Igor*, and still more by the spread of this new intensity to Italian roles like Philip, Fiesco, Procida and Creon. Any description of the discriminating weighting of each syllable and each semiquaver and of the contrasts of tonal colour that he achieved in the music he sang best could suggest either a pedant or a miniaturist; and yet Christoff's singing contained little of either. He was seldom other than a natural singer who exulted in sound and effect, and he put music across on a grand scale as well as with infinite exactness.

The sound was always closer to Chaliapin's than to Pinza's, and yet I have found both in the theatre and on record that no Italianate bass of his generation compares well with Christoff; he dominated for a much longer period than the comparably splendid but short-careered Rossi-Lemeni, he was more authoritative than the mellifluous Cesare Siepi, more consistently interesting than a greatly-gifted and equally Italianate bass, that other Bulgarian Nicolai Ghiaurov. The least restless and firmest sung of any Don Basilio I heard or saw, Boris Christoff's was also the funniest, and I remember Benjamin Britten revelling in the classical means he used to such comical ends.

I got to know Boris when he first came to London for *Boris Godunov*, having heard him initially as Rocco at la Scala the same year; and nearly twenty years later he came to inaugurate the chamber concerts Patricia and I started at Harewood in the late 1960s. Our small son Mark could scarcely believe that the Boris Godunov he knew from records was to sing at Harewood, but with the first notes Boris uttered in his rehearsal he rushed towards him and clutched him round the legs: 'It is *really* Boris!'

The trouble was that at this rehearsal the first note was so long in coming; most of the time had so far been taken up with the discussion of the temperature which would prevail that evening, and with moving piano and spotlight to make quite sure that *all* would be well on the night. In the end, at that rehearsal he sang for perhaps ten minutes, to the discomfiture of his accompanist Janine Reiss; she was even more discomfited that night when, turning pages for her in a fast song, I deposited all the music in her lap. I swore it was the last time I would turn pages in public and was only slightly consoled when Howard Hartog said: 'Well, what can you expect if they bring the music printed on sheets of lavatory paper!'

Most male lovers of singing – and I have yet to meet a female record collector – talk for much of the time about sopranos, and I am no exception. But the thrill – I use the word again, literally I hope – of the best operatic tenor singing is something on its own. It is less 'natural' in its effect than the best sopranos, mezzos, baritones or basses, with its apparently artificially constricted and yet uniquely satisfactory ascent to top notes, its particular brilliance and intensity. If Caruso with his records provides us all with the touchstone of tenor quality, Jussi Björling before and after the last war came nearest in my opinion to establishing a new standard – different of course from Caruso's because the voice was lighter, but unique in the fervour and youthful quality of his singing. I find just as much pleasure in his records as I remember from his performances, and the ardour of his phrasing and matching of sound to music is something I would recommend any other tenor to hear. It is exemplary.

In our own day Placido Domingo is the only tenor who seems to me consistently to match Caruso's or Björling's standards, particularly in his ability to screw the listeners' nerves to the requisite high point. He is a rarity, in that a great though not vast voice goes hand-in-hand with supreme and natural musicianship.

There are genuine lovers of singing who find that Callas's vocal inequalities nullify her unrivalled interpretative gifts, but very few would admit that they were first and foremost connoisseurs of the 'golden voice', and not primarily interested in the music. Nonetheless, you hear the most astonishing selections mentioned as someone's favourite recording of Melba or Selma Kurz or Tetrazzini. Personally, I have always found a Patzak or a Pears incomparably more interesting than an Italian tenor with a vein of gold in the throat but a vacuum six inches above it.

Zinka Milanov could be deemed an exception to any rule. She virtually never made a sound that was other than rounded and golden and perfectly poised. I heard her once in New York in 1946 and then not again until she was nearly fifty, but I shall always cherish affection for that effortlessly beautiful singing. The Tosca she sang at Covent Garden in 1956 was as nearly perfect as anything of the kind I have heard. The voice was immaculately produced, from a smooth top C to the A two octaves and a bit below it; I suspect she had preserved its quality and evenness by invariably singing within her means, not risking more than ninety-five per cent on any night.

If ever the phrase 'the grand manner' meant anything (and it does), it applies to Zinka Milanov's singing of Verdi – listen to her early records of excerpts from *Ballo* and *Forza* and see what I mean. Those round, full tones, the floated top A's and B flats, were the stuff of which legends are made – and in America a legend is what she became, so that when the Met mounted a new *Gioconda* in its first season in the new house, the audience applauded her entry to the auditorium far more enthusiastically than they applauded her successor in the role on stage.

I have a friend in America, a singer who is also highly knowledgeable about singing, to whom I am devoted and with whom I argue. 'No one else today can sing this role,' he will exclaim after a fine piece of singing at the Met. 'I am dedicated to exactly the opposite of that proposition,' I answer, with more emotion than logic. The truth is that I cannot accept that only a big Italianate sound and production can be considered 'correct' or 'beautiful'. Such a notion seems to me restricted, destructive, unhistorical, in the end anti-musical. Because of the sounds they had in their ears when they wrote, the composers of different countries postulated differing types of voice; their music reflects national types without necessarily being folk-orientated or even nationally-based. I rejoice in the differences and respond to them.

As a lover of the human voice, I would not hesitate to say that the natural quality and individuality of Galina Vishnevskaya's has given me in theatre and concert hall and on record a pleasure that is quite unusual. Whether in Glinka or Shostakovich, Prokofiev or Puccini, Beethoven or Tchaikovsky, hers is at all times engaged, committed singing. She may strain for effect, but the natural sound triumphs over all, most of all perhaps in the exquisite *piano* singing of her songs. She and Slava Rostropovich, her husband, used often to dine at Orme Square and very frequently after dinner said 'thank you' with Puccini arias or Tchaikovsky or Glinka songs. I used to ask for Tchaikovsky's 'Why?', and the brooding opening at the measured tempo that she and Slava preferred carried then, and on record has for me still, total fascination. That song seems to me to epitomize her unique, generous gift.

Vishnevskaya was a silvery-voiced but radiant Aida at Covent Garden, a role she acted in an old-fashioned style, nonetheless touching; she sang several times at Edinburgh in 1962, and I shall not quickly forget '*Un bel di vedremo*' as an encore at a Harrogate Festival, which she sang gloriously and which Slava played from memory – also gloriously, but with such a wealth of improvisatory reminiscence during the aria and after she had finished singing as might have made Puccini reconsider his own treatment of leading motifs!

As married couples will, Galya and Slava could disagree and some of their disagreements could come before a performance. They were once in ferocious argument before going on to the platform for Schumann's '*Frauenliebe und Leben*', and Slava grabbed the man who was turning the pages for him (who told me the story), hauled him to his chair, and then placed music on the stand – not the Schumann at all, but a copy of Beethoven's cello sonatas which he persisted in peering at while playing the Schumann cycle, pausing if he felt like it to wait for pages (of the wrong music) to be turned. Galya was suitably and understandably disconcerted.

One of the modern heresies about singing is that nothing good comes from France, that the once great school produces nothing nowadays. I suspect that this is largely a matter of opportunity; a 'school' will naturally decline if its average products cannot use their talents, and it is from many 'average' singers that a few outstanding performers emerge.

In the 1950s and early 1960s I heard many Paris performances and it is true that the operatic level was low – but not quite so true that the singing was bad. Production was at best traditional, mostly non-existent, and morale seemed generally poor. The orchestra and chorus sounded uninvolved, and the stage hands went so noisily about their business that you could usually by curtain-fall identify some by name. The singing, on the other hand, was often very good.

Soon after I started to work at Covent Garden, we were asked to listen to the French-Canadian tenor Raoul Jobin, who had returned to Paris. I went to hear him in *Lohengrin* but, just before the prelude began, it was announced that he was ill and that René Verdière would substitute. Verdière sang Lohengrin in exemplary fashion – one of the best I ever heard, Crespin was an ideally youthful Elsa, Suzanne Juyol was very good as Ortrud, and only René Bianco (my Albert in Algiers twelve years before) as Telramund and Georges Vaillant as the King were on a more routine level.

A few weeks later I went to Paris for another *Lohengrin*, but Jobin was again ill. I went instead to *Louise* at the Salle Favart, where Julien was excellently sung by Verdière (the Lohengrin of my first visit) while a *third* company member sang Lohengrin that night at the Palais Garnier. This was probably Charles Fronval. To have two good Lohengrins in one company is not bad going, but to afford a third seems to me close to riches. That *Louise* too was admirably sung and, with sets by Utrillo, one of the better-looking offerings Paris had at the time.

La Bohème a little later could put forward Janine Micheau and Albert Lance as a nearly ideal Mimi and Rodolfo – Lance was an Australian (Lance Ingram) but he studied in France with a French teacher and became a French singer. *Faust* in the same period had the outstanding Ernest Blanc as Valentin. It was not so much the singing that was bad in France at that period as the general operatic know-how – willingness to invest in new productions, and indeed the money with which to pay for them.

Which is in some ways to digress, though not entirely. I delight in singers with different national characteristics, and am convinced that a Georges Thill or an Alain Vanzo is not less good or less enjoyable to listen to (and that is the crux of the matter) than an Italianate equivalent. What Italian can nowadays (as could once di Stefano) hit his top c in Faust's '*Salut demeure*' squarely and firmly in the middle, as does the Frenchman Vanzo, and then allow a slow *diminuendo* until he is ready without extra breath to descend to the A flat and finish the phrase? (Vanzo in 1978 sang it the same way at every rehearsal and performance, so Valerie Masterson, his partner in *Faust*, told me.)

'I am dedicated to the opposite proposition,' I tell my friend in New York who claims that only one singer is up to a particular role, and, working at the Coliseum with British singers, my proposition must for me be correct. Maybe that is another story, although I must proclaim here that my present work by no manner of means involves a monastic denial of the values with which I started this chapter – a straightforward love of good and interesting singing.

CHAPTER SEVENTEEN

India, 1958-81

IT'S QUITE POSSIBLE I believe to love without understanding, hard to understand without loving. I should never dream of saying 'I understand India', but I should contest any suggestion that I did not somehow and in my own way love the country, to a pitch where for over twenty years the prospect of spending some time there excites me more than such a possibility anywhere else.

It started with a sitar* recital of Ravi Shankar's, to which Ben Britten took Marion and me in 1956. I had never thought much about India before, but Ben had recently been there and what interested Ben tended to interest me. I found an immediate fascination in the new sounds and rhythms and shapes – the shapes far harder to get hold of than the colours or the rhythmic patterns – and soon started to fall under their spell. Nearly twenty-five years later I recognize (but cannot always name) certain ragas†, and with time I have become familiar with the outline of the great classical structures spun from the twin elements of sound and time by Ravi and his fellow-pupil Ali Akbar Khan, the sarod‡ player, and Vilayat Khan the sitarist, by Subbulakshmi and Semmangudi the Carnatic§ singers, and by others aspiring to their eminence. I know enough to see that the experience is sensuous rather than something I analyse intellectually, but it is a strong experience and I have no difficulty in recognizing its intensity.

So it was with India itself. I was asked by the British Council to tour the

---

*A stringed instrument, with adjustable frets, played with a stroke of the fingers or plucked with a plectrum. There are side strings which act as a drone and many 'sympathetic' strings underneath the frets.

†The nearest English word to *raga* would be 'mode'; it is the tonal structure or frame on which all Indian music whether composed or improvised is constructed.

‡The sarod uses metal strings and has a metal finger board. Like the sitar, it is plucked, and has side strings and a number of 'sympathetic' strings.

§South Indian music. Though the earliest treatises on Indian music make no distinction between Northern (Hindustani) and Southern (Carnatic) schools, among other factors now differentiating the two schools, the influence of Persia and therefore Islam on the North extended hardly at all to the South, so that the modern practice and even the modern approach of the two schools is substantially different.

country and give some lectures in the autumn of 1958, and I can't think of any exotic place I've found myself so immediately in sympathy with, the sights, sounds, smells and above all the people, with their enquiring, talkative natures. I saw quickly what a friend meant when she said she loved living in India because she could always be sure of a good argument!

Almost anything Marion and I did on that packed 1958 tour turned out to hold some kind of delight, whether it was wandering the first morning in the grounds of Rashtrapati Bhavan (Lutyens's Viceregal Lodge), where every plant and bird seemed new, or tasting Tandoori chicken at Moti Mahal in Old Delhi, or indulging in that incomparable shopping amidst the saris and the silks and cottons, the boxes and the toys collected from all over India. Novelty became the norm, and, whether we were in Kashmir or Calcutta, Madras or Bombay, Konarak or Fatehpur Sikri, around us crowds bustled, cows meandered, carts trundled, beggars wheedled and kites circled over the perpetually hooting cars as they were manoeuvred through unheeding pedestrians and bicycles by drivers who (Patricia and I much later decided) had all, to judge by their horn-blowing *machismo*, been through driving school in Italy.

My first Indian impressions were gained under peculiarly privileged conditions, as I should be the first to admit – I stayed with the President and went the rounds of Government Houses and VIP hotels. Just as important, my introduction to music and musicians was from that wisest (and most widely knowledged) of Indian musicians, Narayana Menon, himself an accomplished veena* player, conversant with North and South Indian styles and their exponents; as a graduate of Edinburgh University, he was a student from afar of Western musical tradition under Donald Tovey; and, as administrator, destined to become Director General of All India Radio in Delhi and subsequently head of the National Centre of Performing Arts in Bombay.

My next visit was in 1961, in order to negotiate with the Indian Government for a heavy Indian representation at the 1963 Edinburgh Festival. This came after another new and vivid encounter when I saw for the first time Balasaraswati dance Bharatanatyam† at an East–West Conference I was attending in Tokyo. Bala, though hardly young, struck me as one of the greatest dancers in any form I had ever seen. Assurances of her pre-eminence

---

*A seven-stringed, fretted instrument, plucked with the fingers and a plectrum.

†Bharatanatyam. The word literally means *natya* or dance according to Bharata. The use of this word is recent (just over fifty years) but today it is applied to the traditional solo dance as executed by the great dancers of South India, like Balasaraswati, particularly in Tamil Nadu. It is gaining wide currency elsewhere.

– the greatest exponent of Bharatanatyam of her generation, I was told –
were easy enough to take on trust. At first the to me quite new rhythmic
pounding and stamping, the flashing arms and expressive head movements,
suggested an epic art with the dancer's stamina as a main factor; but the
large-scale pieces were interspersed with lyrical, intimate 'episodes in which
the dancer's powers of mime, particularly the subtle, instantly intriguing
hand movements, the control of eye and head expressions, took over from
the earlier, more strenuous activity – and told just as well on the huge, bare
stage of the Tokyo hall.

Something Bala did brought home to me a curious idiosyncracy of Indian
performing artists. At the end of each number she would retreat to the side or
back of the performing area and there relax as if she were out of sight before
drawing herself up for the next item. It was the equivalent of Ravi Shankar
tuning during a performance while maintaining the rhythmic pattern, of
Subbulakshmi's barely stifled coughs in the middle of a solo; if you were not
so to speak in play, you were invisible or inaudible.

The whole affair was enthralling and her programme left me longing for
more, so that her name was quickly added to my list for the 1963 Edinburgh
Festival. The Indian thread which ran through that year's programme
provided an experience not quickly to be forgotten, partly because of my own
sheer pleasure in what was to be seen and heard, partly because I felt a
number of other people were getting the chance of taking seriously
something which had often, at least musically and in England, been treated
as if it had no more than marginal significance. I fancy there were music
critics as well as audiences who now found delight in the virtuosity and new
sounds of Indian music.

Delhi in February 1964 provided the scene of my next Indian encounter,
when further East–West discussions were arranged under American pat-
ronage and the imaginative aegis of Nicolas Nabokov. At one of the sessions
I spoke about English reactions to Indian music and performers, and took
pains to avoid the mistake I had made in 1958 when asked by the formidable
Dr V. K. R. V. Rao to lead an impromptu East–West discussion at the
Music Society of Delhi University. I thought then to take up a small point I
had heard made· by Indian musicians: how was it possible to make
interestingly individual many repetitions of the same precisely notated piece
of music? In the British Council library I found several different recordings
of the Dagger speech from *Macbeth* (I wanted *Hamlet*'s 'To be or not to be'
but there weren't enough records), and tried with their aid to make my point.

But it wasn't listened to – perhaps *Macbeth* was working its old malevolent spell – various pedants preferring to insist on the sacred meaning of the ragas, of different notes and intervals. Compared with this, they said, mere words – and *English* words at that – had no particular significance. They refused to accept the analogy, which was purely to do with performance (the point I was discussing), and proceeded to chop logic as fine as mediaeval theologians and for so long that the Vice-Chancellor gave up in deference more to the late hour than to the resolution of the discussion.

The longing to visit and re-visit the source of what I came to think of as a unique magic remained, and soon after we were married Patricia and I went twice to India, in January and February 1968 (with Patricia's elder son, Michael Shmith) when we took in Nepal as well, and again in 1970; these visits seemed to represent as it were the dividends on an earlier investment.

What was I keen to demonstrate to Patricia and, if possible, make her enjoy as much as I had? Exotic places and sounds of course, with their individual characteristics, and people with theirs, and I wanted to see whether together they would cast on her that peculiar spell I had found whenever I myself had been in India. We kept notes and a diary, and the degree to which we succumbed again to the magic is probably to be found in its entries.

We were met in 1968 in Bombay by Jamshed Bhabha, our host in India, brother of the famous scientist Homi Bhabha (who was killed in an air accident in 1966), a Tata director and the most active member of the Board of the projected National Centre for the Performing Arts, to advise which I was nominally in India. The long drive in a big American car to the hotel was through the shanty town which surrounds any Eastern city. Patricia's diary recorded: 'We passed a slim, graceful girl in a sari, swaying along with one slender hand in the air supporting a large, dried cowpat!'

The day after we arrived we were at a recital by Vilayat Khan, the sitar player, whom I had heard first at Aldeburgh and who played in Edinburgh in 1965. Indians compare him with Ravi Shankar as eagerly as in the 1950s Italians did Tebaldi with Callas. On this occasion, he struck me as having a more restrained style than Ravi, with less frequent repetition of individual phrases, no emphasis on *meend** in lower register, less rhythmical exuber-

---

Meend, literally 'glide', is used to describe any form of Indian equivalent of the Western *portamento*. It is most often and most idiomatically applied to the effect, confined (so far as I know) to plucked instruments of Indian music, when the string is pulled sideways to produce a note higher in pitch than that originally sounded and then slackened to allow the original pitch to sound again. It is a most unusual effect, and in the hands of a master, extremely striking.

ance. There is in general something reflective, even melancholy about his music-making, not only when playing the evening Raga Bhupali. Patricia wrote: 'He will pick up a few notes of the raga, and as it were turn them in his fingers, until the light catches them and they shoot out all manner of colours.' His accompanist, Shamta Prasad, who played tabla for him in Edinburgh in 1965, was very much to my liking, his soft touch and delicate style perfectly matching Vilayat's. Compared with Ravi, Vilayat is more consciously the poet, making fewer concessions to popular taste, also perhaps displaying less fantasy and less architectural sense.

Later in our journey, in Calcutta, he told us of his affection for the old way of life, as exemplified by his musician grandfather and father and by the Maharajah for whom they once worked and who later left relative affluence in East Bengal (now Bangladesh) for relative penury in Calcutta, but still sent Vilayat 101 rupees* every month 'to remind you of our old relationship'.

Our closest and indeed oldest friends in India are the Kerala-born Narayana Menon and his Bengali wife Rekha, a descendant of the poet and philosopher Rabindranath Tagore. Narayana is at home apparently in every culture provided it accepts music, which is a major part of his life; Rekha is equally articulate and sympathetic but contrives to make even agreement sound provocative, a characteristic, we long ago decided, of the naturally peppery Bengali.

We had been to Agra and on our return Narayana expatiated on the Moghuls and their musical proclivities and antipathies. Akbar, the great sixteenth-century emperor, was passionate about music and employed the greatest musician of his age, by name Tansen†, to sing for him. One day, delighted by Tansen's virtuosity and artistry, Akbar asked who had been able to teach him the secrets of such beauty. Would he come to sing at court? No, but you could hear him at his house. The emperor went and was enraptured to find the teacher, Haridas, even greater than the pupil. How is this possible, asked Akbar. Because he sings to honour God and music, came Tansen's reply, and I sing only at your command.

Akbar's great-grandson, the execrable and philistine Aurangzeb‡, took a very different view, which to my surprise Narayana told us was orthodox Muslim at the time. He hated music and banished it from his court. The musicians of Agra organized a procession, with tableaux showing disease and senility. Seeing this from his palace window, the emperor asked what it was

*£1 is worth nearly 20 rupees.
†Tansen (1532–86).
‡Aurangzeb, son of Shah Jehan, ruled from 1658 to 1707.

intended to represent. The ragas and raginis, came the answer, which are dying since being banished from your court. If they are dying, let them die quickly and let them be buried deep, said the emperor.

In 1970 in Bombay, we heard a specially-arranged, two-part recital. Ram Narayan the sarangi* player, originally from Udaipur and the brother of Chatur Lal the tabla† player I had heard with Ravi in 1956, was the soloist for the first half of the programme. The sarangi in Hindustani music is the regular accompanying instrument for vocal music. The many women singers of the north until recently were professional entertainers – prostitute is too strong a word to describe them; courtesan would be nearer the mark. Many of them were patronized or 'kept' by one wealthy person, but some certainly belonged to the oldest profession. Their sarangi accompanists often functioned as pimps and thus acquired a somewhat doubtful reputation. Ram Narayan has restored to the sarangi the status of a solo instrument in its own right, and by his life and conduct destroyed the stigma attached to it.

He started with a big piece, and in the alap‡ his instrument had the richness of a cello and his style something of the wailing quality of *Schelomo*§. Its range is virtually that of the violin and viola combined, and its three strings, tuned in fourths, are bowed, while he stops them as it were from the wrong side with the fingernail. There are sympathetic strings for every semitone he can play and by the end of the quick section he had given us some amazing, gypsy-fiddler gymnastics and high-flying. Afterwards, Narayana Menon complimented him on his incredibly accurate intonation. He finished with a gentle and rather sentimental thumri‖, which I liked very much.

After him came a Kathak dancer, Damayanti Joshi, a leading exponent of the style, which Narayana explained as, like Bharatanatyam, looking to the Natya Sastra for its basis and authority. I rather took to the great bunches of bells which clustered like swarms of bees above each of the dancer's ankles – far more of them than in Bharatanatyam – and she danced a tale of Holi water with some rather charming mime to what Narayana said was a North Indian raga rapidly becoming popular in the South. To finish with, a set piece involving a peacock, brilliantly stylized, and the monsoon, again mimed to perfection, with the arms and fingers indicating the speed and frequency of

*Sarangi: a stringed instrument, bowed, not plucked.
†Tabla: the drums, treble and bass, used to accompany North Indian instrumental recitals.
‡Alap: the free improvisation on a raga whpch usually forms the introductory part of a big-scale concert.
§*Schelomo*: a Jewish lament composed as a cello solo by Ernest Bloch.
‖Thumri: a piece of music in a light, popular, classical style.

257

the raindrops, the ankle bells reinforced by the tabla imitating the sound and impact they made.

Indian sights as well as Indian sounds lie in wait to enthral the traveller. My collateral ancestor Lord Canning was Governor-General at the time of the Mutiny in 1857 – his nickname of 'Clemency' Canning started as a sneer in *The Times* but carries other overtones to a modern generation – and his papers suggest an involvement with India even if no collection of miniatures or treasures remains behind him. My grandfather, King George v, went there only for the Durbar in 1911, to be crowned, and never returned, but according to her biographer James Pope-Hennessy, Queen Mary never got over the beauty of it. So perhaps some of my awe and delight at what I see and hear in India is inherited from her.

Air travel in India I found too frequently bedevilled by an early start – you get up at four-thirty for a plane at six-fifteen. But there is almost invariably reward at the destination. In Udaipur, for instance, we rounded the Maharana's vast palace to see our hotel in the middle of the lake, a fragile, white, flat structure, floating lily-like on the water – a pavilion in a Moghul painting. A curious sound seemed to hover over Udaipur itself like a dust-cloud. Because there was no mechanized noise whatever, the soft murmuring of a great number of people chattering in the city below could be heard quite clearly. Indians are compulsive talkers like Italians, and I thought that this was what Naples must have sounded like in Nelson's and Lady Hamilton's day. The most memorable of several islands in Udaipur's lake is called Jagmandir, and its outstanding feature is its parrots. They roost here in their thousands, and we watched them for forty minutes as they swooped over the lake, turning and splintering emerald green before alighting in the branches of the trees.

From Delhi, it is only a day trip to Khajuraho, with its astonishing group of temples and carvings. When you have admired the individual divine figures, the astonishing portrayals of dancers or temple maidens adorning themselves, tying on ankle bracelets, painting their lips or their eyes, drying their hair, writing letters, bouncing a ball, scratching their backs or caressing their breasts, you return to amazing erotic sculpture. These paeans of praise to sensual enjoyment bear astonishing witness to the all-embracing nature of the Indian outlook; everything – music, dance, sex, contemplation – was welcomed to the complete experience of life which religion not so much accepted as demanded.

You cannot go to India without seeing Agra and Fatehpur Sikri. It is said that the Taj Mahal is, with the Parthenon, the least disappointing of famous buildings, and the truth is that its colour and setting contribute to this view almost as much as design and proportion – the marble makes an effect of ivory against the ideally undistracting blue sky. From there it is forty minutes ride to Fatehpur Sikri. Though I first saw it in 1958, I had forgotten that the great gate, the highest in the world, could be seen for miles across the plain. It is easy to imagine this place humming with courtly activity, with music and dance in the water-cooled central court, with philosophical discussion in the uniquely-shaped little debating room with the emperor's throne on a kind of central stalk, as this small, aristocratic city – only court, nobles, army and priests as inhabitants – plied its fifteen years of doomed activity (doomed because there was no water supply).

Three packed days and nights spent in Nepal left us with impressions mostly in vivid contrast to India. To begin with, Kathmandu is always to be seen against a backdrop of the snow-covered Himalayas, and nothing more dramatic has ever been devised in any theatre. The city itself looks not unlike Srinagar in Kashmir, with much stouter buildings than you find in India. Less spoiled by modern development than Kathmandu is Patan, three and a half miles away and once a capital on equal terms when there was a king in both cities. It made an odd first impression as of Tudor London – pitched roofs, narrow streets with a lot of mud at the sides, small but significant squares, lots of ebullient people.

The Durbar square is a fantastic sight, surrounded by pagodas and temples, several of them with golden roofs – the more roofs a temple has, the higher it rates, as in Japan. The ancient Royal Palace is, according to Patricia's diary, 'a beautiful long building of glowing dark red Tudor brick, its atmosphere oddly Elizabethan because of its richly carved wood-work and overhanging gables.' It could be a set for a Nepalese *Falstaff*.

Uniquely impressive for us is the Buddhist Stupa of Bodnath, colossal in size, thought to be 2,500 years old and ringed by a Tibetan village which dates from well before the Chinese invasion. We wandered among the crowds of Tibetans, and photographed an engaging group of Nepalese untouchables who played and sang and danced what we were told was the Ten Sing tune (composed in 1953 in honour of the hero of Everest and invariably sung it seems in the same key). We climbed to just below the ever-focused eyes which are painted under the spire on all four sides of the Stupa and stared down on the Tibetan village activity. Near the Stupa, there was a holy man walking, unkempt, nearly naked and burnt black, with one withered arm stretched up from the shoulder and pointing permanently at the sky. Was this for holy men a normal type of disfiguration, we wondered, or did it represent the expiation of some horrendous vow?

We were taken to a handsome house near the old Hindu temple square where lives for her allotted span the Living Goddess. In Nepal, they choose a physically perfect infant girl, and bring her up with her family in surroundings of relative opulence. Once a year she must go in procession and be worshipped as the Goddess she is impersonating. But there are snags. At the first sign of blood issuing from her body she is out. A small cut is sufficient and the onset of puberty of course brings automatic disqualification. This is only the start of her troubles. For ten or a dozen years she has been a sort of Vestal Virgin but after her term she cannot resume normal life, nor can anyone marry her without the risk of extreme bad luck. As often as not, since the state pension is not very large, she finishes up in a brothel.

We filed into the courtyard and looked up at a rather haughty beauty of nine, much made up and artificially posing. Our guide said an offering of five rupees was appropriate and I gave it to the oldest of the boys in the courtyard. It was a little sad at dinner to be paying the same sum for a can of imported beer.

An expedition to view the sunrise over the Himalayas involved setting off at five. We started to climb and at Nagakot a notice announced we were 7,133 feet up. The freezing temperature was emphasized by the arrival of three little children, swathed about the head and down to the waist, but without socks, one of the boys walking on his heels to avoid the rest of his bare feet touching the ground. It was light enough when we arrived to see that we were going to be spared the mist which we had feared might obscure the view of the mountains. There they were, pinkly visible though not yet illuminated; with the clouds eddying around near us and below them as we looked. Everest, some seventy-five miles away, was far from the most imposing viewed from Nagakot, and indeed gave the impression of being much lower than the nearer Gauri Shanker.

Suddenly a peak was tipped with gold as the sun rose, then another until the whole range was gilded except for those peaks that had been covered by the clouds, which started to rise from the valleys as if to salute the sun. At the same moment, an exhilarating cacophony of shahnai* and drums rose from the other side of the valley – a wedding symphony, explained our guides; this was a very auspicious day for such a ceremony, Sripanchami, the beginning of Spring.

*Shahnai: a North Indian equivalent of the European shawm, a kind of oboe-like instrument.

The Annapurna range of mountains lay to the north west and these the clouds never covered even for a few minutes. By the end of forty-five minutes Everest had reappeared, everything was starting to take on the colour of day, the weddings were audibly (though invisibly) in full swing, the small children had been photographed with Patricia against a backcloth of the Himalayas, and we were more than a little conscious that we had missed four hours of sleep and I had forgotten to bring the brandy flask.

On my 1958 visit, I had seen Konorak and its Black Pagoda in Orissa State, south of Calcutta, deserted after the monsoon and majestic in a great clearing. In 1968 things were rather different. It was the day Hindus celebrate the dawn of the love between the Sun God and a favourite damsel – Konorak is the temple of the Sun God, planned in the shape of a chariot with great elaborately carved wheels ten feet high. The celebration takes the form of a pilgrimage in which thousands of devotees flock to the temple to bathe in the sea and later to visit the super-sacred Juggernaut Temple in Puri.

The great main temple at Konarak collapsed centuries ago so that it is only the smaller audience chamber and dance hall that one sees; but these make an overwhelming impression. The dancing figures round the hall, much eroded by sea, wind and sand; the great series of erotic sculptures round the first level of the temple; above all perhaps the wheels round its base, the horse figures trampling savages, the Hindu lions subduing the Muslim elephants, and the marvellously subtle and huge figures round the top – these are the glories of Konarak, these and the incomparable grandeur of concept and setting. It was odd to see it crowded and hot when I remembered it deserted and cooled by the monsoon, but the Bank Holiday atmosphere contributed something special. All round the great square meadow in which it is situated were booths for eating, for selling souvenirs, for shows of every kind.

If Kathmandu and Konarak are as different as Wimbledon from Widnes, you couldn't find anything in much greater contrast to Konarak than Cochin. To get to Periyar, the reservoir created about 1890 and now providing power and water storage as well as a game sanctuary, you drive almost continuously through villages, at first past the famous backwaters of Cochin, later over hills, always through what looked like immensely fertile land – on the way up, we noticed crops of coconut, tapioca, rice, tea, pepper, bananas, cardamom, coffee, rubber. The lake is an extraordinary spot, and as you chug about it by boat or sit in the guest house in the middle you constantly catch glimpses of wild pig, black monkeys, Indian bison and elephants. We watched for half an hour a group of thirty or forty Great

Indian Hornbills. These great pterodactyls, as anachronistic as the elephants but much rarer in their natural habitat, circled and wheeled and dived from one tall tree to another a hundred feet up and two hundred yards away, just far enough for the sound of their great throbbing flight to carry to us intermittently.

We were sitting in the dark after our first day listening to what sounded like dozens of elephants all round, bathing and drinking and squirting water, with occasional squeals from the baby elephants. All seemed relaxed and delightful until suddenly a tiger roared, twice, and apparently very close to us. Immediately there was dead silence, as if every living being had frozen: we imagined an elephant with one foot raised, another unable to discharge a trunk full of water. The tiger's roar is a horrendous sound, sudden, very loud indeed, starting *fortissimo* and as threatening as a hostile tommy gun at close range. You *know* it's after you – and we all got up as one the second we heard it and disappeared indoors.

Madras I have purposely left till last. Not only have some of my most memorable experiences of Indian music taken place there, but in 1968 Patricia and I found the place itself from the aesthetic point of view perhaps the most attractive of the great Indian cities. Madras has a spaciousness about it – no one seems to hurry unduly, doubtless partly because of the climate.

I must admit to a strong sympathy with South India, which feels itself very much put upon by the North, especially in the matter of language (Northern, jumped-up, bastard Hindi now replacing English as the national tongue, and not ancient, pure, Southern Tamil). The immediate linguistic issue concerns civil service jobs; obviously the man who takes the exam in his 'native' language has an advantage. But there is more to it than that. Culture in South India is less mixed in its influences, invasion having been from north-west to south-east, and one feels less sense of compromise with alien beliefs in Madras than in Calcutta or Delhi. Perhaps after all it is partly the Northern Englishman in me identifying with the similarly deprived South Indian – the analogy is not so far-fetched.

Madras was to be the outward point of our trip in 1968 and at the airport we were met by, amongst others, Subbulakshmi and Sadasivam, her husband. Subbulakshmi I have described as the Callas of India, the great singer of Carnatic (Southern) music, and so popular that to announce a concert of hers is to guarantee a sell-out, in the open air to as many as 10,000 listeners. In 1958, she was the first Carnatic singer I heard and on the

262

platform she made an impression of size as well as of authority, only to have each, away from musical performance, completely contradicted. At that time, she spoke little English but ten years later her command of the language had vastly improved, which is not to say that she initiated conversation but that she was prepared to bat the ball back firmly over the net if you hit it appropriately in her direction, whereas before I always had the feeling she was going to claim a let.

Subbulakshmi's hospitality is legendary, and Patricia's first experience of it – I had been to Kalki* in 1958 – was to go for tea in order to meet the nonagenarian Rajagopalachari, who then lived next door. He was the sage of South India, the man who followed Dickie Mountbatten as the first Indian Governor General, and in 1968 he still wrote a weekly newspaper column. He used the English language in a gentle and elegant way which seems to be confined to ancient and erudite Indians – I remember Dr Radhakrishnan, who was President in 1961, using it the same way.

We were invited to Kalki for a musical party, and arrived to find dinner set up in the garden for at least a hundred people. Two other Europeans there seemed slightly out of their depth: I heard one of them say to her neighbour with reference to Subbulakshmi, 'Oh, is she a musician? Does she play the sitar?' The neighbour's reaction was rather as if someone in Italy had just heard it suggested Callas was a water-skiing champion. Balasaraswati and her daughter Lakshmi arrived almost last, and Bala and Subbulakshmi giggled like conspiratorial schoolgirls; there was obviously a bond of sympathy between them. Bala was given her private dish of pan† to chew during the music and when it arrived, her eyes rolled as if she were a child getting an unexpected Mars bar.

I found it somehow touching that, while each leading musician so to speak took the floor in turn, the others, together with Subbulakshmi and Balasaraswati, provided the corner stones to the non-existent platform, beating time and generally showing themselves concerned for what was going on; rather like a senior matador in the bull ring. They were not so much with the performer and against the rest of us as demonstrating the brotherhood of art – how often does one use the phrase and how seldom see it brought to life?

Proceedings started with a violin solo from Papa Venkatramiah, a virtuoso in spite of the bastardization of this western instrument. Then came

*Kalki: the home of M.S.Subbulakshmi and T.Sadasivam; also the headquarters of his periodical of the same name.
†Pan: a masticatory of betel nut, lime, and betel leaf.

Semmangudi, whom I remembered with awe and veneration from ten years before. They said he was now nearly sixty, but he looked to me exactly the same, with his bald egg head gleaming and the ash streaks running off his forehead as he got hotter. He is a sublime artist. On this occasion he was surrounded by two other vocalists (one also playing the tambura), a violinist, and a law-graduate who played the mridangam.

He sustained a marvellous intensity, and the precision of his rhythm was astounding, even amongst Indians. The voice itself struck me as pleasing, I should imagine, to the most Western ears, with its forward, open quality, sometimes like de Lucia's, sometimes like Battistini's. Like them he is artist and virtuoso, throwing back his head to emit great arcs of sound, now smooth and serene, now jagged with the Indian equivalent of tonic sol-fa enunciated at speed on the musical line. His joy in his performance was physical as well as spiritual, and the wide gestures of the arms, the wagging of the head, the throwing of the body about, all this fitted the music and you felt that without it it would be more difficult to sing. He sang for an hour and as far as I am concerned it was pure joy, as splendid and evocative and absorbing as an opera by Britten or Janáček, or an hour of Brendel or Curzon playing Schubert. It was not just a compliment to tell him afterwards that he alone could have consoled us that Subbulakshmi didn't sing; it was wholly true.

Subbulakshmi and Sadasivam, together with Bala, have come to epitomize Madras for us and other events there have assumed the character of background, whatever the year, however beautiful the place. In 1968 we drove from Madras to Kanchipuram – 'The Benares of the South' the guide book calls it, and it is almost as sacred and its saris almost as beautiful; we bought a couple, but most of the designs seemed to abjure the traditional for something aimed at the American market.

The enormous Ekambareswara temple, dedicated to Siva, suggests that Indian temples, before the advent of the skyscraper, were the nearest approach to a physical representation of the Tower of Babel. It is attractive in that throngs of people constantly move about it in a purposeful manner, including while we were there a wedding party.

I don't remember music for the weddings but there certainly had been when I was there with Marion and Tony Gishford in 1958, *Nadaswarams*, a kind of baritone *shahnai* (itself a North Indian form of shawm), sounding like trumpets at full blast, and going round in front of us with a temple elephant and great thudding South Indian drums (tavils) as accompaniment. It made a quite marvellous open-air din, more indigenous though less peculiar than the experience in 1981 of hearing a very free version of 'Home, sweet home' played on trumpets and drums as a march at a Christian village wedding near Trivandrum in Kerala! By far the most peculiar music we heard in a temple was in 1981 at Suchindram, also near Trivandrum. There, before temples admitted drums (they are made after all with the skins of animals), they had round a pillar installed stone rods tuned to particular pitches so that they resonated when struck. I had never met such a phenomenon before, but it is a fact that a tune of a rather melancholy hue was obtained from these singing stones, as they call them, and that one could feel the rods vibrating. It was not as brave a sound though as the *Nadaswaram* and drums which accompanied Suchindram's mid-day *puja* (religious rites) and echoed round the ancient vaults.

On our way out of Kanchipuram, we went through the shopping district, which produced a crop of remarkable names: 'Everest Bangle Mart', 'New bright pin men – Washers and Dry Cleaners', 'M. S. Smoothsell', 'Spencer's Kickapoo Joy Juice' (in a *dry* state?).

But soon after we had reached Madras in 1968, I fell ill. Patricia went alone to Balasaraswati's dance recital and I stayed in bed in the hotel, highly conscious that the Indians are right to call the ailment 'breakbone fever' since the possibility of sleeping through the constant aching seemed remote.

Patricia, when she got back from Bala's recital, told me that I might get a pleasant surprise at ten next morning. In walked Bala and Lakshmi, and after a while Bala said, 'Would you like to hear something?', whereupon flute and tambura players entered and sat with Lakshmi (Indian musicians invariably perform sitting cross-legged on the floor). Here was the surprise. For thirty minutes, Bala sang and mimed Padam* (there was no room to dance), which was for me moving and exciting – too exciting I suspect for the recently abated fever. It was marvellous to watch her from so close, with the youthful facial expressions, the touching, beautiful arm and finger gestures, the tiny inflections of head and neck – Indian hand movements seem three-dimensional and ours are flat in comparison. She sang sweetly too, with ample vocal support from Lakshmi, who maintained afterwards that she was singing for the first time when anyone but family could hear her; and she finished with my favourite 'Krishna ni, bega ne baro' ('Come Krishna, come quickly'), which had featured in each one of her Edinburgh Festival programmes.

Bala was always a lady of uncommonly forceful character and nothing if not direct. She was, one must not forget, by caste a Devadasi, one 'Dedicated

*Padam: short, sacred song-dramas.

265

to God', and from the caste which produced temple courtesans as well as musicians. She understands English well but is shy of speaking it. Once, the story goes, she was at a dance conference in Delhi, and listened to an older South Indian lady expatiate in English on the spiritual qualities of the dance and how it had been rescued from its disreputable past. Bala made some comments in Tamil, which only a few present including the previous speaker understood, and which a distinguished Tamil speaker in some embarrassment translated as 'Shrimati Balasaraswati says she is very interested in what has been said and has certain reservations over the way the traditions of the dance have changed over the years.' What she *had* said, unequivocally, could apparently have been more accurately rendered as 'I am interested in what the previous speaker has said. These society ladies have been taking over our profession and they do it very well. But we have retained our art.' Bala did not insist; her retort had been understood by the few she wanted to reach.

No sooner had Bala's contribution to my convalescence finished than along came Subbulakshmi and Sadasivam, who said they could have *their* musicians there in half an hour. I had another thirty minutes of glorious music from the great M.S., with full accompaniment. She is a superb artist and I had by now heard enough Carnatic music to recognize her stature and see why Narayana rated her so highly. It was an unforgettable morning.

For our visit to Madras in 1970, we stayed, initially in their absence, with the Sadasivams, and were told when we arrived that breakfast would be at nine with a goodly company assembled for music afterwards.

The music to our delight turned out to be from Semmangudi. After about fifteen minutes, my English banking neighbour whispered that Semmangudi had warmed up amazingly quickly; we were in full flight, the sound clear and true and, to the Western ear, instrumental, the rhythms of that knife-edge precision which place him in a category almost by himself, the runs and decorations articulated with the clarity of a Horowitz. Maybe it is this unfailing flexibility that so impresses the Western ear, a quality once the *sine qua non* of every great Western singer, now, at least in male singers, for all practical purposes an extinct virtue. The bass range of the mridangam* in these circumstances can bring a peculiarly masculine element to Carnatic music, and with it bouncing, almost jaunty rhythms, even in devotional music. Semmangudi started what we were told was a garland of ragas – several strung together and none of them developed – as a concluding piece. In the course of one of them, called Hamsanandhi, Semmangudi made

---

*Mridangam: South Indian drum, used for accompaniment.

sudden, violent key shifts, out and back without warning or resolution – electrifying, like a flash of brilliant paint in an otherwise brown picture. Is this a quality of this raga or an idiosyncrasy of his?

Towards mid-day, it was over. There was a sudden flurry of clapping, not heralding as I thought the end of a superb performance but the arrival of garlands for Patricia and me. We transferred them almost immediately to Semmangudi and Papa Venkatramiah, which seemed appropriate and I hope was not against etiquette. After the concert, we heard that Subbulakshmi and Sadasivam were coming back specially from Calcutta, and, with innumerable other members of the family, went off to the airport to meet them, carrying garlands. The moment Subbulakshmi entered it, the house became more alive. Somehow the atmosphere was warmer, meals more fun, with her about.

After dinner that evening, music. Everyone has supreme musical memories which pop up as insistently as the smells of childhood; Subbulakshmi and Semmangudi singing together in 1958 is one of mine, and tonight this experience was renewed, twelve years later, she in the middle of a busy concert tour, he complaining like the Irishman that he is voiceless, has a sore throat, and anyhow sang yesterday for an hour and a half – and also the day before. But the magic was not slow in coming.

I first reacted to Indian music in its Hindustani manifestation and in particular to the sound of stringed instruments like the sitar and the sarod. But I believe now that I am even more completely under the spell of the Carnatic, particularly Subbulakshmi's pure, timeless, soaring, visionary art; its impact on me is as strong and true at the time I write as it was twenty-two years ago. Semmangudi deferred to her and had to be drawn into the music, but he soon realized that she was tired and needed assistance and so he played his part, adopting a range which suited her and therefore going from time to time into falsetto so as to keep the octave relationship with her.

Some of his singing was extremely soft and seemed to me of incomparable suggestive power, the soft attacks and adumbrations of phrases reminding me of Peter Pears or Callas or de los Angeles in their subtlety, precision, imagination, colouring. These two supreme artists never apparently appear together in public, but for me the occasion marked a repeat of perhaps the musical high spot of my first visit to India and I found myself praying that this occasion of hearing them together would not mark the completion of the circle. Memories count for a lot in music but it is an immediate art and the reality counts for even more.

I cannot end without a 1981 Madras postscript. The cycle began for me in 1958 was not yet in fact quite complete. By heroic re-arrangement, Subbulakshmi and T.S. postponed their departure from Madras for a concert in Hyderabad in order to give us supper and some music on my fifty-eighth birthday. Semmangudi was there too, proclaiming his age as seventy-three but still, with Subbulakshmi playing tambura and supplying not much more than vocal accompaniment, producing considerably more than a shadow of the accomplishment I had found so beguiling many years before. Nearly ninety minutes of their music in a small room without amplification (that canker of public success in Indian music) was as fine a birthday present as I ever had.

I must not forget too that (as a result of our own re-arrangements) it was followed two days later by Subbulakshmi's superb public concert at Hyderabad in which she displayed vocal and musical prowess of un-diminished perfection. She strikes me as the sort of natural singer an opera company dreams of – tremendously gifted physically, unaffected, beautifully schooled, totally involved in her work and treating it more as a mission than a profession. After the concert, we watched her all but mobbed by crowds of admirers trying to touch her feet as a sign of affection.

In 1981, we found that Bala, after years of heart trouble, had retired from dancing and was confining herself to teaching. Hers was no easy method – five years of basic training, after which pupils *might* be ready to tackle the art itself, was her formula (if the word can be used in connection with someone so spontaneous and individual), and to watch her class, ranging in age from five to fourteen (all girls of course) was a touching experience.

But more was to come. We had been told she would perform in public only to sing accompaniments at the dance recitals of her daughter Lakshmi, and this she did before dinner at her home that night. When it was over, Patricia said it had been marvellous and only one thing was missing: 'Krishna ni, bega ne baro.' Lakshmi had told me she would not include it in her own programme, as she felt it too exclusively Bala's, and Bala had for five years resisted all persuasion to revert to it; the past was the past, she said.

Suddenly, still sitting on the floor, perhaps for old time's sake and knowing it was our favourite, she felt in the mood. For ten minutes we saw and heard her as at her greatest, with such variety of vocal and mime inflection, such invention (things even Lakshmi had never seen her do before), such improvisatory wit and pathos, that her home for a little while was not a place for dry eyes.

Here was no old star putting the clock back, but rather someone of wisdom and resource joyously adjusting time to fit a new kind of present. It was very moving and we left the house with that sensation of emotional involvement which both Patricia and I have always felt with Bala just as we have with Subbulakshmi. Perhaps because we love them – and others – we have come a bit nearer to understanding India.

CHAPTER EIGHTEEN

Achievements and Might-have-beens 1958-74

THE LEEDS FESTIVAL, for which I began to work in 1956, has a long tradition, starting in 1858 with the opening of a new Town Hall. Immediately after the 1939–45 war, plans were made for its continuation as a triennial event (I was on the Programme Committee). As before the war, the concerts were run on a subscription basis and once again they were full, but the 1953 Festival showed a deficit and no further plans were made.

Three years later, the relatively new Yorkshire Symphony Orchestra was also running into difficulties and a West Riding pressure group, headed by Jack Lyons, Norman Watson and Norman Wilkinson, and backed by the *Yorkshire Post* and its chairman Sir Maxwell Ramsden, was pressing for the revival of both orchestra and Festival. The area needed the orchestra, they argued, and it would be unthinkable for the Festival's centenary to go by without an effort to revive that too. They first approached Peter Diamand, of the Holland Festival, but he declined the invitation and said they had the right man on their doorstep, which was me. As they came from the West Riding, they had the gumption to tell me this when inviting me to become the Festival's director.

It was clear that it would be a part-time job until the few weeks before the Festival itself and I had no difficulty in obtaining the necessary leave from Covent Garden. We had a strong committee in Leeds, with aims a little different from those of the past. Nobody was under any illusion about the box office making a profit for charity as it had before the war; indeed, I very quickly convinced them that a properly rehearsed programme was certain to require subsidy itself. To decide what the Festival's core should be presented no problem; the long tradition was based on choral performance, and this we intended to uphold.

We persuaded Herbert Bardgett to return as chorus director – we all considered him the best in the land, and so he was, provided the music he was asked to work on wasn't too modern – and there was no trouble in finding candidates for audition to make up the 300-strong body we planned; nothing less would do for the Town Hall and the Festival tradition, insisted Norman Wilkinson, a pillar amongst local music lovers and that rarity, a genuine enthusiast, from whom I always had immense support and for whom I developed great affection over the years.

I had of course never run anything of this kind on my own and I had no first-hand experience of dealing with committees. I doubt if the Professor of Music at Leeds University, James Denny, took kindly to my appointment, and as chairman of the Programme Committee he had already commissioned Peter Racine Fricker to write a new choral work. I asked the committee to accept from the start that in principle our programme should contain one of the acknowledged choral masterpieces conducted by its greatest exponent, and, if possible, a première of a new work. They had already made up their minds that the Festival should open with Beethoven's *Missa Solemnis*, so my contribution here was to insist that Otto Klemperer should conduct the Beethoven and John Pritchard the Fricker.

The organizational spadework on the artistic side was my responsibility, and I wrote the letters with my secretary at home, selecting and contracting artists, arranging a rehearsal schedule, compiling a souvenir programme and commissioning writers for the daily programmes. In addition, there was a mass of administrative detail that had to be dealt with in Leeds: booking of rehearsal rooms, organization of box office, ticket pricing, publicity, accommodation for artists, a Festival Club, and a hundred and one things which only come to light if what you are running seems likely to prove a success.

My mother had written to invite the Queen to come and she had accepted. The problem from then on was not so much how to cope with her visit as how to deal with the rush of tickets that followed the announcement. The Queen was to go to the Grand Theatre and to two concerts, and the rehearsals for her visit were not without their comic overtones. Every kind of person was press-ganged into appearing as someone else, and to the amazement of bystanders we processed up and down the steps of the theatre, round and round the corridors and the lifts of the Town Hall, in and out of the Gallery of the Great Hall of the University, until we felt we had got it so much into our heads that, whatever improvization was necessary on the day, nothing could go fundamentally wrong. Slightly to the surprise of many of us, it didn't.

Jack Lyons had suggested my deputy a retired general, John Latter, and we quickly made him administrative director. It turned out from my point of view an ideal appointment, as he was a meticulous staff officer by training, with a great sense of humour and a considerable love of music. Nothing was beyond John's administrative capacity, although the West Riding businessman's sometimes inflated estimate of the appropriate relationship of his seat to his sovereign's at either theatre or Town Hall came near to ruffling even John's customary calm.

We had decided to make the centenary event in 1958 as far as possible a national affair. Covent Garden staged Handel's dramatic oratorio *Samson* in the Grand Theatre, with Jon Vickers in the title role and Joan Sutherland in support; we had jazz programmes headed by Duke Ellington in one of the cinemas, Indian music played by Ravi Shankar at the Art Gallery, and a wealth of choral music in the Town Hall, ranging from the *Missa Solemnis*, through Fricker's *A Vision of Judgment* to Walton's *Belshazzar's Feast*, which ended the Festival and had been first heard there in 1931.

But there were to be snags. In the two years since 1956, when I had invited him to take part and he had accepted, Klemperer had become increasingly a prey to illness and had cancelled a number of London concerts. Some three weeks before our opening he was at home in Zürich confined to bed. He fell asleep late one night smoking his pipe; his heavy woollen bedjacket caught fire and he tried to put it out with the bottle of alcohol with which he was customarily rubbed down before going to sleep. The third degree burns were difficult to treat; skin grafting lasted into the following summer and there was no question of his conducting in Leeds.

In the end Jascha Horenstein did a neat, musical job for our opening concert, the Festival as a whole went off well and we started not too long afterwards to plan for 1961 – Leeds was still then a triennial event and only in the '70s did we step it up to alternate years.

The Leeds Festival suffered I believe at this time from a conviction on the part of the city council that it was essentially a rich man's toy and not a Leeds amenity. The view was based I am afraid on my connection with it and also that of Jack Lyons, a prominent Leeds businessman who had succeeded Max Ramsden as chairman in 1956. I sometimes felt indignant not only on behalf of the Festival but of Jack and myself, since we were I was convinced a good team and had weathered a number of storms together. Without him and in spite of an active committee, I doubt if Ken Kendall and I could after 1974 have handed over a going concern (with which Ken continued for a couple more Festivals) to future committees and future artistic directors.

The three Festivals in 1961, 1964 and 1967 had a rather similar pattern. Carlo Maria Giulini was the main visiting celebrity and he was an inspiration to the chorus. Whenever he was on the podium my policy of persuading an international celebrity to give a definitive performance of one of the choral masterpieces seemed justified. I personally remember with a lot of pleasure the extrovert but curiously touching *Stabat Mater* of Rossini, in which Nicolai Gedda's brilliant singing of '*Cujas animam*' will stay in the memory of those who heard it.

At only three festivals after 1958 did we achieve a performance of a commissioned piece: from Alexander Goehr, Richard Rodney Bennett and David Blake. Blake's work won many admirers and had a spin-off in that, as one of them, I asked him, quite soon after I went to work at the Coliseum, to write an opera for Sadler's Wells. New works by no means represented the sum of our contemporary endeavours. In 1961 we secured the first British performance of 'The Dance Round the Golden Calf' from Schoenberg's opera *Moses and Aaron*, not yet then performed in this country.

For me the best moment of the 1961 Festival came when, sitting with Benjamin Britten at Beckett's Park, Britten nearly knocked the Schoenberg score off our knees as a tenor soloist enthusiastically overshot the mark with a phrase ending on high D flat instead of the written B flat. We looked up to see that John Pritchard had simultaneously to retrieve *his* score, which in his moment of shock – and perhaps of delight – he appeared to have flung from the stand. Perhaps I should record that Heather Harper and Janet Baker were two of our 'Naked Virgins' in this (concert) première of Schoenberg.

In 1970 and 1972, we added what might perhaps be seen as a new dimension to the Festival. In collaboration with Deutsche Grammophon, we mounted and they recorded successively Handel's *Israel in Egypt* and *Saul*. We had ideal soloists and conductor and I think the resulting gramophone records did everyone credit. Certainly Charles Mackerras's brilliant conducting of Handel came as a revelation to many. The public sadly seemed disinclined to recognize what was in their midst and did not fill the hall.

I was becoming uncomfortably aware that modern music is exceptionally hard for amateurs, that composers cannot easily change style to suit circumstances, and that the Leeds Festival's long tradition of performance of contemporary music was waning. I believe that to make contemporary music the province of specialists sows disastrous seeds for the future and that an organization like the Leeds Festival, where amateurs perform to a professional standard, has, or certainly had, something to contribute to remove such barriers. A new view of the amateur in connection with contemporary music, appropriate to Leeds, was not during my time evolved, and I often ask myself whether this was an opportunity missed or a reappraisal for which the time was not yet ripe.

I cannot resist one other memory of those Leeds Festivals. Herbert Bardgett was a most resourceful chorus-master in the old tradition. He had with infinite care improved the official translation of *Les Noces*, which of course we were singing in English rather than in Russian. When I enquired of him whether he had passed on his new verbal felicities to the solo singers, he appeared rather puzzled by the question until suddenly light dawned as to why I or anybody else should bother themselves about anything other than what the chorus was singing. 'Oh, you mean the in-between bits?' he asked.

When I was a schoolboy at Ludgrove I was once in a class required to write an essay on capital punishment. We couldn't see the point of the subject and I had no notion then that it would later become for me an issue of importance. I first started to think seriously about it when a POW in Colditz and an American colonel was brought into the camp under sentence of death. The rest of us started to think about the effect of waiting on a prisoner under sentence of death, then the unthinkable nature of a civilian executioner's job. We read some convincing evidence about the lack of deterrent power of the death penalty, and I at least was on my way to becoming an abolitionist.

I was convinced then as now of the illogicality, the primitive ferocity of meeting killing by killing, however much it was judicially controlled; of the brutalizing effect in general of retaining such a punishment; of its ineffectiveness as deterrent; of the total unacceptability of society exacting retribution (an argument much used many years later even by churchmen in the first House of Lords debate, but virtually absent from the second). Since it is widely admitted that neither abolitionist nor retentionist is usually open to argument, each having reached conviction as a result of some almost atavistic urge, it was all the more surprising to many of us that, at the second time of asking, the House of Lords eventually passed the Abolition Bill with a big majority.

I voted with the minority the first time round and was shocked and miserable at the result. Sad too at the lack of reason (as I felt) in some of the retentionist speeches, and only slightly restored in spirits when old Sam Hoare, a one-time Home Secretary, told me afterwards that he was convinced it would turn out differently the next time. He added that it was rare that an ex-Home Secretary, having once known the agony of rejecting an appeal, should in either Lords or Commons vote other than abolitionist – an exception presumably was David Maxwell Fyfe, who as Lord Kilmuir later and by no means ineffectively led the retentionist case.

Reformers are disinclined to let sleeping dogs lie, and after that first vote Victor Gollancz asked me to lunch to find out how serious I was about a cause on which he set great store. With music as an added bond, we became friends, and he soon asked me to join a group which aimed to put pressure on successive Governments. In 1962, we asked R.A. Butler, Home Secretary and a known abolitionist, to introduce a Government measure, or at least provide time for a Private Member's Bill, but he declined. The Prime Minister, Harold Macmillan, agreed to receive a deputation. Victor Gollancz insisted I act as chairman of the group, which it was agreed should consist of Gerald Gardiner (later Lord Chancellor), the Bishop of Exeter, Chuter Ede (Home Secretary in the first post-war Labour Government), Gollancz and myself.

We met in V.G.'s miniscule office to discuss the presentation of our case, agreed we should in turn make a limited point, with none of us speaking for more than three minutes, then trooped off to Downing Street, where the Prime Minister wordlessly received us at the door of the Cabinet Room. Butler was late and I led off with some rather mild remarks about my prison experience and general conviction, kept strictly within time. Gerald Gardiner followed, and introduced a concise, well-argued case by saying that as a man of law he represented probably the social group which had been throughout history the most reactionary over law reform. At this point, the PM permitted himself a clearly audible 'I'd back the Bishops!', which so unnerved an already diffident Bishop of Exeter that he followed Gardiner to no effect at all. Chuter Ede spoke next, with humanity but for nearer thirty minutes than three, and by the time Butler came in, I felt we had muffed our case.

Macmillan was eloquent if diffuse in reply, and, in spite of much reference to the horror of death on the roads (with which subject at one moment I feared he had got us confused), declared his conviction that at some time in the future abolition would be with us. But, in his decided view, not in the life of this Parliament. Butler seemed concerned to defend the current compromise position, which retained capital punishment for killers of policemen but not for poisoners for gain.

Macmillan was right: abolition did not come in that Parliament, but, following another vote in the Commons, a Bill came to the Lords in summer 1965, early in Harold Wilson's first administration. There was a two-day debate and on the second day I made my maiden (and so far solitary) speech in the House of Lords, carefully prepared but of course, as is customary, without notes. My theme was purely humanitarian – since there was no indication that it was a deterrent, why should Great Britain be among the last European countries to retain the death penalty? I had thought to make a plea too for the victims of murder and their dependants but decided at the last moment to cut it out as being too obviously a bid for sympathy, moreover one I had no way of backing up with practical proposals. I was impressed by one of the abolitionist speakers who supported his case with statistics – a difficult thing in what is primarily a moral issue. Individual states of the USA, he said, had between 1918 and 1940 pursued policies over the death penalty which were by no means parallel. Some had started the period abolitionist and finished it retentionist, some the other way round, some had changed more than once, others had been constant to a single view throughout. But in no individual state had the graph of capital murder varied from the pattern which obtained for the whole United States. In other words, the evidence for the death penalty as deterrent was non-existent; the pattern went its way regardless of the state of the law.

Abolition was passed with a handsome majority, even though peers came up from the country to vote retentionist who, like me, hardly knew their way to the building; but to my chagrin, Lord Kilmuir, winding up for the retentionists, made sarcastic play with the fact that no single abolitionist speaker, though basing his case on humanitarianism, had had a word of sympathy for the victims of the criminals we were being asked to feel sorry for. I had missed my chance.

The aftermath was not without embarrassment as far as I was concerned, as some newspapers took it upon themselves to blow up my own part to ludicrous proportions, labelling me a royal rebel and a leading figure in the whole debate, which was a very long way from the truth.

When I left the Edinburgh Festival in 1965, Howard Hartog, to whose intervention I owed much of the success of the mini-Boulez Festival in Edinburgh, suggested to them and to me that I might join the New Philharmonia Orchestra, which as Philharmonia had played at festivals in Edinburgh and Leeds with which I was concerned. Since Walter Legge, its founder and mentor, had retired and made a move the previous year to disband it, the orchestra had reformed under its own auspices as an independent body. Its self-governing status was now jealously guarded, but it felt the need of some guidance from outside. I was invited to be artistic adviser, a curiously anomalous title carrying I never was to know precisely how much delegated administrative authority.

At first I took it literally, and gave my advice on artists and programmes, but very soon the chairman, Bernard Walton the first clarinet, asked me to act on an idea I had put up and told me that he and the orchestra's council expected to be consulted only over conductors. Bernard was an excellent player, one of that splendid band led by Gareth Morris the flautist, Dennis Brain the first horn, and Jock Sutcliffe, oboe, which had given the orchestra its original pre-eminence; and as chairman he showed tenacity and vision. Before long, he told me he felt that he himself must spend more time in the office than he could at present afford. Members of a freelance orchestra like the New Philharmonia are paid by the session rather than salaried, and the suggestion that he should receive money for not playing was distinctly unpopular with his colleagues. They voted him down, and he resigned.

Gareth Morris, who was elected chairman in his place, enunciated a simpler philosophy: he wanted to get on with the playing and let the office do the planning. On the other hand, he reserved the right to criticize the result. He was not difficult to work with but he certainly knew how to criticize. We had the chance of engaging Georg Szell, one of the most renowned and in my view one of the finest conductors around, and I asked Gareth what he thought of the idea. 'I've no objection,' he said. 'Mind you, I don't admire him at all. To me, he's nothing but a bandmaster!' We engaged him, but the chemistry was wrong, and it was hard to tell whether Szell's contempt for the orchestra or their dislike of him was the greater.

Otto Klemperer had for some years been the Philharmonia's 'chief conductor for life' and, when Walter Legge abandoned it, became the New Philharmonia's president. My regard for him dated from soon after the war when I first heard him in London, and a performance of Mahler's Second Symphony in Amersterdam in 1952 convinced me that he was one of the greatest conductors alive. I wrote a highly enthusiastic review in the *Daily Mail* and was amazed years later to be told by Lotte Klemperer that her father had been pleased enough by the article to preserve it. He conducted at my first Edinburgh Festival, and I was instrumental in persuading him to conduct at Covent Garden, the arrangements for the new *Fidelio* being made during my time there although the results were seen and heard after I left.

The removal of a tumour on the brain (the result of a fall from the rostrum) during the war had left him indistinct of speech and with only partial use of his right side. To get a telephone call from him was therefore awkward. One summer afternoon, with David Webster away from Covent Garden, I received such a call. It transpired that, with a view to the forthcoming *Fidelio*, he wanted to see the Opera House's orchestra pit. I rustled up Morris Smith, the orchestral manager, and alerted Sergeant Martin, the head commissionaire, to the augustness of our visitor and, since he was lame, to the help he would need getting up and down stairs. From the stalls, he inspected the pit and pronounced himself satisfied.

Passing the box office, he asked what they were queuing for. 'Tonight is a ballet première: Stravinsky's *Agon*,' I told him. 'I should like to come,' said Klemperer – moreover he wanted three tickets, aisle seats. I promised to arrange it, and begged him to stay for the last ballet, which was *Daphnis et Chloe* with Margot Fonteyn. At the interval he said he had vastly enjoyed *Agon*. As, after *Daphnis*, I pushed my way towards him through the departing balletomanes I heard him calling to me over their heads, 'Awful music! Frightful music!' – a sentiment I could not help in my heart of hearts echoing.

One of the joys of working with the New Philharmonia was regular contact with Klemperer. A conductor we had engaged once cancelled with 'flu. Klemperer was in London between recordings and I was rather pleased with the formula I hit on: 'I have been trying to make up my mind whether it is ruder to ask you to substitute for Kletzki or not to ask you, and have decided that *not* to ask you is the ruder. Will you do it?' He laughed, and did the concert. Much of what he conducted for us in public was also recorded, and half the programmes were arranged round EMI's needs.

His pre-war rages were famous, like Toscanini's, but I only saw him angry once. He wanted to do Mahler's Eighth, a work requiring vast forces, and with representatives of gramophone company, chorus and orchestra, we were in his sitting room at the Hyde Park Hotel discussing details. He told the chairman of the New Philharmonia Chorus, Charles Spencer, that he wished a particular protégé to play for its rehearsals; Spencer politely reminded him that the chorus had its own regular pianist, and stuck to his guns until Klemperer, supported on his stick, half rose like a wounded dragon from his seat at the end of the sofa and for thirty seconds roared at him with the fire of ancient days. Later, Lotte assured us that her father could never cope physically with so complicated a work and we quietly let the project drop.

It was not the only such project which disappeared. Klemperer had worked in opera all his life and missed the theatre – when Patricia and I went to see him after the Covent Garden *Fidelio*, he was sitting up in his chair and positively purring. 'I don't believe you have conducted this opera at all,' she said. 'You never look like this after a concert!' To which he grunted, '*Ich bin*

Theatermensch' ('I am an old theatre hand'). He wanted to record Gluck's *Orfeo* with Janet Baker, and I went to discuss casting and schedule with him. He seemed flummoxed when I asked him which version he would perform, and Lotte said: 'I don't believe you've ever conducted *Orpheus*' (they both pronounced it as if it were a German opera) 'in your life!' 'Yes, I have.' 'When?' 'In 1918,' he said.

In the late 1960s, there was something like a Klemperer-cult in London. His concerts sold out almost as soon as they were announced, as did his records, and young musicians were as keen to hear him conduct as he was to go to their concerts or rehearsals – he got easily bored and listening to music got round that problem. He favoured Lorin Maazel at first, but his favourites were Pierre Boulez and Daniel Barenboim, the latter mainly in those days as pianist. Before his own concerts, he liked a few people (who included Patricia and me) to go to his dressing room perhaps half an hour beforehand to talk quietly while he composed himself for the work ahead. We were sitting once like this with Boulez when suddenly Klemperer said, 'Mr Boulez, are you married?' 'No,' said Pierre. 'Very good!' came the reaction. He did not approve of the modern way in which all young pianists, even conductors, are friends and form some sort of mutual admiration society. 'In my day, Furtwängler and Bruno Walter and Kleiber and I *hated* each other! It was more healthy!'

Patricia and I used to ask Klemperer to lunch every now and then, and on one such occasion he rang her up in the morning to say, 'May I borrow your piano after lunch? I want to play two things: one song, and one opera!' His song was a Hymn of Hate by the Jews for the Germans in a somewhat Kurt Weill-like idiom; his opera, as he himself said before he started to play, was basically post-Strauss and post-Mahler, 'not modern enough for today'. It was not half bad, but his piano playing, with dexterity confined to the left hand, made turning the pages (my job) very hard indeed. Often I was lost like him in a morass of wrong notes and, occasionally, long before either of us had reached the bottom of the page, he would mutter '*Genug!*' and urge me to turn.

Mark was a favourite of his from the moment they first met. He was sitting in a chair when Mark came in and he put his arms out and said simply, '*Komm!*' Mark sat on his lap, watched with pleasure while the great man during lunch palmed pepper-grinders to make them disappear, and offered him a cigarette afterwards ('Alas, Mark, you are too young and I am too old!'). Klemperer never failed to ask after him, nor to point out, when we took him to tea at the Hyde Park Hotel, that it was Mark he had invited and who brought us rather than the other way round. Mark liked him in return and used to refer to him as 'Dr Plemperer'.

With Klemperer, the sardonic was never far away. He said to Peter Diamand once about me: 'You call him George, do you?' 'Yes,' said Peter; 'Don't you?' 'Of course not,' said Klemperer. 'He is my employer.' My affection for him grew during these New Philharmonia years, whose climax came with the Beethoven bi-centenary in 1970. The Festival Hall had reserved the Beethoven symphonies for him in early summer and the BBC asked if they could televise them. John Culshaw, once of Decca and by then for several years head of TV music, could get no answer from Lotte and, in despair, he asked me to set up a lunch. He was shocked to find that Lotte's main reservation was that Klemperer might possibly have a stroke or heart attack during the performance and that the BBC might continue to film. John went pale at the idea; the guarantee was given and the TV films were made, and I hope preserved for posterity. They make a fitting epitaph for a very great man.

Klemperer was an eagle amongst conductors, and that he survived sufficient vicissitudes to kill a village was in itself remarkable. After his serious illness of 1958–9, he seemed if anything to redouble in spirit, his best performances having even greater certainty. He had to be half-dragged on to the platform and was barely able to make the ordinary gestures. Yet the music he recreated was entirely his own; the NPO played for him as for no one else – some said, no orchestra unused to him could have played for him at all – and their Beethoven with another conductor was entirely different. As a performer, he was architect first, poet second, but the most famous tunes came out filled with meaning and balanced in a way which eluded lesser men. That he took the classics slowly became an article of critical faith in London; and it is true that he often did, but by no means always. He once conducted a whole programme of Mozart in C major or minor (an odd idea in prospect but one which came off in practice), and, after the *Jupiter*, Patricia and I met Boulez going back to congratulate him. We agreed that it must have been one of the fastest *Jupiters* ever heard in the hall, yet next day one of the critics wrote parrot-like that the concert was dominated by Klemperer's usual slow tempi. Even when it was slow, the music had enormous vitality, and I came to believe that part of the secret lay in the spring and elasticity that he somehow gave to the accompaniment; the bass line was never soggy, always lively and full of bounce.

Patricia and I were on holiday in Beirut when we heard of his death. We loved that dauntless old man very much.

Carlo Maria Giulini was the other conductor I worked with most closely during my NPO time. He is a North Italian, associated particularly with Italian opera; his British career started at Glyndebourne, and his fame with *Don Carlos* at Covent Garden in 1958. He conducted often while I was at the Edinburgh Festival, at five Leeds Festivals for which I was responsible, and during this period recorded with Philharmonia as well as conducting a number of concerts.

Carlo's approach to music was intensely serious. He told me he had as a radio conductor in Rome conducted most of the classical and some of the modern repertory, little of it with so deep a knowledge that the performance came from his heart. He was determined to avoid doing the same now that a second and more serious career was opening to him. As a result, his repertory was notoriously small. Just as notorious was his reluctance to make any compromise over casting, rehearsal or the other conditions surrounding a performance, and to this he added before long a basic reluctance to be away from home for any length of time. He would not take over the chief conductorship of the NPO when Klemperer died.

Nevertheless, to work with him was an immense pleasure. In winter 1966, he conducted *Rigoletto* at the Rome Opera, and I took Patricia there as a birthday treat. He knew we were coming but I had no idea what his attitude to her might be. He knew Marion, Patricia and I were not married, and he was after all a devout Roman Catholic. The performance, in spite of a rather austere production by Eduardo de Filippo, was one to treasure and I need not have worried about Carlo's friendliness. His wife asked us to have supper with them, and we went back to their apartment – you can't call those spacious Italian dwellings 'flats'. We discussed the performance in great detail, and talked of the sad state into which he felt Italian opera, especially at la Scala, had fallen, of the prospects in England in general and at New Philharmonia in particular. When I looked at my watch I saw to my horror that it was nearly four o'clock in the morning. I asked him to ring for a taxi, but he said he would drive us; there was no prospect of sleep for him after a performance until five or six. In the end he took us to our hotel through a Roman dawn and I understood a little more about the different demons which drive different performers.

Carlo used regularly to stay at Harewood for an early run-through with the Leeds Festival Chorus, and at the first Festival after my mother died conducted Beethoven's *C Minor Mass* in her memory. He became disenchanted with opera over the years. Nonetheless, he was a superb operatic conductor and I suspect opera lost more than the symphonic world gained when he gave up the one and went over wholly to the other. In concert he has his peers, while in opera he was a king.

After I had been at New Philharmonia eighteen months and had guided them through the difficult period following the crisis (Rosemarie Schnutz and I worked very hard to avert disaster and secure a future), I conceived my job as being primarily to instal a good and experienced manager, and then to draw back into the more literal meaning of the term 'adviser'. This was easier said than done; a self-governing orchestra is an awkward body. Pressures and jealousies develop within it, everyone theoretically has an equal say and, however much control may be delegated to the orchestral council, everything – detailed planning, foreign tours, policy – may be turned upside down at the next annual general meeting. Moreover, in London, a balanced programme – proportion between bread-and-butter works and something more enterprising, between what is chosen for recording, what for individual performers and what because it represents the orchestra's strength – is hard to achieve because planning is done in competition with the other London orchestras, who perform in the same hall, as does the BBC.

I often used to think that it would have been far easier to devise an orchestra's programmes for a provincial city like Manchester, Liverpool or Leeds. In London, it was hard to do more than cobble together a compromise between an initial plan and what would in the end satisfy the irritatingly egalitarian, first-come first-served principles which (quite properly, I fear) govern the Festival Hall's programming policy. There were four independent orchestras in London, as well as the BBC's Symphony Orchestra, to say nothing of visiting bands, all competing for some 150 symphonic dates at the Festival Hall and for basically the same spoiled, choice-bloated, fickle public. Novelties drove the crowds away because there was so much else to go to which required less effort, and too-stereotyped programmes resulted in half-empty houses because people preferred to hear the best-known works conducted or played by the best-known names. It was hard for a young conductor to make his name in this atmosphere. Hard too, when you had worked as a middle-man in London music for some years, not to agree with Beecham who once said something to the effect that 'The average Englishman may not know much about music, but by God he likes the noise it makes!' That, one sometimes thought, and nothing more.

In early 1965, I was telephoned at my Edinburgh Festival office and asked to go round urgently to see Anthony Quinn the film actor. Next day at the

Hilton Hotel I was ushered into a room which looked as though some kind of party had recently been taking place in it. Nobody appeared to be Quinn, and nobody took much notice when I went in. Eventually a general on the pay-roll located him next door, where the party seemed to have moved, and he came in to greet me. Had I ever been to Rhodes? No. It was the greatest place on earth, and would I like to run a festival there? I said I didn't know; I had another job.

Maps of the island were produced and a scheme explained whereby Quinn himself would buy some land, partly for his own use, partly in order to establish an artistic colony, and he would underwrite a festival that would put the island on the map and contribute to its economy.

Quinn was too rushed to explain any more – he had to go to Paris, or New Mexico, or Rome – and he handed over to a Mr Salounios, a Greek from Rhodes, most agreeable and full of further explanations. Rhodes depended a lot on its tourist trade and great hotels had been built and throve throughout the season. But during the summer, the island was easy of access and many people came just for the day. The Tourist Board was keen to keep them (and their money) for longer, and a festival might be just the thing. Anthony Quinn had involved himself because he loved Rhodes, and also because it was difficult for a foreigner to buy land there. If he founded a festival, they might make an exception. Would I be interested? I said I could not possibly tell without seeing the local possibilities, whereupon Quinn was consulted by telephone and I was invited – bidden – to fly out next day, all expenses paid. I said I could not possibly do that, but might manage in about a fortnight's time, when I had to spend a few days in Italy. I could go on to Greece from Rome.

This seemed to satisfy them, though surprise that I would not go next day was not concealed. I was then asked to stop in Paris on my way as Mr Quinn would be there and wanted a conference with the Italian architect whom he had chosen to build the complex and who could go with us to help spy out the land. Another conference, this time at a hotel in Paris, again with Quinn mostly busy in another room but popping in from time to time to see how our multi-lingual session was getting on, again with maps of the site but this time with some fairly concrete proposals by the architect. As if afraid he might not be seen to be showing enough interest, Quinn freed himself for a quick lunch, or part of one.

In due course, Patricia and I presented ourselves at Rome Airport, where we met the architect and flew to Athens, which I had never seen. Mr Salounios met us, took us on a whirlwind tour of Parthenon and Acropolis, and next morning we flew to Rhodes, exchanging – this was early March – European winter for southern Mediterranean spring. It is a delightful island at that time of year, bright with flowers and a tourist's paradise, unspoiled and beautiful. Mr Salounios showed us round the town, with its harbour, its castle, and its square near the *Hammam* (Turkish bath; the baths, like the best food in Rhodes, remain Turkish). We measured the castle's courtyard to guess at the seating capacity, and wondered if *Seraglio* could be fitted in front of the *Hammam*. We motored round the island and saw its villages nestling on hillsides away from the sea so as to keep out of view of predatory pirates, its churches with their ikons, and got as far as the adorable Lindos, the prettiest village in Rhodes. We were shown a great hippodrome – not unlike an amphitheatre, but longer, since it was for horse-races, not spectacles, and with slighter banks of seats at the sides – and I wondered whether it could be the site for the first truly Mediterranean *Les Troyens*, which itself might become the centrepiece of an annual festival. I found out that there was no concert hall as such but looked at local cinemas and discovered their seating capacities, and I asked about the state of local and imported music. I enquired whether Italian artists would be welcome festival visitors (the Italians had after all occupied Rhodes for some time), and tried, with no success, to find out something about what musical resources might be available from the mainland, and their likely cost.

What should I do next? Send in a specimen programme with a budget, came the answer. We said goodbye, with assurances about meeting again soon, and I busied myself in the aeroplane working out a sketch programme and budget, filled in some figures when I got back, and sent the results off, as instructed, to Mr Salounios and to Anthony Quinn himself.

The trip for four people cannot have cost nothing, with fares and hotel bills for four days, but to this day I have never heard another word about the Rhodes Festival project – of commendation, query, or rejection; not even an acknowledgment of my letter and the figures I sent. Perhaps another project took its place, perhaps there is a drawer somewhere stuffed with abortive festival plans for Rhodes, Famagusta, Hammamet, Acapulco – all unacknowledged because the order has gone out to save money, if on nothing else, on stamps.

I never had the heart to ask for a consultation fee and a year later it had all begun to feel like a practical joke. If so, it was a singularly enjoyable one for the victim. And I had begun to rather like Quinn.

Nearly a year before Patricia and I were married, I was asked to report for the magazine *Opera* on the opening in September 1966 of the new Metropolitan Opera House in New York.

The opening, with Samuel Barber's commissioned but no more than worthy *Anthony and Cleopatra*, was nonetheless a great occasion, and next day I went to see Rudi Bing. He reminded me that a couple of years before he had written to me to say that he planned to retire in 1968, once he had coaxed the new building into life, and that the Board would be looking for a successor as general manager. They might ask his advice; would I be interested in being considered? I had answered that I did not know the American scene and that the Met and its ways seemed rather remote from all that I had been accustomed to at Covent Garden, with its permanent ensemble, but that any position in the operatic world must of course interest someone like me, not least one so prestigious as this.

Bing now proposed that I should lunch with him and Anthony Bliss, the president of the Board (the equivalent of chairman in England). In the end, Bing could not make the lunch, but Bliss and I got on famously. He wanted me to stay on and see other opera in America, but I had obligations in England. We agreed that I should return with Patricia, take in more performances at the Met and visit San Francisco and Detroit, where the National Company, newly formed under Met auspices, was performing; and perhaps meet members of the Board. To keep all this on an 'informal' basis, I could write for *Opera* about what I saw and heard.

We fell in love with San Francisco (and made great friends with the Opera's distinguished president, Bob Miller, and his wife), found much to criticize in the rules the National Company had made for itself (among other things, no truly experienced singers to set an example to the younger ones), and continued to find a kindred spirit in Tony Bliss. It soon transpired that Bing was not taking well to the idea of the talks Bliss had been having with me (although he himself might be held to have initiated them), and I did not get a very friendly feeling from the members of the Board that I met a day or two before flying back to England.

Within a few weeks Bliss had resigned, out-manoeuvred apparently by Bing, who told the Board in effect that it was clear that the president would like to make a change of general manager rather sooner than planned and that he would therefore prefer to tender his resignation as from that moment. The choice was not a hard one; if they did not back Bing they risked chaos.

I was fascinated years later to read an account of all this in Bing's amusing book *5000 Nights at the Opera*, in which my introduction to the scene is presented as a consequence of Bliss's keenness on ballet. He planned, Bing said, to use my Covent Garden experience of opera and ballet companies working together to change the nature of the Met. This the Board would not wear. There was enough truth in this to prevent it from being *pure* fiction. But only just enough.

I must make it clear that I was at no time offered a job at the Metropolitan. Discussions never went beyond the preliminary stage. But I have often asked myself what I would have done if an offer had been made. The Met was at or near the top of the operatic ladder – it certainly thought of itself as the world leader – and to work there obviously had its attractions. But there were snags. Fund-raising was a part of the general manager's function, and I have no gift for that, nor inclination to develop one. Then I found that maintenance of the announced programme without risk of cancellation had become so paramount a consideration that at one time (possibly still) the practice was to have one singer for a given role in the dressing-room, another in Manhattan within twenty minutes call, and a third no more than an hour away. This struck me as financially wasteful, and the result of elevating something desirable to the level of a fetish. It was obvious too that the new building was going through massive teething troubles, which were evident even on the first night when a stage revolve stuck, and, worse still, the opening weeks were bedevilled by union problems that entailed wholesale postponements.

The trickiest part of the job seemed to be centred on what was expected by its audience of the Met. American critics often wrote seriously about opera as a form and Bing had emphasized production values from the moment he arrived – with his German and Glyndebourne background, it could hardly have been otherwise. But audiences still for the most part required massive voices and would not have noticed what an ensemble was like if they had met it. I enjoy good singing more than the next man but sheer vocal power is not among my highest priorities. I was also very much aware that I knew nothing at all about America and very little about American taste – and above all I should not have found it easy to be an exile from Europe, from England, most of all from Harewood. I doubt whether sufficient euphoria would have been generated by an offer, if it had come, to overcome all that. Particularly the last.

In 1968, an old friend of Patricia's, Claudio Alcorso, who was then chairman of Australian Opera, wrote to her to say that the British-based member of their Board (Stephen Arlen of Sadler's Wells) had resigned; would I take his place? Claudio was in London shortly afterwards, and I accepted. Australian

Opera had always had an 'overseas' director, and I felt I knew the European scene and its performers and could contribute to their work by correspondence and, less often, by attendance on the spot.

Probably I was attracted to the idea of visiting Australia because it was Patricia's country, but I am certain that the sympathetic personality of Claudio Alcorso had something to do with my interest in Australian Opera. As I was gradually to find out, he was the ideal kind of 'new' Australian, an Italian who had before 1939 set up his own business in Tasmania, been interned during the war but somehow transcended the experience so that his thinking was very much an Australian's. I never heard anyone talk more persuasively about the country and its future. Australian Opera, he felt, should stop looking exclusively to Europe. Its products were going to remain basically European, but its outlets, apart from Australia, could be in China and Japan and perhaps in South America. Claudio was not only persuasive, but patient as well, and these two qualities made him an ideal chairman, able to reconcile the often opposed points of view one would find on the Board, which unfortunately included several 'representatives', each of them keen to put forward the brief he felt was his mandate.

Patricia and I cut our second Indian trip in half to spend a fortnight in Australia in early 1970. (I seemed always to have made fairly frequent trips abroad but mostly within Europe; with Patricia we seemed to fly inter-Continental almost more than to Paris or Milan, and it is odd that I never visited America, for instance, between 1946 and 1966 and yet have made at least one journey there every year since that initial return.) I was partly prepared for what I found in Australia; from first contact, you could not but find the country refreshingly alive and invigorating and it would have been hard not to respond to friendly, intelligent people, the sparkling climate of Sydney, and the sheer beauty of much of what we saw – though I was surprised that this never seemed to be a first topic of conversation with the average Australian.

We flew once with Patricia's close friends David and Patricia Wynn to Coonawarra in South Australia, which was then (he's since sold it) David's most productive and highest quality vineyard – he is a wine-grower of rare skill in a country that produces some of the best wine I have drunk outside France. The welcome we had from Patricia's family and friends in Australia, of whom David and Patricia were only two, would have convinced any kind of doubter, and I had not started out as that. In addition, the Australian Opera performances (of Gilbert and Sullivan, on which I am no expert) seemed fine. Our conversations were stimulating and constructive, but the

Music Director, Carlo Felice Cillario, who is an admirable conductor, quickly showed that he was more interested in performance than in working to develop a company. Soon after we left he resigned, and back in England I was asked to recommend someone to take his place – there was apparently no one suitable in Australia. I thought immediately of Charles Mackerras and Edward Downes, and indeed approached Charlie to see if he would return to his native land. He said he would – but only as a guest. With Ted Downes matters were different. He had joined Covent Garden about the same time as me seventeen years before, and I had always felt that, as well as being an experienced and admirable conductor, he was essentially a builder, which was what attracted me to him so far as this job was concerned. He seemed intrigued, but it was not long before I found that his wife was inclined to blow cold on the idea. A year or two back Ted had accepted to take over there as Music Director (which I did *not* know), given up all his European engagements with this in view, and had then been completely let down over the subsidy he had been promised for the company. Had he not been lucky with a number of good European contacts, he would have been without work for quite a lengthy period. Ted was prepared to write it off to experience but Joan was not.

But Ted agreed in principle to take the job, and a few weeks later, in March 1971, we went out with them both to find the company in Melbourne, in a theatre which was far from air-conditioned and where the heat was so extraordinary that I became convinced that the clothes I was soaking would eventually have to be burned. I remember well-based performances of *Otello* and *Turandot*, *Bohème* and *Faust*, the last-named a new production, and the considerable capacity inside the company excited Ted's enthusiasm. He took over in early 1972 and started his regime with new productions in Melbourne of *Rosenkavalier* – its first Australian performance – and *Rigoletto*, each with strong and willing casts.

Australian Opera had – still has as I write – a very curious kind of 'joker' in its hand, the snag being that the joker is always played by other people. There is a Sydney and a Melbourne orchestra, each under the control, not of the company at all, but of the Elizabethan Theatre Trust. The orchestras travelled little but alternated between opera and ballet mostly in the cities where they belonged. The Melbourne orchestra was the junior of the two but, with masses of rehearsal, Ted coaxed them to perform miracles in *Rosenkavalier*. The experience turned the orchestra from something of little account to a body which had already progressed beyond the foothills and was striding up the mountain of achievement. (I believe this is the natural result of rehearsing *Rosenkavalier* for the first time, and I put the opera down for the future soon after starting work at the Coliseum.)

Australian operatic life was to disclose other hidden dangers. Patricia and I were due to go to Australia for Ted's 1972 opening. We landed in Sydney before going on to Melbourne, and were met by the press officer of Australian Opera who showed us that morning's papers, which carried reports of an upheaval inside the company. I was warned to be on my guard as the press would lie in wait for us.

It is a bad habit in Australia for journalists to ask visitors their impressions as they step on to Australian soil, when they can have none except of extreme fatigue, and I was duly asked for my reactions and comments on the situation. I said I had no knowledge of it and therefore no comment, but next morning I read in a respectable Melbourne paper that I had said 'I know nothing about it, but let's hope it's not as nasty as on paper it looks.' My stepson, who worked for another newspaper, knew the journalist in question, who told him: 'Well, he didn't say anything and I felt I had to put in something!' So visitors to Australia be warned: 'No comment,' sacred elsewhere, has little validity there.

At that time Australian Opera's thinking was aimed towards the opening of the Sydney Opera House which was scheduled for September/October 1973 and which we were to attend. Ted and I and others discussed the possibilities open to the company. He had it in mind to open with Prokofiev's *War and Peace*, which he had already performed in concert form, albeit much cut, at a Leeds Festival for which I was responsible. The idea seemed imaginative, and he wanted to tie in this great effort with the commissioning of an Australian opera from Peter Sculthorpe; in the event it was not ready. Other works would be slightly less exacting – *Nabucco* from the previous Melbourne season, a revival of Puccini's *Trittico* with the fine Australian tenor Don Smith, and Mozart's *Magic Flute* in a new production conducted by Charles Mackerras, which would be seen by the Queen when she performed the official ceremony some weeks after the opening night.

The Sydney Opera House is unquestionably a witness to man's continuing instinct for beauty and was, by the time of the opening, with its sail-like white grace, something of a symbol of Sydney and indeed of Australia as a whole. It was also an example (and widely quoted as such) of the incompetence of planning by committee, particularly one ruled by changing political masters. The architect, a Dane of genius by the name of Utzon, had been jettisoned some years before and replaced by New South Wales 'specialists', who had yielded to the advice of, I am ashamed to say, an English 'specialist', which was to transfer the functions of the concert hall, intended to be housed in the smaller auditorium, to that of the opera theatre, which of course had bigger resources with its wing space and its flying tower. As a result, by opening night the concert hall had a useless backstage area and flying spaces doomed never to be used – Utzon had designed the 'sails' of his building to hide what he thought of as the ugliness of flying towers! – and the opera theatre had no wing space and no possibility of flying. Nonetheless, the opening night went off to considerable acclaim and was a vivid and exciting experience, and it was satisfactory to have been in on some of the planning.

By September 1973, a new General Manager, John Winther, a Dane with considerable experience of operatic planning and an excellent musician in his own right, was in charge. This seemed a logical and good choice. I had not met him before but found immediately that he was suspicious to the point of paranoia of any interference by Board members in what he conceived of as his function. He had never met such interference in Europe, where the English idea of trusteeship vested in Boards was unknown, and he shied away from it in Australia. The trouble was that I was the member of the Board deputed to report on artistic matters and to act as liaison between the artistic planners and the Board. Nothing I said could persuade John that I was on his side, but the last thing I achieved as a member of the Board in 1973 was to write a long report arguing in some detail plans for a *Ring* cycle for Australia. There had not been one within living memory, it could, a couple of roles apart, be cast from the company, and it was the kind of enterprise that would complete the coming-of-age process which Ted had started with *Rosenkavalier*. But the *Ring* project has proved abortive apart from two or three concert performances of *Rheingold* conducted later by Mark Elder, with concert follow-up of the rest of the cycle planned for the future.

Soon after the opening Claudio resigned, as he felt his work was done and was keener to prove that you could grow wine in Tasmania than opera in Australia. He was an ideal chairman, and I once heard him at a seminar for Australian artistic enterprises proclaim a truth: 'There is always a risk that the central funding body will warm to an organization which keeps its books in apple-pie order, never risks a deficit, is punctual with its returns. That it produces nothing exciting somehow becomes secondary. But I maintain that the body which generates artistic excitement, however chaotic its records and chancey its finances, is the one which is delivering the goods and giving value for money.'

Before long, Ted resigned too because, I was told, Richard Bonynge had been appointed co-Music Director without Ted being consulted.

The new chairman of Australian Opera was obviously in favour of any British connection being with Covent Garden, and so, with limited possibilities of getting away from my new job at English National Opera, I resigned.

Needless to say that was far from the end of visits to Australia, as Patricia for all her English and Yorkshire acclimatization, like all Australians, remains very much an Australian at heart, and our subsequent visits have taken us more than once to Sydney, Melbourne and Adelaide, usually with some element of business on which to hang the trip. I have been a willing fellow traveller and the journeys have taken us into Melbourne's Dandenongs to look for (and find) Lyre birds, to North Queensland to see beautiful and rare aboriginal cave paintings in an area officially designated as 'wilderness' near the tiny town of Laura, and to Lizard Island North of Cairns to spend a few days' holiday inside the Barrier Reef – even to the famed Melbourne Cup, the only race in the world which earns a city a public holiday. But not so very often to see Australian Opera, whose vicissitudes I have tended to follow from a distance.

CHAPTER NINETEEN

Harewood
1947-81

As I GROW older and, I hope, more mature, I have increasingly 'found' myself in Harewood. It was only natural that the aftermath of the war should bring big changes from our lavish, pre-war style of living, with its four or five house parties a year – racing, shooting, Christmas, my grandmother Queen Mary's annual visit – with some form of elaborate entertainment by day and over twenty sitting down to dinner at night.

Nonetheless, however much times had changed after the war, my mother almost invariably dressed for dinner, and when we had guests the men usually wore dinner jackets. We still constantly had people to stay, often because they had business to do in the neighbourhood, sometimes because they were connected with one of my mother's public services – WRAC, Red Cross, Girl Guides, Leeds University – not quite so often just because we wanted to see them. The household was run by my mother and Marion in, so to speak, double harness, an arrangement which by its nature could not be wholly satisfactory; my mother took overall financial responsibility with help from me in cash and kind. She ran the house to her liking and timing, but our guests as well as her friends were often mine and later Marion's.

Entertaining at Harewood continued, for Leeds Festivals, which had been an early feature of my mother's life in Yorkshire, and for York Races, when Sir Victor Sassoon among others used to stay with us (to help my mother's racing interests, he leased the Stud from us for a period). Christmas of course was a family affair, with Gerald, his wife Angela and their son Henry at Harewood as well as Sophie and Erwin Stein, and of course my three sons. My mother enjoyed carols and the Queen's speech, Father Christmas and stockings, the Christmas service in church and presents in the library – both as part of an old tradition she had known all her life and as part of a new one she had helped to evolve at Harewood.

When my father died, my mother and my father's first cousin Tommy Lascelles (Sir Alan Lascelles, the King's Private Secretary) were named as executors and until the death duties were paid, which was mostly but not entirely achieved by 1951, there was no question of my either wanting, nor probably obtaining, control over the estate. My father's land agent – indeed my grandfather's, since he arrived at Harewood in 1923 between my birth and christening – was Nigel FitzRoy, who had been twenty-four years in the saddle by the time my father died. He was a stimulating and agreeable companion whom already before the war I had got to know well, mostly on our daily rides, horseback being his standard means of transport around the estate. We had cemented our friendship when I worked for the War Agricultural Committee, of which he was vice-chairman. He fought to keep the estate together, in spite of death duties, and to a considerable extent he succeeded. Neither he nor my father were at heart agriculturalists, any more than I am, and the war had caused the estate itself, always run on somewhat *laissez faire* principles, because of national shortages to deteriorate.

In the late winter of 1952–3 Nigel FitzRoy fell ill with pneumonia, and I understood that he could not battle through another winter without help. I knew, I thought, precisely the right man to be his assistant, and accordingly rang up Neville Ussher, my onetime fellow ADC in Canada and the father of one of my first godsons. Luck was with me: 'By pure coincidence,' he said, 'I put my farm on the market two days ago. It's too small to be workable.' He agreed to come to Harewood to discuss the whole affair, seemed to like what he saw, and went away to talk to his wife Marguerite.

Within a few days, Nigel FitzRoy had died, and I took only a day or two to make up my mind to ask Neville to take his place. He told me he was not fully qualified, in terms of exams and membership of the right organizations, but when I pressed him he accepted. After Canada, he had had a career of varying agricultural fortune: a job in the Ministry of Agriculture in London, which ill-suited him as a countryman; a period as land agent during which he fell out with the owner; some time as a junior partner in a Warwickshire land agency; and then three or four years as a farmer on his own. The experience was, in its way, perfect for the job I was offering him; he acquired the right letters after his name during the course of a few years at Harewood, and I have never had cause to do other than rejoice at the decision we both took. Not only is Neville the most loyal friend and one of the liveliest companions I have ever known, but he is a dedicated professional, for me an understanding partner, and with it all over the years a diplomatic and judicious adviser to my mother as well as to me.

With such an apparent paragon, there had to be a snag, and I already knew what it was: he found music a bore, and took years to accept that an interest in it could be part of the make-up of otherwise rational beings.

Neville and Marguerite Ussher came to Harewood in 1953, just before the Coronation, and he is still active after virtually thirty years at Harewood. During this time, we have played tennis and gone shooting together; we have plotted finance and planned survival; we have organized the technical process known as 'dedicating' woodland; we have cleared up after the tempestuous gales of 1962 and after the Foot and Mouth of 1960; we have installed a pig farm with a 500-sow herd and a turnover of 4,000 pigs at any one time, and built up milking herds free of TB and brucellosis and the buildings to house them in. In addition, we have got the House Opening business at Harewood into a state when it would but for inflation be quietly profitable. I say 'we' because without Neville none of it might have happened, or would certainly have happened differently.

Gradually, as the years went by and I became used to decisions about Harewood coming my way, and then to accepting that whoever I consulted it was my responsibility and mine alone to take them, I tended to identify more and more with the place, with its present inhabitants and their security, and with its past. The land-owner who talks possessively about *his* fishing and *his* shooting and the swans which nest in *his* lake is perhaps not aware that he is using symbols to show how closely *he* is bound to what he 'owns', not the other way round. He is not so much a feudalist as in love with where he lives.

It is no part of my brief (nor my belief) to advocate feudalism out of its time (when I imagine it worked no worse than most accepted systems), but I firmly believe that the land possesses whoever lives on and off it at least as much as the owner possesses the land, and the relationship which is built up in this way is just as real as between man and woman, and probably a deal more secure. For my own part, I came early to love Harewood and its heritage, and to rejoice in the feeling that I belonged to it, as I suspect my father did before me. When we used to drive into Leeds, he always looked back at the house from Lofthouse Gates 'in case it isn't there when we get back'; and I was not in the least surprised when Patricia, driving with me up the Great North Road and later the M1, said that she knew when we had crossed the invisible Yorkshire boundary because I heaved a sigh of relief and spoke with more animation than before!

Eighteen months or a year before she died, my mother told me that she had been wondering whether she should leave Harewood and move south – on doctors' advice, she said, because of the heart murmurings she and they had detected. She might move to near Sandringham, which she loved. I suspected then that the prospective upheaval was less for medical reasons than because she was being advised to get clear of Harewood before the breaking of scandal that would follow Mark's birth and my divorce. But I have since wondered whether the core of the matter was not somewhat different, and concerned rather with her gradual acceptance that it was no longer *her* responsibility to care for our little bit of the country to which she had given much of her life, but mine. I don't think I consciously or subconsciously elbowed her out and she was not given to discussion of that kind (nor I suppose was I), so that she never dropped a hint that such thoughts were in her mind; but I suspect my aunt knew and understood it, as the same kind of thing must have happened to her at Burwarton.

Mark was born about nine months before my mother died and of course she knew all about him, but I had the impression she would have done anything rather than raise the subject herself. We in fact talked about him only once, and she received what I had to say in total silence and made no comment of any kind, except to ask on the subject of a divorce: 'What will people say?'

Her death was enviable. James and Jeremy had already started their Easter holiday at the end of March 1965 and I was at Harewood with them. We all four went for a walk after lunch. My mother had complained for some time about her heart, but the doctors had given her reasonable clearance while warning her not to do too much – she was after all nearly sixty-eight – and we had put it down to a certain hypochondria, to which she was by no means immune. We were down by the lake when she stumbled and fell and I helped her to a seat, asking what was the matter. She said rather faintly, 'I don't really know.' I supported her while the boys ran off to get a car to take her home. There was no apparent crisis and I had no idea that in the quarter of an hour which intervened before the car came, she had died quite peacefully in my arms. Somehow the shock was cushioned by the lack of struggle involved, and I don't believe either of the boys was more frightened than I was. I suppose she would have wanted that, as, although she liked her due, she also disliked fuss and bother – of any kind.

In the 1960s, her presence and her personality floated in a slightly Chekhovian way round our lives, particularly at Harewood, where I think she sometimes found three grandchildren frequently in the house too noisy. Something not wholly tangible disappeared when she died. It was not simply the loss of a beloved parent, traumatic as that inevitably is; and it was more than just the disappearance of the lower-échelon trappings of royalty – ladies-in-waiting, official visitors, foreign tours, uniforms in peacetime, our own occasional visits to Buckingham Palace. I mourned her of course as a son mourns a parent, but I missed her too as a grown-up misses someone in whom he has always found a point of certainty. Harewood was her home just as much as mine, and the post-war atmosphere that I valued above most things was very much her creation. I am glad that, for whatever reasons, they did not succeed before she died in dislodging her from her home.

During my initially unsuccessful attempts to persuade Marion to give me a divorce, my return visits to Harewood alone – often by train through over-familiar scenery (what else can you call what you pass through regularly by train?), occasionally by plane to Yeadon – these return visits were more like coming home than any other home-comings I have known. Here I felt free, here life continued unless you chose to jump off, which in Yorkshire was the last thing that crossed my mind. Just to walk round the lake at Harewood was a form of renewal.

When I came from London alone, I used to have meals with the Usshers, trying not to bore them with my woes – they were Marion's friends as well as mine – but to talk mostly about mutual interests. Neville has more than a streak of the Irishman in him and his stories, as they say, lose – have never lost – anything in the telling. Village life, as Neville describes it, is seldom without incident, whether of gangs out to steal the remaining lead off the roofs, of the uncharitable behaviour of neighbour to neighbour, or of trees that might fall and do untold damage to life and property – we are on Neville's insistence insured against an aeroplane crashing at Harewood during House Opening and landing on a bus full of American millionaires, whose heirs would instantly claim colossal compensation. Neville feels safer, and the premium is understandably not high.

Neville is a true countryman and perhaps his greatest foible is his gun-dogs. He trains them of course himself and volubly, constantly, and often successfully, controls them. Shouts of 'All dogs, sit!' precede and follow him everywhere, and he is once recorded to have gone away shooting with his wife and to have installed himself at the first stand with a firm 'Sit down and shut up!' to find he had left his dogs at home and was addressing only Marguerite.

Shooting and dogs are much more in Neville's line than horses and Horse Trials. The first Harewood Three Day Event, mooted by Nigel FitzRoy, was in an advanced state of preparation when he arrived. From the outset we scorned the single day and insisted on starting at the top with a promise of taking our turn with Badminton for any international event allotted to Great Britain. I never got truly interested in the dressage day; but the middle day, with its solo runs over steeplechase and obstacle courses, could be thrilling, and year after year we betook ourselves by Land Rover round the individual fences and watched the jump-off on the final day, with high quality show-jumping as a special bonus afterwards.

In 1959 we had our only international year, with teams from various countries limbering up for the Olympics the following year, and a great concourse assembled to watch them. Marion and I had a fluent Russian-speaker helping with the children that year, and she and they were with us going from one major obstacle to another. Horses went individually perhaps five minutes apart, and we knew that a Russian was due next. As he appeared out of a wood, the loudspeaker went into action to instruct a Steward to halt him because the competitor next in front was stuck in a fence. The Russian appeared convinced it was a plot and did his best to ride on, and only our nanny's intervention prevented an international incident.

We stopped the Horse Trials while we were, so to speak, at the top, as the February after our international year, Foot and Mouth disease broke out at Harewood and we were faced with the horrors of destroying all cloven-hoofed beasts on the farm. Before Foot and Mouth we had had pedigree Red Polls; afterwards we reverted to store cattle until we could, by culling and selection, build up our milking herd again. I was away, but I heard that the slaughter and burning of the carcasses had a traumatic effect on everyone on the estate; and we had to take the decision to abandon non-agricultural luxuries like Horse Trials with their uneconomical use of grassland, and concentrate on farming.

Neither Patricia nor Mark came to Harewood until we were married, which was when he was three. Mark took to it very quickly, in spite of initial difficulty in finding his way around, and a year after arrival he was at the village school at nearby Arthington. Here he found wealth was mostly assessed by the number of cattle in family ownership and, when asked if he lived in a cottage, replied, 'It's more like three knocked together.' Cottage or not, he soon found himself as much at home at Harewood as in London and life in the country came quite naturally to him.

Drawing seemed also from an early age to come naturally to him, and he was constantly experimenting with new graphic techniques. As a little boy, he took easily to opera. We decided *Carmen* was the ideal opera for a child to start on – an exciting story, full of action; vivid, tuneful music, divided into short lengths so that boredom should never set in so to speak permanently – and it was *Carmen*, when Sadler's Wells was on tour in Leeds, that we chose for him. He knew the story and had heard the opera on record, but nearly fell out of the box with excitement during the prelude and was far from wanting to take advantage of our offer to take him home the moment he was bored – an offer renewed for everything we took him to until he was old enough to decide beforehand for himself if he wanted to go.

At an early age he used to do a mime of the death of Boris as a result of coming in when I was playing Boris Christoff's second recording and demanding to know the story, and *Boris* was a favourite recording for a number of years. Gradually, the influence of his pop-orientated brothers has caused the level of noise from his record-player to assume heroic proportions, but he has so far continued to come often to operatic performances with us. And, whatever his other interests, the country seems to be his milieu and Harewood his home.

It did not take long either for Patricia to become at least an honorary Yorkshirewoman. She had inevitably heard a lot about the county and its inhabitants before coming up to Harewood for the first time after we were married, and neighbours were generous with hospitality from the start.

Football she took to immediately, which was just as well. I loved football in general and Leeds United in particular as a boy, and my interest revived many years later, in the 1950s, at a time when Leeds United's fortunes were at a low ebb. I became the club's president a week or two before Harry Reynolds became chairman, and only a month before Don Revie became manager. Harry Reynolds, the Leeds businessman who was the architect of the club's renewal, told me that Don asked him for a letter of recommendation as player-manager to another club; as he wrote, Harry realized he was signing away just the man who could restore the club's fortune. And he was right. Leeds's stock rose from the time Reynolds and Revie took office.

When I became president just before Christmas 1961, Leeds were in the bottom half of the second division and in the last game of the season we avoided relegation to the third. Two years later, Leeds were second division champions, twelve months further on we were only beaten in the Cup Final at Wembley in extra time and pipped by Manchester United as first division champions on decimal points.

This was the start of ten years of excitement and achievement which brought two first division championships to Elland Road, League and FA Cup victories at Wembley, two Inter-Cities Fairs Cups, and half a dozen seconds in one competition or another – 'Runners up! Runners Up!' used to be the taunt at some grounds, but a few years earlier it would have seemed a compliment.

I went to most home games and, between 1965 and 1972, before I started work at the Coliseum, to away games as well, and watching Leeds became something of an obsession. Loyalty has not since faded but it will take time to restore the faith Don Revie and his team inspired in those years – belief first in their integrity, later in their skill, conviction (to use the old phrase) that Don was a rare leader of men. He welded together an ensemble – that is what a team is – which was the envy of others, and he and I used sometimes to talk into the night about how you build football teams and operatic ensembles and then inspire them so that the whole is greater than the sum of the parts. (Don couldn't take the idea that singers went off in mid-season to sing elsewhere and yet remained loyal members of an ensemble!)

During that decade, Leeds became a team of all the skills, from the start with a defence second to none, later with a fine attack as well; but it took the southern journalists years to recognize it and, once they had done so, to admit it in print. The difference between Leeds and other leading sides of the period was, I believe, one of conviction and passion, and I once heard Jack Charlton, for most of those years the lynch-pin of the side, declare his contempt for another player precisely because he lacked this quality of passion and involvement.

I used particularly to enjoy matches against European clubs because they were the least predictable. There was almost sure to be skill on display, and always the chance you might sweep them aside, as we did against Ujpest Dosza of Budapest in a Fairs Cup game of 1966; we were deservedly 4 up at half time, and we went to Budapest to defend a 4–1 lead and played one of the most hectic and in the end heroically defensive games I ever saw. It ended 1–1 after the Hungarians had threatened to overrun us in a do-or-die opening, only to lose steam after we had equalized part way into the second half. Or you might yourselves get swept aside, as happened in a replay at Elland Road against Zaragoza, who were 3 up inside a quarter of an hour – Jack Charlton was heard to murmur to the foreign referee, 'Hey, ref, can we start again! We weren't ready!'

To name names invites inadvertent omissions, but football and its folklore involve names. If I remember Willis Edwards and Wilf Copping from the Leeds of my boyhood, I must not forget the lion-hearted Billy Bremner from the 1960s and 1970s; nor Norman Hunter of the fearsome tackle; Jack Charlton, Terry Cooper, Willy Bell and Paul Reaney, who at one time or another formed part of Leeds's nearly impregnable defence. Forwards included Allan Clarke, whom they called 'Sniffer' because of his nose for goals, Peter Lorimer with his reputation for the hardest shot in football, Mick Jones, who broke his elbow in the last stages of our winning Cup Final and never fully got back into the game, and Eddie Gray, an injury-prone Scot of prodigious skill who nearly beat Chelsea on his own at Wembley (we lost the replay days later) and is one of the few still playing from Revie's side.

Don initially founded his team on the skill and experience of Bobby Collins, who while at Leeds regained his place in the Scottish side before breaking his leg badly in 1965; and replaced him with the Irishman Johnny Giles, whose canny domination of midfield was the foundation of many a Leeds victory. A journalist wrote that you could not understand what Don had done for Leeds until you travelled with them and felt the family feeling. I went quite often abroad with them and that journalist was right. Bobby Collins was once asked his opinion of the Club and said: 'They are very, very thorough, and very, very kind.'

For part of the period of Leeds's pre-eminence, I was president of the English Football Association, a more onerous job than it sounds. You were expected to preside at annual general meetings and that, with motions, counter-motions, amendments and votes, this was no sinecure. Early in my time of office came the World Cup of 1966 held in England. A few weeks before it started, we heard of the death of the FA's experienced and likeable chairman, Jo Mears. There was no vice-chairman prepared to take over, but, having left the Edinburgh Festival, I was happy to dash round the country supervising the social side of the great competition, an enjoyable experience culminating as it did in an England win in the final at Wembley.

But my heart was with Leeds and nothing in football gave me as much satisfaction as the gradual build-up of trophies, from the League Cup in 1968 to the League Championship in 1969, the FA Cup in 1972, and the League Championship again in 1974, our finest year and our best team. That Don Revie subsequently left to become manager of England was more of a shock than a surprise; he had put together a supreme team and I could understand that he could not bear to preside over its disintegration.

Patricia and I went to Mexico with the England side defending the World Cup in 1970. The men I used to meet in Board rooms all over England assured me that they had made a host of good friends in football and I believed them; I did too. But I also watched the back-biting, the manoeuvring to stab in the back, until respect for that 'official' aspect of the game began to disappear. In Mexico, Patricia and I were looked at rather askance for spending time with Don Revie and Joe Mercer, Manchester City's manager (both there as radio and television commentators) and I was not much surprised when the following year it was suggested I might step down as president. Nevertheless, I should be a little sad if the prospect of watching a game failed to fill me with expectation. I am glad to say it still does.

Within a year of arriving in Yorkshire Patricia was also learning to shoot, not content with going out with me but, with an Australian's sense of involvement, insisting on seeing if she too could do it. She can, too. Until 1972, when I started to work at the Coliseum, we spent a lot of time in the country, with a great deal more exercise and quite a lot more shooting than eventually became possible, and with frequent expeditions to see Leeds United play in those heady years of the club's greatest success.

We heard a lot of music in London as well as spending a great deal of time at Harewood, and I don't remember a more care-free period than these years after 1967, when my responsibilities in London were less than they subsequently became, when those at Harewood were agreeably shared, and when the prospect of heading through life on a relatively even keel became, for the first time for a number of years, a genuine possibility.

I am grateful for those years. During them and since we built up our private legend – when we went to London, our friends in Yorkshire thought we were off for a shopping and cultural spree, whereas I have usually had a job there; and our London friends were convinced that life in the country was either a round of parties or constant early bed, whereas the intricacies of the estate at Harewood provide plenty of preoccupation. So convinced were we that a new pattern had evolved, in which Harewood would be our base and London somewhere to do some part-time work, that we eventually decided to sell our spacious house in Hamilton Terrace, in St John's Wood, and look for something much smaller.

Within eight months of the sale, and before we had settled into the much smaller house near Primrose Hill, I had been offered a new job at the Coliseum for Sadler's Wells, the kind of job I could not refuse, and our efforts to economize by leaving the big London house had been turned firmly and uncomfortably upside down. But this job counts still as 'work in progress' and cannot therefore for a number of reasons figure more than marginally in this book.

After my mother died, we soon made up our minds to step up efforts to make Harewood as nearly self-supporting as possible. The opening of famous houses to the public is nothing new and people visited them regularly in the eighteenth century – but in little parties of a dozen or so rather than in hundreds as now. Harewood had visitors in the 1770s within a year or two of being lived in, and was regularly open between the wars, with the proceeds going to designated charities. My mother accepted opening as a necessary post-war invasion of privacy – the privacy she valued so highly that she planted shrubs at strategic points to prevent anyone looking over the railings at her when she was in the garden – but it was only after her death that we embarked upon it as one of Harewood's major assets.

We were perhaps impelled towards this new view by a reference in a book by Lord Montagu of Beaulieu, who estimated house openers not only by the number of visitors they attracted (although this was obviously a crucial factor) but also by the way in which they set about getting them there and entertaining them when they had arrived. We all belonged, Edward Montagu said, in one of two categories, Amateurs or Professionals. Some of the greatest houses came into the first category, because they appeared to suffer the invasion rather than welcoming and organizing it; and some of the smaller houses came into the second, because of the capable way they tackled the problem of attracting visitors and then making them feel comfortable – and incidentally prepared to part with their money. Harewood was, in Edward's view, in the first category, but we struck him as among the most likely to make the leap into the second. We prepared to jump.

The most important thing was to plan an advertising campaign that would attract visitors at times of day and on days which were as yet far from operating to full capacity. Harewood cannot cope with 10,000 or 15,000 people on a single day without making them queue to go round the house, to buy food or even an ice cream; the layout is not suited to cope with more than the 4,000 or 5,000 we regularly get at Bank Holidays, and to alter that would be to change the place's character – and change it for the worse – in the process probably alienating those who now come regularly because of an atmosphere they have grown to appreciate.

We decided to open every day of the week from the end of March to October, in later years extending our season to include, though more selectively, part of the autumn and winter. Apart from Christmas and the New Year, when we would have a party staying, we felt we should relinquish the downstairs rooms which we had hitherto inhabited on an everyday basis; so we withdrew upstairs and took over one of the spare rooms as a sitting room and another as dining room, and made the entire ground floor available to visitors. It is curious how comforting it is to feel that rooms one has lived and worked in but given up are still in use and not 'lost'; certainly that was my reaction to moving from what had been my sitting and work room for the eighteen years since my father's death.

Patricia and I had discussions with Neville Ussher about introducing an additional attraction – something that would draw visitors and at the same time add to rather than detract from the existing amenities and ambience of Harewood. After one or two visits to others in the same line of enterprise, we decided to set up a Bird Garden, which we felt would fit easily into the landscape round the Stables. The Stables themselves would form the Bird Garden's headquarters (office, food preparation and storage, acclimatization and sick rooms for birds), and we decided to concentrate on exotic rather than British birds.

We knew from the start that the success of the whole enterprise depended on the recruitment of the first curator. We advertised, and to vet the applicants enlisted the help of Len Hill, whose Birdland at Bourton-on-the-Water had seemed to us a model of the kind of thing we wanted to do. After a week we asked for a progress report. 'I know them all,' said Mr Hill. 'Five are no good, five are possibles. But the right man hasn't yet written. I must give his memory a jog!' Peter Brown, whose application resulted from the memory jog, made a splendid job of everything, not least the layout and design of the aviaries, and including the all-important choice of exhibits and the difficult business of assembling them.

The Bird Garden has given Patricia and me – and fortunately a large number of other people as well – a great deal of pleasure. We have come to love birds we had never really known before – the dusty-blue Crowned Pigeons from New Guinea, with their Ascot hats and their Edwardian strut; the various Touracoes from South America, with their brilliant scarlet under-wings; the contrasting varieties of Grackle from everywhere – we had always thought of them as just starlings, but found them both glamorous and in some cases close to extinction; the elegantly-strolling Stanley Cranes from South Africa, which dance in spring; the Macaws from Brazil, which now fly free round the house when the weather is fine, and screech at the wind when it's foul. Our flock of Flamingoes came from Santiago in Chile and a dozen years after their arrival we still have nearly the original group; the Penguins, with a glass-fronted pool through which you can observe their aquabatics at meal-time, from Chile.

Two architects, John Carr and Robert Adam, worked on Harewood from 1759 to 1772; Sir James Barry did some of it over in early Victorian style in the 1840s, and my parents modernized some sections and restored others in the 1930s. In 1973 Patricia and I, not content with restoring the hall to its original Adam form and colours (my parents had left it in its Victorian state), decided to embark on cleaning the outside of the house. Over the years it had soaked up industrial grime from Leeds and Bradford, and had turned from the colour of honey to something much nearer soot. For weeks after the sand-blasting was over, the contents of even unopened drawers and wardrobes showed a fine film of sand; but the process was infinitely worthwhile both financially, since the cost has since gone up at least five-fold, and aesthetically, as Harewood, in spite of Barry's additions, is now the kind of complement to the Yorkshire landscape that Carr and Adam originally contemplated and that Capability Brown made a setting for.

Jacob Epstein's great alabaster carving *Adam* now dominates our repainted hall; this is the most important work of art I have been able to introduce to the collection my family has made over the centuries. It reached Harewood by a curious route. With other Epstein carvings whose reception in the years just before 1939 had been little short of causing a scandal, it was acquired and exhibited in a kind of sideshow as near-pornography. When Dicky Buckle wanted to borrow this collection for the great Epstein Exhibition of 1961 in Edinburgh, we found that the owner would not lend, but was prepared to sell – for the quite simple reason that he would have to pull down the side of the flimsy building in which he exhibited the pieces if he were to remove them.

Dicky assured me that these Epsteins would be a very sound investment, so Jack Lyons and I put up the money, which we subsequently recouped by sales in the years after 1961. Adam stayed with us and we exhibited him in the Stables before deciding he could form the centrepiece of our rehabilitated hall. We had a mock-up model made and moved it about to see where it would look best, and finally Neville Ussher supervised the removal, not missing the opportunity of photographing the cranes and pulleys and the team of estate workers who swung Adam carefully into position.

Epstein apparently owned the great alabaster pillar from which Adam was carved for a number of years, and used to contemplate it to find out how best to put it to use. In the end, he exploited the narrow form of the pillar to give Adam a quite primordial power, as if the vast figure were struggling against unseen restrictions – as indeed the sculptor himself had been obliged to do in order to conjure this immensely striking form from the original pillar. I get huge pleasure every time I see Adam in his new home, and am not in any way put off when visitors ask if it is a portrait of the original architect, Robert Adam.

Music has had its place in the all-the-year-round use of Harewood since we devised a regular series of six chamber concerts to take place each winter. The acoustic in the Gallery is good, and our own pleasure in what is played is doubled because my work with the English National Opera since 1972 almost precludes our going to London chamber recitals; this way we get them at home at weekends.

We started in 1968 with programmes from Boris Christoff and the Janáček String Quartet, the latter appearing only a few weeks after the infamous invasion of Czechoslovakia and the downfall of Dubček. Their Haydn and Dvořák seemed quite conventional; but Janáček's first quartet, with which they finished their programme, was played with such fire and conviction as to amount to something like a declaration of faith, a manifesto. I believe profoundly in the music, but I have never heard it sound more convincing than in that emotional context.

Over the years, the pianist Alfred Brendel has become for us not only a much-admired artist but a friend as well, and quite often he and his wife have come to Harewood for extended weekends, which have usually included a rather diffident offer from Alfred to play before dinner some Schubert he had been practising – an offer that has regularly resulted in some of the loveliest music-making I know anywhere at the present time. Alfred is a townsman, and picnics in what passes for the English spring have been on the whole less successful than the impromptu (and of course also the scheduled) recitals.

As part of our efforts to use Harewood to the utmost, we built a children's adventure playground, a marvellous affair of logs and spars, ropes and wooden bridges. Our friend Jack Charlton, once of Leeds United and now manager of Sheffield Wednesday, opened it one hot summer's day, making the typically generous point that if such a thing had existed in his own day, however far from where he lived, he could not have been kept away from it – which is of course what we hoped would still be true. The children who watched and listened to him saw Jack attempt the course, and he was at first defeated by a contraption of ropes on which you are supposed to swing yourself from one side to the other of a wooden 'moat'; when I had tried it in strict privacy before breakfast, I inevitably fell at the same obstacle. But the rest turned out not beyond the capacity of the average fifty-plus.

It is not always easy to justify to doubters or ill-wishers that families who have built and then lived in large houses for perhaps hundreds of years should continue to do so in the differently adjusted present; and there is only limited point in insisting that without the vast sums of private money that go to keep ancient buildings with their collections warm and water-tight – private money which could go much further for purely selfish ends if deployed in more modern surroundings (but perhaps with less satisfaction to the spenders) – a large chunk of this aspect of the national heritage, to use the by no means inaccurate jargon, would disappear within a generation. There are too many such houses to be within the competence of the National Trust, and those of less than national importance would presumably be lost.

As I see it, a house with surroundings and an inheritance like Harewood's can contribute very considerably to the well-being of people who choose to visit it, and the scale and nature of that contribution must be a major preoccupation of those who are privileged to hold it on trust for a generation or so. That trust is both a pleasure, which is obvious if the place is your home, and a burden, because the expense involved is enormous and the ingenuity required to keep the contribution vital very great indeed. But it is worthwhile; and as long as we can maintain Harewood contributing to the environment in the widest sense of the word, I shall have no twinge of conscience in staying here.

Biographical Notes

ALFONSO, XIII, King of Spain (1886–1941). Born after his father's death, therefore King as soon as his masculine sex established. Married Queen Victoria's grand-daughter, Princess Victoria Eugénie. Reigned from 1886 to 1931.

ALICE, Princess, Countess of Athlone (1883–1980). As daughter of the Duke of Albany, she was Queen Victoria's grand-daughter and married Queen Mary's brother, Prince Alexander of Teck, who was made Earl of Athlone in 1917.

ANNAN, Noel (b.1916). Fellow of King's, Cambridge, 1944–56, Provost, 1956–66; Provost of University College, London, 1966–80.

ARLEN, Stephen (1913–72). From General Manager of the Old Vic, in 1951 he was appointed General Manager of Sadler's Wells and then Administrative Director. In 1966 he became Managing Director of Sadlers Wells and in 1968 was responsible for the Company's move from Rosebery Avenue to the London Coliseum.

ASHTON, Frederick (b. 1904). Choreographer to the Royal Ballet at Covent Garden, 1933–70, and its Director, 1963–70.

ASQUITH, Anthony (1902–68). Film director of distinction, whose only operatic excursion was a production of *Carmen* at Covent Garden in 1953.

ATHLONE, Earl of (1874–1957). Husband of Princess Alice, brother of Queen Mary. Governor General of South Africa and of Canada, 1940–45.

BADER, Douglas (b.1910). Lost both legs in flying accident in 1931, but rejoined RAF in 1939 and fought as pilot with distinction, winning DFC and DSO before becoming a POW. Retired 1946.

BARBER, A.T. (b.1905). Captain of Oxford and Yorkshire Cricket XI's and a master at Ludgrove School, where I started my education.

BATTISTINI, Mattia (1856–1928). One of the most famous Italian baritones of operatic history, whose legacy of gramophone records supports his claim to fame. His career lasted from 1878–1926.

307

BIOGRAPHICAL NOTES

BECHI, Gino (b. 1913). Italian baritone of outstanding gifts.

BERENSON, Bernard (1865–1959). Lithuanian-born American art critic and historian, specializing in Italian Renaissance painters.

BERG, Alban (1885–1935). Austrian composer, who studied with Schoenberg and whose operas, *Wozzeck* and *Lulu*, are possibly the most successful avant-garde works composed since Wagner.

BERNAC, Pierre (1899–1979). Distinguished French baritone, from 1935 associated with the music of Francis Poulenc, with whom he gave innumerable recitals.

BESSBOROUGH, Earl of (1880–1956). Governor General of Canada, 1931–5.

BING, Rudolf (b. Vienna 1902). Operatic manger of Glyndebourne Opera, before and after 1939–45, of Metropolitan, New York, 1950–72. He founded the Edinburgh Festival and directed it from 1947–9.

BJÖRLING, Jussi (1911–60). Swedish tenor of world renown and wide-ranging repertory.

BLOND, Neville (1896–1970). Businessman who served in both world wars and was first Chairman of the English Stage Company.

BLUNT, Anthony (b. 1907). Professor of History of Art, University of London, and Director of Courtauld Institute, 1947–74, Surveyor of King's Pictures, 1945–52, of Queen's, 1952–72.

BÖHM, Carl (b. 1894). Austrian conductor, Generalmusikdirektor before the war in Dresden, after it in Vienna.

BORENIUS, Tancred (1885–1947). Born in Finland, lectured at Slade School of Art on History of Painting, and was appointed Professor of this subject at London University, 1922.

BOULEZ, Pierre (b. 1925). French composer and conductor, who studied with Messiaen and was the leader of young modern musicians until well into the 1960s.

BOYNE, Lady (1883–1976). My father's sister, married in 1906 to Gustavus Hamilton-Russell, who was nineteen years her senior. She had six children, three of whom were killed in the 1939–45 war.

BRITTEN, Benjamin (1913–76). English composer in all forms. Companion of Honour after composing *Gloriana*. Order of Merit, 1965.

BROOK, Peter (b. 1925). One of the most brilliant stage directors of post-1945 period.

BUCKLE, Richard (b. 1916). Ballet critic, writer, connoisseur. His exhibitions in 1954 commemorating Diaghilev, in 1956 on Film, in 1961 of Epstein, in 1964 commemorating the 400th anniversary of Shakespeare's birth, made him famous.

BUMBRY, Grace (b. 1937). American mezzo-soprano, who appeared successfully in Europe, including a famed Venus in Bayreuth, before singing at the Metropolitan, New York, from 1965.

BUSONI, Ferruccio (1866–1924). Composer of distinction and one of the greatest pianists of musical history.

BUTT, Clara (1873–1936). Famous contralto singer, married to the baritone Kennerley Rumford.

CANNING, George (1770–1827). Politician and Statesman. Foreign Secretary and later Prime Minister, the only British PM to die in office. Espoused the cause of Greece again the Turks, and spoke up for South American independence from Spain with the resounding phrase that it was 'necessary to call the new world into existence to redress the balance of the old'.

CANNING, Lord (1812–62). Younger child of the statesman and Prime Minister, Lord Canning was the last Governor General of India (during the Mutiny) and the first Viceroy. *The Times* sarcastically called him 'Clemency' Canning, and he died worn out soon after the end of his tour of duty.

CARUSO, Enrico (1873–1921). Probably the most famous tenor who ever lived. His presence in a cast virtually guaranteed success for some twenty years – he died at forty-eight – and he was a prime factor in the early success of the gramophone.

CASELLA, Alfredo (1883–1947). Italian composer, theorist and pianist.

CEBOTARI, Maria (1910–49). A beautiful, talented and versatile Russian-born soprano; after the war a member of the Vienna opera.

CHALIAPIN, Feodor Ivanovich (1873–1938). Russian bass of world-wide fame. Noted above all for his singing of Russian music, particularly of the title role in *Boris Godounov*.

CHARLTON, Jack (b. 1935). Played football for Leeds United and England (member World Cup winning side 1966). Later managed Middlesborough and Sheffield Wednesday.

CHRISTIE, John (1882–1962). With his wife, the soprano Audrey Mildmay, founded at Glyndebourne, his country house, the well-known Festival of Opera, 1934.

CHRISTOFF, Boris (b. 1914). Bulgarian bass, resident in Italy and famous in particular for his Boris Godounov and Philip II in *Don Carlos*. He sang regularly in London from 1949 to 1974.

CLANRICARDE, Lord (1832–1916). Grandson of the Prime Minister George Canning and son of a later cabinet minister, Uncle Hubert seems to have carried little of the intelligence and integrity of his grandfather into his own life, but much of the unsavoury reputation of his father.

CLARK, Kenneth (b. 1903). Pursued a distinguished career as art connoisseur and historian.

COATES, Albert (1882–1953). English conductor, born in St Petersburg and worked there as chief conductor and artistic director. Active in opera in England between the wars.

COBURG, Duke of (1884–1954). A posthumous son of Queen Victoria's fourth son, the Duke of Albany, he became Duke of Coburg in 1900. During 1914–18 war he was stripped of his British honours. His daughter was the present King of Sweden's mother.

COLLINGWOOD, Lawrance (b. 1887). English conductor and composer; active in Russia before joining the Old Vic in the 1920s. He remained there conducting the entire repertory until 1946 and returned afterwards as a guest.

CRANKO, John (1927–73). Danced in Capetown and for Sadler's Wells Ballet, but his talents were for choreography. He produced *Midsummer Night's Dream* for Britten at Aldeburgh, and choreographed Britten's only ballet, *The Prince of the Pagodas*, at Covent Garden. The climax of his career came with his direction of the Stuttgart Ballet from 1961 until his death.

CROSS, Joan (b. 1900). English soprano, active at the Old Vic and Sadler's Wells, 1924–46, and at Covent Garden before and after 1939–45 war. Created roles in five Britten operas: *Peter Grimes*, *The Rape of Lucretia*, *Albert Herring*, *Gloriana*, *The Turn of the Screw*, and was active as a teacher after she left the stage.

CROZIER, Eric (b. 1914). Writer, and producer for Salder's Wells during the war, of *The Rape of Lucretia* at Glyndebourne in 1946. For Britten, wrote libretti of *Albert Herring*, *Saint Nicolas*, *Let's Make an Opera* and *Billy Budd* (with E. M. Forster).

DEL MAR, Norman (b. 1919). Conductor, associated at first with Sir Thomas Beecham and the Royal Philharmonic Orchestra, later with Benjamin Britten and the English Opera Group.

DE LOS ANGELES, Victoria (b. 1923). A great Spanish soprano specializing in lyric operatic roles and Spanish songs of all ages.

DE LUCIA, Fernando (1860–1925). Italian tenor of outstanding gifts whose gramophone records, many of the greatest beauty, are still listened to as examples of a style of singing, often called '*bel canto*', which disappeared when he and Battistini, its last examplars, sang no more.

DENT, Edward Joseph (1876–1957). Born in Ribston, Yorkshire, he was Professor of Music at Cambridge, 1926–41. Opera was his enthusiasm and he wrote extensively and persuasively on the subject.

DE SABATA, Victor (1892–1967). Outstanding Italian conductor, as much at home in the German classics as the Italian operatic repertory. Music director of la Scala until 1953, after which time a heart condition caused his virtual retirement.

DE VALOIS, Ninette (b. 1898). Born in Ireland, she danced at Covent Garden and for Diaghilev before embarking on her life's work, which was to found and direct Sadler's Wells (later the Royal) Ballet, 1931–63.

DEVINE, George (1910–66). Actor and director, whose early career seems only a preparation for taking charge of the English Stage Company in 1955.

DIAMAND, Peter (b. 1913). Brought up in Berlin, in 1933 he became Artur Schnabel's private secretary. During the war, he was in prison or in hiding in Holland, where he founded the Holland Festival in 1948, which he directed until 1965, when he became director of the Edinburgh Festival.

DOBROWEN, Issay (1891–1953). Russian conductor, active in Germany and, after 1948, at la Scala.

DOUGLAS, Norman (1868–1952). English writer, of whose output *South Wind* (1917) is the most famous.

DOWNES, Edward (b. 1926). Conductor, first with Carl Rosa, then at Covent Garden, 1952–72, when he became music director of Australian opera, 1972–6.

DROGHEDA, Earl of (b. 1910). Managing Director of the *Financial Times* from 1945 and from 1971 Chairman; Chairman, Royal Opera House, Covent Garden, 1958–74.

DUNCAN, Ronald (b. 1914). Poet, playwright and farmer, his plays *This way to the Tomb* and *The Eagle Has Two Heads* were mounted with great success in the years after the war. He wrote the libretto for Britten's opera *The Rape of Lucretia*, founded the Devon Festival and the English Stage Company.

DUNN, A.T.B. (1861–1902). Old Etonian who played soccer for England as forward and full back. Arthur Dunn Cup presented in his memory and played for each season.

DU PRÉ, Jacqueline (b. 1945). The greatest cellist ever born in England, she was stricken with multiple sclerosis in the early 1970s.

EBERT, Carl (1887–1980). German producer and opera manager, who left Berlin in 1933 and from 1934–59 was the main influence on the artistic life of Glyndebourne. From 1956 to 1961 he was Intendant at the Berlin Städtische Oper.

ELIZABETH, Queen, The Queen Mother (b. 1900). As Lady Elizabeth Bowes-Lyon, she was one of my mother's bridesmaids in 1922; she married the Duke of York, later King George VI, in 1923.

EVANS, Geraint (b. 1922). Welsh baritone, active at Covent Garden since

1948 and all over the world since his Glyndebourne successes of the 1950s.

FERRIER, Kathleen (1912–53). Outstanding English contralto, famous as a concert singer but well known too for her Lucretia in Britten's opera and as Gluck's Orfeo.

FISCHER-DIESKAU, Dietrich (b. 1925). German baritone, as distinguished in Opera as in Concert and Recital.

FLAGSTAD, Kirsten (1895–1962). Norwegian soprano whose world-wide fame as a Wagnerian began in 1935 with her debut at the Metropolitan, New York, before which she had had an extensive career mostly in Scandinavia. She returned from South America to occupied Norway during the war on a German visa, and was for a period ostracized in America as a collaborator; but it was eventually established that her concern was entirely for her husband, who was in Norway suffering from an incurable disease.

FORSTER, E. M. (1879–1970). Leading English novelit of first half of twentieth century, all of whose novels were published before 1925.

FOX, Robin (1913–71). After service in Second World War, he was an agent and theatrical impresario.

FRANGÇON-DAVIES, Gwen (b. 1896). English actress, famous in classical and modern plays and as singer of the role of Etain in Rutland Boughton's *The Immortal Hour.*

FRY, Christopher (b. 1907). English dramatist whose poetic plays swept England in the 1940s and 1950s.

FURTWÄNGLER, Wilhelm (1886–1954). The leading German conductor of his generation

GIBSON, Sir Alexander (b. 1926). Scottish conductor, Music Director of Sadler's Wells, 1957–9, since when he has been Chief Conductor of the Scottish National Orchestra. Founded Scottish Opera in 1962.

GIGLI, Beniamino (1895–1957). Probably the most famous, certainly the most popular, Italian tenor since the death of Caruso.

GIULINI, Carlo Maria (b. 1914). Italian conductor. Active at la Scala, Milan, and in Britain at Glyndebourne, the Edinburgh Festival and Covent Garden.

GOBBI, Tito (b. 1913). Leading Italian baritone from pst-war until his retirement in 1979. Noted for the intelligence, musicianship and detail of his characterizations.

GOODALL, Reginald (b. 1901). Conductor at Sadler's Wells (première of *Peter Grimes* in 1945), Glyndebourne (*The Rape of Lucretia*), and Covent Garden. In the late 1960s he emerged, with a new production of *The Mastersingers* at Sadler's Wells, as one of the great Wagnerian conductors of his generation, and a complete *Ring* followed at the Coliseum.

GRAHAM, Colin (b. 1931). Operatic producer and administrator, associated with Sadler's Wells, English National Opera and with Benjamin Britten. For the former he produced such successes as *War and Peace*, for the latter the first performances of *Noyes Fludde, Curlew River, The Burning Fiery Furnace, The Prodigal Son, Owen Wingrave, Death in Venice.* Founded and directed the English Music Theatre, 1975–8.

GRAY, Cecil (1895–1951). English critic and composer, friend of Peter Warlock and Bernard van Dieren.

GUTHRIE, Tyrone (1900–71). Distinguished theatrical and operatic producer and administrator. Administrator at the Old Vic and Sadler's Wells, 1939–45, and responsible for many successful stage and operatic productions all over the English-speaking world.

HALL, Peter (b. 1930). Director of plays, films, and operas; Director of Royal Shakespeare Theatre, 1960–73; of National Theatre from 1973.

HAMILTON-RUSSELL, Hon. Gustavus (1907–40). Eldest son of Lord and Lady Boyne. Killed at Dunkirk.

HARTOG, Howard (b. 1913). Music publisher, later artists' agent. Helped us start (and manages) the chamber concerts at Harewood.

HAREWOOD, Florence, Countess of (1859–1943). My paternal grandmother. Daughter of Lord Bradford, who was for a time Master of the Horse to Queen Victoria.

HAREWOOD, Henry, 5th Earl of (1846–1929). My paternal grandfather. Captain Grenadier Guards, Lord Lieutenant of West Riding of Yorkshire. His interests were hunting, fishing, racing and the opera.

HEBER-PERCY, Algernon (1903–61). Served Grenadier Guards, retiring as Brigadier in 1955.

HILL, Derek (b. 1916). Painter, traveller, lover of the arts.

HOTTER, Hans (b. 1909). German bass baritone specializing in Wagnerian repertory.

HOWARD, Robin (b. 1924). Served in 1939–45 war, losing both legs. Founded London Contemporary Dance Company.

HOWELL, Gwynne (b. 1938). Welsh opera singer for Sadler's Wells and later Covent Garden.

HOWES, Frank (1891–1974). English music critic and writer; on the staff of *The Times* from 1925 and its Chief Music Critic from 1943–60.

HUNTER, Ian (b. 1919). Administrator and impresario, working with Glyndebourne and as assistant to Rudolf Bing at the Edinburgh Festival, whose director he became in 1950. Since 1955, he has been an agent and director of festivals.

BIOGRAPHICAL NOTES

HUROK, Sol (1888–1974). Russian-born American impresario.

INGRID, Queen of Denmark (b. 1910). Daughter of King Gustav VI of Sweden; a great-grand-daughter of Queen Victoria's, therefore my mother's second cousin.

JAFFE, Michael (b. 1923). A contemporary of mine at Eton and Cambridge. Since 1973 Director of the Fitzwilliam Museum, Cambridge, and Professor of the History of Western Art.

JERITZA, Maria (b. 1887). Viennese soprano (born Brno, Moravia) of legendary fame.

JOHNSON, Edward (1878–1959). Leading operatic tenor, originally in Italy (where he was the first Parsifal) and then in America, where he sang at the Metropolitan, 1922–35. In 1935 he became General Manager of the Metropolitan, a job in which he was succeeded by Rudolf Bing in 1950.

JURINAC, Sena (b. 1921). Soprano born in Jugoslavia, but active particularly as member of Vienna State Opera from 1944.

KEMPE, Rudolf (1910–76). German conductor, much of whose career was built abroad, at Covent Garden from 1953, and the Metropolitan, New York, 1954–6. He was conductor of the Royal Philharmonic Orchestra, and just before his death of the BBC Symphony Orchestra.

KETELBY, Albert (1875–1959). English composer, mainly of light music, and conductor, particularly of gramophone records.

KIRSTEIN, Lincoln (b. 1907). Founder and Director of New York City Ballet and its school, he was instrumental in taking Balanchine to America. By his writing and influence he has affected America's, and particularly New York's, artistic life for fifty years.

KLEIBER, Erich (1890–1956). Fiery and talented Austrian conductor particularly of opera, whose son Carlos has inherited talents which perhaps even surpassed his father's.

KLEMPERER, Otto (1885–1973). Great German conductor in Prague and Hamburg before becoming music director in Cologne in 1917. The apex of his German fame came with his directorship of the Krolloper, Berlin, 1927–33, but the advent of Hitler meant retreat to America, where he was operated on for a tumour on the brain following a fall from the podium. Much of his post-war conducting was done in England.

KONETZNI, Hilde (b. 1905). Austrian soprano of considerable fame.

KRAUSS, Clemens (1893–1954). Austrian conductor.

KRIPS, Josef (1902–74). Viennese conductor, whose efforts were mainly responsible for creating the post-war Viennese ensemble.

KUBELIK, Rafael (b. 1914). Czech conductor and composer, son of the

314

famous violinist Jan Kubelik. Chief conductor in Brno, 1939–41, Music Director of Covent Garden, 1955–8.

LASCELLES, Alan (b. 1887). My father's first cousin and executor. He served in France, 1914–18, and was later Private Secretary successfully to the Governor General of Canada, Kings George V and VI, and Queen Elizabeth II.

LASCELLES, Hon. Edward (1887–1935). My father's brother, five years younger than him. He served in the Great War, became private secretary to Arthur Balfour, but was most at home as a countryman, particularly as master of the Bramham Moor hounds.

LAURI-VOLPI, Giacomo (1892–1979). Leading Italian tenor renowned among other things for his unfailing and stentorian top notes, one of which he sang (and had recorded) on his eightieth birthday.

LAWRENCE, Marjorie (1909–80). Australian soprano, whose European career began in France in 1932; at the Metropolitan, New York 1935–41, in which year she was struck with polio. She appeared after the onset of her illness in a few stage performances and many concerts.

LEAVIS, F. R. (1895–1978). Lecturer in English, Cambridge University, from 1936.

LEGGE, Walter (1906–79). English impresario, responsible for some of the finest gramophone records made from the early 1930s. Married to the soprano Elisabeth Schwarzkopf.

LENYA, Lotte (b. 1898). Viennese-born singing actress who married in 1926 the composer Kurt Weill, many of whose subsequent works were written for her.

LEY, H. G. (1887–1962). Organist; head of music at Eton in my time.

LIEBERMANN, Rolf (b. 1910). Composer and operative administrator. Intendant in Hamburg, 1959–73, at the Paris Opéra, 1973–80.

LYTTELTON, Anthony (Lord Chandos) (1920–80). At Trinity College, Cambridge, while I was at King's; a stockbroker and music-lover.

LYTTELTON, Humphrey (b. 1921). Son of an Eton master (subsequently famous for his published correspondence with Rubert Hart-Davis), Humphrey won considerable renown as a jazz trumpeter and band leader.

LYONS, Sir Jack (b. 1916). Industrialist and philanthropist. Chairman, Leeds Festival, 1956–72.

MACKERRAS, Sir Charles (b. 1925). Australian conductor, most of whose activity has been in Europe. Sadler's Wells, 1948–54, English Opera Group, 1955–60, Hamburg State Opera, 1965–70, Music Director Sadler's Wells/ENO, 1970–7.

MALIPIERO, Gian Francesco (1882–1973). Italian composer, who wrote new operas, edited old music (notably Monteverdi and Vivaldi), and attempted with Casella to lead a renaissance of Italian music.

MARKEVICH, Igor and Topazia (b. 1912 and 1922 respectively). Igor is a composer and conductor of Russian birth and Swiss domicile. His wife was born Topazia Caetani.

MARTINELLI, Giovani (1885–1969). Leading Italian tenor, much of whose career took place in Americ, particularly at the Metropolitan. He made many gramophone records, and late in his career reappeared at Covent Garden (1937) singing the first Otello of his career and, opposite Eva Turner, the only Calafs.

MASTERSON, Valerie. Leading British lyric soprano for d'Oyly Carte Company, and from 1970 for Sadler's Wells/ENO. Has sung extensively in France including Aix Festival and Paris Opéra.

MCCORMACK, John (1884–1945). Irish tenor of world-wide fame. Gave up opera in 1923 and spent the rest of his life singing concerts.

MELCHIOR, Lauritz (1890–1973). Danish tenor, who became the most famous Wagnerian of his generation.

MENON, V.K. Narayana (b. Trichur 1911). Indian musician, writer and administrator. Educated at Madras and Edinburgh Universities, served with BBC, 1942–7, when he returned to India. Director General All India Radio, 1965–8, active member International Music Council, UNESCO.

MENUHIN, Yehudi (b. 1916). Violinist and conductor. His fame came as a child prodigy and he recorded the Elgar violin concerto with the composer conducting in 1932.

MILANOV, Zinka (b. 1906). Yugoslav soprano, whose international fame began with performances of the Verdi Requiem at Salzburg under Toscanini in 1937. From then until her retirement in 1966 she was leading soprano at the Metropolitan, New York.

MITCHELL, Donald (b. 1925). Writer on music and critic.

MOISEIWITSCH, Benno (1890–1963). British pianist born in Odessa; a fiery and brilliant interpreter of romantic music.

MOLYNEUX, Hon. Richard (1873–1954). Served in Sudan and South African war, and in France, 1914–18. Groom-in-waiting to King George V and Extra Equerry to Queen Mary after 1936. A lover of the fine arts.

MUNNINGS, Sir Alfred (1878–1959). Painter, specializing in horses and their riders. President of the Royal Academy.

MUNTHE, Axel (1857–1949). Author of *The Story of San Michele* and creator of the fashion for Capri.

MYSAKOVSKY, Nikolay Yakovievich ·(1881–1950). Russian composer of considerable fecundity.

NABOKOV, Nicolas (1903–78). Russian, later American, composer, who wrote for Diaghilev in 1928 but in later life spent time in musical politics and in the organization of international festivals.

NARES, Owen (1888–1943). Famous British actor.

NELSON, John, Maj. Gen. Sir (b. 1912). Commanded 3rd Battalion Grenadier Guards, 1944–5 (DSO), and after a distinguished military career was GOC Berlin, 1966–8.

NEVEU, Ginette (1919–49). Great French violinist, killed in plane crash.

NEWMAN, Lt. Col. Charles (1904–72). A civil engineer by profession, commanded No. 1 Commando in raid on St Nazaire, where he won the VC.

NUREYEV, Rudolf (b. 1939). Russian ballet dancer and choreographer, who defected from Kirov ballet in 1961. Appeared frequently with Royal Ballet at Covent Garden, and subsequently all over the world.

ORD, Boris (1897–1961). English organist and conductor. Organist and choir-master at King's, Cambridge, 1929–57.

OSBORNE, John (b. 1929). Playwright, whose *Look Back in Anger*, produced at Royal Court Theatre, 1956, heralded a new theatrical outlook variously described as 'angry young man' by those who half-liked it, and 'kitchen sink' by those who didn't.

PASERO, Tancredi (b. 1893). Leading Italian bass.

PATZAK, Julius (1898–1974). A self-taught Viennese singer, who before the war in Munich and after it in Vienna was the most versatile and most musical tenor singing in German.

PICCAVER, Alfred (1884–1958). Tenor, born English, brought up in America, famous for twenty-seven years as leading tenor in Vienna.

PIPER, John (b. 1903). Painter of distinction, who designed most of the first stagings of Britten's operas.

PIPER, Myfanwy. Wrote libretti of *Owen Wingrave* and *Death in Venice* for Benjamin Britten. Married the painter John Piper in 1935.

PLOMER, William (1903–73). Poet and writer, responsible for libretti for Britten of *Gloriana* and *Curlew River*.

PLOWRIGHT, Joan (b. 1929). Actress, whose early fame was gained at the Royal Court Theatre. Married to Laurence Olivier.

PONSONBY, Robert (b. 1926). Artistic Director Edinburgh Festival, 1955–60, Administrator Scottish National Orchestra, 1964–72, Controller of Music at BBC since 1972.

RAO, Dr V. K. R. V. (b. 1908). Formerly Professor of Economics at Delhi University and later Vice-Chancellor. Minister of Education, 1969–71.

RENNERT, Günther (1911–78). Leading German operatic producer. Intendant in Hamburg, 1946–56, Munich, 1967–78.

REVIE, Donald (b. 1927). Professional footballer for Leicester, Hull, Manchester City, Sunderland, Leeds, then Leeds's manger from 1961–74. Played several times for England, and was manager, 1974–7. Since 1977 Team Coach, United Arab Emirates.

RHODES, Wilfred (1877–1973). Cricketer: Yorkshire and England.

RICHARDSON, Tony (b. 1928). George Devine's assistant at Royal Court Theatre, he directed *Look Back in Anger* and a host of other successful productions.

RICHARDSON, W.P. (1885–1974). His career as land agent took him from the Fawkes family at Farnley in Yorkshire to county land agent to the West Riding, and finally to war-time activity as Chief Executive Officer to the West Riding War Agricultural Committee.

RICHTER, Sviatoslav (b. 1915). In the opinion of many, the greaest pianist to emerge from Russia since the end of the war.

ROBBINS, Jerome (b. 1918). American choreographer and director of successful muicals and Broadway shows.

ROSEBERY, Lady (b. 1892). Wife of 6th Earl of Rosebery and a keen amateur pianist. She was on Council of Edinburgh Festival from its inception.

ROSEBERY, Lord (1882–1974). Son of the Prime Minister, Captain of Surrey Cricket team 1905–7, MP 1906–10, served in First World War, Regional Commissioner for Scotland, 1941–5, Secretary of State for Scotland, 1945.

ROSTROPOVICH, Sviatoslav (b. 1927). Russian cellist, the greatest virtuoso on his instrument since Pablo Casals; it an accompanist and conductor of the highest calibre.

ROTHSCHILD, James A. de (1878–1957). Born in Paris, he was Liberal MP for Isle of Ely until 1945.

ROWLATT, Charles (1894–1959). Educated at Eton and Oxford. Severely wounded in 1914–18 war, returned as assistant master to Eton, where he was a House mater and later rose to be Vice Provost, 1952–9.

RUBINSTEIN, Artur (b. 1888). Polish (later American) pianist of world-wide fame.

RYLANDS, George (b. 1902). Fellow of King's, Cambridge, lecturer in English and occasional stage director (notably *Hamlet* with Gielgud in 1945).

SCHNABEL, Artur (1882–1951). Composer and pianist, one of the greatest exponents of the classical Viennese school.

SCHOEFFLER, Paul (1897–1977). From 1925–38, a leading member of Dresden ensemble, from 1938–65 in Vienna.

SCHOENBERG, Arnold (1874–1951). Composer and teacher.

SCHWARZKOPF, Elisabeth (b. 1915). German soprano, who came to fame as a member of post-war Viennese ensemble.

SEEFRIED, irmgard (b. 1919). Born in Germany but came to fame as leading exponent of the Viennese style in the famous post-war ensemble.

SEMMANGUDI, R. Srinivasa Iyer (b. 1908 at Tirukkodikkaval). Numerous awards for his singing. Principal Academy of Music, Trivandrum; director Central College of Carnatic Music, Madras.

SERAFIN, Tullio (1878–1968). Leading Italian operatic conductor.

SHANKAR, Ravi (b. 1920). Brother of Uday Shankar, for whose troupe he danced and played. A pupil of Alauddin Khan, he plays sitar and introduced the joys of Indian music to many Westerners.

SMITH, G.O. (d. 1943). As centre forward he played for Oxford, Corinthians and England, his twenty-one internationals still a record for an amateur. Scored century in University Cricket match of 1896. Headmaster of Ludgrove, 1902–22.

SOLTI, Georg (b. 1912). Hungarian, later English, conductor. Music Director in Munich and Frankfurt before filling the same post at Covent Garden, 1961–71.

SPENDER, Stephen (b. 1909). Poet and writer associated with new writers of the 1930s who were led by W. H. Auden. In 1941 he married the pianist Natasha Litvin.

STABILE, Mariano (1888–1968). Italian baritone who sang Falstaff at the opening of Toscanini's last period at la Scala, 1922. He was still singing the same role there in 1951 and elsewhere until 1961.

STOKOWSKI, Leopold (1882–1977). One of the world's greatest virtuoso conductors. Born in London, active in America, where he turned the Philadelphis orchestra into one of the world's greatest.

SUTCLIFFE, Herbert (1894–1978). Cricketer: Yorkshire and England.

SUTHERLAND, Joan (b. 1926). Famous Australian soprano, active at Covent Garden from 1952, later all over the world.

SWAYNE, Sir Ronald (b. 1918). Served No. 2 Commando, 1940–45, taken prisoner after raid on St Nazaire. Chairman Overseas Containers Ltd.

SZIGETI, Joseph (1892–1973). Hungarian violinist, famous all over the world for his supremely musicianly playing.

TAUBER, Richard (1892–1948). German tenor, adopted Austrian and later

British nationality. Sang opera until just before his death; as a singer of popular songs, rivalled only by John McCormack.

TEBALDI, Renata (b. 1922). Italian lyric soprano.

THORPE, Jeremy (b. 1929). MP, 1959–79, and leader of the Liberal Party, 1967–76. In 1973 he married my first wife, Marion.

TILL, Barry (b. 1923). Ordained in 1950. Chaplain and Dean at Jesus, Cambridge, he was Dean of Hong Kong, 1960–64, where I stayed with him. Now Principal of Morley College, London.

TOOLEY, Sir John (b. 1924). General Administrator Royal Opera House, Covent Garden, since 1970.

TRACEY, Edmund (b. 1927). Musician, critic, and administrator. From 1964 has worked for Sadler's Wells and English National Operas as dramaturg.

TRAUBEL, Helen (1899–1972). American Wagnerian soprano of ample voice and proportions.

TUCKER, Norman (1910–78). After study to become a professionl pianist, joined the Civil Service and was Director of Sadler's Wells Opera, 1947–66.

TUCKWELL, Barry (b. 1931). Australian musician and leading player of French horn. After a number of years as an orchestral player, he concentrated on solo and chamber work.

TURNER, Eva (b. 1892). One of the most famous of English sopranos, particularly for her assumption of the title role in *Turandot*.

VALK, Frederick (b. Germany, d. 1956). Active in Germany and Czechoslovakia until the advent of Hitler, when he came to England, playing in *Thunder Rock*, and appearing as Shylock and Othello, and in many other plays.

VANSITTART, Robert (1881–1957). Permanent head of Foreign Office, 1930–38. Advocate of 'unconditional surrender' as opposed to negotiated peace.

VINAY, Ramon (b. 1912). Chilean tenor (originally baritone), the outstanding Otello of his generation.

VISHNEVSKAYA, Galina (b. 1926). Leading Russian soprano, at Moscow's Bolshoi Theatre, 1952–74, when she and her husband Rostropovich left the Soviet Union.

WALLENSTEIN, Alfred (b. 1898). American cellist and comductor.

WALTON, William (b. 1902). Leading English composer.

WEBER, Ludwig (1899–1974). Austrian bass, particularly renowned for his roles in Wagnerian opera.

WEBERN, Anton von (1883–1945). Austrian composer, pupil of

Schoenberg's, creator of a number of outstanding works of unprecedentedly short duration.

WEBSTER, David (1903–71). General Manager Bon Marché and Lewis Ltd, Liverpool, before in 1945 becoming General Administrator of Covent Garden, where he continued until 1970.

WELITSCH, Ljuba (b. 1913). Bulgarian soprano, who came to world-wide fame immediately after the war with the Vienna Opera Company.

WEST, Christopher (1913–67). Worked at Shakespeare Memorial Theatre, then Covent Garden, 1949–59, producing première of Tippett's *The Midsummer Marriage*. Later worked in United States, where he died.

WIDDOP, Walter (1892–1949). Yorkshire dramatic tenor, at his best in Wagner, of whose music he made a number of admirable records. Sang at the Albert Hall the night before he died.

WILSON, Steuart (1889–1966). English tenor and administrator. He sang Tamino in a pioneering performance of *The Magic Flute* at Cambridge in 1910, but, wounded in the 1914–18 war, sang mainly concerts until becoming head of music at the BBC and then deputy general administrator at Covent Garden, 1949–55.

WINDSOR, Duke of (1894–1972). Eldest son of King George v. Proclaimed King, January 1936, abdicated December 1936 to marry Mrs Wallis Simpson. Governor of the Bahamas, 1940–45. After the war lived in France.

Index

323

INDEX

INDEX

INDEX

Drogheda, Joan, Countess of, 221
du Pré, Derek, 34
du Pré, Jacqueline, 34, 71
Duchess of Malfi, The (Webster), 70
Dunbar, Sir J. Greig, 183
Duncan, Ronald, 103, 124–5, 127, 135, 146,
   177, 178, 180, 217
Duncan, Rose Marie, 124, 125
Dunn, Arthur, 21
Dussurget, Gabriel, 127–8

Eastwood, Geoffrey, 79
Ebert, Karl, 114, 126
Ede, Chuter, 275
Edinburgh Festival, 84–5, 154, 173–4,
   183–200, 201, 253, 254, 277, 281
Edward VIII, King, *see* Windsor, Duke of
Edwards, Michael, 89
Edwards, Willis, 11–12, 299
Elder, Mark, 290
Elektra (R. Strauss), 111, 165
'Eleven Jewish Poems' (Shostakovich), 133
Elizabeth, Queen, the Queen Mother, 24
Elizabeth II, Queen (formerly Princess
   Elizabeth), 90, 103–4, 137, 169, 220, 271;
   opera for Coronation, *see Gloriana*
Elizabethan Theatre Trust, 288
Ellington, Duke, 272
Elphinstone, John (later Lord), 55, 58, 64,
   68, 73
English Opera Group, 144, 177
English Stage Company, 177–82
Entertainer, The (Osborne), 180
Epstein, Jacob, 186–7, 304
Epstein, Kathleen, 188–9
Erb, Karl, 245
Erede, Alberto, 145, 226
Esca, Pina, 42
Esdaile, Alfred, 178
Eton, 18–19, 22–4, 29–30, 81, 85
Eugene Onegin (*Yevgeny Onegin*;
   Tchaikovsky), 135, 203, 208–10
Evans, Dame Edith, 85
Evans, Sir Geraint, 26, 152–3
Exeter, Bishop of, 275

Falconer, Sir John, 183
Falkner, Keith, 117
Falstaff (Verdi), 108, 145, 240–1
Fantastic Symphony (Berloiz), 192
Farebrother, Harcourt, 43, 45

Fatehpur Sikri, 259
Faust (Gounod), 250–1, 288
Faust Symphony (Liszt), 190
Favaretto, Giorgio, 126
Fayer, Yuri, 170
Ferrauto, Augusto, 42
Ferrier, Kathleen, 83, 130, 241
Ffrangçon-Davies, Gwen, 36
Fidelio (Beethoven), 100–1, 239, 242, 277–8
Finney, Albert, 189
Fischer von Erlach, Johann Bernhard, 101
Fischer-Dieskau, Dietrich, 148, 244
Fisher, Sylvia, 147, 151, 155, 164
FitzRoy, Nigel, 293, 296
Flagstad, Kirsten, 101, 239, 245
Fledermaus, Die (Johann Strauss), 71, 243
Florence, 111, 113–14
Fonteyn, Margot, 168, 192, 231
football, 21–2; *see also* Leeds United
Football Association, 300
Forbes, George, 45
Forster, E.M., 86–7, 90, 104, 131, 144
Forza del Destino, La (Verdi), 42
Fountain of Bachshisherai, The, 169
Four Sons of Aymon, The, 191
Fox, Robin, 178, 181, 182, 189
Frantz, Ferdinand, 154, 246
Frau ohne Schatten, Die (R. Strauss), 95
Freischütz, Der (Weber), 164
Frick, Gottlob, 246
Fricker, Peter Racine, 271
Friedrich, Karl, 93
From the House of the Dead (Jańček), 51, 125
Froude, Richard, 9–10, 25
Furtseva, Madame, 201, 203, 204, 205,
   210–11, 211
Furtwängler, Wilhelm, 100–1, 110, 124

Gal, Hans, 200
Gamelin, General, 69
Gardiner, Gerald (later Lord), 275
Gaulle, Charles de, 31
Gedda, Nicolai, 273
George V, King, 2, 14–17, 258
George VI, King, 17, 18, 103
Ghiaurov, Nicolai, 247
Giannino (restaurant), 113
Gibson, Sir Alexander, 190
Gielgud, Sir John, 31–2, 36, 71, 160
Gigli, Beniamino, 95, 112, 141
Gigli, Rina, 112

INDEX

Lascelles, Mark (author's son), 11, 194, 218, 219, 220, 247, 279–80, 295, 297–8
Lassalle, Nancy, 221, 222
Latham, Elizabeth, 155
Latter, Major General John, 271–2
Laufen, 64, 66
Lawrence, Martin, 240
Leavis, F.R., 88
Lee, Jennie, 197
Leeds Festival, 118, 125, 141, 170, 173, 270–4, 281, 292
Leeds United FC, 11–12, 298–301
Legge, Walter, 171, 198, 276
Lehmann, Liza, 200
Lehmann, Lotte, 36, 165–6, 229
Leigh, Adèle, 157
Leighton, Lord, 117
Leitner, Ferdinand, 114
'Lélio' (Berlioz), 192
Lemeshev, Sergei, 208, 209–10
Leningrad, 206
Lenya, Lotte, 190
Lessing, Levinson, 206
Let's Make an Opera (Britten), 139
Lewenstein, Oscar, 177, 180
Lewis, Richard, 156, 160
Ley, Dr Henry, 23
Liddell, Alvar, 185–6
Liebe der Danae, Die (R. Strauss), 154
Lied von der Erde, Das (Mahler), 237
Liepa, Marius, 211–12
Litvin, Natasha, 147
Lloyd, David, 29
Lloyd, Gwynedd, 104
Lohengrin (Wagner), 250
London, George, 163
London Opera Centre, 174
Look Back in Anger (Osborne), 178–9
Lorimer, Peter, 300
los Angeles, Victoria de, see de los Angeles
Louise (Charpentier), 164, 250
Lubbock, Roger, 123
Lucas, Brenda, 192
Lucia di Lammermoor (Donizetti), 164–5, 237
Ludgrove (prep. school), 21–2
Lulu (Berg.), 116
Lyons, Sir Jack, 186–7, 270, 271, 272, 304
Lyttelton, Anthony, (later Lord Chandos), 89
Lyttelton, Humphrey, 23, 72

Maazel, Lorin, 191, 279
Macbeth (Shakespeare), 36
Macbeth (R. Strauss), 93
Macbeth (Verdi), 88
McCloy, J.J., 73
McClure, John, 74
McCormack, John, 12, 238
McCracken, James, 185, 186
Mackerras, Charles, 175, 273, 288, 289
McLaglen, Victor, 12
Macmillan, Harold, 275
MacMillan, Kenneth, 190
MacWatters, Virginia, 151
Madama Butterfly (Puccini), 31, 238, 244
Madras, 262
Magaloff, Nikita, 115
Magic Flute, The (Mozart), 29, 101, 160, 163, 289
Mahler, Gustav, 237, 241
Malcuzynski, Witold, 77
Malipiero, Gian Francesco, 104
Manon (Massenet), 134
Markevich, Igor, 154, 214–15
Markevich, Topazia, 18, 214–15
Marriage of Figaro, The (Mozart), 31, 100, 107, 175–6, 238, 242
Martin, Sergeant, 278
Martinelli, Giovanni, 237, 244
Martyn, Denys, 83, 99, 100, 110
Martyr de Saint Sébastien, Le (Debussy), 114
Marulli, Ettore, 42
Mary, Princess, Countess of Harewood (author's mother), 2, 5, 13, 14, 17, 18, 20, 26–9, 31–2, 33, 37, 69, 77, 78, 81, 83, 90, 91, 92, 95, 97, 98–9, 100, 102, 117, 118, 137, 189, 203, 271, 281, 292, 294–6, 302
Mary, Queen, 2, 5–6, 13, 15, 18, 27, 91–2, 103, 119, 137, 258
Masked Ball, see Ballo in Maschera
Massey, Ilona, 80
Masterson, Valerie, 245
Mattoni, André von, 197–8
Mayer, Louis B., 80
Mayer, Tony and Thérèse, 136
Mears, Jo, 300
Medea (Cherubini), 232–3
meend, 255
Meistersinger von Nürnberg, Die (Mastersingers; Wagner), 21, 107, 116, 134, 152, 156
Melchior, Lauritz, 79

329

INDEX

Meneghini, Battista, 100, 226, 233
Mengleberg, Willem, 94
Menon, Narayana, 189, 192, 253, 256
Menon, Rekha, 256
Mercer, Joe, 300–1
Metamorphosen (R. Strauss), 94
Metropolitan Opera Houe, New York, 285–6
Mewton-Wood, Noel, 135
Micheau, Janine, 127, 250
Midgley, Walter, 151
Midummer Marriage, The (Tippett), 156–7
Midsummer Night's Dream, A (Britten), 140, 148
Milan, 108–10, 112, 112–13; *see also* la Scala
Milanov, Zinka, 245, 248
Mildmay, Audrey, 83
Miles, Bernard, 36, 239
Miller, Robert Watt, 285
Minotis, Alexis, 232–3
Miraculous Mandarin, The (Bartok), 192
Missa Solemnis (Beethoven), 191, 271
Mitchell, Donald, 130
Mitropoulos, Dimitri, 111
Mödl, Martha, 246
Moiseiwitsch, Benno, 37
Montagu, Lord, of Beaulieu, 302
Montgomery, Lord, 130
Month in the Country, A (Turgeniev), 36
Moosburg, 52
Morison, Elsie, 160
Morris, Gareth, 277
Moscow, 205
Moses and Aaron (Schoenberg), 273
Mravinsky, Yergeny, 205
mridangam, 266
Munich, 52
Munich Opera, 154
Munnings, Sir Alfred, 3–4
Munthe, Axel, 105

Nabokov, Nicolas, 254
Nabucco (Verdi), 289
Naples, 42–3, 112
Narayan, Ram, 257
Nares, Gordon, 89
Nares, Owen, 36
National Company, 285
Nelson, Sir John, 45, 46
Nepal, 259–60
Neri, Giulio, 111

New Philharmonia Orchestra, 146, 219, 278–82
New York City Ballet, 169
Newman, Colonel Charles, 53
Nicholson, William, 188
Nicolai, Elena, 224
Nilsson, Birgit, 239
Noces, Les (Stravinsky, 274)
Nocturne (Britten), 141
Noni, Alda, 110, 240
Nono, Luigi, 191
Norma (Bellini), 136, 225–6, 228–9, 229–30
Nowakowski, Marian, 32
Noye's Fludde (Britten), 139
Nureyev, Rudolf, 167

Oberto (Verdi), 112
Oedipus Rex (Stravinsky), 125
Ogdon, John, 192, 200
Olaf, Crown Prince, of Norway, 31
Olimpia (Spontini), 111
Olivero, Magda, 112
Olivier, Laurence, 180, 181
Onassis, Aristotle, 233, 234, 235
Opera (magazine), 121–2
Opernball, Der (Heuberger), 116
Ord, Boris, 87–8
Orfeo ed Euridice (Gluck), 100, 279
Osborn, Franz, 118
Otello (Verdi), 109–10, 159–60, 237, 288
Othello (Shakespeare), 36

Palghat Mani, Iyer, 199–200
Palio, 111
Pasero, Tancredi, 110
Patriot for Me, A (Osborne), 180–1
Patterson, Harry, 56
Patzak, Julius, 100, 101, 107, 242, 245
Pears, Peter, 87, 125, 129, 130, 135–40 *passim*, 141–2, 142–9 *passim*, 160, 191, 245
Pelléas et Mélisande (Debussy), 39
Peter Grimes (Britten), 71, 129, 130, 146, 152, 155, 238
Petrified Forest, The (Robert Sherwood), 36
Philharmonia Orchestra, *see* New Philharmonia Orchestra
Philip, Prince, (Duke of Edinburgh), 103, 137
Philippeville, Algeria, 37
Phillips, Anthony, 199
Piccaver, Alfred, 36
Picchi, Mirto, 99, 111

330

INDEX

INDEX